# REPORTING THE SECO

REPORTING THE SECOND WORLD WAR

THE PRESS AND THE PEOPLE 1939–1945

Tim Luckhurst

BLOOMSBURY ACADEMIC
LONDON • NEW YORK • OXFORD • NEW DELHI • SYDNEY

BLOOMSBURY ACADEMIC
Bloomsbury Publishing Plc
50 Bedford Square, London, WC1B 3DP, UK
1385 Broadway, New York, NY 10018, USA
29 Earlsfort Terrace, Dublin 2, Ireland

BLOOMSBURY, BLOOMSBURY ACADEMIC and the Diana logo
are trademarks of Bloomsbury Publishing Plc

First published in Great Britain 2023

Copyright © Tim Luckhurst, 2023

Tim Luckhurst has asserted his right under the Copyright,
Designs and Patents Act, 1988, to be identified as Author of this work.

For legal purposes the Acknowledgements on p. vii constitute an extension
of this copyright page.

Cover image: One of a series of watercolours of London's Waterloo
Station during WWII by Helen McKie © SSPL/Getty Images
Cover design: Graham Robert Ward

All rights reserved. No part of this publication may be reproduced or transmitted
in any form or by any means, electronic or mechanical, including photocopying,
recording, or any information storage or retrieval system, without prior
permission in writing from the publishers.

Bloomsbury Publishing Plc does not have any control over, or responsibility for, any
third-party websites referred to or in this book. All internet addresses given in this
book were correct at the time of going to press. The author and publisher regret
any inconvenience caused if addresses have changed or sites have ceased
to exist, but can accept no responsibility for any such changes.

A catalogue record for this book is available from the British Library.

A catalog record for this book is available from the Library of Congress.

ISBN: HB: 978-1-3501-4949-6
PB: 978-1-3501-4948-9
ePDF: 978-1-3501-4951-9
eBook: 978-1-3501-4950-2

Typeset by RefineCatch Limited, Bungay, Suffolk
Printed and bound in Great Britain

To find out more about our authors and books visit www.bloomsbury.com
and sign up for our newsletters.

CONTENTS

List of Illustrations	vi
Acknowledgements	vii
Introduction	1
1 A Brief History of Newspapers	5
2 Barons, Abdication and Appeasement	9
3 The Phoney War	25
4 Churchill, Norway and Dunkirk	43
5 Class Unity and the Myth of the Blitz	57
6 The Battle of Britain	65
7 Air Raid Shelters, Fairness and a New Home Secretary	73
8 Morale, Intimidation and Censorship	91
9 Britain and Russia: 'One Touch of Hitler Makes the Whole World Kin'	109
10 The Beveridge Report: Banishing Want from Cradle to Grave	127
11 Peculiar Problems: Reporting the Americans in Britain	139
12 'Bomb Back and Bomb Hard': Allied Bombing of Germany	155
13 Concentration Camps	171
14 VE Day, General Election and Atomic Bombs	185
Conclusion	197
Notes	205
Bibliography	237
Index	245

ILLUSTRATIONS

3.1	A group of children arrive at Brent station near Kingsbridge, Devon, after being evacuated in 1940.	31
7.1	A mother and child sleep in a trench shelter in London during the Blitz, November 1940.	76
7.2	A female Fire Guard using a stirrup pump on the roof of a building in London, 1941.	80
7.3	A British airman is amongst a group of civilians crowded around the window of a shop in Holborn, London, to look at a map illustrating how the RAF is striking back at Germany during 1940.	84
9.1	David Low, 'The Scum of the Earth, I Presume', *London Evening Standard*, 20 September 1939. Low's cartoon lampoons the cynical alliance between Nazi Adolf Hitler and Communist Josef Stalin. (dmg media licensing)	111
9.2	Philip Zec, 'German Murderer and Russian Body Snatcher', *Daily Mirror*, 20 September 1939. Zec's cartoon condemns the division of Poland between Hitler's Germany and Stalin's Soviet Union. (mirrorpix)	112
9.3	A huge crowd gathered outside the British Museum to hear Harry Pollitt, General Secretary of the Communist Party of Great Britain, make a speech about aid to Russia, 1941.	117
9.4	Philip Zec, Hitler: 'I can eat anything', *Daily Mirror*, 24 June 1941. Zec's cartoon marks the beginning of Operation Barbarossa, the German invasion of Russia. (mirrorpix)	118
11.1	A US serviceman having tea with the former mayor of Winchester, Mr Edmonds, and his wife and daughter in the garden of their home during 1944.	140
14.1	Norman Pett's VE Day cartoon for the *Daily Mirror* depicted Jane naked for the first time, 8 May 1945. (mirrorpix)	186

ACKNOWLEDGEMENTS

This book builds upon a project to present case studies of newspaper coverage of significant controversies during the Second World War that has occupied much of my academic career. It incorporates elements of work and ideas that I originally outlined in articles for academic journals, and adds thousands of hours of meticulous research and analysis in newspaper archives physical and digital. Each hour represents a small repayment of the debt of gratitude I owe to journalists and editors who died before I was born. Their work is often dismissed as ephemeral. I hope to demonstrate that it is tremendously valuable to historians who endeavour to understand the past as it was understood by those who experienced it.

As a young journalist, I reported wars and conflict in Romania, Iraq, Kuwait, Kosovo, Northern Ireland and Serbia. This book was inspired by those experiences. It is dedicated to my outstanding family. My wonderful wife, Dorothy, has supported and encouraged me throughout. I can never thank her enough. Huge thanks also to our excellent children Phoebe, Toby, Georgia and Molly, for their outstanding kindness and generosity. My research is informed by the work of superb journalists with whom I have had the privilege to work. Alan Ruddock (1960–2010), editor of *The Scotsman* between 1998 and 2000, set a compelling example of principle and intense decency. I was proud to serve as his deputy and successor. Ian Bell (1956–2015), the Orwell prize winning political journalist who wrote with exceptional style and intelligence for *The Scotsman*, demonstrated the power of a truly great columnist. Thanks to Peter Wright, Editor Emeritus of Associated Newspapers, for alerting me to the value of quality popular journalism and Kim Fletcher, editor of *British Journalism Review* for publishing my musings. Roger Mosey, Master of Selwyn College Cambridge, with whom I worked at BBC Radio 4's Today Programme and at BBC Radio Five Live, sets an example of calm intelligence and great kindness.

I am a journalist and editor who became an academic. This book owes a great deal to both halves of my career. At the University of Kent, where I served between 2007 and 2019 as Professor of Journalism and founding head of the Centre for Journalism, I am grateful for the support and friendship of my collaborator Lesley Phippen and John Wightman, lecturer in law and former Dean of Social Sciences. Many thanks also to the Kent students who studied my module 'Reporting the Second World War' for your interest and encouragement. For hours of stimulating conversation and debate my intense gratitude to Graham Majin, then my PhD student, now a Senior Lecturer at Bournemouth University. For the inspiration to write newspaper history, my sincere thanks to Mark Connelly of the University of Kent and Stephanie Seul of the University of Bremen. For his generosity and wisdom my thanks also to Tim Crook of Goldsmiths, University of London.

Acknowledgements

My research was supported by expert staff at the British Library and Cambridge University Library. I am particularly grateful to the staff in the Cambridge University Library Reading Room who found for me printed wartime editions of *Tribune*. For initial intellectual training that eventually bore fruit, and the kindness that allowed me to make the most of my undergraduate degree, eternal gratitude to two superb academics at Robinson College, Cambridge, Martin Brett, my Director of Studies, and Mary Stewart, my tutor. My thanks to colleagues at South College, Durham for your help, support and interest in your Principal's research. Finally, to my friends Professor Rob Lynes, Principal of Stephenson College, Durham, and Tim Williams, always a fine historian and now a consultant on cities based in Sydney, Australia. To both, thank you for your unfailing wisdom and kindness.

INTRODUCTION

Historians have explored extensively the BBC's broadcast journalism during the Second World War. Newspaper journalism of the era has received less attention. This is regrettable because, while the BBC grew dramatically in scale and prestige between 1939 and 1945, newspapers mattered greatly throughout. In May 1940, when Mass Observation (MO), the innovative and ambitious social research organization, produced its 'Report on the Press', it found: 'almost everybody reads newspapers, whether regularly or irregularly, thoroughly or cursorily'.[1] MO's interest in Britons' reading habits was not limited to scale. The social scientists wanted to know why people read newspapers and whether they believed what they were told. MO's answer to the first question was admirably concise: 'the general reason is that newspapers provide topics for the day's conversation: they tell what is happening, and what is happening is what people want to talk about. Without newspaper news there is scarcely any generally accepted basis for conversation except the weather'.[2] MO argued that newspapers were 'a social necessity' and concluded that '[newspapers] are a kind of currency, passing on the news of the town – to everyone. Consequently, newspaper reading becomes a habit, like smoking or drinking or going to the films'.[3] The smoking analogy is instructive. In wartime Britain, 'There was always a far greater demand from the public for cigarettes and tobacco than suppliers could fulfil, though after 1941 this eased somewhat when tobacco leaf was included in the terms of the US Lend Lease programme.'[4] Indeed, tobacco use reached a peak in the 1940s. The highest rate of smoking in the UK was recorded in 1948, when 82 per cent of men and 41 per cent of women were regular smokers.[5]

When German forces invaded Poland from the north, south and west on 1 September 1939, Britons were already the 'world's most avid newspaper readers'.[6] The habit of buying one or more daily national newspapers extended throughout every social class. Eighty per cent of British families read one of the mass circulation London dailies, the *Daily Mail*, *Daily Mirror*, *Daily Express*, *News Chronicle*, *Daily Herald* or *Daily Sketch*. Two-thirds of middle-class families shared this habit – though many also bought a sophisticated title such as *The Times*, *Daily Telegraph*, *Manchester Guardian*, *The Scotsman* or *Yorkshire Post*.[7] Sunday newspapers were also immensely successful. Indeed, newspapers may have been more popular than God. A wartime survey found that 60 per cent of men and 80 per cent of women professed faith, but two-thirds of them admitted they never went to church.[8] Those who read newspapers bought them constantly, voluntarily and often from meagre household incomes. A survey conducted in 1934 by Political and Economic Planning found that a sample of 100 British families bought each week: 95 morning daily newspapers, 58 daily evening titles and 130 Sunday newspapers.[9]

The BBC's audience grew rapidly between 1939 and 1945 and so did its staff. To a greater extent than ever before or since, the corporation secured the trust and affection of its listeners. It emerged from the conflict 'as both a symbol and an agent of victory'.[10]

Too often overlooked in accounts of the BBC's wartime accomplishments is any understanding that newspapers also served colossal audiences of engaged readers and, crucially, that they could and did perform roles the BBC could not.

When the war ended, newspapers had been overtaken as purveyors of news by the speed of radio. However, their circulations grew by an average of 86.5 per cent between 1937 and 1947.[11] Between 1938 and 1945 daily sales rose from nineteen million to 24 million.[12] In 1943, the Wartime Social Survey estimated that four out of five men and two-thirds of women read a daily newspaper.[13] To achieve such growth despite the simultaneous expansion of the BBC, Britain's newspapers learned to work in informal partnership with the national broadcaster. From the summer of 1940, newspaper editors began to recognize that the BBC would provide their readers with essential news and information about the war. They adapted to play new roles. These included the provision of context, human colour and comment. Across the ideological spectrum, editors took advantage of their freedom to express trenchant opinions. This, BBC editors and producers could not do. Crucial, though not most prominent among the newspapers' wartime duties, was to hold the government to account on issues that mattered to ordinary Britons. Newspapers spoke truth to power on topics of ethical concern. Examples of such accountability journalism include coverage of the overseas evacuation of children, air raid shelter policy and the treatment of black American soldiers posted to the United Kingdom. Journalists raised sharp ethical questions about plans for post-war social policy, the area bombing of German cities by the RAF and the use of atomic bombs against Hiroshima and Nagasaki. They noted growing evidence of Nazi brutality towards the Jewish people and struggled to comprehend its nature and scale. They were scathing about the labyrinthine bureaucracy that grew to serve the wartime state and drove their readers to the edge of apocalyptic fury. Through their letters pages, they offered a public platform to an eclectic range of opinions including those of organizations such as the Bombing Restriction Committee whose members condemned the bombing of German civilians by the RAF as 'un-British', 'unsporting' and 'un-Christian'.[14]

Of course, newspapers more often conformed to the wishes of the wartime coalition and endorsed government policies. They faced pressure including bullying and intimidation by ministers when they did not. National titles functioned as tools of propaganda as well as publishers of dissenting opinion, but the government did not control them. The BBC's position was more complex and certainly more constrained. It remained formally independent of the Ministry of Information only because it suited the government that the BBC should appear to retain autonomy. In fact, it could only offer the government line and had done so throughout the era of appeasement in close collaboration with the Foreign Office. This is not to suggest that it lied. On the contrary, as Jean Seaton, historian of the BBC, has explained: 'The BBC's accuracy and objectivity was in itself a propaganda weapon – a demonstration of the superiority of democracy over totalitarianism.'[15] The BBC offered accuracy in the interests of a wartime coalition united in the joint causes of national survival and the defence of democracy. It did not offer challenge.

That newspapers could and did challenge and dispute policy in wartime owed much to reluctant acceptance by government that this was a duty owed by a free press to democracy. Emergency regulations introduced by parliament in the summer of 1940 granted the Home Secretary power to suppress newspapers. Herbert Morrison, Home Secretary between October 1940 and May 1945, used it against the Communist *Daily Worker*. Encouraged by Winston Churchill, Morrison also deployed his powers to threaten and cajole the *Daily Mirror* and *Sunday Pictorial*. Churchill resented newspaper criticism deeply. However, Britain fought in the name of democracy, and victory would require the support of the United States where press freedom is protected by the first amendment to the Constitution.

Understanding the complex symbiotic relationship that existed between newspaper journalism and accountable government in wartime requires a grasp of how Britain's free press came into being. Since the 1960s, radical media historians have sought to challenge and deconstruct the account upon which British journalists, politicians and informed citizens have long relied. These scholars, inspired by George Boyce's essay, 'The Fourth Estate: The Reappraisal of a Concept',[16] base their view of British journalism's origins on the argument that journalism did not, as liberal historians believe, escape from official control in the nineteenth century. Instead, it continued to serve the interests of economic and social elites.[17]

Why freedom should inspire newspapers to promote radical causes remains a mystery to liberals, but the radicals' confidence that it should serves a political as well as a scholarly purpose. It seeks to consolidate media history as a discrete discipline, and it provides campaigners against an unregulated newspaper market with an intellectual rationale for reform. The revisionists borrow techniques from academic history, but their real motive appears less noble. They dislike Britain's raucous, audacious and impertinent newspapers precisely because such titles are powerful enough to speak truth to power on behalf of their readers and entertaining enough to secure reader loyalty.

The radicals object that such titles are privately owned, profit-seeking enterprises. They accuse them of selling news as if it is a commodity while portraying as a public good journalism that seeks to entertain rather than inform. They object that Britain's free market in newspapers unregulated by the state supports the existing liberal economic model instead of working to overthrow it. They fear what Sir Brian Leveson described as free journalism's potential 'to create undemocratic concentrations of power and undermine freedoms and the public good'.[18]

This book stems from an older tradition. It defends the three-centuries-old consensus, dating from the abolition of press licensing in 1694, which argues that British newspapers have performed a valuable service to democracy precisely because they are not regulated by the state. It stems from the understanding of newspapers I have acquired not simply through intense academic study, but also via extensive hands-on experience as a broadsheet editor and columnist. I believe that Britain's distinctive status as a democracy without a written constitution imposes on journalists a duty they must perform if our representative institutions are to function properly.

Generations of Britons understood, not least because they were taught to understand, that, in the United Kingdom, checks and balances on power are exercised in the public interest by the courts and the press. They recognized that this is additionally important because Britain's democracy is distinctive. At Westminster, executive and legislature (government and parliament) are not legally separate as they are in the United States. Our ministers sit in the House of Commons and lead a parliamentary majority. This hybrid arrangement has given British governments unparalleled power to ensure their legislation is passed: a level of executive power that is absent from other democratic traditions. To balance this power, this country has a free press untrammelled by state regulation and able to scrutinize parliament and government without prior restraint and in the public interest.

Radical journalism history was invented to challenge this account. The cultural historian Mark Hampton warns that it may be produced through minimal attention to empirical evidence. He suspects that it reveals more about the author's theoretical perspective than the contents of popular newspapers.[19] Adrian Bingham, Professor of Modern History at the University of Sheffield, has offered the additional insight that 'entrenched stereotypes [have] prevented historians from properly understanding the nature of popular newspapers'.[20] Bingham further – and tellingly – observes that: 'Many generalisations have been made about newspapers, but there has been far too little detailed investigation of their contents'.[21] The liberal tradition in media history recognizes that for-profit and ideological newspapers do not obliterate human agency and that journalism in representative democracies is a communication activity through which societies define, maintain and repair themselves.[22] Close reading of British newspapers offers a rich source of evidence for historians. It follows that I have written this book from the liberal perspective and after extended immersion in newspaper archives both physical and virtual.

Throughout my analysis I judge newspapers' performance against the 'six things news can do for democracy', as defined by Michael Schudson. These I consider the most illuminating academic description of what newspaper editors understood to be their first duty in wartime Britain. They include: the duty to inform citizens about events that they need to know about; investigation of issues that government prefers not to discuss; analysis of complex and significant topics; promotion of social empathy between classes and groups; mobilizing their readers to take action or protest; and promoting representative democracy.[23] During the Second World War, editors understood that Britain was engaged in a struggle for national survival. Their obligation to democracy also included a duty to promote the war effort and scrutinize its efficiency.

My focus is on newspapers rather than correspondents. Although they could operate only with the permission of the War Office, the work of war correspondents was read avidly. However, their work has received considerable attention. Philip Knightley's *The First Casualty* offers an excellent starting point for readers unfamiliar with their wartime role.[24] Richard Collier's *The Warcos* provides compelling colour.[25] Among accounts penned by the correspondents themselves, I recommend *Looking for Trouble* by Virginia Cowles,[26] Clare Hollingsworth's *The Three Week's War in Poland*,[27] Hilde Marchant's *Women and Children Last*[28] and *The Desert War* by Alan Moorehead.[29]

CHAPTER 1
A BRIEF HISTORY OF NEWSPAPERS

In Britain, passionate and often intemperate argument for and against press freedom was vivid in the aftermath of the American Declaration of Independence (1776) and the French Revolution (1789). Between 1783 and 1806, the governments led by Prime Minister William Pitt opted for vigorous repression, employing a battery of powers including laws of seditious and blasphemous libel that made criticism of the state and prevailing social order a criminal offence. To these were added newspaper stamp duty and taxes on both advertising and paper. During Britain's extended wars with revolutionary France – and particularly in the fraught atmosphere generated by the summary dismissal of British soldiers after victory at Waterloo in 1815 – Whig and Tory politicians alike believed consumption of newspapers by the poor would pose a grave threat to the social order. They particularly feared the consequences that might flow from paupers reading titles that advanced the arguments made by the English radical Thomas Paine (1737–1809) in *Rights of Man*,[1] his stirring case for democracy and equality. In 1819, publishers of weekly political periodicals were required to register their titles and to pay financial bonds of between £200 and £300. Repression proved ineffective, however. Prosecutions for libel often appeared to enhance the credibility of radical titles and many ignored the stamp duty and published illegally. Indeed, the radical press flourished among working-class readers. In the summer of 1836, Lord Melbourne's Whig government decided to make an emphatic change of direction. It reduced stamp duty by 75 per cent in the hope that sales of respectable, legal newspapers would expand. At the same time, new powers of search and confiscation brought fresh pressure to bear on the publishers of illegal unstamped radical titles. This pincer movement worked. Sales of legal titles expanded rapidly and, in 1855, parliament repealed stamp duty entirely. Members of Parliament had been convinced that making cheaper professional newspapers that supported legal reform would kill the radical press.

In the decades following repeal, the positive economic and social consequences predicted by liberal campaigners for press freedom followed fast. A tsunami of new titles flowed onto the market and entrepreneurial editors and proprietors soon worked out how to make their publications appeal beyond a small, highly educated elite. Establishment titles such as *The Times*, *Daily Telegraph* and *Morning Post*, replete with verbatim accounts of parliamentary speeches and wordy exegeses on foreign policy, were joined by popular titles such as the *Daily Mail* (1896), *Daily Express* (1900) and *Daily Mirror* (1903). Contemporaries recognized that these new newspapers contained a 'new journalism' and the pious amongst them condemned it instantly as 'feather brained',[2] but every title, whether austere or entertaining, competed in a free market established and defended according to shared principles. Commercially successful journalism was a bulwark of Britain's slowly emerging representative democracy. Freed by profit from reliance on state or party it could represent public opinion courageously and without deference. While Queen Victoria reigned (1837–1901) and in the subsequent decade of Edwardian liberalism (1901–10), Britons enjoyed a plural and diverse free press capable of informing, educating and entertaining them. The liberal assertion that a free press could detect and expose crime, protect public health and safety and prevent the public from being misled by individuals or organizations – including their government – appeared to be vindicated. The instinct to censor, prohibit and prosecute with which government had responded to every new idea since Gutenberg's printing press arrived in England at the end of the fifteenth century was in abeyance. The outbreak of war in 1914 demonstrated that it was not dead.

Every democracy acknowledges that national security demands secrecy about the operational aspects of military activity. The British government recognized early in the First World War that such limited control would not meet its needs. It concluded that, to sustain modern warfare, newspapers would have to be recruited to the patriotic cause. Editors and proprietors faced social and legal pressures to comply. Their correspondents obtained access to the battlefields on terms that accorded much higher value to the operational requirements of the military than to free speech. The terms on which newspapers published were choreographed to tell the government's narrative from the recruiting office to the grave. Correspondents got close enough to the action to write stories that dazzled and fascinated the taxpayers back home, but they rarely risked blighting their readers' appreciation with troubling narratives about grotesque wounds, squalid death or perpetual terror. Hosted by armies that fed, housed and conveyed them, these journalists formed close bonds of trust with the military conducting officers who chaperoned them. Such proximity spawned a version of Stockholm syndrome.[3] Many journalists became willing allies of military/political authority. It exploited them to create a narrative amenable to its interests. These were, as defined by the American communications theorist Harold Lasswell (1902–78): to mobilize hatred against the enemy; to preserve the friendship of allies; to procure the co-operation of neutrals and to demoralize the enemy.[4] Through the pages of their willing newspapers and compliant editors, British journalists served these purposes and their government's national propaganda campaign. Public faith in newspapers suffered.

Journalism's failure to report accurately the 'faceless corpses, the scattered limbs, the heaped-up bodies and the stench of death'[5] angered soldiers. Veterans returning home from the front expressed fury about the inaccurate portrayal of battles in which they had fought. British soldiers from the first generation recruited via compulsory conscription preferred to produce and read their own trench newspapers.[6] Titles such as *The Wipers Times*, a satirical magazine published by British soldiers fighting in the Ypres salient (and who struggled to pronounce Ypres), lampooned savagely the reporting of their activities by British national newspapers.[7] Official censorship undoubtedly played a vital role in generating the propaganda-laced accounts that emerged from the Western Front. The British government controlled news at source, restricting newspapers' access to any material that might damage home morale, help the enemy or offend allies. Other factors were also in play. These included self-censorship by journalists and their editors, exploitation of newspapers by a government determined to maximize pro-war propaganda, and remoteness of journalists from the battles they purported to describe. Beyond these political and economic factors, it is clear that many journalists were overwhelmed by the scale and nature of slaughter in this first mechanized war. Some responded by 'reverting to earlier narratives of heroic war'[8] which proved inadequate and inappropriate.

Many British survivors of the Western Front, returning to their homes with painful memories of comrades killed or maimed – and the terror and suffering they had shared, regarded war correspondents and their newspapers with contempt. In addition to the spontaneous literature of correction contained in their trench publications, soldiers and those who sympathized with them responded in wartime and afterwards with poetry and literary fiction that depicted journalists unfavourably. Sarah Lonsdale describes Siegfried Sassoon's (1886–1967) poem 'Fight to a Finish' in which the author, a recipient of the Military Cross for his heroic service on the Western Front, 'fantasises about soldiers returning from the War running through the grunting and squealing "Yellow Pressmen" with their bayonets'.[9]

In 1914, British newspaper readers had expected war reporting to be exciting and revelatory. In the second half of the nineteenth century, technologies including the electronic telegraph and photography had transformed the coverage of news. Readers had enjoyed the results in coverage of the Crimean War (1853–56), American Civil War (1861–65) and Franco-Prussian War (1870–71). British readers of the ambitious and highly profitable new popular titles had relished, in particular, daredevil reporting from the Second Boer War (1899–1902) between Great Britain and the two Boer (Afrikaner) republics – the South African Republic (Transvaal) and the Orange Free State. In these conflicts, professional correspondents travelling independently had eclipsed serving soldiers as sources of reporting from the front. Moreover, by the end of the nineteenth century, the work of pioneers such as William Howard Russell (1821–1907) of *The Times* and Archibald Forbes (1838–1900) of London's *Daily News* had generated a tradition of bold, adventurous journalism capable of attracting readers and, occasionally, speaking truth to power. The Japanese decision to ban American correspondents from the front during the Russo-Japanese War of 1904–5 offered a warning that such freedom to report would no longer be tolerated. In fact, it did little to reduce popular expectations, and the damage to newspapers' reputations when this model of heroic, independent reporting was curtailed was consequently greater.

By 1918, newspaper journalism had lost some of the aura of glamour with which it had been associated. Surviving members of the Front generation now believed that newspapers had failed to do their duty and were vulnerable to manipulation by government. At the same time, Britain's military and political leaders shared a new understanding that newspapers could be exploited in ways that rendered them valuable as agents of state propaganda. Between 1918 and the outbreak of the Second World War in September 1939, several incidents reinforced the impression that Victorian liberal ideals concerning the value of a free press were in grave jeopardy.

CHAPTER 2
BARONS, ABDICATION AND APPEASEMENT

On the evening of Wednesday, 18 March 1931, Britain's Conservative leader of the opposition Stanley Baldwin uttered the phrase, which, more than any other, has endured to stigmatize British newspapers, even in the twenty-first century. Baldwin spoke at an eve-of-poll rally in support of Duff Cooper, the Conservative candidate in the St George's by-election in which the Conservative Party faced a challenge from the United Empire Party (UEP). The UEP was a political hybrid launched, funded and promoted by the newspaper barons Lord Beaverbrook, owner of the *Daily Express* and *London Evening Standard*, and Lord Rothermere, owner of the *Daily Mail* and *Evening News*. Sometimes the barons' pet party fought elections in its own name. At other times, Beaverbrook, the dominant character in this unequal partnership, was content to support a Conservative candidate who would promote the UEP's commitment to British Empire free trade and its hostility to Mr Baldwin. In St George's, Westminster, a rock-solid Conservative seat, an independent Conservative, Sir Ernest Petter, declared his intention to stand against Duff Cooper. To begin with, Petter really was independent, but the press barons confronted him with an offer he could not refuse. Either he accepted their backing and fought the by-election on their terms and with the active support of their newspapers, or they would put up a UEP candidate who would. Petter bowed to the barons' ultimatum. In return, Beaverbrook paid his election expenses and spoke in his support at sixteen venues in the constituency. Cooper, a loyal supporter of Baldwin, knew the power of the barons' newspapers. In his autobiography, he recalled:

> Servants have little time to read a newspaper in the morning, but if they do cast an eye on one in the West End of London it will almost certainly be the Daily Express or the Daily Mail. In the afternoon, when they have more time at their disposal, they will turn to the Evening News or the Evening Standard. These four papers were my chief opponents, and every issue of them was devoted to damaging my cause.[1]

The rank snobbery speaks for itself. Duff Cooper was grand and immensely wealthy. However, his cause was also Stanley Baldwin's and, in Cooper's support, Baldwin told his audience in Queen's Hall, Westminster that Beaverbrook and Northcliffe used their newspapers to exercise 'power without responsibility – the prerogative of the harlot throughout the ages'. His speech, ably finessed by his cousin, the poet Rudyard Kipling, contained several pithy denunciations. He accused the barons' newspapers of 'direct falsehood, misrepresentations, half-truths' and 'the alteration of the speaker's meaning by publishing a sentence apart from the context'. The barons themselves were exercising 'insolent plutocracy'. Moreover, although Baldwin's animosity was personal, it was also justified. The reputation of British newspapers was at a low ebb during the 1930s. Later in the decade, failures over the abdication of King Edward VIII and appeasement of Adolf Hitler would further damage their status. In each of these episodes, Britain's national newspapers would illustrate that popular and elite titles had drifted away from the liberal, fourth estate ideals on which were built their freedom from censorship and burgeoning circulations.

Our Victorian ancestors really did believe that newspapers were more than commercial products. They regarded a free press as an estate of the realm brought into being to inform and enlighten public opinion. By providing detailed and accurate information about the state of the nation and the world, newspapers would strengthen representative democracy and protect the country against revolutionary sentiment. They would scrutinize government on behalf of an increasingly informed and slowly expanding electorate. At their best, newspapers would speak truth to power and hold to account those who exercised it, whether as politicians, public servants or businessmen. The delusions that truth does not exist, that reality is socially constructed, and that journalism creates news rather than describing it did not exist. Newspapers were trusted to provide a forum for debate capable of promoting and sustaining ideals of free speech such as those described in 1859 by the philosopher John Stuart Mill in his essay, *On Liberty*. To this day, professional journalists believe this is what they do. By 1938, however, journalists richly deserved their depiction in *Scoop*, Evelyn Waugh's coruscating satire. Their most notorious employers certainly deserved Waugh's vivid creations, Lord Copper and his Megapolitan Newspaper Corporation. *Scoop* pinpoints, too, the scale and lavish wealth of Britain's newspaper industry in the late 1930s. Standards had fallen below Victorian ideals, but circulations were still growing in this last decade before BBC Radio became a significant competitor for news audiences. The final pre-war Audit Bureau of Circulations (ABC) list, published in 1939, shows the largest popular Conservative title, the *Daily Express*, with an average net daily circulation of 2,510,019 copies. On the left, the *Daily Mirror* also sold approximately 2,500,000 copies according to figures compiled by its proprietors. The *News Chronicle* was the dominant Liberal daily with a circulation of 1,298,757. The *Evening Standard*, a London title with an interest in national affairs, sold 384,419 copies per day. These titles, together with the broadsheet establishment favourite, *The Times*, its competitor, the *Daily Telegraph*, and the Labour Party's favourite broadsheet, the *Daily Herald*, failed utterly to speak truth to power about an event of far greater significance to the British public than any by-election. This was the abdication crisis of 1936 which saw the king replaced by his reluctant brother and ministers conspiring to change the head of state before parliament or people could express an opinion on the matter.

Attempting a first draft of history in the immediate aftermath of Edward VIII's abdication, the American historian Marshall Knappen concluded that Britain's press had failed in its duty to democracy.[2] Sixteen years after the abdication, George Young observed: 'The voluntary discretion of the English papers concealed from the public a situation which the people of the United States were watching with excitement, France with amusement, and Canada with some anger and alarm.'[3] Richard Cockett argues that, through the power of informal and peculiarly English establishment contacts, the government 'preserved a blanket of censorship on the press about a matter that was front-page news in almost every other country for weeks before the storm broke in Britain'.[4] Mick Temple notes that no story 'illustrated the strength of press self-censorship more than the British press's response to the Abdication Crisis of 1936'.[5] British newspapers certainly did a formidable job of keeping the secret. For months before they made their readers aware of it, foreign titles had reported the king's affair. American titles were determined to follow the adventures of Wallis Simpson, a woman many considered an all-American success. They paid particular attention to her second divorce at Ipswich Assizes on 27 October 1936 where she was awarded a decree nisi on the grounds of adultery by her English husband, Ernest Simpson. Such coverage often relied on conjecture; American correspondents in London were accustomed to relying on reports in British newspapers, but that source of information was closed, and official sources were obstructive. However, despite these difficulties, commuters taking trains home from Manhattan could read titles such as *Liberty* magazine, which printed 2.5 million copies of an edition detailing the affair and advertised it on billboards proclaiming, 'THE YANKEE AT KING EDWARD'S COURT'.[6] In Portland, Oregon, students launched a 'Simpson for Queen' campaign with the slogan 'God Save the King'.[7]

Meanwhile, official efforts ensured that little of this reporting reached the British public. Imported titles that covered the affair were intercepted at ports or censored with scissors by distributors who feared they might be sued.[8] Public figures who discussed the king and Mrs Simpson found their comments unreported. In November 1936, Willie Gallacher MP (Communist, West Fife), told parliamentary lobby reporters: 'I see no reason why the King shouldn't marry Mrs Simpson if he wishes. Naturally, the charmed circle in this country would be upset, but we Communists certainly shouldn't worry about it. Good luck to him, and good luck to her.'[9] Not a syllable of this appeared in British newspapers. Editors and proprietors colluded with government to manage the crisis. Newspapers did not inform Britons about events which they needed to understand. They failed to interrogate government. They did not mobilize protest or promote the principles of representative democracy. Lord Beaverbrook, owner of the market-leading *Daily Express*, responded to the king's request for help 'to protect Wallis from sensational publicity at least in my own country' by working to persuade other newspapers to ignore the story.[10] In subsequent discussions with Stanley Baldwin, by then prime minister, Beaverbrook argued that the king should be allowed to marry the woman he loved.[11] Baldwin, the Cambridge-educated son of a provincial industrialist, had first served in government as financial secretary to the Treasury between 1917 and 1921. In 1935, he entered his third and final term as prime minister, following a successful general election campaign in which his national alliance secured 430 seats in the House of Commons of which 386 were occupied by his Conservative MPs. The Labour opposition held only 154 seats. Baldwin believed the electorate would be appalled by a marriage between their king and a divorcee. White records that the prime minister told his king: 'I might be a remnant of the old Victorians, but my worst enemy would not say to me that I did not know what the reaction of the English people would be to any particular course of action, and ... so far as they went, I was certain that that would be impossible.'[12]

Editors, including Geoffrey Dawson of *The Times* and C.P. Scott of the *Manchester Guardian*, visited Downing Street during the crisis and spoke to members of the Royal court. Cecil King, chairman of Mirror Group Newspapers, would complain, 'The people behind the *Mail*, the *Express* and *The Times* were all actively involved.'[13] However, none of these newspapermen felt obliged to inform their readers. The foreign press had been discussing the relationship between Edward and Mrs Simpson for ten months before the British public read about it. The first hint that a serious crisis was developing only appeared in the British press following a speech on 1 December in which the bishop of Bradford, the Right Reverend A.W.F. Blunt, spoke of the king's 'need of Divine grace'. His opaque but entirely deliberate indication that the king faced an acute moral and constitutional crisis was understood as he hoped it would be. Led by the *Yorkshire Post*, regional papers in Leeds, Bradford, Manchester, Nottingham, Darlington and Birmingham reported his comments.[14]

The Press Divided

The dam was breaking. It collapsed entirely following a meeting between the king and the prime minister at Buckingham Palace on Thursday, 3 December. The king had intimated that he wished to marry and the Cabinet had advised him against it. Now he confirmed that he intended to go ahead. In its edition of Thursday, 3 December, *The Times* quoted with approval the *Yorkshire Post*'s explanation that the real rationale for Dr Blunt's words lay in 'certain statements which have appeared in reputable United States journals, and even in some Dominion newspapers and which cannot be treated with indifference'. In an article headlined 'KING AND MONARCHY', it described a 'grave constitutional issue to be raised by a conflict between the King's intentions and the advice of his ministers'. At one highly successful English local newspaper, the *Kent Messenger*, the editor-proprietor highlighted the column with slashes of ink from his fountain pen. At the end he wrote 'see next page'. There, on page sixteen of *The Times*, he marked with additional slashes a column replicating comments about Dr Blunt's speech from the *Yorkshire Post*, *Yorkshire Observer* and *Birmingham Post*.

On Friday, 4 December, Stanley Baldwin made a statement in the House of Commons. He explained that the king sought a Bill of Exclusion that would allow him to marry Wallis Simpson without her becoming queen and exclude any children of the marriage from succession to the throne. Baldwin said the Cabinet had denied his request.[15] The prime minister's statement made newspaper silence impossible. Now the British press divided openly into two distinct camps that had started to emerge during the private machinations between editors, proprietors and ministers.

One group supported Baldwin's insistence that the king could not marry Mrs Simpson and remain king. This group shared the prime minister's view that the crisis must be resolved in Cabinet without debate in parliament or press. It defended the institution of monarchy over the rights of the monarch himself. It consisted mainly of elite titles, including *The Times*, *Daily Telegraph* and *Manchester Guardian*, which feared debate would embroil the king in political controversy, divide the country and damage British prestige. Siebert writes that they believed: '[A]ll discussion of possible solutions should be avoided in the public prints until after a final settlement had been made.'[16]

The second group, known as the King's Party, sympathized with Edward's wish to marry. It included the *News Chronicle*, *Daily Mail*, *Daily Mirror*, *Daily Express*, *Evening News*, *Evening Star* and *Evening Standard*. Precise positions varied. The *News Chronicle* supported a morganatic marriage. The *Daily Mirror* demanded democratic debate. On 5 December, it told the prime minister: 'The Nation Insists on Knowing the King's Full Demands and Conditions. The Country Will Give You a Verdict.'

Forewarned and Forearmed

One week elapsed between first reports of the relationship in British newspapers and the king's abdication on 10 December. Many Britons were flabbergasted. Edwin Pratt Boorman, editor-proprietor of the *Kent Messenger* was not. In the autumn of 2012, Geraldine Allinson, chairman of the Kent Messenger Group, showed the author around the building at Larkfield near Maidstone in which her family's newspapers were published until 2012. In the abandoned executive suite was an old, brown paper package. A label, handwritten in black ink, revealed the contents: 'Copies of newspapers dealing with the abdication of Edward VIII and accession of George VI, December 1936'. Inside were US, British and French titles from the autumn and winter of 1936, several bearing Pratt Boorman's handwritten notes. The collection, which remains in my possession, includes the county edition of the *Kent Messenger* for Saturday, 12 December, bearing the headline 'THE KING: HOW KENT RECEIVED THE NEWS'. Accompanying it are British newspapers, including the Cadbury family-owned, London evening newspaper, *The Star*, its competitor, Associated Newspapers' *Evening News*, the *News Review* – 'Britain's First Weekly Newsmagazine' – and copies of American titles, including *Time* magazine and an edition of New York's *Literary Digest*. Prominent in Pratt Boorman's collection of foreign newspapers, I spotted a copy of *Paris Soir*'s edition of Wednesday, 28 October 1936, carrying a front-page story: '*La presse et la radio des États Unis annoncent le mariage d'Eduard VIII avec une Américaine*' ('Press and radio in the United States announce Edward VIII's marriage to an American woman').

American and French newspapers in Pratt Boorman's bundle reveal that he was determined to obtain uncensored accounts of the affair and that he knew how to get them. Handwritten notes and underlining in his copies of the *Literary Digest* and *Time* indicate that he read detailed coverage before he informed his own readers. His conduct provides a case study of the British establishment's concerns about Edward's relationship with Mrs Simpson and the future of the monarchy.

Most intriguing in the bundle are two galley proofs, made by hand-stamping the composed decks of type onto sheets of newsprint. In the hot-metal era, these were prepared so editors could correct copy and assess its merit before allocating it to a page. These proofs preserve pre-publication versions of reports that would explain the abdication crisis to hundreds of thousands of readers. Their survival emphasizes the issue's sensitivity and that Pratt Boorman was intimately involved in every aspect of his newspaper's coverage.

Striking in the *Kent Messenger* proofs is a story explaining the newspaper's silence regarding the crisis throughout the weeks when it was openly discussed abroad. Headlined 'Friendship with Beautiful Mrs Simpson', it explains: 'Along with other newspapers, the *Kent Messenger* has been bound by that reticence with which the affairs of the Royal family are treated by the British press, but now that the matter has become a national issue, this no longer holds.' The explanation implies a formal convention that did not exist. Nevertheless, it offers an accurate account of the informal conspiracy through which Britain's pre-war elite prevented public discussion of issues it considered uncongenial. George Orwell captured this process superbly when writing about 'the pre-war silliness' of British newspapers:

> One of the most extraordinary things about England is that there is almost no official censorship, and yet nothing that is actually offensive to the governing class gets into print, at least in any place where large numbers of people are likely to read it. If it is 'not done' to mention something or other, it just doesn't get mentioned. . . . No bribes, no threats, no penalties – just a nod and a wink and the thing is done. A well-known example was the business of the Abdication. Weeks before the scandal officially broke, tens or hundreds of thousands of people had heard all about Mrs Simpson and yet not a word got into the press, not even into the *Daily Worker*, although the American and European papers were having the time of their lives with the story.[17]

The owners' own lobby-group-cum-club, the Newspaper Proprietors Association (NPA), had decided on a policy of silence.[18] Other newspapers would proclaim the policy of concealing truth from their readers appropriate and virtuous. The arch-conservative *Morning Post* declared that it was 'no part of the function of the Press to publish gossip possibly injurious to such an institution as the monarchy'. Some British editors resented so profoundly American coverage of the affair that they retaliated by suggesting that American newspapers were equally guilty of protecting the powerful from embarrassment. *Time* noted that a British accusation that American journalists voluntarily concealed the president's disability was at least exaggerated:

> Although the infirmities of President Roosevelt have been freely chronicled and pictures have been published in the US which show him hobbling about, the London *Daily Telegraph* salved its conscience for omitting the Mrs Simpson story by declaring: 'Actual view of the President's disability never fails to surprise the public. Neither the reporters nor the photographers have prepared them for it.'[19]

Ignorance was not quite complete. For those in the know, there were early hints in the British press that a crisis was looming. However, this was Delphic stuff which left all outside the social and political elite mystified. Edwin Pratt Boorman of the *Kent Messenger* was part of this elite and his access to foreign newspapers ensured that he was earlier informed than almost all of his readers. It is plain that, in common with several fellow members of the NPA, he shared the prime minister's moral concerns. An article in *Literary Digest* appears to have captured his interest. It begins: 'Nobody mentioned the King. For that matter, no British newspaper mentioned that Mrs Simpson was his friend. But minutes before the Baltimore belle slipped out of Ipswich Assizes with her second divorce in her pocket, a million conversations were being launched around the world with the phrase: "Now that she's free . . . ?"'[20] In Pratt Boorman's edition, the words, 'second divorce in her pocket' are heavily underlined.

His disapproval is confirmed in the galley proofs. Explaining that some readers may have heard about the scandal from relatives and friends in the United States or Canada, the *Kent Messenger* notes in bold text: '**To most people, especially those belonging to the middle classes, it came as a shock. They were almost unanimous in their condemnation of the proposal that the King should marry Mrs Simpson.**' Then, reverting to plain type, it explains: 'Their principal objection was that Mrs Simpson had been married twice before.'

The grandest of Britain's establishment broadsheets, *The Times* rode to the prime minister's defence with an adamant declaration that such a marriage was not merely unpopular – an assertion for which neither it nor the *Kent Messenger* had a shred of evidence – but also unconstitutional. Relying entirely on conventions which, in the absence of a written constitution, were all it could summon in evidence, *The Times* explained that the king had asked Mr Baldwin to secure consent for him to marry Mrs Simpson according to the morganatic principle whereby she would become his wife but not queen. This, it insisted in an extended leader column, was simply not possible:

> He desired to marry Mrs Simpson, but not to confer upon her the rank of Queen Consort of England, which in the present state of law cannot be denied to the King's wife. His proposal therefore required a change in the law; and, if the King desires a change in the law, he must ask his Ministers to move Parliament accordingly.[21]

Despite his profound personal concern for the king's happiness, the prime minister had no choice but to conclude that such a marriage would 'affect the succession to the throne'[22] and, according to the 'established constitutional position',[23] any such change must require 'the assent of all the self-governing dominions'.[24] Such assent would not be forthcoming. Therefore, with infinite regret but no hint of personal preference, Mr Baldwin had been constitutionally compelled to tell the king he could not follow the dictates of his heart. The abdication that followed was the king's decision alone and had been reached in the absence of any pressure from the Cabinet.

The argument that the British establishment did what it was compelled to do, not what it wanted to do, when confronted by Edward VIII's request is more convenient than constitutional. It ignores Baldwin's acute desire for stability and the ingredients for crisis that existed in Britain during the years before the abdication. Martin Pugh notes that threats to liberal democracy were real.[25] Economic conditions had given rise to extremist movements of right and left. Fascism in Italy and National Socialism in Germany were destabilizing Europe. Edward VIII's affair reached British attention just as the Spanish Civil War that had erupted in July 1936 threatened to provoke a wider confrontation between totalitarianism and constitutional democracy. Fear of instability and war abounded. The Conservative Baldwin led a National government and, in dealing with the crisis, had support from the parliamentary Labour Party. Labour's Clement Attlee, the leader of His Majesty's Loyal Opposition, was a dedicated monarchist and his priorities during the crisis were indistinguishable from Baldwin's. He was determined that the monarchy must endure unscathed and certain that Edward VIII would discredit it.[26] Attlee and Labour made sure that no party-political split emerged to intensify division in the country.

In the newspaper industry, intense competition for readers stimulated a brief spasm of truly populist journalism once the king's intentions were known. Thus, the *News Chronicle* supported a morganatic marriage and the *Daily Mirror* demanded full democratic debate. On 5 December, it told the prime minister: 'The Nation Insists on Knowing the King's Full Demands and Conditions. The Country Will Give You a Verdict.' However, only a week elapsed between the first reports of the relationship in British newspapers and the king's abdication on 10 December. The press did not have time to repair its reputation. It would damage it still further as furore over the abdication gave way to a prolonged and grave crisis over appeasement.

Newspapers and Appeasement

The policy of appeasement, the umbrella term for assorted diplomatic, economic and strategic gestures to avoid war with Nazi Germany and Fascist Italy by soothing and placating the European dictators, is most commonly associated with the Conservative leader Neville Chamberlain. Chamberlain certainly pursued appeasement with vigour, but he did not invent it. Stanley Baldwin was the dominant figure in British Conservative politics during the 1920s and 1930s. In 1935 he entered his third and final term as prime minister with a substantial majority following the General Election of Thursday, 14 November. Chamberlain, then serving as chancellor of the exchequer, had urged his colleague to fight the contest on a commitment to rearmament. The Cabinet had seen compelling evidence that Hitler was building large, modern armed forces. As chancellor, Chamberlain feared that, if the Conservatives were elected without advertising an explicit pledge to build stronger armed forces, they would face accusations of dishonesty when later obliged to spend heavily on weapons of war. Baldwin did not make rearmament a central theme of his campaign. Facing an explicitly pacifist Labour opposition and aware of profound public hostility to war, he acknowledged a need to modernize Britain's defences but promised that there would be 'no great armaments'.[27] Having meekly turned a blind eye towards the relationship between Edward VIII and Mrs Simpson, most British newspapers now adopted an equally supine attitude to the question of appeasement. Their approach would serve Chamberlain well when, in late May 1937, he replaced Baldwin as prime minister.

When Neville Chamberlain moved into 10 Downing Street, Hitler's willingness to ignore international agreements was already starkly apparent. German troops had entered the Rhineland on 7 March 1936. In moving his forces into this border territory between Germany and France, the Nazi leader breached the Treaty of Versailles by which the First World War was formally concluded in 1919. Under the terms imposed on her in defeat, Germany was 'forbidden to maintain or construct any fortification either on the Left bank of the Rhine or on the Right bank to the west of a line drawn fifty kilometres to the East of the Rhine'.[28] Any breach of this agreement was recognized explicitly as a hostile act. Baldwin's government acquiesced and so set a standard of caution his successor would emulate and then exceed. To reinforce his policy and secure for it the public support he craved, Chamberlain would build a system of newspaper management that used many of the informal channels that had worked for Baldwin during the abdication crisis. However, faced with escalating territorial demands from Hitler, the new prime minister would also use the institutions of government in his efforts to tame, manipulate and mislead journalists and their readers.

Thirty years ago, in his *Twilight of Truth: Chamberlain, Appeasement and the Manipulation of the Press*, Richard Cockett showed how the Chamberlain government 'consciously set out to control and manipulate the press' while, 'for domestic consumption, maintaining the fiction of a liberal democracy' with free and independent newspapers.[29] Cockett argues that Chamberlain paid close attention to briefings from Sir Nevile Henderson, Britain's ambassador to Berlin. Henderson warned repeatedly that Hitler was acutely sensitive to criticism in British newspapers. Following one meeting with the Führer, he concluded that any prospect of enduring peace was stymied by British criticism of the Nazi leader. Hitler told Henderson: 'Nothing could be done until the press campaign against him in England had ceased.'[30] The ambassador would later explain: 'It would not have mattered so much had Hitler been a normal individual, but he was unreasonably sensitive to newspaper, and especially British newspaper, criticism.'[31]

The dictator's control of the German press was absolute and his understanding of democracy poor. He imagined Chamberlain could compel editors directly. In fact, the prime minister had no legal powers of prior restraint. British newspapers were free to oppose him and to condemn his policy if they chose to do so. Instead, many national newspapers supported appeasement as the prime minister wished them to. In the absence of formal power to censor, Chamberlain's achievement was to persuade them that his policy was in the national interest and that hostility to it would weaken Britain's influence abroad. This he achieved through a mixture of old-fashioned establishment contacts with proprietors and editors and innovative use of the government machine.

Chamberlain maintained a friendship with Lord Kemsley, owner of the *Daily Sketch* and the *Sunday Times*. He was extremely close to Geoffrey Dawson, editor of *The Times* and a zealous appeaser. Lord Astor, owner of *The Observer* needed no persuasion; he and his wife, the society hostess Nancy Astor, regarded Chamberlain as a prophet. For help to influence the mass-market *Daily Express*, *Daily Mail*, *Daily Mirror*, *News Chronicle* and *Daily Telegraph*, Neville Chamberlain relied on assistance from two colleagues, Sir Joseph

Ball, chairman of the Conservative Research Department and George Steward, the first official ever to occupy a role as the prime minister's personal press officer.

Colin Seymour-Ure explains that Steward's career in press relations began in 1915 at the foreign office. A career civil servant, he was later transferred to the Treasury and then to Downing Street where he prepared press briefings for Ramsay MacDonald, Labour leader first of the minority Labour government that held office between 1929 and 1931 and later of the national government 1931–35.[32] Steward first offered briefings to parliamentary journalists under MacDonald in 1930.[33] His role would expand substantially when Chamberlain took office.

Cockett shows how Chamberlain's team exploited the parliamentary lobby system of unattributable briefings to accredited correspondents. To achieve his master's ends, George Steward decided that all significant information about government policy must reach lobby correspondents from his lips or those of a loyal minister. By making regular, scheduled lobby briefings he tamed many of the most influential correspondents. If they reported what he told them without attribution, as lobby rules required, they would remain privileged insiders. That their readers would thus be persuaded that these ostensibly objective insights into government thinking were unalloyed truth was, of course, the whole point. Steward made the lobby correspondents dependent upon him. Willingness to promote the government's line would guarantee access to Chamberlain's thinking. Refusal to comply might mean exclusion and professional failure. Compliance was the norm. James Margach, in 1938 a young lobby correspondent for *The Times*, observed that relations between government and the journalists who were supposed to hold them to account became 'too cosy and comfortable'.[34] He lamented that Steward's success was not due to manipulative skills alone. Rather, the lobby correspondents themselves were too keen to be considered 'honorary members of a power establishment and ex-officio members of a political system . . . as allies, legmen and buddies'.[35]

It is a reflection on the paucity of quality newspaper history in Britain that nothing published since has seriously challenged Cockett's excellent interpretation. Close reading of newspapers certainly confirms that, with the exception of the *Yorkshire Post* and the *Daily Telegraph*, Conservative newspapers supported the prime minister's zealous pursuit of appeasement. Some did so more slavishly than others and none more slavishly than Geoffrey Dawson's *Times*. My first case study examines editorial treatment of the notorious Munich agreement, by which Chamberlain imagined he had secured what he described to a cheering crowd in Downing Street as 'peace for our time'. This he had accomplished by proposing the transfer of the Sudetenland to Germany without first securing Czech consent. Accepted by Hitler, this Anglo-French proposal left the Czechs with no option but to concede territory without which the remainder of Czechoslovakia became militarily indefensible.

Reporting the Munich Agreement

The Munich agreement was debated in the House of Commons on Monday, 3 October 1938. Geoffrey Dawson's *Times* did not wait to hear the parliamentarians' views before expressing fawning adoration for the prime minister. 'The volume of applause for Mr Chamberlain, which continues to grow throughout the globe, registers a popular judgment that neither politicians nor historians are likely to reverse', it declared.[36] Britain's most prestigious broadsheet newspaper went on:

> The peace concluded at Munich is a peace dictated at bottom by the peoples who would have suffered in case of war; and not least insistent, though with difficulty articulate, were the German people. One fundamental truth that Mr Chamberlain's diplomacy brought into light was this – that even in a totalitarian state the people will have their influence in last resort upon the party.[37]

Then, not content with the implausible suggestion that Hitler had come to the negotiating table under pressure from the German people, *The Times* concluded with a prediction that combined cloying praise for the prime minister and a nod towards his background in business with a Panglossian view of the future: '[T]he world will reach the goal which is known to be Mr Chamberlain's dearest ambition, of an era when the race for armaments will be seen for the madness that it is and will be abandoned because it has ceased even to be profitable.' Such coverage was precisely what George Steward was deployed to achieve for his employer. It was not entirely typical.

Like *The Times*, the leading popular Conservative newspaper, the *Daily Express*, seized the opportunity to comment on Munich before the parliamentary debate. Indeed, it commented twice. A front-page leader column reflected its proprietor's rigid conviction that war was disastrous for business and should be avoided at all costs. Headlined 'Make this "Cheerful Monday"', this boisterous piece declared:

> Back to normal today. Aftermath of Crisis Week news still fills many columns of news space, and our reporters are still following the German troops into Sudetenland, still watching the Poles, the Hungarians and the Czechs to keep you well informed. **But** throughout the Daily Express today you will find news features – peace-time features. So, back to normal! Back to our peace-time occupations.[38]

The front-page leader then issued a bold invitation to buy friends and family members 'a peace gift' to get trade moving again. The *Express* took a more considered view of appeasement in its conventional leader column. This questioned whether Britain's defensive strength was adequate to maintain peace: 'We fear it is not. Is it soon to be made adequate? We, the public, demand that it shall be. Mr Chamberlain must give us his answer.'[39] Lord Beaverbrook's most powerful organ went on to explain the consequences of weakness. 'Britain accepted the Munich agreement because our defences were not in a condition enabling us to make any other decision', it explained. Finally, it demanded arms and isolation. Once strong enough to do so, Britain should 'not mean to attach ourselves to any other Power in Europe. We shall follow the path of isolation.'[40]

At the other end of the Conservative spectrum, the *Yorkshire Post*, under the inspiring editorship of Arthur Mann, described the terms agreed at Munich as 'harsh and unconscionable'. Hitler had threatened war to get what he wanted, and Britain had bowed to his demands. 'How is it possible', asked the influential regional broadsheet, 'that we should feel confident that a man so minded will really prove peace-minded in future?'[41] The *Daily Mail* praised Chamberlain's achievement and seized the opportunity to criticize his opponents: 'The Government's calm statement of the facts was in striking contrast to the frothy diatribes of the Socialists. . . . While Mr Attlee cried of the "shameless betrayal" of the Czechs, Sir Samuel Hoare [Home Secretary] in his reasoned winding-up speech last night, showed convincingly that Czecho-Slovakia itself owes its survival to the four-power agreement.'[42] That the *Mail*'s leader writer recognized how little Czechs were likely to endorse this opinion, he acknowledged in his concluding sentence: 'The British people endorse the Prime Minister's admiration for the "restraint, dignity, and magnificent discipline of the Czechs".'[43]

George Steward's achievement was not complete. Unanimity of opinion did not exist in the Conservative press, but on the right opposition to appeasement was a minority taste and only the *Yorkshire Post* expressed it consistently and vigorously. Among Arthur Mann's most telling condemnations of Chamberlain was a leader he published on the twentieth anniversary of the end of the First World War. Calculated to offend the prime minister, it denounced 'a policy of appeasement indistinguishable from a surrender to threats' and accused its architects of a 'tragic lack of conviction'. It concluded: 'We have not cared deeply enough for the things we won in 1918.'[44]

Left-of-centre newspapers felt no compulsion to praise the prime minister, though they too came under persistent pressure to avoid comment that might anger Hitler. Their major handicap was Labour's failure to articulate a plausible alternative to appeasement. The most popular of the Labour titles, the *Daily Mirror*, reflected this absence of leadership in its coverage of Munich. On its front page on 3 October, the *Mirror* published the king's thanks that peace had been preserved. George VI told his subjects: 'The time of anxiety is past' and he did not hesitate to praise Chamberlain: 'After the magnificent efforts of the Prime Minister in the cause of peace, it is my fervent hope that a new era of friendship and prosperity may be dawning among the peoples of the world.'[45] Beside this Royal praise, the *Mirror* published an account of Hitler's 'visit to his new empire' and noted that 'he goes like a conqueror into his new dominions in Czechoslovakia'.[46] The following day, after the debate at Westminster, the *Mirror* reflected on the fragility of Chamberlain's achievement: 'And so, once more in listening to the latest debate against the background of the latest Nazi triumph, it was impossible not to wonder ruefully where else Hitler will be marching when the next debate is due.'[47] The *Mirror* feared the 'further strengthening until it becomes invincible of the Nazi domination of Europe'. It believed that peace could only be guaranteed by strength and encouraged rapid and extensive rearmament, but it could identify no clear alternative to compromise and deterrence. It feared the creation of 'a world so armed and so explosive that it will blow itself to bits'.[48]

As Neville Chamberlain deployed it, appeasement incorporated elements including pacifism, isolationism and deterrence. His constant was resolute certainty that press and public shared his enthusiasm for it. Daniel Hucker shows that the prime minister misled himself. At his most deluded, Chamberlain misinterpreted press support that he had won through bullying and persuasion as evidence that his policy was genuinely popular. When newspapers did criticize it, he ignored them or dismissed their criticism as misrepresentation.[49]

Among the Conservative titles the *Daily Express*, *Daily Mail* and *The Times* could be relied upon to champion appeasement as an inherently virtuous policy. Their support was precious because these titles offered a combination of scale and prestige. Between them, the two mass-market titles reached between seven and nine million readers daily. Circulation and readership of *The Times* was smaller, but newspaper influence depends on more than scale alone. Crucial also is who reads and how instrumentally. *The Times* was read and trusted by opinion formers in parliament, the City and England's universities.

The left-of-centre press, while loathing Hitler, had grave doubts about any alternative to appeasement and was hampered by the Labour Party's reluctance to offer clear leadership. However, newspapers of the thinking left identified grave flaws in Chamberlain's approach. Thus, the *Manchester Guardian*'s leader column on 3 October 1938 cautioned:

> Now that the first flush of emotion is over it is the duty of all of us to see where the 'peace with honour' has brought us. The Prime Minister claims that is has brought us 'peace for our time'. It is an inspiring claim, and if it proves to be a just one, he will have earned a high place in history.[50]

This intelligent and ambitious newspaper of liberal dissent was not persuaded that Chamberlain's pride could be justified. It urged MPs to scrutinize the Munich agreement forensically and it argued that complete solidarity between Britain, France the United States and the Soviet Union would be essential if democrats were to oppose effectively the emerging alliance between Hitler's Germany and Mussolini's Italy. The leader concluded: 'To discard Russia (which has seemed to be Mr Chamberlain's aim) would be to tie ourselves bound to the Berlin-Rome axis. If indeed we gained "peace for our time," it would be the peace of the shorn lamb.'[51] Four days later, the *Manchester Guardian*'s doubts had intensified. It still hoped that: 'Mr Chamberlain's surrender to the blandishments of the dictators is less complete than his earlier utterances and actions suggested.' It hoped that new arms, soldiers, sailors and airmen could reinforce British diplomatic influence. However, it demanded 'an entire change in our foreign policy' and insisted that, without one, 'ordinary men and women' would not be convinced that 'the diplomacy our armaments are to serve' would be anything but 'weak and truckling'.[52]

Over appeasement, newspapers did not fail as utterly as they had failed during the abdication crisis, but few challenged Chamberlain's policy thoroughly or consistently. Those that did mount intelligent opposition, amongst which the *Yorkshire Post* stands out as a proud example of editorial integrity and independence, failed to dent the prime minister's confidence in his own virtue.

In 1937 and 1938, the viciousness and modernity of warfare in Spain and China brought disturbing images to British newspapers, cinema newsreels and magazines.

Aerial bombardment of cities aroused new and vivid awareness that modern warfare could not be restricted to the battlefield. Civilians in cities, towns and villages throughout the land would become targets for bombers. *The Times* special correspondent George Steer's account of the destruction of the Basque city of Guernica by German warplanes on 26 April 1937 offered a particularly alarming glimpse of the terrors that might be inflicted. It was widely read and shared in Britain and around the world. Steer reported that Guernica was a 'horrible sight, flaming from end to end'. He explained that: 'In the form of execution and the scale of the destruction it wrought . . . the raid on Guernica is unparalleled in military history. Guernica was not a military objective. . . . The object of the bombardment was seemingly the demoralisation of the civil population. . .'[53] His report, translated into French and published in the French Communist newspaper *L'Humanité*, inspired Pablo Picasso's outstanding modernist image, 'Guernica', which toured the United Kingdom in 1938 and was seen by many thousands in locations including a car showroom in Manchester.[54]

Between 1937 and the beginning of war, both houses of parliament spent many hours discussing how to protect civilians against bombing, many of them during intense debates over the Air-Raid Precautions Bill which sought 'to secure that precautions shall be taken with a view to the protection of persons and property from injury or damage in the event of hostile attack from the air'.[55] Juliet Gardiner notes that, in February 1939, a local government report had offered a bleak assessment: 'In a country the size of England, there is, in the condition of modern war, no place of absolute safety.'[56]

This was the context in which newspaper editors sought to explain, interpret and depict appeasement to their readers. A generation scarred by the ghastly toll of mechanized warfare between 1914 and 1918 now faced new and awful threats. That statesmen should exercise every reasonable effort to avert them seemed only reasonable. The nuanced question was whether Chamberlain's efforts always qualified as reasonable. The evidence is that a minority of British newspapers, mainly but not exclusively on the left, concluded that they did not. They reached this conclusion many months before the German seizure of rump Czechoslovakia demonstrated the worthlessness of the Munich agreement in March 1939.

However, in noting that the spirit of press freedom was not entirely dead during the era of appeasement, I suggest only that British newspapers offered a small fraction of the editorial diversity required to invigorate democratic accountability. Remote from London, Arthur Mann of the *Yorkshire Post* found the integrity and strength of character to identify appeasement's flaws, condemn them and offer reasoned alternatives. The *Manchester Guardian*, similarly insulated by distance from pressures applied by the prime minister and his servants, raised pointed questions. Those who published in London felt the formal and informal pressure from Downing Street more directly.

Neville Chamberlain announced that Britain was at war with Germany in a radio broadcast on the morning of Sunday, 3 September 1939. He told the millions listening: 'You can imagine what a bitter blow it is to me that all my long struggle to win peace has failed. Yet I cannot believe that there is anything more or anything different that I could have done and that would have been more successful.'[57] Newspapers had suggested that he might have done more, but they had not identified clear alternatives, still less had they advertised or promoted better ideas. Britain's national newspapers entered the Second World War widely read but little trusted. Nothing that they achieved in the last months of 1939 or the first months of 1940 would shift public scepticism. Indeed, when, two years after the war in 1947, Clement Attlee's Labour government established the first Royal Commission on the Press, the behaviour of newspapers during Chamberlain's pursuit of appeasement was a justification for this unprecedented interference in the independence of newspapers.[58] Richard Cockett suggests that contemporaries assumed the press barons had simply 'supported a policy that was conducive to a profitable and stable trading atmosphere'.[59] In May 1940, Mass Observation's Report on the Press found, 'The general curve of distrust of the news has been rising during the last year.'[60] Newspapers' timid reporting of abdication and appeasement augmented the legacy suspicion that they could not be relied upon that had endured since the First World War.[61] The consequence of voluntary self-censorship, it was encouraged by a prime minister who set out to manipulate journalists, their editors and proprietors and pioneered new techniques to achieve his aims. Mass Observation added that, 'Since the war has broken out ... distrust of the press has increased.'[62] In analysing newspaper performance during the first months of war, we shall see that intense shock was required to persuade the British press to do its duty according to liberal principles.

CHAPTER 3
THE PHONEY WAR

If British readers did not entirely trust their newspapers in September 1939, we should be clear that they neither trusted nor admired the BBC to anything approaching the extent to which they would trust and admire it when the war ended. On the left of British politics, resentment of the corporation's pro-Establishment stance during the General Strike of 1926 remained vivid. The BBC had done even less than newspapers to question appeasement. It had denied access to the airwaves to politicians such as Winston Churchill who argued against Chamberlain's diplomacy. Most powerfully corrective to any romantic delusion that the BBC entered the war already beloved by millions is the plain truth that it was small, dull and meekly obedient to the demands of ministers. Newspapers in contrast were read by a vast audience that included all but the very poorest Britons. Some of them were tremendously entertaining.

Five popular titles, the *Daily Express*, *Daily Mirror*, *News of the World*, *The People* and the *Sunday Express* had a combined circulation of more than thirteen million in 1939.[1] All of the popular titles offered a great deal more than hard news. Strip cartoons were a staple and would become additionally popular as the war ground on. In September 1939 the *Daily Mirror* was running five regular cartoons. Jane, created by the artist Norman Pett and based initially on his wife and from early 1940 on the model Chrystabel Leighton-Porter, was a beautiful and scantily clad girl about town. She would become a potent symbol of British cheerfulness in the face of adversity and was described by Winston Churchill as the country's 'secret weapon'.[2] Jane was the British serviceman's favourite and had pride of place at the top of page five. Buck Ryan (a crime-fighting private investigator), Beelzebub Jones (a wild western farmer), Belinda (Belinda Blue Eyes, a perpetual waif and British equivalent of the American Little Orphan Annie) and the hapless Buggles all appeared on page twelve, above the crossword and beside the *Mirror*'s horoscope 'Message of the Stars' by Ann Maritza.[3] Such horoscopes, which also included 'Fortune Forecast' in the *Daily Mail* and plain 'Horoscope' on the woman's page of the *Daily Express* were immensely popular.

Film was also well loved. Between eighteen and nineteen million cinema tickets were sold each week in the late 1930s[4] and Hollywood studios were enjoying a golden age. The top grossing releases of 1939 included *Gone with the Wind* and *The Wizard of Oz*. Glamorous movie stars, such as Vivien Leigh, the 25-year-old British star of MGM's *Gone with the Wind*, and other big names, including Hedy Lamarr, James Stewart and Clark Gable, appeared frequently in news stories and pictures. The newspapers paid additionally close attention when Hollywood names visited the UK which, ever keen on career-boosting publicity, they frequently did.

Newspapers, particularly the mass circulation dailies, offered an eclectic and engaging mix of content designed explicitly to attract, engage and retain readers. The British popular newspaper diet of 1939 was not quite as expansive as the novelist Jay McInerney's recipe for tabloid success, 'Killer Bees, Hero Cops, Sex Fiends, Lottery Winners, Teenage Terrorists, Liz Taylor, Tough Tots, Sicko Creeps, Living Nightmares, Life on Other Planets, Spontaneous Human Combustion, Miracle Diets and Coma Babies',[5] but it achieved a genuinely broad appeal. And, although they did it in less detail and plainer English, popular newspapers reported the serious news agenda as assiduously as their sophisticated broadsheet rivals. Indeed, many families bought one of each. Buying and reading newspapers was a normal part of everyday life. They were as common as mobile telephones are in the twenty-first century and even more easily available. Home delivery was common, street vendors were ubiquitous. Chalked boards and paper flyers advertised the latest headlines and stimulated casual purchase. Coupon offers, competitions and star columnists encouraged loyalty to an individual title. In 1939, 2,510,019 copies of the *Daily Express*, 2,500,000 of the *Daily Mirror*, 1,532,683 of the *Daily Mail* and 1,298,757 of the *News Chronicle* were sold every weekday. The *News of the World* alone sold 3,750,000 copies on Sundays.[6]

We know that families gathered around their wireless sets to hear the prime minister declare war via the BBC. These people and many more also read the news in their daily newspaper the following morning, Monday, 4 September. In their newspapers, they consumed comment that BBC newsreaders could not supply and analysis that sought to explain and contextualize events. The *Daily Mirror*'s headline reflected its admiration for those who had opposed the prime minister's appeasement of Germany; it read 'Britain's First Day of War: Churchill Is New Navy Chief'[7] and explained Churchill's appointment as First Lord of the Admiralty, a position he had previously occupied during the First World War. A sub-heading explained the early impact of war on everyday lives: 'Petrol Will Be Rationed', it announced before noting that one new member of the nine-strong war cabinet had been driven away from Downing Street 'by a woman chauffeur in uniform'.[8]

At the opposite end of the ideological spectrum, the *Daily Mail* worked hard to keep its readers informed, producing new editions throughout the night. The final edition, a 6.00 am special, carried on its front page the latest news about the sinking of the British liner *Athenia* in the mid-Atlantic. 'The Admiralty issued a report at 4 a.m. that the *Athenia* has sent out an SOS saying that she had been struck by a torpedo', it reported. 'At 5 o' clock this morning it was reported by the Admiralty that the liner was sinking rapidly.' The *Mail* noted that *Athenia* was carrying 1,400 passengers, 160 of whom were American.[9] Also on its front page was a report of a speech by Neville Chamberlain, not the one he had made the previous day, but an early morning address to the German people via French radio in which the prime minister advised any German citizens who dared to listen that Britain's quarrel was with their government, not with ordinary Germans.[10]

Newspapers remained more popular than the radio as sources of news, but they were already adapting to compete with the new medium. Treating as news information to which readers had enjoyed live access the previous day made no commercial or editorial sense. Editors made every effort to ensure that their titles carried fresh stories with engaging new details and perspectives projected on the front page. Popular as well as elite newspapers were broadsheet in design and this allowed ample space for a range of stories.

Voluntary Censorship

When war was declared, the British press remained free, at least in theory. Rear-Admiral George Pirie Thompson, a veteran submariner, was the government's deputy chief press censor. He would spend five wartime years as chief press censor. His title tells its own story. Despite its inadequacies, the government recognized the obvious: formal press censorship laws were incompatible with the principles of democracy Britain must defend. However, the absence of a censorship statute should not divert our attention from the oppressive system of voluntary censorship that was in place. This had as its first objective the duty to protect national security. Awareness of the concomitant obligation to keep the public informed came a poor second. This system was, at first, almost comically inept. In his memoir, *Blue Pencil Admiral*, published in 1947, Thompson describes blundering, myopia and inconsistency as censors sought to manage a barrage of news copy, photographs and anxious requests for guidance.

Before the war, a shadow Ministry of Information (MoI) had experimented with a censorship staff made up entirely of retired military officers. Their work had failed to impress. So, when German forces entered Poland, Thompson's team had expanded to include 'a motley crew – retired naval, army and RAF officers, barristers, solicitors, publishers, journalists, teachers, art critics, advertising agents'.[11] He describes as chaotic their first encounter with enemy action, the aforementioned sinking of the passenger liner *Athenia*. Censors were overwhelmed by the volume of articles and telegrams pouring into their office. An atmosphere of barely suppressed panic appears to have infected the operation.

When Thompson arrived in the MoI's wartime offices in the Senate House of the University of London, the commissionaire in the courtyard proved reluctant to accept that he was not a German spy. Inside he found the Director of Press Censorship, Admiral Usborne, 'sitting alone on the ground floor trying to deal with four telephones at the same moment'.[12] He recalls Admiral Usborne's forlorn and indignant response to one call: 'Hallo – Director of Censorship speaking – who's that? The *Daily Mail*? No, I don't know anything about the British Expeditionary Force and if I did, I couldn't tell you.'[13]

Thompson soon refined his objectives. He must 'decide, day by day, hour by hour, just how much war news your favourite newspaper and the BBC could give you without at the same time telling the enemy what *he* wanted to know'.[14] In the first half of his task he was assisted by the MoI's control of official information. Reporters from all Britain's national and regional newspapers were housed in a vast newsroom of the ground floor of the Senate House. Here, they would listen as ministry officials read official communiqués from the armed forces and other government departments. These contained information that had been approved for publication. It reflected the military hierarchy's intensely cautious mindset and rarely contained any colour or detail. However, this official boilerplate was easy to use. Reporters could simply send it to their newspapers where their editors could as simply publish it.

Harder to handle was livelier copy sent by newspaper editors who needed censorship guidance. This they sent to their reporters in the Senate House newsroom who would then take it to an MoI censor for correction and approval. This could be a painfully slow process. Censors were meticulous and intensely cautious. Any remotely complex or sensitive story would send them scurrying for guidance from representatives of the Admiralty, War Office, Air Ministry or Foreign Office. Each kept staff in the newsroom.

Pandemonium descended mere days after Neville Chamberlain's formal declaration of war. British newspapers knew soldiers of the British Expeditionary Force (BEF) were heading for France as soon as the army began embarkation on 4 September. They immediately began submitting for censorship articles describing the BEF, its personnel and their equipment. Some copy tried to assess the British troops' value to allied strategy. Unfortunately for readers, military advisers in the MoI newsroom were operating under rigid instructions from the War Office: the BEF was not to be mentioned. All articles whether filed from France or written in Britain were to be stopped (or 'held' to use the jargon of the time). At first, editors accepted this on the understanding that some British soldiers were still crossing the channel. Reporting might render them vulnerable to attack by U-boats.

By 10 September, the BEF was ashore in France and busy constructing field defences on the Franco-Belgian border. Now newspaper editors began to lose their patience. They were not persuaded that the Germans had failed to notice that there were British soldiers in France. Given the speed and apparent ease with which the Wehrmacht was crashing through Poland, they thought their readers might appreciate morale-boosting news that Britain was actively contributing to the defence of allied territory. Admiral Usborne and George Thompson sympathized and made the editors' case to the War Office. It remained obdurate. The BEF must remain a secret. Then, on 12 September, French radio broadcasting from Paris announced that British soldiers had landed in France. The French bulletin was audible in Germany and even the densest British military buffoon knew German military intelligence must have heard it. Continued British silence would surely be ludicrous.

The War Office appeared to accept defeat. A military adviser arrived at the MoI with consent to pass for publication news that the BEF had arrived on the Continent. It was already nine o' clock in the evening and perilously close to first edition deadline for the national titles. They had to work fast. Detailed articles and colour features, some reporting the mood among the soldiers on the ground, were submitted for immediate censorship. At the War Office, the general staff were appalled. The detail and flavour of the material newspapers were submitting to the censors went far beyond bare facts. Thompson recalls that 'at 11.30 p.m. the Ministry of Information was informed that the permission previously given had been withdrawn and there must be no news in the papers about the landing in France of the British Expeditionary Force'.[15]

This was no longer a case of preventing publication. Tens of thousands of copies of national newspapers had already been printed. At London mainline railway stations, they had been loaded onto trains for distribution throughout the country. Early editions were already on their way to provincial cities. Still, the War Office remained stubbornly and absurdly inflexible. Every effort must be made to prevent people reading the forbidden news. Police were sent to stations to take bales of newspapers out of railway carriages. Newspaper vans were halted and their contents seized. George Thompson describes the bedlam:

> Editors rushed down to their offices from their beds to get some sort of edition of their newspaper printed. It looked as if most of the population of the United Kingdom were to be without their morning newspaper. Proprietors of great newspaper organisations, editors and other men of influence were ringing up one Cabinet Minister after another insisting that permission given to publish an item of news could not possibly be cancelled at so late an hour. American correspondents – who are not prone to hide their feelings – swore at the censors over the phone.[16]

Such lunacy could not endure. At about 2.30 am, the War Office realized that its orders were unenforceable. Continued efforts to implement them would be more embarrassing than effective. An emergency directive was sent to all newspapers via the Press Association's private telegraph service lifting the ban and authorizing publication. This was one of two methods used by the MoI to communicate censorship decisions to newspapers. The other method was via letters sent through the conventional mail service. These were marked 'Private and Confidential – Not for Publication'. Plainly mail delivery was slower, but it had the advantage that any censorship message contained in a letter would be seen only by the editor or his very senior staff. Messages sent by telegraph had the advantage of speed but they might be read by anybody in a newsroom.

At first wartime censorship decisions were intensely restrictive. All the service representatives in the MoI newsroom were cautious, but the Royal Navy, fiercely proud of its status as 'the Senior Service', was notoriously conservative. Thompson recalls that, long after the Army and the Royal Air Force learned to appreciate the value of publicity, 'it was seldom that any naval news of real interest or importance was allowed to come out, unless from the lips of the Prime Minister or the First Lord of the Admiralty, until so long afterwards that all interest in the event had vanished'.[17] A proud submariner himself, Thompson cites the example of His Majesty's Submarine *Triumph* which struck a German mine in the North Sea on Boxing Day 1939.

Triumph sustained immense damage. Eighteen feet of its hull were blown off entirely, water poured in and *Triumph* found itself unable to dive in enemy waters, with its pumps working flat out to prevent sinking. In a voyage that would have stirred readers' hearts and inspired great affection for its brave crew, the battered submarine survived atrocious weather and attack by German bombers to limp home to the Firth of Forth. So intense was naval suspicion of journalists that 'it was not until September 1941 that the British public and the world were told this magnificent story of the heroism and fortitude of the British sailor'.[18] The Admiralty's view was stark. It would not reveal that a warship had been damaged.

This was a period of trial and error. British journalists chafed and harried officials to secure greater clarity and speedier decision making. American journalists were blunt and frequently incredulous. The difference was not just cultural. For the Britons, the censorship of news copy was voluntary even if they did accept it willingly. Reporters from overseas were compelled to submit their work to the censors. The British government owned or controlled the radio transmitters and cables through which the Americans could file reports to the United States. It imposed censorship in return for access. These arrangements persisted throughout the period known colloquially at the time as the 'bore war' and now universally by the American coinage 'the phoney war'.

For fighting between British and German forces, the term 'phoney' is largely accurate. Until the Norway Campaign of April and May 1940, British forces were not engaged in fighting on land. Military inaction and cautious, bureaucratic censorship conspired to produce dull and homogenous coverage of the war. Much editorial energy was concentrated on coverage of the home front. A snapshot of the reporting of evacuation in the first week of September 1939 offers a representative flavour of newspaper content. Official communiqués dominated coverage and made it harder for newspapers to distinguish their reporting from that of rivals. This does not mean that they did not try.

Evacuation

Even before Chamberlain declared war, the government implemented its plan to evacuate to safety zones children, mothers, hospital patients and blind people from congested areas thought vulnerable to bombing. In retrospect, it is hard to fully comprehend the fear of aerial bombardment that made parents willing to hand their children over to the care of strangers. Equally difficult to grasp is the political consensus that, in advance of any actual bombing of British cities, convinced ministers that a colossal exodus was essential. In his superb but oft-neglected memoir, *Living Through the Blitz*, Tom Harrison, one of the founders in 1937 of Mass Observation, explains why bombing inspired unique terror.[19]

Harrison credits an Italian general, Giulio Douhet, as the architect of the theory that deliberate and indiscriminate, large-scale bombing of civilian populations would shatter morale and spread panic. Douhet believed that such bombing would cause complete collapse on the home front thus undermining organized military forces. He urged Italy's Fascist leader, Benito Mussolini, to use mass bombing raids on cities to 'hammer the *nation* itself to make it give in'. Acknowledging that such attacks would 'be an inhuman, an atrocious performance', he insisted they would be completely effective.[20] Such certainty that air raids were the modern, scientific way to win wars was shared on the left and right of British politics. When he was prime minister, Stanley Baldwin warned that 'the bomber will always get through' and warned of 'tens of thousands of mangled people – men, women and children – before a single soldier or sailor' was harmed in combat.[21] Labour's Clement Attlee agreed entirely. He explained that Labour believed 'another world war will mean the end of civilisation'.[22] As early as 1934, Winston Churchill warned the House of Commons that London lay naked before 'the cursed hellish invention of war from the air'.[23] He described Britain's capital as 'the greatest target in the world, a kind of fat, valuable cow, fed up to attract beasts of prey'.[24] On the right, an unspoken certainty was widespread that the working classes lacked the moral fibre to withstand the suffering bombing would impose. The left's equal certainty that their natural supporters would bear the brunt in bombing raids produced a functionally identical enthusiasm for evacuation.

On 1 September, the front page of the *Daily Express* reported 'Evacuation Today'.[25] Inside it published a map showing the nine dedicated roads along which children would be moved out of London. It explained that public transport by rail and road would be disrupted and advised readers not to travel unless it was absolutely necessary. Further coverage revealed the scale of the exercise: 'Three million people begin to leave their homes today in history's greatest exodus. ... They will be scattered throughout the counties between Land's End and the Wash within the next four days.'[26]

This reporting was all extracted from information in official news communiqués. Thus, the Labour-supporting *Daily Mirror*'s treatment of evacuation contained many elements that were identical to those in the Conservative *Daily Express*. It contained the same detail of traffic disruption, the same advice to 'Travel only if compelled'.[27] Only where their own reporters could provide eyewitness reporting did these two mass-market behemoths show the character that made each attractive to its own very different readership. Thus, the *Mirror* sent a photographer and a reporter to Hugh Myddelton Junior School in Clerkenwell, east-central London. Here, in language calculated to boost morale, it depicted happy girls skipping as they waited to board evacuation buses.

Figure 3.1 A group of children arrive at Brent station near Kingsbridge, Devon, after being evacuated in 1940.

Herbert Morrison, Labour leader of London County Council, advised parents to 'Help your children to go away in a cheerful mood. Keep calm. Keep a cheerful British smile on your face.'[28] A headline declared: 'We'll see the Children are Happy'.[29]

The *Express* was equally determined to promote the government's desire to maintain civilian morale. It had sent a staff reporter to 'a village somewhere in Buckinghamshire' in anticipation of the arrival of children evacuated from London. The *Express* journalist wrote: 'Lights were burning in cottages and big houses as women prepared spare rooms and put hot water bottles in the beds in which London's children will sleep.... Everyone was looking forward to the coming of the children.'[30]

The Times was no less determined to depict evacuation in a positive and optimistic light. Indeed, its commitment to appeasement was not yet dead. It still dared to hope that fighting might be avoided through last-minute diplomatic endeavours. Its editorial on 1 September explained in detail the scale of the evacuation scheme, the road closures necessary to make it work and the demands on the railway network. It concluded that: 'The Government are fully justified in believing that their decision will cause no sort of flurry and encourage no silly rumour of the imminence of attack. For the decision is only part of the policy of taking precautions while still hoping and working for a time when they will be unnecessary.'[31]

Adopting a less upbeat tone four days later, *The Times* reflected on the emptiness of a London without children: 'During the last few days countless mothers and fathers must have been thinking, as the trains drew out from the big cities, "These are our jewels: we are sending them away for safe-keeping."'[32] It also identified a class division among evacuees:

> In well-to-do houses there may have been other valuables too which had to be removed to the country or lodged in the bank.... But in the poorest homes the children were the only treasure: and now they are gone the parents must be feeling destitute indeed.... To be in London now is to know what the town of Hamelin must have been like after the Pied Piper had set his long pipe of smooth straight cane to his lips again.[33]

In recognizing the particular distress of working-class families, *The Times* identified an issue that would soon make evacuation controversial. Juliet Gardiner reminds us that at the outbreak of war just under 1.5 million Britons were officially unemployed. The real figure was probably higher. In large cities poverty was common and the poorest parents simply could not afford to feed, wash or dress their children properly.[34] Many of the children evacuated came from these cities and so evacuation became a process of introducing poor urban Britons to much wealthier ones with homes in the countryside. Neither social group was familiar with the habits or lifestyle of the other and some genuine shock and outrage occurred. Infestations of head lice caused acute distress.

An editorial in *The Times* of 15 September 1939 makes plain the strength of feeling among its readers. The top people's newspaper might contemplate a compromise peace with Germany, but it would not stand for dirty working-class children in clean upper middle-class homes:

Some of the really bad features of this migration cannot, of course, be tolerated at all. The insanitary cases, verminous or diseased, must be treated at once as infringements of the public health requirements and be subjected to medical and judicious disciplinary treatment. The Ministry of Health acknowledges that the billeting of this type of person in respectable homes is unreasonable. As official language errs on the side of moderation, the word 'unreasonable' should be construed by the local authorities as synonymous with unjustifiable and indefensible.... Lice in particular are a 'minor horror of war' and complaints of children thus affected come from all parts of the country, not only those from districts where cleanliness was known to be difficult.[35]

In the Communist *Daily Worker*, loyal to the policy of revolutionary defeatism promoted by its owner, the Communist Party of Great Britain, columnist Charlotte Haldane responded furiously, wielding lice-infested evacuee children as weapons for social reform:

Now that the unfortunate, underfed, poorly clad and not always very clean kiddies from some of our terrible city slums have poured into the reception areas, those very people who turned away from their urgent needs with callous indifference are raising the roofs of [their] mansions with cries of verminous, diseased, unclean.... The children are the nation's treasure, their care the nation's responsibility. Nothing should be too good or too expensive for them.[36]

Touching on infestation with delicacy, the *Daily Express* achieved cautious balance by restricting its coverage to a report of parliamentary debate. 'While MPs from all parties praised the smooth working of the evacuation scheme, there was an angry scene at the first mention of vermin', wrote the *Express*'s parliamentary reporter on 15 September:

It came from Captain Thornton-Kemsley (Cons. West Aberdeen) who said it distressed him, but he thought it his duty to read a letter from a rector in his constituency saying that children from Glasgow had arrived in this condition. Mr. Buchanan, one of the Glasgow Socialist M.P.s. shouted: 'It's a damn shame, a terrible thing to say; You are asking the fathers to fight and yet you come here with villainous and slanderous accusations against their children.'[37]

The *Manchester Guardian* captured the acute sensitivities involved in this most uncomfortable meeting of different tribes in a report from the prosperous little town of Wilmslow, eleven miles south of Manchester city centre. On Saturday, 7 October, its correspondent accompanied Miss Florence Horsburgh MP (Conservative, Dundee), Parliamentary Secretary to the Ministry of Health, on her visit to see how the evacuation scheme was working. Wilmslow was providing homes to many city children and its solid, middle-class, church-going citizens were disgruntled. Mr S.B.L. Jacks, Chairman of the Wilmslow Urban Council, told the *Guardian*'s reporter:

> Wilmslow is a high-class residential area with many large houses, a number of small semi-detached houses and cottages. Many children have been billeted in the large houses, but experience has shown that, however much or little trouble the householder takes with the children, they are acutely uncomfortable in an atmosphere to which they are not accustomed. There have been cases of lice, dirt, filthy and vicious habits. Every such case creates a bad impression in the neighbourhood and makes it more difficult to billet satisfactorily.[38]

Mr Jacks was forthright. He told Miss Horsburgh: 'It is obviously unfair and only asking for trouble to put a clean child in a dirty home or a dirty child in a clean home.' He sought a promise that compulsory billeting would end. The parliamentary secretary did not give him what he wanted. She thanked Wilmslow for giving evacuee children 'an extraordinary welcome' and told residents: 'You have tackled a difficult job and you have succeeded.'[39]

Dismissal of Leslie Hore-Belisha

Plainly, tensions aroused by evacuation offered newspapers of varying political complexions the chance to shine light on disparities in wealth, manners and personal hygiene between Britain's middle classes and the urban poor. Equally plainly, newspapers seized this opportunity. Their coverage offers an early example of the freedom from policy censorship British newspaper journalists would enjoy throughout the war. With the sole exception of the communist press, with its comparatively tiny circulation and rigid adherence to a policy line dictated from Moscow, no British newspaper wished to compromise British military security. Editors retained, however, the right to challenge the way in which the war was being fought. They rarely exercised this right during the phoney war which endured from September 1939 to April 1940, but the dismissal of a minister in January 1940 sparked newspaper criticism.

Isaac Leslie Hore-Belisha was born in London in 1893. His father, Messod Belicha, a Sephardic Jewish merchant from Morocco, died when he was an infant. Hore-Belisha's widowed mother married Sir Charles Hore, Permanent Secretary to the Ministry of Pensions, hence the double-barrelled surname. He was educated at Clifton College in Bristol, a public school with a significant military tradition. Leslie Hore-Belisha had served in cabinet since 1936. Angus Calder notes that: 'Belisha Beacons, the road safety device he had introduced before the war, still testify in Britain's streets to his talent for self-publicity.'[40] He was a popular minister. The public and not a few journalists on the popular newspapers admired him because he was an enthusiastic belligerent in a cabinet still dominated by reluctant converts to war. Hore-Belisha had been Secretary of State for War since May 1937. In this role he had introduced to the army reforms which had caused consternation among traditionalists. Critics of the Chamberlain government would assert that residual resentment of these changes and anti-Semitism lay behind his dismissal. Chamberlain insisted that the difference was purely professional. He admired Hore-Belisha's 'exceptional qualities of courage, imagination and drive' but reluctantly concluded that 'he has the defects of his qualities ... impatience and eagerness, partly for a self-centredness which makes him careless of other people's feelings'.[41]

Critics on the left of British politics were not persuaded. Major General A.J. Trythall writes that, 'The most widely held contemporary journalistic view, particularly on the left, was that Hore-Belisha had been sacked as a consequence of a plot hatched against him by senior army officers who resented his measures of military reform and democratisation.'[42] Hugh Cudlipp, writing in the *Sunday Pictorial*, alleged that, 'The Public will not stand for this abject surrender by Chamberlain to the high-caste brass-hats. You haven't heard the last of Leslie Hore-Belisha or of his miserable mean dismissal.'[43]

For the *Daily Mirror*, the secretary of state for war's departure was an important story which dominated its front page on Saturday, 6 January 1940. The headline was 'Belisha Resigns'. This was technically true because, on dismissing him as secretary of state for war, Chamberlain had offered Hore-Belisha the Board of Trade, which he had rejected as a humiliating demotion. The *Mirror* made it clear that it did not regard this as a resignation. Its report began:

> A sensational change in the war cabinet was announced last night. Mr Leslie Hore-Belisha, the man responsible for purging the army council of its old men, has resigned the office of War Minister. Actually, he has been dismissed because the generals objected to his reforms and made representations to the Premier.... Despite the denials of policy differences in the letters that have passed between Mr. Hore-Belisha and the Premier, it is obvious that a War Minister does not resign unless he has been repudiated by his chief on a major issue. It was, in fact, a revolt by the generals. Hore-Belisha's 'live wire' methods, his demand for a democratic Army has roused the opposition of the military caste – the old gang of the Army Command. The old gang took their case to the Premier, and Mr. Chamberlain, anxious to appease the generals, decided to sack his War Minister. It is the first victory of the generals.[44]

The *Mirror* was angry and it did not restrict its fury to the front page. Hore-Belisha's involuntary departure also provided the ammunition for its leader column. This was topped by a single-word headline: 'BOMBSHELL!' The leader writer spelled out its significance:

> What is behind the sudden and surprising departure of Mr. Hore-Belisha from the Cabinet of Antiques in Downing Street? He is (for a Minister) young. He has proved himself a man of ideas and energy. So far as we know, much of the recent modernisation and reform of the Army methods, much of the Army's recent mechanisation, together with a part at least of such remarkable achievements as the passage of a big expeditionary force to France, may be set to his credit. At any rate, his name is known to the men at the front, to the men in training at home, and to the civilian public.[45]

The *Manchester Guardian* was less outspoken about this departure from government than the *Daily Mirror*, but it shared some of the popular title's suspicions. The *Manchester*

Guardian described the war minister's resignation as 'a tremendous surprise'. It opined that 'Mr Hore-Belisha has been one of the few successful Ministers in the National Government' and noted that 'No other Minister, Mr Churchill excepted, has had so great a popular appeal'.[46] Press Association copy published alongside the *Manchester Guardian* correspondent's column reported: 'Those in a position to know something about what has been going on behind the scenes suggested last night that interests high up in the military caste, who for a long time have been opposing the democratisation of the army by the War Minister, have won their campaign'.[47]

Alert to the controversy surrounding Hore-Belisha's departure, and determined to advertise it to its readers, the *Manchester Guardian* chose to summarize treatment in other national newspapers.[48] *The Times* was determined not to stir controversy. It suggested that the minister may have been too tired after his hard work to create an army large enough to meet wartime demands, praised his efforts and insisted that 'there is no reason to suppose that this retirement marks the extinction of a political career that has been distinguished at least by the one most essential quality of drive'.[49] The liberal *News Chronicle* took a harder line:

> Mr Hore-Belisha's departure will certainly be a serious loss to the Government's efficiency and is almost certain to weaken its standing in the country.... The nation has a right to know more and will certainly demand that it shall be told.... What is the attitude of the Army and in particular of the High Command to this change? For some time past, gossip has been unpleasantly busy with stories of a whispering campaign against the War Minister in high Army quarters.[50]

The Labour movement's quality title, the *Daily Herald*, went straight to the point: 'Mr Hore-Belisha's removal from the War Office will create a national sensation ... the public will want to know why he has been sacked in this way.'[51] The *Daily Express* regretted his departure: 'Mr Hore-Belisha was one of the most efficient Minsters.... Mr Oliver Stanley is a most unsatisfactory appointment.'[52] The *Daily Mail* was not entirely happy either: 'Mr Hore-Belisha has not been getting on well with the generals and he goes. The public hopes that the course of events in the critical days to come will not cause the country to regret his departure.'[53]

Hore-Belisha's dismissal confounds simple explanation. Early in his career as secretary of state for war he had modernized the army with energy and imagination. In doing so he had aroused anger among traditionalists. Some of their resentment included elements of anti-Semitism. Henry Pownall, who served as chief of staff to Lord Gort, commander of the BEF, obnoxiously described Hore-Belisha as an 'obscure, shallow-brained, charlatan, political Jewboy'.[54] By December 1939, Chamberlain understood that his war minister was causing tensions in the BEF, not least because of his intervention in plans for defensive fortifications in France. The so-called 'Pill Box Affair' arose after Hore-Belisha visited the BEF in Northern France and, on his return to London, criticized the High Command for failing to build enough of these concrete defensive emplacements.

Trythall notes that, as a National Liberal politician in an overwhelmingly Conservative government, he lacked political support.[55] Certainly, Chamberlain concluded that Hore-Belisha had made himself unpopular with the High Command and particularly with Lord Gort. He could safely be reshuffled.

Following a meeting with him on 20 December 1939, the prime minister noted in his diary that his war minister 'did not and could not see where he had gone wrong and only thought he had been treated with great injustice and prejudice'. Chamberlain believed that, while the country was at war, 'nothing could be worse than perpetual friction and want of confidence between the Secretary of State and the C-in-C in the field'.[56] He decided to replace him as war minister with a more collegiate politician. This was a miscalculation that backfired badly, provoking press coverage that Chamberlain loathed. His reaction followed the pattern he had developed while defending appeasement. Newspapers that dared to question his leadership must be bullied back into line, and they were. Cockett suggests that, following Hore-Belisha's exit from government on 5 January 1940, 'the press relapsed into a mood of resentful acquiescence', in which newspaper editors and proprietors were convinced that the War Cabinet was unfit for purpose, but felt compelled not to attack the government for fear of fracturing national unity; 'the press was prepared to attack the government in detail, but hung back from criticising Chamberlain himself or the individuals in the government because that would split the nation and help the Germans'.[57] This pervasive mood of sullen, resentful acquiescence is well illustrated in my own case study of press coverage of a parliamentary by-election contested in the depths of the phoney war.[58]

A By-election during the Phoney War

The Central Southwark constituency fell vacant following the death of its Labour member of parliament, Colonel Harry Day. Under the terms of a wartime electoral truce between the major parties, Day's demise should not have precipitated a formal contest. The truce stipulated that wartime vacancies in the House of Commons would be filled by a nominee of the party in possession without opposition from the other two.[59] However, in Central Southwark a candidate, heavily backed by the Communist Party of Great Britain but standing under the guise of 'Labour anti-war candidate',[60] provoked a contest. Charles Searson was a Labour member of Southwark Council but his candidature flagrantly breached Labour Party policy. Labour had declared its support for war in September 1939. By challenging this decision, Searson threatened to expose the extent of anti-war sentiment among Labour's pacifist left and so to undermine party unity. Two previous wartime by-elections, one in Clackmannan and East Stirling, the other in Stretford, Greater Manchester had demonstrated that anti-war policies had some electoral appeal. Now the Communist Party of Great Britain spotted a chance to use a 'front' candidate to make its revolutionary defeatist case in a capital that anticipated enemy bombing and in which public enthusiasm for the fight was lukewarm.

The Communist Party during the Phoney War

MI5, Britain's domestic security service, feared during the phoney war that Josef Stalin's USSR would use the Communist Party of Great Britain (CPGB) as a weapon against the British state. Christopher Andrew, official historian of MI5, shows that, in November 1939, penetration by Soviet agents persuaded Lord Halifax, the foreign secretary, to purge the Foreign Office Communications Department. In January 1940, a Soviet intelligence officer who had defected to the United States came to the UK. Walter Krivitsky told MI5 that a Soviet intelligence network was active in Britain.[61] Senior MI5 personnel believed Soviet agents often used ordinary Communist Party members. Their colleagues at the MoI feared that CPGB campaigns might fracture public morale. At the time of the Central Southwark by-election, the Party was wedded to the Nazi-Soviet non-aggression pact, signed in Moscow on 23 August 1939 by the German foreign minister Joachim von Ribbentrop and his Soviet counterpart Vyacheslav Molotov. In domestic terms, this meant the British Communists promoted the Comintern's declaration that war between the Western democracies and Nazi Germany was an 'imperialist war' and therefore inimical to the interests of British workers. In practical terms this meant that they pursued a policy of revolutionary defeatism. This sought to exploit the conditions of war to bring about the revolutionary overthrow of the British state.

Press Coverage of the Central Southwark By-election

Paul Addison advises us that, during the phoney war, the government was acutely sensitive to any evidence of anti-war feeling.[62] It understood that by-elections offered an opportunity for the expression of popular discontent. Although there was no Conservative candidate in the ballot held in Central Southwark on 10 February 1940, Searson's candidature offered Labour supporters a chance to turn against their party's leadership by supporting the candidate opposed to the conflict and the electoral truce with the Conservatives. It also obliged Labour to fight the seat. The party's official candidate was John Martin, like Charles Searson a local councillor, unlike his communist-backed opponent a loyal advocate of official Labour policy. A third candidate also emerged and was condemned as a 'freak' by the *London Evening Standard*.[63] Later famous as a campaigner against capital punishment, Mrs Violet Van der Elst (1882–1966) was born Violet Dodge, the daughter of a washerwoman and a coal porter. She married the Belgian inventor of Shavex, a successful brushless shaving foam. When her husband died, she deployed the substantial profits Shavex had earned to pursue issues dear to her heart. Describing herself as 'The Great Personality Who Will Fight for You',[64] Mrs Van der Elst campaigned on a variety of promises including more generous old age pensions, better homes at lower rents and enhanced health services. These she promoted in a self-financed election newspaper, *The Voice of the People*, which she paid her employees to distribute.[65] Speaking from her chauffeur-driven open-topped car to a bemused crowd of working people on Walworth Road, Violet Van der Elst, whose family home was Harlaxton Manor, a grand residence also known as Grantham Castle, made a revealing claim. The *Daily Express* columnist William Barkley was there to witness her performance. Concerned that she was encountering scepticism regarding her eligibility to represent poor Londoners, she declared: 'It is thrown against me that I have a castle, but I have given many poor people a happy time there. Send me to Parliament. I will see that babies have nourishment when they are born.'[66] William Barkley concluded that the official Labour candidate would win. He was right. John Martin took the Central Southwark by-election with 5,285 votes to Charles Searson's 1,550, a majority of 3,735. Violet Van der Elst came third with 1,382 votes.

The by-election was fiercely contested. Communist activists from around the country flooded the streets of Central Southwark promoting the policies and slogans their party had chosen for Charles Searson's campaign. They deployed a classic 'front' tactic, embracing Searson without labelling him as one of their own. The CPGB's newspaper, the *Daily Worker*, promoted him relentlessly. Indeed, all of Searson's election literature was printed on the *Daily Worker*'s presses. The Communist Party knew the Nazi-Soviet pact had damaged its reputation and dismayed many members. It cherished the opportunity to promote a more positive message. Addison observes that: 'In the war years it was still an article of faith among "progressives" – people who were not Marxists, but optimists for mankind – that the Soviet system was a great and inspiring experiment in science and democracy.'[67] Searson's Communist foot soldiers hoped the government's attitude to the Russo-Finnish War, then raging along the Mannerheim Line, could be exploited to secure progressive votes. Knightley argues that: 'No one seemed prepared to question the fact that the allied efforts to help the Finns against the Russians greatly exceeded their efforts to help the Poles against the Germans.'[68] Searson questioned it. The guide to canvassers the CPGB prepared on his behalf insisted, 'The present government will not be content to fight Germany . . . it will drag this country into yet another war with Russia.'[69] Additional CPGB slogans targeted Searson's appeal at ordinary voters unconcerned by global affairs. These included, 'Welfare not Warfare, Vote Searson' and 'Stop the War, and Open the Schools, Vote Searson'.[70] A sticker declared, 'Say the Nazis "Guns not butter", Says Chamberlain "Guns not butter", Vote Searson Labour's Stop the War Candidate and GET BUTTER.'[71]

This fiercely contested parliamentary by-election, fought before British soldiers had engaged in land warfare against the Germans and before the bombing of any British cities, offered newspapers a real opportunity to demonstrate their value to democracy. The potency of by-elections as gauges of popular sentiment was apparent to politicians and newspaper editors. The issues raised by the Communist-supported Searson were vividly controversial in Labour-supporting communities. Indeed, senior Labour politicians including the party leader, Clement Attlee campaigned in Central Southwark. The press was not yet subject to newsprint rationing. It had ample space in which to report arguments between the pro- and anti-war candidates. Such reporting might have offered a respite from the MoI's stranglehold on military news. It might have taken Charles Searson's anti-war message to the rest of the United Kingdom and stimulated debate. Instead, newspapers chose not to advertise views considered deeply unhelpful by both the Chamberlain government and the official opposition.

I have scrutinized in detail coverage of the Central Southwark campaign in daily newspapers including *The Times*, the *News Chronicle*, the *Daily Express*, the *Daily Mirror*, the *Manchester Guardian*, the *Daily Herald* and the *Daily Worker*. I have also examined reporting and commentary in the *New Statesman and Nation*, a weekly political title, directed at opinion formers on the left of British politics, which gave meticulous attention to controversies in the Labour Party and the broader Labour movement. My analysis reveals that the mainstream press put hostility to the Communist Party before service to the electorate and declined to treat the contest as a plausible test of public opinion. There was, however, a brisk and vigorous battle between the Communist *Daily Worker* and the Labour-supporting *Daily Herald*.

The latter, owned since 1929 by Odhams Press (51 per cent) and the Trades' Union Congress (49 per cent), was a mass-market newspaper with populist instincts. Its editorial policy followed the cautious social-democratic approach of its minority shareholder and the Labour Party's National Executive Committee. The *Herald* began the by-election campaign by running a column by Arthur Greenwood, deputy leader of the Labour Party in which he did not directly mention Central Southwark, although it was plain that this was why he was writing. He mounted a steadfast defence of the electoral truce, explaining that by-elections in wartime 'would not give a reliable verdict'.[72] The electoral register was out of date, the blackout required to protect London against bombing would make voting difficult and the demands of the wartime economy required overtime working that was incompatible with political campaigning. The following day, Labour's leader Clement Attlee weighed in with a speech in which he denounced British Communists and their supporters as 'Stalin's Ventriloquist's dummies'.[73] Throughout the campaign, the *Daily Herald* avoided mention of Charles Searson's name. The Labour Party was determined to avert the confusion Searson and the CPGB sought to sow by their description of him as 'Labour's Stop-the-War Candidate'. Labour supporters who relied on it for news might have wondered why the by-election was taking place.

Readers of the *Daily Worker* were left in no doubt. The Central Committee of the CPGB appointed the *Worker*'s editor and dictated editorial policy. It was a party propaganda newspaper on the *Pravda* model. It had clear objectives in Central Southwark: to exploit divisions in the Labour Party between the pro-war leadership and grassroots anti-war opinion, and to promote fear that Neville Chamberlain's government might use the Soviet Union's invasion of Finland to justify war against the USSR. In the *Daily Worker*, every example of internal dissent against the Labour Party's war policy attracted coverage. On 4 January, the front page carried a report revealing that the annual conference of the University Labour Federation had voted to adopt an anti-war stance.[74] The same edition declared Communist support for Charles Searson. It celebrated 'his years of labour to clean up the slums of the borough and re-house the people' and proclaimed his ambition 'to rouse the 36,000 local voters against the imperialist war'.[75]

Determined to maximize the impact of his candidature and its potential to damage the Labour Party, the *Daily Worker* would insist in all of its coverage that Searson was, in fact, a Labour candidate. Communists should support him, it explained, because he shared with them respect 'for the cause of peace, progress and solidarity with the Soviet Union'.[76] The *Daily Herald* was much less austere than its Stalinist rival. It offered a diet of morale-boosting content including the cartoon strip 'Christa and Wanda, the Fuehrer's Secretaries' and the tale of the five Mair children who walked 29 miles from their evacuation digs in Buckinghamshire to the family home in Islington because Joyce (five) yearned to see her mother.[77] The *Daily Worker*'s ideological fervour appears to have made limited impact on local residents. Although their streets were flooded with CPGB activists from all over England – many offering the party's newspaper for sale – Mass Observation detected overwhelming political apathy. One observer noted: 'People seem very fed up with the by-election.'[78] Another heard a Communist complain: 'Some of them don't even know that Labour isn't against the war.' A canvasser said: '[M]ost of them just look at you with a face like a dying colt.'[79]

Beyond this ideological catfight between the *Daily Herald* and the *Daily Worker* in which the latter showed sharper claws, press coverage of the Central Southwark by-election was desultory and trivializing. The *Daily Express* enjoyed ridiculing Violet Van der Elst and accurately predicted that Labour would hold the seat on a low turnout. *The Times* restricted its coverage to just six brief mentions all published between 23 January and 13 February. The most extensive, two paragraphs published on polling day, reported that 'electors' were asking: 'Why should there be an election at all in view of the political truce.'[80] The absence of attribution and the use of the plural 'electors' strongly suggests that this was the newspaper's opinion as well.

The *Manchester Guardian* paid little attention to proceedings in Central Southwark and, when it did mention the contest, was almost as wedded to the official Labour Party line as the *Daily Herald*. On polling day it promoted Labour's message that: 'A victory for the so-called "Stop-the-War" candidate would be received with rejoicing by the German propaganda machine, but it would be a defeat for the true cause of peace and social freedom.'[81] Lord Beaverbrook's *London Evening Standard* showed no greater interest in this by-election on its home territory. On the morning the writ was moved it simply recorded that there would be an election.[82] When the result was declared, it explained that the contest had 'brought freak candidates into the field' and produced 'a dreadful result' for the Labour Party whose victorious candidate had secured only half the number of votes won by his predecessor.[83]

* * *

Such meagre and ideologically compromised reporting of the Central Southwark by-election exemplifies the prevailing tenor of British newspaper journalism during the phoney war. They were willing to advertise class tensions over evacuation policy because these mattered greatly to readers of all classes. Lice could not be ignored, but the reporting did not blame ministers for their presence. The angry response to Leslie Hore-Belisha's departure had shown that resentment of the Chamberlain government extended beyond the Labour and Communist titles. To the failure of appeasement had been added early evidence of the prime minister's reluctance to fight the war energetically. Newspapers were not enthusiastic about the government or its approach, but they remained unwilling to pinpoint ministerial incompetence in wartime. It would take the shock that saw Chamberlain replaced by Winston Churchill to remind editors that readers in a democracy at war require honest, diligent and watchful newspapers. Even then several would be slow learners. United in their commitment to victory, British newspapers only gradually proved their determination to speak truth to power. On one issue, however, they were alert: distinction on the grounds of social class. Evacuation from the cities had demonstrated the depths of misunderstanding that existed between rich and poor. Now the suggestion that children should be taken abroad to safety revived this most potent of British sensitivities. Newspapers were beginning to understand that a democracy fighting totalitarianism must show that its defence of the freedom to speak and dissent was not exclusively theoretical.

CHAPTER 4
CHURCHILL, NORWAY AND DUNKIRK

By early April 1940, sullen resentment of the Chamberlain administration was turning into acerbic criticism in the popular left-wing press. The *Daily Mirror*'s Cassandra, pseudonym of the columnist William Connor (1909–67), was among the sharpest critics. In his column on Friday, 5 April, Connor lambasted the prime minister for appointing Sir Samuel Hoare to the Air Ministry. Hoare, a convinced appeaser, had served in Conservative and National governments during the 1920s and 1930s. He resigned as foreign secretary in December 1935 when his plan to partition Ethiopia between Fascist Italy and its indigenous population was denounced. Later, he served as Chamberlain's home secretary and was an architect and defender of the Munich Pact. Now, ridiculing Hoare's potential as a credible opponent to Hitler's air marshal, Herman Goering, William Connor warned his readers: 'The Nazi roar in the air is answered with a polite squeak' and questioned whether Hoare was 'the strong, ruthless, resourceful character who will sweep the Nazis from the skies?' Connor thought it highly unlikely: 'Will he smash all the red tape and official humbug that is slowly strangling the growth of the Royal Air Force? . . . I am not asking that new wine should be put into old bottles – all I want is that somebody shall come and take the political empties away.'[1]

The blithe complacency that inspired such appointments had been vividly on display the previous afternoon when Chamberlain addressed the National Union of Conservative and Unionist Associations in London. Explaining why he felt able to abandon his duties as war leader for long enough to speak to them, the prime minister told his party faithful: 'I listened-in this morning, to hear if there were anything stirring on the other side of the Rhine. But there was nothing but the stale old threats.'[2] Then he made a prediction that would soon appear as oafish as it was smug. Hitler 'has missed the bus', he said, explaining that he had anticipated a German attempt to overwhelm Britain and France before they could make full defensive preparations. Now it was too late, the allies were ready and Hitler had missed his chance. The *Daily Express* noted that Labour's deputy leader, Arthur Greenwood, was equally confident: 'Hitler never was on the bus', he told a party meeting in Richmond, south-west London, 'he is a rat in a trap.'[3]

German Invasion of Denmark and Norway

Such reassurances influenced public opinion. There was evidence that city dwellers had stopped worrying about air raids, black-out precautions were being overlooked, evacuees were returning home. Mass Observation recorded that people were 'beginning to doubt that this is a war at all'.[4] It took five days for harsh evidence to emerge that it was indeed war and Britain's leaders had been entirely outwitted. Just after 4.00 am on 9 April, German forces crossed the Danish border in a preliminary step towards their conquest of neighbouring Norway. Denmark's Royal Army fought bravely but briefly against overwhelming German invasion forces. It was all over in twelve hours.

The news dominated the British press on Wednesday, 10 April. A short news item on the front page of the *Daily Mail* captured the significance of Denmark's defeat. Reuters news agency had listened to a shortwave radio broadcast from Germany. It reported Berlin's message that: 'The first and last purpose of the German measures in Denmark and Norway is to force Britain to her knees.'[5] The *Mail*'s banner headline confirmed that fighting had now begun in earnest: 'Big Naval Battle off Coast of Norway', it declared. The story below reported that warships of the Royal Navy were fighting the German fleet. Battle was raging 'over a 400-miles line from Skagerrak to Narvik'.[6] All leave had been cancelled for soldiers of the British Expeditionary Force and RAF airmen. Mr Chamberlain had gone to the House of Commons to condemn 'Germany's latest act of brutal aggression', noted the *Mail*, but Winston Churchill was not in the House of Commons. He had spent his day and, the 4.00 am edition explained, most of the night, in the 'famous Map Room of the Admiralty'.[7]

The Times of 1940 did not carry news on its front page. This was reserved for notices of births, marriages and deaths and assorted small and personal advertisements. Comprehensive coverage appeared inside and included a prescient editorial. This explained that Norway had pledged to fight and Britain and France had promised military support by sea and land. However, it noted, soberingly, 'The Norwegian Army is very small, the population being less than that of Finland and the period of service shorter . . . their only hope of prolonged resistance lies in making the fullest possible use of the natural defensive qualities of their rugged country.'[8] A longer political leader column on the same page confirmed that *The Times* remained loyal to Neville Chamberlain. Having listened intently to the prime minister's speech in the House of Commons, the leader writer opined: 'We are facing the facts of this menace to the independence of free peoples, and facing them in the fullest consultation and collaboration with France.' He concluded by quoting Chamberlain: 'I have no doubt', Mr Chamberlain said, 'that this further rash and cruel act of aggression will redound to Germany's disadvantage and contribute to her ultimate defeat.'[9]

The *Daily Mirror* dedicated space on nineteen pages to detailed and colourful coverage. Its front-page headline focused on the overnight drama: 'GERMAN FLEET HUNTED: ALLIES IN RUNNING SEA FIGHT'. It also spotted a story that would cause its favourite Conservative, Winston Churchill, great pain: 'Mr. Giles Romilly, nephew of Mr. Winston Churchill, was arrested by the Germans after they had captured Narvik, the Norwegian iron-ore port yesterday. Mr. Romilly is a London journalist.'[10] The Germans would soon recognize that Romilly (1916–67), a reporter for the *Daily Express*, was a nephew of Winston Churchill through the first lord of the Admiralty's wife, Clementine Churchill. Poor Giles would be held for much of the war in the infamous Colditz Castle. However, the *Mirror* had more than a sharp instinct for news, it had a sharp tongue too. Cassandra pointed out that Britons should not be surprised by the latest evidence of Hitler's territorial greed or the enthusiasm with which German soldiers fought to satisfy it. 'This is the country against whose people, as distinct from their rulers, we are told that we have no quarrel', he lamented, referring back to Chamberlain's naivety at Munich and beyond; 'It's like making friends with a pack of jackals led by wolves.'[11]

In Germany, those wolves were in ecstatic mood. The Nazi-controlled German press celebrated too. *Der Angriff* (in English, 'The Attack'), a Berlin-based title established in 1927 by Joseph Goebbels, then leader of the Berlin branch of the Nazi Party, described the seizure of Denmark and Norway as 'one of the most brilliant feats of all time'.[12] *Volkischer Beobachter*, the party's own national newspaper, declared simply, 'Germany saves Scandinavia'.[13] The irony is that British failure to defend Norway was as much Winston Churchill's fault as it was Chamberlain's.

The Norway Debate

As first lord of the Admiralty, Churchill summoned and deployed the poorly equipped British Expeditionary Force that suffered humiliating defeat by superior German land forces backed by impressive air power. He had expected the Norwegians to fight with the ferocity of their Viking ancestors and had described them as 'beyond all challenge the most formidable and daring race in the world'.[14] When they proved ineffective against the Germans, Churchill would benefit spectacularly from his own failure. His ascent to the premiership came as an almost total surprise, even to his most enthusiastic supporters. On 7 May 1940, when MPs gathered in the House of Commons to debate the failed Anglo-French campaign in Norway, no British newspaper anticipated that it would culminate with the resignation of Neville Chamberlain and the formation of a government led by Winston Churchill.

The Times remained predictably staunch in its loyalty to Chamberlain. In its initial report of the debate, it emphasized Chamberlain's warning that, 'we should not exaggerate the extent or the importance of the check we have received'. The withdrawal of British troops from southern Norway, whence they had been expelled by force, 'was not comparable with Gallipoli' and British losses 'were not really great in number nor was there any considerable or valuable amount of stores left behind'. Readers should take care not to be fooled by 'the false legend of German invincibility'.[15] In its editorial, *The Times* sought to deflect criticism of the prime minister. It acknowledged that his 'explanation of the course of the campaign in Norway follows lines that had been largely anticipated and defends the supreme direction of operations to the fullest extent that seems possible'.[16] However, it insisted that to dwell on any omissions in Mr Chamberlain's argument 'would obviously be unjust'. It noted that, 'Since all three Service Ministers are to speak in the course of the debate, it must be for them to demonstrate, so far as it may be safe to do so, that the general plan was carried out by the staffs with full efficiency.'[17] Churchill, as first lord, was the senior service minister. He would wind up the debate on the government's behalf. Important Conservative contributors plainly believed he was culpable. A notable example was Admiral of the Fleet Sir Roger Keyes. Speaking in his capacity as the Conservative MP for Portsmouth North, Keyes addressed the House clad in full naval uniform adorned by medals. An admirer of Churchill, Keyes nevertheless made it plain that he considered the first lord primarily responsible for a badly misconceived military operation in Norway. Chamberlain, happily persuaded that the debate was going as he had hoped, concluded his own contribution with a plea for 'the cooperation of all parties in work which everyone recognises to be the prime need of the day'.[18]

Through its editor, Geoffrey Dawson, *The Times* had maintained warm personal relations with the prime minister throughout the spring of 1940. Dawson's biographer, John Evelyn Wrench, notes frequent one-to-one meetings between Dawson and Chamberlain. These Dawson would record meticulously and with pride in his personal diary. A typical entry for 9 February recalls 'a long, friendly, discursive talk with the Prime Minister who was in very good form, looking fit and well on top of his job'.[19] Most often these meetings took place at 10 Downing Street. Sometimes the pair would meet in Oxford or at Cliveden, the country home of Waldorf and Nancy Astor, keen appeasers and providers of lavish hospitality to their powerful friends.

The frequent presence at Cliveden of leading advocates of appeasement had spawned pre-war conspiracy theories – first published by the communist journalist Claude Cockburn in his private newsletter, *The Week* – about an establishment cabal determined to concede British interests through compromise with Nazi Germany. Geoffrey Dawson, a member of the Anglo-German Fellowship, was portrayed as a leading member of this 'Cliveden Set' and he resented it profoundly when the 'conspiracy' re-emerged in the mainstream press. He described publicity given to the 'Cliveden Gang', 'Cliveden Front' or 'Cliveden Set' in the *Daily Express* and *Evening Standard* as 'grotesque reactions' to innocent social gatherings.[20] More candidly, his biographer acknowledges that Dawson and his wife, Cecilia, were 'fairly frequent visitors to Cliveden' where they enjoyed the company of 'prominent individuals' from the worlds of British and American politics.[21]

Plainly, it would take a catastrophe for Dawson to withdraw *The Times*' support from his friend and ally. Their relationship involved a proximity to and affection for power which compromised Dawson's editorial independence and undermined his newspaper's capacity to serve the public interest. Even as the reality of British failure in Norway became apparent, Dawson refrained from direct criticism. For *The Times*, the worst that might be said of Chamberlain's government was that there was 'abundant room for improvement'. As for the prime minister, his sole fault was loyalty. 'Mr Chamberlain's weakness has always been his devotion to colleagues who are either failures or need a rest', lamented Dawson in a self-penned editorial.[22] However, he immediately diluted this mildest of rebukes with another dose of sycophancy: '[T]he testimony of those (no inconsiderable number) who have been admitted from time to time into the mysteries of the Cabinet room is that he stands out in those surroundings for vigour, courage, dispatch of business and the capacity for weighing alternatives and coming to a definite conclusion.'[23]

Even as Chamberlain's failure became apparent, *The Times* stood four-square behind him. The *Daily Mirror* saw a much less varnished picture. It seized on Sir Roger Keyes' contribution to the first day of the Norway debate. This featured on the front page, where the *Mirror* described it as 'a dramatic speech' and one of several 'heavy salvos of criticism fired at the government'.[24] But the *Mirror* also gave front-page billing to the Conservative

MP for Birmingham Sparkbrook, Julian Amery's famous reworking of Oliver Cromwell's speech dismissing the Long Parliament. Cromwell had directed his ire at parliament. Amery aimed his at one man: Neville Chamberlain. He had considered Chamberlain a true friend. Now he was merciless. Reminding the House of the words Cromwell had used after he judged that parliament was no longer fit to conduct the nation's affairs, Amery directed his gaze towards the prime minister's seat on the front bench and concluded: 'You have sat too long here for any good you have been doing. Depart, I say, and let us have done with you. In the name of God, go.'[25]

Several newspapers would misrepresent this as an attack on the whole government. The *Mirror* understood it perfectly; 'In Name of God, Go, Premier Told' ran the headline on another front-page story. It concluded by recalling that, when Cromwell had made the same demand in 1653, 'The Long Parliament went.'[26] Still reluctant to advertise overt disloyalty to a prime minister in wartime, the *Mirror*'s editorial stopped just short of calling for Chamberlain's resignation. Instead, it condemned the government for multiple failures and asked: 'What is the good of closing ranks behind leaders who are always too late?' It warned that 'the patience of the nation is dwindling to vanishing point'. Finally, it concluded that, despite alarming evidence that Britain was not offering effective resistance to German aggression, 'Mr. Chamberlain retains his blind confidence in victory.'[27] Beside the leader appeared a cartoon depiction of Britain's War Horse crushing a prostrate and panic-stricken Neville Chamberlain beneath its hefty flank.[28] The *Daily Mirror* was setting the standard for sharp analysis of complex and significant topics. It spoke truth to power in words that reached a mass readership.

As the Norway debate opened, the *Daily Mail* perceived a greater threat to Winston Churchill than to Neville Chamberlain. It described the first lord of the Admiralty as, 'in the midst of one of the biggest battles of his political life'.[29] The *Mail* regarded Sir Roger Keyes' speech 'as a political bombshell of the first importance'.[30] However, despite its Conservative stance, it was not afflicted by the sycophancy amounting to self-censorship that enfeebled *The Times*. It observed that Chamberlain's own speech was 'regarded even by the most loyal Conservatives as largely ineffective and much too apologetic in view of the crisis facing the Government'.[31] The *Daily Mail* anticipated that Labour would seize the opportunity to force a vote and try to bring down the government. Nevertheless, it noted that the opposition did not expect to succeed, 'Labour men feel that in the last resort most of the rebel Conservatives who have met and talked in recent days will obey the crack of the party whip.'[32]

The *Daily Express* paid close attention to Sir Roger Keyes' criticism of the Norway campaign. It reminded readers that Keyes, who had commanded successful naval operations in the First World War, had offered his services as a commander of the British Norwegian Expeditionary Force.[33] A profile of the 68-year-old retired admiral recalled that Keyes had led the 'famous raid on Zeebrugge on St George's Day 1918' when 'blockships filled with concrete were sunk to block the exit of U-boats using the Bruges canal'.[34] The leading popular Conservative title reported from Westminster that: 'It was generally felt in the lobbies last night that the debate had damaged the prestige of the Government.' It did not expect Labour to force a vote of confidence and explained that 'the Socialists' (the *Express* always used this description of Labour) 'feel that direct challenge to the government would rally the Government's supporters and give a false impression of the feeling in the House'.[35] The *Express* recognized Julian Amery's speech as direct criticism of the prime minister. It reported his words briefly in a column headlined: 'Amery to Premier: Get out!' and summarized his message as 'There must be a change of our governmental machinery.'[36]

In its editorial, the *Daily Express* declined to condemn Chamberlain directly. He had taken military advice from the 'professional heads of the Navy, the Army and the Air Force . . . And now their judgment is brought into question.' The prime minister had been right 'to demonstrate to the world that our championship of small nations was something more than talk. That we meant it. That we would act upon it.'[37] And, if this was to damn Chamberlain with faint praise, the *Express* had identified a minister it did admire. It celebrated Winston Churchill's appointment as 'Minister with a special responsibility for military operations' and believed the public would also welcome his new additional role: 'Mr. Churchill is the right choice for the post. He is qualified by experience of war and study of war.' If the written message was oblique, Sidney 'George' Strube's three-column cartoon, which dominated the page alongside the single-column editorial, was not. It depicted Winston Churchill and Neville Chamberlain sheltering in a sand-bagged bunker under bombardment by enemy warplanes. Churchill held a machine gun; Chamberlain a sheet of paper. The caption read: 'Winston's New Job: Neville: "Go ahead, Winston, you're the new supervisor of all military operations."'[38]

In his excellent *Six Minutes in May: How Churchill Unexpectedly Became Prime Minister*,[39] Nicholas Shakespeare has reconstructed meticulously the scenes in the division lobbies after Labour seized its chance to force a vote on the motion for adjournment. The government chief whip, David Margesson had not begun to consider the possibility that a significant number of Conservative MPs might rebel until the concluding speeches of the two-day debate. By then, any opportunity to impose discipline had passed. It would probably have failed anyway, given the anger prevalent on Conservative benches, notably among younger MPs already serving in the armed forces. Whips and ministers worked frantically to bully these rebels into compliance. Assorted threats were issued, including claims that the king would be obliged to invite Labour to form a government if Chamberlain were humiliated and that Germany would invade Holland instantly if the government fell. The Conservative Duff Cooper, who had announced during the debate that he would vote against the government, noted 'a young officer in uniform, who had been for long a fervent admirer of Chamberlain, walking through the Opposition Lobby with the tears streaming down his face'.[40]

The government's majority fell from the 213-vote margin it expected on a whipped division to just 81. Now, Lord Halifax, the foreign secretary, made plain his intense reluctance to serve as prime minister. Labour leaders, Clement Attlee and his deputy, Arthur Greenwood, set out the terms on which they would join a government of national unity. They would serve under Winston Churchill. Rebel Conservative MPs insisted they would not support any government that did not include Labour and Liberal ministers. Richard Toye notes that the *Daily Express* carried a report that Chamberlain would stand down,[41] but he was still prime minister on the morning of Friday, 10 May 1940 when one of the government whips' threats to potential rebel MPs came true: the Germans invaded Belgium and Holland. Churchill was summoned to Buckingham Palace at 6.00 pm. There King George VI invited him to form a government. At 9.00 pm, Chamberlain made his resignation public in a broadcast on the BBC. Radio ownership was widespread in 1940. Approximately 73 in every 100 households owned a receiver, so the outgoing prime minister's statement was heard in households throughout the country. However, Richard Toye notes that a Mass Observation survey found that listeners considered the corporation's coverage 'insufficiently vivid'.[42] Newspapers would convey a greater impression of drama and significance.

A New Prime Minister

The editorial in *The Times* the following morning conveyed a sense of shock and dismay. It briefly recounted the facts that Chamberlain had resigned and that Labour had agreed 'to take their share of responsibility as a full partner in a new Government, under a new Prime Minister, which would command the confidence of the nation'.[43] Next, it lamented that, given the critical military situation, Labour had not seen fit to 'give their support to the present War Cabinet without prejudice to reconstruction at the earliest practicable date'. It concluded: 'There may be divisions of opinion about the capacity of leaders, but there is none whatever about the purpose all leaders have in view; and the fighting services, which are now moving to a vast and vital grapple with the enemy, can rest assured that their spirit and their courage express the resolution of the whole people.'[44] *The Times* printed too early to include in its editorial news of Churchill's appointment.

The *Daily Express* was not constrained by an early print deadline. It carried a banner headline announcing the German invasion of Belgium and reported that 'British and French reinforcements were pouring across Belgium this morning into the first great battle of the western war'.[45] Beside this story, its political correspondent, Guy Eden, explained that Mr Winston Churchill was now prime minister. He noted that 'Representatives of the Socialist and Liberal Parties will enter the new Cabinet' and that Churchill had persuaded Chamberlain to continue to serve as a minister.[46] The *Express* explained that Churchill was loathed in Germany. A German news bulletin had described him as the 'most brutal representative of the policy of force – the man whose programme is to dismember Germany – this man whose hateful face is well known to all Germans'.[47]

If the *Daily Express* welcomed Winston Churchill as a warlike leader who might strike fear into German hearts, the liberal *Manchester Guardian* was equally pleased and determined to explain his value to its readers. It gave the circumstances of his appointment in a succinct news story.[48] Further detail appeared in an analysis by its political correspondent. This explained the key role played by Labour Party leaders in securing Neville Chamberlain's resignation and the significance of their consent to his remaining a minister in a coalition Cabinet led by Churchill. The *Guardian*'s expert also revealed that the Labour negotiating team intended to play a full part in the new government. It sought seats at the Cabinet table for its leader and deputy leader, Clement Attlee and Arthur Greenwood, and for Albert Alexander, a senior figure in the Cooperative movement, Herbert Morrison and Ernest Bevin. True to its ideals, the *Guardian* was adamant that 'Sir Archibald Sinclair must receive a post as leader of the Liberal Party'.[49]

The news of Churchill's appointment had broken late on the evening of Friday, 10 May and coincided with the shock German advance into the low countries. The Sunday newspapers would have time to offer deeper, more reflective coverage than their daily counterparts. The Astor family, owners of *The Observer*, had long disapproved of their editor, James Louis Garvin's close friendship with and support for Winston Churchill. Now, with his employers' friend Chamberlain deposed and Churchill installed as prime minister, Garvin could speak with candour. This he did in an extended column on Sunday, 12 May. 'Despite the conventional predictions that for all his genius he would never arrive', wrote Garvin, 'Mr Churchill becomes Prime Minister at sixty-five. He takes the helm in a hurricane.'[50] Calling on the new Cabinet to 'become a band of brothers like Nelson's captains', Garvin dared to hope that the inclusion of Labour and Liberal ministers would help 'constitute a great Government'. He was certain that Churchill had unanimous backing and described his friend as 'the choice of both Houses and of all parties' adding that 'his premiership is welcomed with enthusiasm by the nation and the empire'.[51] In Garvin's account, the nation desired a complete change and Churchill would deliver it.

The *Sunday Times* regretted that the unity necessary to face the 'direct fury' of German attack could only be achieved through Chamberlain's resignation. Nevertheless, its editorial called for unity and explained that Winston Churchill 'possesses many qualifications for leadership in war'. He was a former soldier who had studied military history. He could 'be trusted to deal fairly with all sections of the Coalition which he now leads'.[52] Still, the Kemsley family-owned title, then entirely independent of *The Times*, as the *Manchester Guardian* was from *The Observer*, did not hesitate to lavish praise on the outgoing prime minister. Neville Chamberlain had 'inherited a situation full of dangers and difficulties that were not of his making. He faced them with a skill and resolution that are not unappreciated now, but will be even better understood when history has laid bare the hidden facts behind successive crises.'[53]

The reticence with which the *Sunday Times* greeted Churchill's elevation and its combination of sympathy and respect for his predecessor reminds us of the importance of perceiving historic events as contemporaries did. In May 1940, Winston Churchill was not a universally popular leader and Britain's diverse and plural newspaper press reflected the full range of opinions which greeted his premiership. Richard Toye explains that that the War Cabinet would take the view that: 'While on the whole the attitude of the Press had been helpful, it was unfortunate there was a certain tendency to encourage inquests rather than to concentrate on the tasks ahead.'[54] On the extreme left, the Communist *Daily Worker* was adamant in its hostility to the new government. Its front page simply reproduced a statement published by the Communist Party of Great Britain. Winston Churchill's coalition represented: 'the greatest possible danger to the people of this country and to the future of democracy, Socialism and peace. It will not only intensify the war abroad. It will carry through the most intensive attacks against the working class and the standards of the people.'[55] The *Daily Worker* described Churchill as 'the man of Gallipoli'.[56] It called on the Labour Party to deny him support and warned that Labour opponents of the war were being prevented from speaking at the Labour Party conference then meeting in Bournemouth.

Dunkirk: Reporting the Miracle of Deliverance

The spirit of independence many newspapers had displayed as the Chamberlain administration staggered towards collapse did not survive the German Blitzkrieg in western Europe. The devastating speed with which German forces seized Holland and Belgium and advanced through France is a familiar story. For all who wish to understand it thoroughly, this author recommends Julian Jackson's excellent *The Fall of France*.[57] For the British Expeditionary Force, it culminated in the rescue of 224,320 British soldiers from the port of Dunkirk and the beaches between Dunkirk and De Panne in Belgium between 26 May and 4 June 1940. Winston Churchill, powerfully aware that retreats do not win wars, accurately described Dunkirk as a 'miracle of deliverance'.

The broadcaster J.B. Priestley first defined it in British memories through his 'Little Ships' *Postscript*, transmitted by the BBC immediately after the main evening news bulletin on Wednesday, 5 June. Priestley's eloquence and reassuring, warm Yorkshire accent helped to promote his prediction that 'our great grandchildren, when they learn how we began this war by snatching glory out of defeat, and then swept on to victory, may also learn how the little holiday steamers made an excursion to hell and came back glorious'.[58] There is, however, an additional reason why the depiction of Dunkirk as a colossal moral triumph took root quickly and has remained powerful. There were no newspaper correspondents available to challenge the romance with harsher depictions of chaos, suffering and squalor. A few correspondents did struggle back to the beaches with the soldiers whose feats they had been sent to report. Once there, they had no means by which to communicate with their news desks. They had abandoned their typewriters and had no access to radio transmitters or telegraph wires.

All newspaper reporting and analysis of Dunkirk was written by reporters and columnists at home and at the mercy of the naval press officers. These servicemen's first objective was to portray the senior service's colossal achievement. In this endeavour, they had the active support of the Ministry of Information. As a tool with which to manipulate journalists, helpful persuasion is often more effective than censorship, and so it proved. In an extended essay by its correspondent Evelyn Montague, grandson of its famous former editor, C.P. Scott, the *Manchester Guardian* adopted the desired tone even before the evacuation was complete. Montague witnessed the disembarkation of rescued soldiers from Royal Navy warships. His opening paragraph began, 'In the grey chill of dawn today in a south-eastern port war correspondents watched with incredulous joy the happening of a miracle.'[59] He explained how men who had 'seemed certain to be cut off' and who had been 'completely outnumbered, out-gunned, out-planned' and 'all but surrounded' were discharged 'safe and sound on British soil'.

The *Daily Mirror* was no less enthusiastic about a rescue mission that left virtually all the British army's armour and artillery in France. 'BLOODY MARVELLOUS' was the headline on its leader column on the same Saturday that Montague's essay appeared: 'For days past, thousands upon thousands of our brave men of the B.E.F. have been pouring through a port somewhere in England, battle-worn, but, thank God, safe and cheerful in spite of weariness.'[60] The *Mirror* was clear about who deserved credit for the rescue of this 'gallant force' from 'the trap planned for them by Nazi ruthlessness'. Throughout the difficult and dangerous operation, 'the Navy has toiled night and day, without sleep for scores of naval officers and men.'[61] A naval press officer was conveniently on hand to confirm that His Majesty's senior service 'is doing forty-eight hours' work every twenty-four hours.'[62] Beside the editorial appeared a large cartoon by Philip Zec (1909–83), the *Mirror*'s brilliant and dedicated graduate of Saint Martin's School of Art. It depicted a beaming sailor carrying a bloodied but smiling squaddie off a burning beach.[63]

The Times' view of Dunkirk was rose-tinted from the beginning. It soon became positively rapturous. While the evacuation continued, it cautioned that: 'The troops and their leader have had more than their share of sheer ill-fortune; but they have the more reason to look back on their achievement with the sense of duty well done and to the future with resolution and hope.'[64] Twenty-four hours later, with thousands more soldiers safely home, it reflected that Hitler must have thought he had the BEF trapped like rats in a sack, but Hitler did not understand Britain. *The Times* explained that the soldiers of this great seafaring nation 'retire to the seashore as outposts falling back upon an impregnable position, the great stronghold of sea-power, which can cover the last stages of their retreat and then offer an impassable barrier to attack'.[65] If this optimistic myth-making did not actually mention Horatio Lord Nelson or Sir Francis Drake, what followed certainly conjured names and romance from Britain's national story. Winston Churchill was 'a leader behind whom a resolute nation may face the heaviest blows of fortune unafraid', declared the newspaper that had fought harder than any other to keep his predecessor in office. The prime minister's 'We Shall Fight on the Beaches' speech to the House of Commons, 'breathed the spirit of Shakespeare's England. Whatever happens to Englishmen and Frenchmen, England and France are unconquerable. If necessary, we shall fight field by field and street by street' until Hitler's 'foul contagion is purged from the face of civilisation.'[66]

Dawson would not be the first newspaper editor to make a prediction that would soon be rendered risible. However, his optimism that Britain's alliance with France would endure was excessive. Marshal Pétain sought armistice terms on 17 June. The armistice was signed at Compiègne on 22 June, in the railway carriage used for the German armistice of 1918.

The *Daily Mail* was not above sentimental myth-making. Celebrating Dunkirk as 'a withdrawal unmatched in warfare', it called for medals to be awarded to 'the fishermen and others who played a magnificent part in a great exploit.'[67] However, realism about the consequences of the BEF's evacuation also featured in its editorials. The *Mail* warned its readers that Hitler's forces had 'cleared Holland, Belgium and Northern France of all opposition except the stubborn rearguard at Dunkirk' and it noted that, while the BEF was 'not broken or disintegrated', it had 'lost large quantities of material and weapons'.[68]

New Restrictions on the Press

Between September 1939 and June 1940, British newspapers faced few obstacles beyond birth pains in the Ministry of Information's voluntary censorship scheme and the service departments' reluctance to share interesting news. There was no rationing of newsprint and the powers of press censorship available to government were derived entirely from Defence Regulation 3. This meant that censors had authority only to prevent publication of news that would 'aid the enemy in his military effort'. The regulations meant that censorship covered facts, but not opinions: it was security censorship, not policy censorship. In June 1940, Churchill's new government considered imposing tougher regulation of newspapers. At its meeting on Tuesday, 11 June, the War Cabinet considered a memorandum by the minister of information, Duff Cooper. One of the prime minister's close allies, Cooper had replaced Sir John Reith at the MoI on 12 May. Now he advanced proposals designed to appeal to his leader's desire for national unity in the face of harsh adversity. Duff Cooper's paper was entitled 'Compulsory Censorship'. It summarized the government's dilemma:

> The fundamental weakness of the present system is that there is no effective sanction at all for breaches of Censorship Regulations. Submission to Censorship is voluntary; it is no offence to ignore the censoring of matter, even if submitted; and the only relevant offence which has been created by the Defence Regulations is the offence of publishing information which would be likely to be useful to the enemy.[69]

Diagnosing the problem was easy. Duff Cooper recognized that there was no simple solution. He outlined two schemes: a system of 'compulsory censorship',[70] whereby newspapers would be forbidden to publish anything which had not been censored, and a 'compulsory sources' scheme under which they would be forbidden to publish 'any matter on a list of defined subjects except official communiqués'.[71]

Duff Cooper acknowledged the 'scope of the problem'.[72] His paper advises that any scheme would have to deal with eleven London daily papers, 133 provincial dailies and 760 London, provincial and suburban weekly newspapers. It would also face opposition from a public brought up to believe that press freedom was the birthright of every Briton. The information minister believed a free press was a vital component in Britain's political settlement. His Labour and Liberal colleagues in the new coalition government ascribed to the same belief. Indeed, throughout the war, they would demonstrate the certainty of their belief by defending newspapers' editorial freedom against demands for new restrictions. In June 1940, the War Cabinet concluded that draconian censorship was not achievable. However, it was not prepared to proceed as if withdrawal from Dunkirk changed nothing. Hitler's armies had shattered the French army, the largest in Europe. The retreat to Dunkirk had revealed the BEF's lack of preparedness and the inferiority of its armour and artillery. The threat of invasion was real.

Duff Cooper did not rush to decide. Instead, he consulted MPs before imposing two new defence regulations, 2C and 2D. The former gave ministers power to exclude 'any material calculated to foment opposition to the war'.[73] The process by which this would be achieved was to be fast and straightforward. The home secretary would issue a formal warning to any newspaper he considered to be in breach of the regulation. If the editor failed to comply, the minister could prosecute and, if successful, prevent publication. Regulation 2D gave the home secretary additional power to close any newspaper that systematically published material calculated to foment opposition to a successful prosecution of the war.

The Communist *Daily Worker* spotted the danger early. Plainly, its embrace of revolutionary defeatism and depiction of the war as an imperialist conflict inimical to the interests of British workers would render it vulnerable. Before they were approved, it warned that the new defence regulations would, 'bring back into Britain provisions for the penalisation of the expression of opinions unknown since the days of Charles First'. The state would have the legal power to 'make the expression of a reasoned opinion honestly held an offence punishable by penal servitude'.[74] The *Daily Worker*'s prediction was prescient. In early 1941, it would become the only British daily newspaper to be banned during wartime. However, as Britain fought on through the summer of 1940, government resentment of press criticism grew more intense. The defence regulations gave ministers new weapons with which to threaten and intimidate newspaper editors and proprietors.

When the minister formally announced the new arrangements in late July, the mainstream press offered a measured response. *The Times* insisted that voluntary censorship worked and accepted the government's assurances that it 'was not going to resort to compulsion'.[75] It reported a speech in Hendon by Harold Nicolson, parliamentary secretary to the Ministry of Information. The junior minister said he trusted, 'that no strain through which we might have to pass would lead any foolish person to imagine it would be necessary to suppress free comment and free speech on the part of the Press'.[76] The Ministry of Information 'was not an Ogpu [Soviet secret police force] or a Gestapo. It did not desire to dictate to the citizens of this free country what they should think, say, feel or hear'.[77] The *Manchester Guardian* took a similarly sympathetic view of the government's approach. Censorship of the press was still voluntary, it concluded, having digested Duff Cooper's announcement.[78] It took analysis by an influential weekly news title, *The Economist*, to recognise that something really might change. The Ministry of Information's new approach was misconceived, it argued. Newspapers were not the problem. The real risk was that government might operate without effective scrutiny by the fourth estate. For *The Economist*, 'The Government has already ample power to put a stop to both irresponsibility and obstructionism. ... Indeed, the chief safeguard against blindness and obstruction in places even higher than the Press is the maintenance of a free forum for all news and views that do not stand in the way of waging the war'.[79]

It was a compelling argument. The value of loyal opposition had begun to emerge as newspapers sought to promote efficiency in the war effort. Dunkirk changed the collective mood, uniting titles of left and right in uncritical praise for Navy and government. The impulse to question, scrutinize and challenge would only emerge with real clarity as the United Kingdom faced German bombing of its town and cities. The

Economist anticipated it intelligently. Honest criticism of government and policy could function extremely well as an aid to victory, but there could and should be no sympathy for opponents of the war. The cause was just and this was a war of national survival. Newspapers must be critical friends of the national coalition. And, when German bombing of Britain became intense, the 'blindness and obstruction' against which *The Economist* had warned would manifest itself. In the War Cabinet, hostility to reporting and comment that criticized ministers and their policies would not be reserved for anti-war communist titles alone.

CHAPTER 5
CLASS UNITY AND THE MYTH OF THE BLITZ

The 'Myth of the Blitz' is the historian Angus Calder's description of a set of values and narratives about British national character and behaviour that emerged in 1940. Calder makes it plain that myths are not lies. Rather, they are stories that serve a useful purpose, and which have roots in observable conduct and evidence. He argues that popular understanding of Dunkirk, the Battle of Britain and the Blitz itself is informed by the Myth. Calder writes: 'Like the Armada when "God blew and they were scattered", the bloodless miracle of the Glorious Revolution, or the providential triumph of Trafalgar, these were events in which the hand of destiny was seen.'[1] He defines these moments in British history as ones that flatter 'the dominant particularism within Britain' and which support 'a myth of British or English moral pre-eminence, buttressed by British unity'.[2] This idea of unity, and, particularly, of class unity in the face of adversity, is among the most enduring elements of the Myth. It is expressed most succinctly in the belief that, under the threat of invasion and the reality of bombardment from the air, Britons were 'all in it together'. My case study from the summer of 1940 confirms what the experience of mass evacuation had already revealed: class unity in wartime Britain was manufactured from fragile components. It deals with a topic that was, briefly, intensely controversial: the evacuation of children to safety overseas.

Overseas Evacuation

In early June 1940, as the last remnants of the British Expeditionary Force departed from the Dunkirk beaches, a perception of grave social injustice smouldered at home. Influential voices on radio, in newspapers and in parliament were determined to fan it into flame. They included the BBC's then most popular broadcaster, J.B. Priestley, Nazi Germany's most notorious English language propagandist, William Joyce – a.k.a. Lord Haw-Haw – and national mass-market newspapers of all political persuasions. The topic that united this diverse range of opinion was the private evacuation to the United States and Canada of a number of children with wealthy and influential parents. They included: John Julius Norwich, son of the Conservative politician, Duff Cooper; Paul Channon, son of Conservative MP Henry (Chips) Channon; Jeremy Tree, son of Ronald Tree, the Conservative MP for Harborough in Leicestershire; Viscount Bayham, son of the Earl of Brecknock; Shirley Catlin – now remembered as Baroness (Shirley) Williams of Crosby (1930–2021) – daughter of Vera Brittain and Sir George Catlin; and Angela Lansbury, daughter of the Communist politician, Edgar Lansbury, and the Irish actress, Moyna Macgill.

Together with her four-year-old brother, one atypical example, five-year-old Jessica Mann, the daughter of German Jewish refugees from Nazi Germany, was 'put into the charge of a stranger hired to take us across the Atlantic'.[3] Having fled anti-Semitism in Germany with little more than their qualifications, her parents were determined to ensure that she could not fall into Nazi hands. Mann spent two years in Canada and one in the United States. In *Out of Harm's Way: The Wartime Evacuation of Children from Britain*, she recalls vividly the resentment occasioned by what was sometimes known as 'seavacuation'. While researching her book, Mann heard children who escaped the United Kingdom described as 'horrid little cowards [who] ran away', unpatriotic and traitors.[4] It is clear that a vivid and plausible sense of social injustice informed such opinions.

Before placing his son Paul aboard a liner, Chips Channon took leave from his duties in the House of Commons and 'spent an hour in Westminster Cathedral … burning candles, listening to the service and praying for the welfare and safety of my beloved child on his transatlantic trip'.[5] What followed when parents and son reached London's Euston Station, whence Paul would travel to his ship, underlines vividly the privileged status of many overseas evacuees. Channon writes: '[T]here was a queue of Rolls-Royces and liveried servants, and mountains of trunks. It seemed that everyone we knew was there on this very crowded platform.'[6] Mann notes that lists of children evacuated overseas at their parents' expense included 'many "establishment" surnames', among them, Mountbatten, Bowes Lyon, Sitwell, Guinness and Hamro.[7]

Queen Elizabeth surely sought to insulate the royal family from popular resentment of such rationing-by-price when she explained, after a bomb hit Buckingham Palace, why she and King George VI chose not to send Princesses Elizabeth and Margaret Rose to Canada: 'The children will not leave unless I do. I shall not leave unless their father does, and the king will not leave the country in any circumstances, whatever.'[8] Such manifestations of the 'all in it together' message would advance the government's ambition to depict Britain as a national family united under royal leadership. Spencer Leeson, headmaster of Winchester College and chairman of the public schools' organization, the Headmasters' Conference (HMC), took a less inclusive approach. He wrote to *The Times* in defence of parents' rights to 'remove younger boys and girls to places of safety for the time being'. Leeson celebrated the generosity of Dominion governments that had offered to accept young evacuees and, eliding the reality that many parents of HMC children were evacuating their sons and daughters privately, noted that a public scheme was now in place to facilitate such evacuation.[9]

The scheme operated by the Children's Overseas Reception Board (CORB) was revealed to the House of Commons on 2 July 1940 by the under-secretary of state for Dominion Affairs, Geoffrey Shakespeare. It was an emergency project to evacuate British children between the ages of five and sixteen years to homes in Britain's overseas Dominions: Australia, Canada, New Zealand and South Africa. It was authorized by the War Cabinet on 17 June but ministers had no time to discuss it and it is not clear that they would have approved if they had. Shakespeare presented it mere moments before an urgent message was delivered informing the War Cabinet that French troops had ceased fire and providing an account of Marshal Pétain's approach to Hitler seeking 'a means to put an end to hostilities'.[10] Sir Martin Gilbert, Churchill's biographer, believes the official record implies consent that was not really granted:

Shakespeare presented the scheme, as it was on the Cabinet agenda. He knew that the Prime Minister had reservations, but when someone came in with the news about France, Shakespeare had to leave because he was not in the Cabinet. He felt he had presented the scheme, it was never discussed but no one had dissented, so he could proceed.[11]

CORB was born following pointed questions about the private evacuation of children to the Dominions in the House of Commons on 12 June. Geoffrey Shakespeare was appointed chairman of an interdepartmental committee charged with urgent work to create a state-funded scheme.[12] Among its principal justifications was the widespread perception that rich parents were buying their children's safety by evacuating them to the United States or Canada.

Shakespeare was painfully aware of 'constant reiteration by Lord Haw-Haw' that the benefits of overseas evacuation 'are exclusively for the rich'.[13] Nazi propaganda broadcasts raised the issue, incessantly. Transmitting to Britain from Germany, English-speaking Nazi broadcasters, such as the Irish-American William Joyce (1906–46), sought to attract listeners away from the BBC and claimed 'to give the listener in foreign lands something quite new – the truth'.[14] Joyce, or Lord Haw-Haw as he was known, following the *Daily Express*'s description of his accent as 'English of the haw-haw, damnit-get-out-of-my-way variety',[15] ruthlessly exploited the assertion that Britain's richest families were getting their children away from danger at the expense of the poor. Throughout May and June 1940, Haw-Haw advertised the Nazi theme that Britain's political and social elite were imposing unjustified suffering on decent working people, who would find their lives much improved if Britain were subject to National Socialist rule. Stigmatizing Britain's governing class as 'the rich, the wealthy, the plutocratic caste', Haw-Haw asserted that the rich had provoked the war in order to profit from it, but 'now that the worst is about to come to the worst, they quietly vanish from the scene'.[16] CORB would counter such arguments. Geoffrey Shakespeare told MPs: 'the essence of our scheme is that there should be no discrimination and no special facilities for a privileged few'. Instead, he proposed 'a balanced migration representing a cross-section of British children'. He believed, 'Nothing would so undermine public morale as to grant such facilities to a privileged few. Such a policy would militate against the spirit of resolution and tenacity with which we intend to prosecute this war to a final conclusion.'[17] The most senior politician to contribute to the debate was Clement Attlee, lord privy seal, leader of the Labour Party and Churchill's de facto deputy. He praised the work Geoffrey Shakespeare had done to prepare CORB and confirmed that: 'I think it absolutely right that there should not be privilege for one lot of people as against another. I think it is right that a fair sample of the population should be sent overseas.'[18] If some children were to escape the threat of Nazi invasion and bombing, MPs agreed they should come from every class and region of the country. Successful applicants to the scheme should be selected according to their suitability as ambassadors for Britain at war and irrespective of parental wealth.

Plainly then, by the second half of June 1940, there was broad consensus in the House of Commons that the CORB scheme was necessary and that it would advance social justice. Newspapers and the BBC had helped to shape that perspective. Even while the evacuation from Dunkirk was still underway, *The Times* reported, 'it is realized that the decision would not be easy for any parent. At the same time many would probably feel that a temporary parting would be a small price to pay for escape from the sort of ruthless bombing which Poland, Norway, Holland, Belgium and France have all experienced.'[19] In his *Postscript* broadcast on the BBC Home Service immediately after the main 9.00 pm radio news bulletin on Sunday, 16 June 1940, J.B. Priestley drew the cause of overseas evacuation to the attention of millions. He did so while recounting his first experience of night-time duty as a Local Defence Volunteer preparing to defend his home on the Isle of Wight. Priestley anticipated imminent invasion by 'half-crazy German youths, in whose empty eyes the idea of honour and glory seems to include every form of beastliness'.[20] He concluded that: 'while one nation is ready to hurl its armed men at another, you must, if necessary, stand up and fight for your own'.[21] Priestley believed it would be easier to fight if loved ones were removed from the combat zone. He wished 'we could send all of our children out of this island, every boy and girl of them across the sea to the wide Dominions and turn Britain into the greatest fortress the world has known'. This done, 'with an easy mind, we could fight and fight these Nazis until we broke their black hearts'.[22] Priestley was distinctive among BBC broadcasters in that he was allowed to mix news and comment in his broadcasts. His yearning for an inclusive scheme of overseas evacuation reflected his socialist beliefs. It was influential. Addison and Crang, in their book, *Listening to Britain*, explain how, during this critical phase of the war, the Ministry of Information's Home Intelligence department compiled reports on popular morale. Between 18 May and 27 September 1940, MoI regional officials filed daily summaries covering the entire country.[23] These suggest strong initial support for overseas evacuation. On Monday, 17 June, the Home Intelligence team in Manchester reported that: 'Evacuation of women and children to Dominions (J.B. Priestley's suggestion) has caught popular fancy.'[24] The following day, Home Intelligence in Reading reported: 'Middle class like the idea of sending children to Canada' and Birmingham found: 'Working class supports idea of Canada for children.'[25] On Tuesday, 19 June, the Home Intelligence summary of regional reports revealed that many men 'would be glad to see women and children go to Canada'. It noted that: 'The number of women making enquiries about taking or sending children to the Dominions is hourly increasing.'[26] Nottingham reported: 'Compulsory evacuation of children to Canada much discussed.' Cardiff found residents convinced that children should be sent abroad if necessary and Manchester found evidence that: 'Delays in arrangements for evacuating women and children to Canada is causing bitter comment.'[27]

With fear of invasion at a peak and loathing for Neville Chamberlain's recently departed administration still vibrant among working-class Britons, J.B. Priestley's suggestion was gaining momentum. However, Home Intelligence soon identified the emergence of differences of opinion based upon social class. Many working-class mothers expressed reluctance to send children abroad if they could not accompany them. In Newcastle, MoI staff found overseas evacuation was primarily a topic of interest to the middle classes. In London, West Ham parents were 'opposed to children going alone'.[28] Priestley had brought the issue alive and now mass circulation newspapers of left and right weighed in.

On Wednesday, 3 July, the market leading, conservative *Daily Express* set a tone rivals would follow. In a leader column headlined, 'To Go – or Not to Go? The Rich Go First', the *Express* protested that 'while the Government is arranging to evacuate the 20,000, there is another kind of evacuation. It is carried out by well-to-do parents who can pay their children's passage and arrange for them to be supported by relatives or friends overseas. Poorer parents whose children are left behind feel a grievance and a just grievance, at the children of the rich who are being sent to safety.' The leader writer noted that Geoffrey Shakespeare had promised to intervene if wealthy private evacuees took up shipping space required by children chosen for the CORB scheme. The *Express* urged the Minister to be decisive: 'The public feels that all available space should be taken over by the government and the rich should take their turn with the rest.'[29]

At the other end of the political spectrum, the Labour-supporting *Daily Mirror* deployed America's first lady, Eleanore Roosevelt, to assist its criticism of class bias in overseas evacuation. Mrs Roosevelt had broadcast from Washington DC a personal plea to eradicate bureaucratic obstructions and transfer many British children to the United States. The *Mirror* reported that: 'The suggestion that so far only children of titled and wealthy Britons have been evacuated to the United States is strongly criticized by the American Committee in London for the evacuation of children.' It warned that Mr Justin Weddell, chairman of the committee, blamed British bureaucracy 'for the fact that the children so far sent have belonged to families that have well-to-do friends in the States'.[30] A week later, the *Mirror* identified children who had just arrived in New York aboard the 24,189-ton luxury liner SS *Washington*. They included: 'Viscount Bayham, son of the Earl of Brecknock and grandson of the Marquis of Camden, and the two daughters of Lord and Lady Mountbatten'.[31] The *Mirror*'s sub-heading was 'Only the Rich Go'.

Its architects depicted CORB as an antidote to class bias, although their own motives included a desire to strengthen links between the Dominions and the mother country. The *Manchester Guardian* welcomed the scheme, noting that overseas evacuation ships would soon be 'filled with young emigrants from all classes of the community'.[32] It acknowledged that any decision to send children abroad was fraught with risk: 'Parents who are considering sending their children to safety overseas must themselves weigh the dangers to be faced in this country against the risks to which every ship that leaves our shores is subjected.'[33] However, the liberal title recognized an appetite for overseas evacuation among its readers. 'Salford parents of school children between the ages of five and fourteen continue to show an active interest in the scheme for overseas evacuation', it reported,[34] noting that more than 300 families had registered for the scheme. The following day it reported: 'one of the busiest days which the evacuation department at Salford education offices has ever experienced.... There were more than two hundred registrations yesterday and this brings the total to date to well over 500.'[35]

Some *Guardian* readers, however, proved resistant to an egalitarian approach. A prominent news story on 3 July recorded an offer by the American, Australian and Canadian federations of university women of 'overseas homes for the duration of the war' to children of British graduates. The British Federation of University Women described the offer as 'most generous' and invited its local associations to advertise it 'without delay to members and other graduates'. It promised to 'see that children of graduates in this country are domiciled with the families of graduates overseas'.[36] If this was not rank snobbery, it was certainly directed at a tiny and elite audience. National membership of the British Federation of University Women did not exceed 4,000 at the beginning of the Second World War.[37] Despite its commitment to equality, many *Guardian* readers were university educated and their newspaper did not hesitate to appeal to their sense of themselves as a class apart.

The *Manchester Guardian*'s letters page reflected its readers' interest in overseas evacuation. Josiah Wedgwood, the Labour MP for Newcastle-under-Lyme, wrote to explain its military significance. His argument reflected J.B. Priestley's certainty that he would fight better if his family were safe. Wedgwood wrote: 'No man can fight well if he is anxious about his immediate dependents.' He warned that civilian panic would mean 'roads will be choked whatever standstill orders are given . . . the wife will wander west and the husband east in desperate anxiety to shelter each other. No risks, no bayonets even, will stop this.'[38] On the same page, T.W.L. MacDermot, secretary of the Canadian Head Masters' Association, informed readers that his association and colleagues in the Head Mistresses' Association 'are willing at once and during the coming year to look after as many boys and girls as their schools can hold'. These were private schools. The *Guardian*'s letters pages also carried correspondence offering places at private schools in South Africa.

The popular, conservative *Daily Mail*'s initial response to the CORB scheme was more humane than ideological but it too stressed equality. On 20 June, it reported that: 'Ships are to sail almost immediately carrying the first batch of 20,000 children from Britain to the Dominions.' It noted that 'passage will be free' and that 'there is a desire in the Dominions to have a complete cross-section of British life, comprising children from all classes'.[39] By 1940, the *Mail* had long been determined to serve its large female readership. In Adrian Bingham's words, the newspaper 'moved the female reader from the margins to the centre of editorial calculations, ensuring that the definition of "news" was radically altered, that the boundary between "public" and "private" was redrawn, and that the visibility of women in public discourse was transformed'.[40] Hence, determined to interpret the issue through the experiences of real families, the *Mail* sent Ann Temple, author since 1936 of its immensely popular 'Human Case-Book' column, to meet Mr and Mrs Smith who were anxiously divided over whether to send their four children overseas.

Ann Temple found Mr Smith adamant that a combination of security and the availability of food in Canada and the United States clinched the issue: 'Safety for their minds as well as for their bodies. We don't want their minds and nerves ruined for life. And there's food to think of. They'd be better off in those countries even if the war did spread.' Mrs Smith was 'not yet convinced that rooting them up out of their home, packing them off across the world over dangerous seas, to live with strangers for an unpredictable length of time is the best for them'. In Temple's account, the argument was settled when 'four healthy, strapping, sunburnt youngsters' rushed back into the house from the garden. They were 'ravenously hungry' and for the *Mail's* columnist, if not for their mother, the case for sending them abroad was made: 'Food stops this argument every time.'[41]

Winston Churchill did not agree. Had Geoffrey Shakespeare's scheme not avoided his scrutiny in cabinet, it might never have been launched. In the event, it did not last long. The government announced the postponement of CORB on 16 July. With Britain under imminent threat of invasion, the Royal Navy could not spare warships to protect vessels carrying evacuees. Clement Attlee told the House that the government could not take responsibility for conveying thousands of children overseas without adequate protection. The decision prompted immediate demands for a simultaneous ban on private evacuation. James Griffiths, the Labour MP for Llanelly, said that, if it was not possible to take 'all kinds of children from all kinds of homes and all classes', then 'the government ought not to permit well-to-do children to leave the country'. Mr Griffiths wanted 'to put it very strongly ... that it is very desirable that we should make it impossible for any impression to gain ground in this country that class distinction is to operate at a time like this.' He said working-class people 'resent it and feel indignant if rich people are looking after their own children and allowing the children of the poor to stand all the risks'.[42] Griffiths views were echoed on the Conservative benches.

Addressing MPs immediately after the postponement of CORB, Winston Churchill said ministers had been 'deeply touched' by offers of hospitality from the Dominions and the United States. They would 'take pains to make sure that in the use that is made of these offers there shall be no question of rich people having an advantage, if advantage there be, over poor'.[43] The *Daily Worker* was not convinced. It reported that angry MPs 'overwhelmed the Government with accusations of class discrimination against children.... The most frequently repeated criticism was that wealthy people were sending their children abroad while poor parents were now prevented from doing so. Members of the Government who have sent their children abroad were particularly strongly criticised.'[44]

Was overseas evacuation as sought after as newspapers suggested? As we have seen, Home Intelligence reports detected early support for CORB. However, reports soon noted that the greatest clamour existed among middle-class parents. Less affluent families opposed evacuation to the Dominions unless mothers could accompany their children (which CORB did not permit). In Islington in early July, Home Intelligence found 'mothers not anxious to send children to Dominions and need reassuring that children will not be whisked away without their consent'.[45] The scheme was formally abandoned after the sinking of the passenger vessel SS *City of Benares* 600 miles out from Liverpool in the North Atlantic on the evening of Tuesday, 17 September. When she was torpedoed, *Benares* was carrying 90 CORB children to Canada. She was also carrying private evacuees. Class segregation determined the likelihood of survival. The CORB children were sleeping in bunks deep in the bowels of the ship. Children moving overseas at their parents' expense had first-class accommodation closer to the lifeboats. Eighty-one children lost their lives in the disaster.

Barbara Bech was a private evacuee travelling on the *Benares* with her sister, brother and mother. She recalled total segregation between first-class passengers and the CORB children. So complete was it that the first time she realized the CORB children were on board was when they were rushed on deck after the torpedo struck. Some were as young as five years old and several were in flimsy clothing (they had all been in bed). Barbara's brother, Derek, recalled hearing the children crying: 'The torpedo struck where the children were, many were trapped in the cabins, some were injured, some were killed and then when they reached the lifeboats ... a lot of the lifeboats capsized. One or two of them obviously drowned immediately.' The Bech family all survived and Barbara and her brother, who had been enjoying the luxury of first-class travel, joked that the sinking was 'a waste of good ice cream'. Thirteen of the 90 CORB children survived alongside six of the ten private evacuees on board.[46]

* * *

So, was newspaper pressure for overseas evacuation ever justified by actual public opinion? Or did the newspapers foment class division at a time when the MoI was desperate to avoid it and the government alarmed that it might undermine national unity? Parallel pressure from popular titles of left and right displayed a mutual demand for fairness that would emerge as a key feature of mass-market journalism in wartime Britain. However, on this occasion, fear of class division led newspapers and politicians to exaggerate demand for overseas evacuation among the poor. Details of those registering for the CORB scheme, as well as those evacuated privately, suggest that overseas evacuation appealed disproportionately to parents accustomed to sending their children away from home, not least to boarding schools.

Achieving fairness in access to essential services was to be a pervading concern among ministers during the Blitz. Controversy over access to overseas evacuation offered early proof that it would be difficult. On 10 October, Geoffrey Shakespeare answered a parliamentary question about the numbers of children who had left the country privately and under the government scheme. He revealed that 4,579 British children had gone to the Dominions under private arrangements and a further 1,617 private evacuee children had gone to the United States, giving a total of 6,196 children evacuated privately. Only 2,666 children had been evacuated successfully under the state scheme.[47]

Ian Kershaw warns us that: 'It is generally hard, knowing the end of a story, to avoid reading history backwards from the outcome.'[48] The controversy over the CORB scheme that manifested itself in national newspapers in the summer of 1940 illustrates the importance of his warning. The Children's Overseas Reception scheme rarely features in histories of the period. It matters because, like the more familiar fury about dirty working-class evacuees that preceded it, newspaper treatment of CORB illustrates that the 'all in it together' spirit of the Blitz was not instinctive. It had to be nurtured.

CHAPTER 6
THE BATTLE OF BRITAIN

The Battle of Britain began on 11 July 1940, just five days before the CORB scheme was suspended. It has a unique place in British history. Remembered above all for the courage of the RAF fighter pilots Winston Churchill christened 'the few',[1] it was exceptional in other ways too. For newspapers, the new defence regulations and security censorship rules were only the beginning. Paper supply was a new problem. Publishers were accustomed to importing paper on which to print multi-page, mass circulation newspapers. Supplies became harder to obtain following German occupation of Norway and Denmark, the reallocation of merchant shipping to essential imports and the threat from U-boats. Official demand for paper products to supply wartime essentials such as ration books would further limit the availability of newsprint. In June, newspapers were restricted to their current circulations and their pagination was restricted. They would go on shrinking for the next three years, reaching at their smallest just four or six pages with little space for anything but the most urgent war news.

Angus Calder shows that MoI staff had, by this time, three 'broad methods of imposing their ideas on the public through the mass media'.[2] The ministry could suppress news, promote or invent stories it wanted to appear or offer selective access to journalists it considered trustworthy in return for positive coverage. Initial newspaper reporting of the Battle of Britain followed the promotion route: the Air Ministry issued bulletins and the newspapers reported them. An example of the homogeneity this produced can be taken from a comparison of five front-page reports published on Thursday, 11 July in the *Daily Mail*, *Daily Mirror*, *Daily Express*, *Daily Telegraph* and *Yorkshire Post*.

The *Mirror*'s headline declared 'RAF's Battle Score 37'.[3] The *Express* had precisely the same figure and additional patriotic fervour. Its headline read '37 German Raiders Down – Three Spitfires Attack Fifty, and Win. A Day of Glorious Deeds'.[4] The *Yorkshire Post* based its story on exactly the same information from the Air Ministry but demonstrated slightly greater precision. Its headline explained '14 Nazi Planes Down, 23 Badly Damaged – RAF Pilots' Best Day'.[5] The *Daily Telegraph* offered another optimistic interpretation of the figures. Its headline read: 'RAF Put 37 Raiders Out of Action – 14 Shot Down: Others Unable to Get Home'. The report that followed hinted that 'unable' was an extrapolation not a fact. It noted that 'in addition to the 14 machines definitely shot down, 23 were so badly damaged that they were unlikely to reach home'.[6]

The *Daily Mail* blended precision and patriotism in its summary of the Air Ministry's briefing. Patriotism took precedence. Its headline declared a 'Big Air Victory'. The standfirst broke the 37 Luftwaffe victims into two categories: '14 Germans Shot Down, 23 Crippled in Battle'.[7] A short news item in *The Times* hinted that the road to victory over the Luftwaffe might not be entirely easy. This noted that: 'The Royal Air Force has gone a step further towards recognition of the Air Defence Cadet Corps (ADCC) by indicating that, if members of the RAF who have attested, but have not been called up, will report to ADCC squadrons, they will receive training which will have a definite relation on their future career.'[8] This, however, was plainly intended to encourage voluntary enlistment by those too young for conscription. It was, therefore, entirely consistent with the Air Ministry's objectives.

In the *Daily Mail*, early coverage of the battle combined loyal reporting of official accounts with vivid patriotism and conscientious attention to the interests of female readers. The *Mail* had shifted its stance since the war began. Gone now were the days when its proprietor, Harold Sidney Harmsworth (1868–1940), the first Viscount Rothermere, befriended Hitler and described the Führer's leadership of Germany as 'great and superhuman'.[9] During the years of appeasement, Rothermere had travelled frequently to Nazi Germany. He had praised that country under national socialism as 'A Nation Reborn'[10] and in 1936 asserted that: 'Natural sympathies due to ties of race and instinct, are fast developing between the British and German nations.'[11] However, in June 1939 Rothermere surrendered control of his newspapers to his son Esmond Cecil Harmsworth (1898–1978), who would become second Viscount Rothermere on his father's death and was a much less ideologically driven proprietor. Now the new owner and his similarly low-profile editor, Bob Prew, were content to put an inglorious past behind them and adopt a robust patriotic tone.

Their *Daily Mail* would promote the war effort and boost civilian morale. It applied all that it had learned about presentation to augment its efforts and please its readers. A fine example of such journalism appeared very early in the Battle of Britain under the headline 'Legless Pilot Dances'. It tells a heart-warming tale of personal heroism that subsequently became familiar to generations of Britons who learned about it at school. It inspired the 1956 film *Reach for the Sky*. It is the story of Flying Officer Douglas Robert Stuart Bader, aged 30. The *Mail* recalled the accident in 1931 when 'coming out of a slow roll over Woodley Aerodrome, Reading, he crashed and for weeks struggled against death in hospital'. It revealed that his legs were amputated and, although he soon learned to fly again using artificial legs, the RAF rejected his applications to return to active service until the war began. It described his marriage in 1938 to 'Miss Olive Thelma Exley Edwards'. Meticulous in its reporting of a triumph over adversity with vivid appeal to its readers, the *Mail* sent its reporter to interview Bader's mother, now Mrs Hobbs, wife of the rector of Sprotbrough, near Doncaster. She told the journalist, 'I wish I could tell you adequately the story of how he had to face life again without both legs.' Prior to his accident, Bader had been a first-class rugby player, as well as a pilot, and had hoped to represent his country. He had struggled to rebuild his life and, his mother explained: 'It was amazing to watch his courage and the gradual return of his sunny disposition.' Now, as the first paragraph of the *Mail*'s account explained, he was the pilot who 'in a fierce aerial fight, shot down a Dornier 17 into the sea during a weekend raid'.[12] He had also learned how to dance and drive a car. The *Mail* portrayed the hero in uniform and smiling for the camera.

The *Daily Mail*'s treatment of Bader's story was an example of expert presentation, not an exclusive. The genius who promoted Flying Officer Bader as a role model worked for the government. *The Times* made plain the attribution, reporting that: 'The Air Ministry news service disclosed on Saturday that a pilot of the RAF Fighter Command who lost both his legs in a crash before the war shot down a Dornier 17 into the sea in a recent raid.' The Ministry was thorough. It furnished *The Times* with details tailored to its readers' taste. Bader had 'passed through Cranwell [home since 1920 of the RAF College], where he was known as a fine games player and was captain of cricket'.[13] *The Times* did not carry a picture, nor did it send a reporter to find Mrs Hobbs at her rectory near Doncaster.

Like its conservative rival, the *Daily Mail*, the Labour-supporting *Daily Mirror* displayed its populist flair to full effect. For its editorial team, Douglas Bader was the 'Greatest Hero of them all. . . . Britain's most amazing RAF Fighter Command Pilot'. The *Mirror* did not interview his mother. Instead, it sent a reporter to Bagshot in Surrey to meet the hero's mother-in-law. Mrs Edwards said, 'The more fights he can fly himself into, the better he is pleased.' He was encouraged by the love and support of her daughter. The *Mirror*'s man did not leave without an exclusive picture. On its front page, Douglas Bader and his bride were depicted in a photograph taken at their wedding reception in 1937. The *Mirror* declared that 'the story of his courage thrilled Britain'.[14]

The *Manchester Guardian* decided that its readership would not appreciate such naked and mawkish populism. For it, Bader merited only two brief and sceptical paragraphs. They read like an apology for reporting official briefing and an attempt to damn with faint praise. As the fifth of seven stories in its 'Our London Correspondence' column, the provincial broadsheet noted: 'Everybody who was in the Air Force or who was interested in rugby football eight or nine years ago knew D.R.S. Bader, the Harlequins and RAF fly half, whose crash robbed him of his legs, cut short a brilliant service career and destroyed good prospects of an England cap.' However, the *Guardian* was not prepared to concede that he was unique. It acknowledged that Bader:

> must be the only completely legless Air Force officer to pilot a machine in action. But a few years ago, there was a squadron leader commanding a balloon unit who, in spite of having one artificial leg, was allowed to keep in training by 'limited flying' of a few hours a month. He wore a plain wooden peg-leg – he was known to the Service as 'Peggy' – which he inserted into a cylindrical cigarette tin screwed to the rudder bar.[15]

The *Daily Telegraph* was not sceptical, nor was it entirely candid. In a brief single column report its air correspondent, Major C.C. Turner, reported: 'I learn that the Hurricane pilot who, although he lost both legs in a pre-war crash, shot down a Dornier 17 in a weekend raid was Flying Officer D.R.S. Bader.'[16] Major Turner did not disclose the identity of his source, but his article leaves the reader in no doubt that he learned all he knew about Bader from the Air Ministry.

In the treatment of Douglas Bader's exploits by mass-market popular newspapers and their broadsheet counterparts, we can see the emergence of a type of diversity that came to typify wartime journalism. Supplied with the facts they needed to tell a compelling story, the popular titles sought additional colour with which to enhance its impact on and appeal to their readers. The *Mirror* and the *Mail* sent reporters to obtain the additional human-interest detail and pictures they needed to bring the story alive for their readers. *The Times*, *Guardian* and *Telegraph* relied on the expertise of specialist correspondents and editors to demonstrate insider knowledge of the RAF and reliable expert contacts. Each newspaper sought to serve its readers by offering them distinctive angles and perspectives tailored to their particular interests. The facts came from the Air Ministry, but this most dynamic and ambitious of official sources knew the newspapers needed to inject elements of original journalism. Those responsible for promoting the RAF's young heroes understood that national newspapers must receive more than official communiqués. They required help to maintain the identity and character that distinguished them from their competitors.

The relationship worked for both parties. Hence, the *Daily Mail*'s willingness to comply energetically with the ministry's strictures did not go unrewarded. It secured access to compelling stories. A fine example appeared on Wednesday, 17 July when the *Mail*'s reporter, Collie Knox, became the first newspaper man to be admitted to an RAF training school. His report, published across four columns, described: 'Hundreds of young men, of all classes and creeds – sons of the rich and the poor, men about town, chemists' assistants, clerks, from all schools and universities, from every type of home – fitted but two hours since with their Air Force blue, passing with swinging arms through the Gate of High Adventure.' He offered 'a message which will cheer the hearts of all parents whose sons have left them for "somewhere in England". All is very well with the young men. Never in my service career had I witnessed such keenness, such spirit. Nor did I deem it possible that any vast organisation could give to each recruit such individual attention and care.' Had Collie Knox been employed as an official spokesman, he could not have done a better job of promoting the RAF and consoling the parents whose sons had been summoned to defend their country. Indeed, his ostensible independence enhanced the impact of his message. Throughout his four gushing columns of newsprint, the *Mail* praised and extolled 'the newest training methods which make the personnel of the RAF the world's best'.[17] For the Air Ministry, the *Mail* reporter's privileged access had secured positive coverage. From the *Mail*'s perspective, enthusiastic embrace and bold presentation of Douglas Bader's story had smoothed the path to an exclusive story. Newspaper treatment of his exploits had helped to produce and promote an enduring tale of heroic exceptionalism.

Calder argues that the evolution of the Myth of the Blitz was largely spontaneous, but to the extent that it was manufactured: 'it was a propaganda construct directed as much at American opinion as at British, developed by American news journalists in association with British propagandists and newsmen – and was all the more strongly accepted by Britons because American voices proclaimed it'.[18] The Ministry of Information's glorification of the RAF and championing of class equality were not intended for British readers alone. An even more important audience existed in the United States.

Isolationism, the belief that America should avoid all involvement in European wars following its searing experience between 1917 and 1918, had widespread support in 1940. It was reinforced by questions about why, if it was a democracy, Britain still retained an empire, whether its notoriously stiff and stuffy official bureaucracy was capable of fighting a modern war and, crucially, why its class system was so rigid and hierarchical. In the spring of 1940, columnist Mollie Painter-Downes, in London for the *New Yorker* magazine, had reminded her readers that 'the British attitude toward the hope of American intervention is now one of weary but complete resignation to the belief that in this war the Yanks will not be coming.'[19] Among the powerful resentments fuelling American isolationist sentiment was dislike of Britain's class-ridden social order. This offended Americans' ingrained certainty, enshrined since 1776 in their declaration of independence from the United Kingdom, that 'all men are created equal'. The Britons of 1940 did not appear equal and American mass media did not depict them as such. Calder notes that in the United States in 1940 'a Disneyland conception of England as a country of villages, green fields and Wodehousian eccentrics'[20] clashed with a harsher reality of inequality, injustice and snobbery.

The disharmony was depicted in the *New York Times*. This great liberal title greeted the formation of Britain's wartime partnership between Conservatives and Labour by reporting that some observers 'see in the new government evidence of a trend towards breaking down the class social structure which existed in England before the war'. Nevertheless, writing from London, its correspondent Robert P. Post did not anticipate immediate equality. He warned: 'Class distinction is very strong in this country. It will take some time before it breaks down completely.'[21] The *New York Times* also advertised views expressed by British socialists. Thus, H.G. Wells, the prolific author of novels, short stories and social commentary, received extensive coverage when he asserted that the RAF had initially failed to achieve ascendancy over the Luftwaffe because in the years before the war the Air Ministry 'had been drawing on a select social class and not upon the entire population'. Now, Britain had learned that, in combat, 'The council schoolboy, the odd lad from the garage is as good as any other sort of airman.' But Britain remained a 'country with a mere frustration of democracy'. To make equality real, 'We have to put an end to the advantages and respect our people have accorded so heedlessly and good humouredly to titles, precedences and privileges.'[22]

Intensely welcome though he was in the drawing rooms of Britain's rich and well-connected, CBS Radio Correspondent Ed Murrow also heard levelling opinions. Murrow enjoyed 'a terrifically wide acquaintanceship among the English-who-matter'.[23] However, between dinners at the fashionable Ivy Restaurant in Covent Garden and at 10 Downing Street, Murrow enjoyed discussing with the political theorist Harold Laski 'the inequities of the British class system'.[24] As the Battle of Britain began, his wife Janet Murrow wrote one of her regular duplicate letters home from London to both her parents, Charles and Jennie Brewster, and her husband's parents, Roscoe and Ethel Murrow. It let them know that: 'Ed will be going off to the coast and other hot spots to see what can be seen – in order to tell you about it.'[25] Murrow's mission, in which he would be ably supported by American and British newspaper reporters, would be to convince the American people that, despite its faults Britain was worthy of their support and admiration.

The journalists began the process with their reporting from the Kent coast in August 1940. The local newspaper proprietor, H.R. Pratt Boorman, editor-proprietor of the *Kent*

Messenger recalled that the south-eastern corner of his county was 'known by the Nazis as "Hell's Corner".[26] A group of reporters, including Vincent Sheean of the North American News Agency, Ed Beattie of the United Press and Drew Middleton of Associated Press, travelled down from London together to this location from which, as Middleton wrote, 'You could be on your back, with glasses, and look up and there was the whole goddam air battle.'[27]

If Middleton's description betrays a hint of breathless excitement, it is not misleading. Any reporter who has covered conflict knows that adrenaline plays a role as important as any commitment to public service. Indeed, adrenaline and commitment make excellent partners. They can be seen working seamlessly together in the work of Ben Robertson of *PM*, a passionately left-leaning New York evening newspaper, launched on 18 June 1940 by editor Ralph Ingersoll, a veteran of the *New Yorker* and *Time* magazine and financed by Marshall Field III, heir to a Chicago department store fortune.[28] *PM*'s launch credo was: '*PM* is against people who push other people around.'[29] It described itself as: 'One newspaper that can and dares to tell the truth.'[30] *PM*'s biographer notes that, 'maintaining the power of British and French colonial empires was distasteful for many of the newspaper's staff' but they all 'detested fascism'.[31] Robertson certainly shared his paper's radical, anti-isolationist views. He expressed them in his reporting from Shakespeare's Cliff, a mile west of Dover. Robertson noted later that he first understood the passions that motivated his countrymen during the American Civil War while reporting the Battle of Britain: 'It was not we who counted, it was what we stood for. And I knew now for what I was standing – I was for freedom. It was as simple as that.'[32]

Ben Robertson was one of 150 correspondents who gathered on the cliff to witness the fighting, two-thirds of them were American. Richard Collier describes them working amidst 'fluttering swarms of white butterflies ... squatting among ripening redcurrant bushes to cover the aerial tournament'.[33] Collier captures the mood acerbically, noting that: 'They had brought along their typewriters, their cameras and their binoculars but somewhere back in their London hotel rooms they had left behind their objectivity.'[34] The presence of female correspondents on the clifftop may have added an additional frisson of excitement. The *Daily Express*'s Hilde Marchant was there. So, too, was Virginia Cowles, the Vermont-born society beauty, reporter and columnist whose work had already appeared on both sides of the Atlantic. In 1937 and 1938 Cowles had achieved the impressive feat of reporting from both sides during the Spanish Civil War. Now employed principally by the *Sunday Times* she was determined to promote the British cause. On 29 June 1940, she broadcast from London to the United States on BBC radio. Her commitment was overt: 'Reports current in America that England will be forced to negotiate a compromise – which means surrender – are unfounded and untrue', she told her listeners. 'The Anglo-Saxon character is tough. Englishmen are proud of being Englishmen. They have been the most powerful race in Europe for over three hundred years, and they believe in themselves with passionate conviction. . . . When an Englishman says: "It is better to be dead than live under Hitler", heed his words. He means it.'[35]

Vincent Sheean, on Shakespeare's Cliff for the North American Newspaper Alliance, compared the RAF's defence of the skies over Kent to the Republican defence of Madrid during the Spanish Civil War. For Ben Robertson of *PM*, the aerial battle conjured images of American settlers defending their stockades.[36] Raymond Daniell, London bureau chief of the *New York Times*, did not regard partiality for the British cause as a flaw: 'Neutrality of thought was a luxury to which war correspondents in that first World War could afford to treat themselves. We, their successors, cannot.'[37]

These American reporters were greatly assisted by the news department of the Foreign Office and the American Division of the MoI. Initial plans to ensure that Britain's story would be told effectively in the United States had been prepared before the outbreak of war. Offering early evidence of his willingness to support the British cause, Ed Murrow, already resident in London as European director of CBS, had offered valuable advice. Winston Churchill's new government now ensured that 'practically all America's news about the war passed through London and was accordingly shaped by the publicity and censorship structure of the British government, or indirectly by the partiality of the press corps'.[38] The unity of purpose that existed between British and American newspaper reporters at the beginning of the Battle of Britain endured as it reached its peak.

For modern Britons, Battle of Britain Day, 15 September 1940, marks the moment when daylight combat between the aircraft of RAF Fighter Command and their German enemies reached its climax. The Royal Air Force shot down 56 German aircraft. This achievement is believed to have convinced the German High Command that the Luftwaffe's tactics would not deliver the air supremacy required to make a seaborne invasion feasible.[39] Close perusal of British national newspapers published in the week beginning Sunday, 15 September 1940 suggests that a sense of climax was certainly apparent to contemporaries. The *Daily Mail*'s banner headline on Monday, 16 September declared 'Greatest Day for the RAF'.[40] The story beneath reported that: 'Hitler's air force returned to mass daylight raids yesterday and the RAF gave them the most shattering defeat they have ever known.' The figures that followed appear wildly exaggerated to modern eyes. Plainly, the Air Ministry regarded them as optimistic and encouraging. The *Mail* explained that: '350 to 400 enemy planes were launched against London and south east England. . . . Of these no fewer than 175 were shot down, four of them by AA fire. All these are "certainties" for the total does not include "probables".'[41] The *Mail* added that six heroic firefighters had prevented the destruction by fire of St Paul's Cathedral.[42]

There was widespread awareness that the Luftwaffe had adopted a new approach. *The Times*' aeronautical correspondent identified it in his report. 'Other tactics having failed to outwit our defences', he wrote, 'they sent over in quick succession large formations of bombers, protected by hordes of Messerschmitt fighters.'[43] The *Daily Mirror* noted that the German High Command was claiming successful raids on 'docks and harbour facilities', including Bromley gas works. Berlin said its bombers had 'set oil dumps on fire' and 'hit industrial plants in Woolwich'.[44] It offered an example of the heroic response by Londoners by reporting that: 'Chelsea pensioners tried to fight fires started by incendiary bombs that hit the Royal Hospital.'[45] The *Mirror* also issued dire warnings for younger readers in a report about a fully loaded Dornier bomber shot down by the RAF on the edge of a golf course in Kent. It reported three had been killed and seven seriously injured after 'souvenir hunters rushed to the blazing plane'.[46]

Reporting the Second World War

During the Battle of Britain, Raymond Daniell's distaste for neutrality was widely shared by his British counterparts. Newspapers saw it as their duty to support the government and Royal Air Force. Criticism was not muted. It was absent. Indeed, the mass circulation popular dailies revelled in their support for the RAF. They embraced Air Ministry briefings as foundations upon which to construct glowing accounts of aerial combat and the pilots who engaged in it. They knew their readers wanted such uplifting accounts. The elite titles exhibited only slight reticence about the stories that were fed to them. They had no alternative source of information, but their coverage displays a sensitivity to their readers' pride and sophistication. Such readers were also hungry for information, but elite broadsheet editors sensed that facts and analysis might satisfy them. And, if their less passionate version of patriotism was not quite enough for all, editors were well aware that many families bought a popular title as well as their *Times*, *Telegraph* or *Manchester Guardian*. A different approach to patriotic fervour had commercial value as well social cachet.

CHAPTER 7
AIR RAID SHELTERS, FAIRNESS AND A NEW HOME SECRETARY

'The Myth that the British were Bombed and Endured stands, supported by the Big Facts', writes Angus Calder,[1] and Calder is right. Shock and depression were not uncommon responses to the destruction by enemy bombs of hearth and home. Looting and worse occurred in devastated cities. Families grieved their dead. However, Britons did prove resilient and personal diaries suggest that, for many, remaining cheerful, where possible, was a spontaneous response. In August 1940, as bombs began to fall near her family home in Brockley in the south-east London suburb of Deptford, Mass Observation diarist Olivia Cockett wrote: 'Should say the raids these last few days have increased the enthusiasm for the war, odd as that should sound.'[2] Eileen Alexander, a Cambridge graduate living in Hampstead found room for humour. Sir John Anderson, a family friend and the home secretary after whom Anderson shelters were named, had told her a story about his visit to a bomb site in Croydon. Anderson, whom Alexander describes as normally 'dull to yawning point', told her that he had seen 'an enormous bomb crater in a working-man's back garden[3]. The man pointed to a few scraps of shattered metal at the bottom of the crater and said rather shyly, "That was my Anderson Shelter." "Oh", said Sir John – rather fatuously as he admitted himself – "You weren't in it then?"'[4] Ed Murrow of America's CBS radio network reported that, although the British capital was taking a pounding, Londoners were acclimatising to the threat. They had 'become more human, less formal. There's almost a small-town atmosphere about the place. . . . There's been a drawing together.'[5]

Yet, that 'drawing together' did not overcome class distinction. Its endurance was felt particularly strongly in the provision of air raid shelters. Homes with gardens could install Anderson shelters. Those with extensive cellars had an additional advantage. For millions of poor Britons, living in close packed urban dwellings, only public shelters were available, and their availability, quality and cleanliness varied greatly. Many, in poor areas of London and Britain's provincial cities, were surface shelters built hastily from brick and concrete. For those who could afford it, an illegal black market in private air raid shelters emerged quickly and soon led to prosecutions. A court report published in *The Times* in early August 1940 reveals that Norman Jones and Francis Webster, employees of Leyton Borough Council, had admitted stealing and selling household shelters distributed free by the council. The pair had identified homes in Leyton from which the occupants had been evacuated and sold the shelters allocated to them to willing buyers. Jones got six months' imprisonment with hard labour. Webster six weeks with hard labour.[6]

We have seen the pressure that evacuation imposed on any ideal of class unity. The bombing of Britain's cities by the Luftwaffe exacerbated that pressure, initially when, in

September 1940, night raids on London became routine and intensive. In the most heavily bombed areas, public surface shelters offered poor protection. Juliet Gardiner explains that more than 5,000 such shelters existed in London alone. Their very basic construction, brick walls topped by a slab of concrete approximately nine inches thick, made them particularly vulnerable to high explosive blasts, with the concrete slab too often crushing the occupants as the walls collapsed.[7] People were reluctant to use them. A report in the *Daily Mirror* on 14 September revealed the solution chosen spontaneously by some Londoners who had lost their homes to the Luftwaffe and urgently needed places of safety. Under the headline 'Homeless find Refuge in the Underground', a *Mirror* reporter explained: 'Away from the sound of guns and bombs for the first time in days, hundreds of homeless people from the East End of London slept peacefully on the platforms of London underground stations.' The *Mirror* reminded its readers that orders had been given 'at the outbreak of war' that tube stations 'should not be used as shelters'. Now, need had rendered that ruling unenforceable and bombed-out Londoners streamed into the tube stations 'from bomb-torn districts of the East End'. Mrs K. Stenner, a young mother nursing her baby son, Ronnie, told the *Mirror* that she had seen their home 'wiped out by bombs'. She and her family had tried sleeping in a public shelter above ground 'but bombs dropped all around us'. A policeman had recommended the underground. 'Why didn't they let people use the stations before?' Mrs Stenner asked, 'They're the best shelters in London. Why, we didn't even know the sirens had gone till a porter told us.'[8]

Spontaneous flight to the tube stations was hard to prevent, but the government was not instantly persuaded to give it official approval. Indeed, on 16 September the home secretary gave the *Daily Mail* an interview in which he declared himself 'unshaken in his opposition to the building of deep shelters'.[9] Sir John Anderson listed his three core objections to underground air raid shelters. They would take too long to build. They would require the use of large quantities of scarce building materials; and he was 'very much against the practice of gathering large numbers of people together in an air raid'.[10] This objection to mass sheltering revealed residual fear that mass panic might ensue. Plainly, having witnessed a full week of heavy raids on the capital, Sir John remained certain that national security required people to do as they were told. He told the *Daily Mail* that he was 'satisfied that the brick-and-concrete surface shelters offer the same protection' as underground alternatives. He insisted: 'Their standard of safety has exceeded all expectations. We are going ahead with them.'[11]

Such certainty could not persist. In fact, even while he sought to use the mass-market *Daily Mail* as a tool with which to encourage obedience, Sir John was exploring alternatives to the crude surface shelters against which Londoners were voting with their feet. *The Times* reported that he was 'examining with the London Passenger Transport Board and the police authorities the possibility of making some use of the Tube railways for air raid shelters without interference with the transport system'. While the Home Secretary consulted, explained a *Times* parliamentary correspondent, 'People are already beginning to resort to underground stations having bought tickets.' There was much overcrowding in 'the larger public shelters at night' and considerable 'movement of people from communal and garden shelters near their own homes to larger shelters elsewhere'.[12]

The *Mirror* enlisted the pen of Tom Wintringham, a former Communist who had led British volunteers in the International Brigade during the Spanish Civil War. In the summer of 1940, Wintringham had turned his military skills to new use by training Local Defence Volunteers, the forerunners of the Home Guard, at a school in Osterley, Middlesex. He emerged as an eloquent and innovative advocate of improvised resistance to Nazism. He used his column to argue for the 'use of a number of Underground railways as permanent shelters where people can sleep quietly and fairly comfortably'. Identifying the source of stubborn bureaucratic resistance to such innovation he concluded: 'London can go on living and fighting. But not on Civil Service lines. We are in the front lines. [It is] time we organised in a front-line way.'[13] A front-page story in the same edition added detail to *The Times*' account. The home secretary and minister of home security had initiated a discussion with the London Passenger Transport Board about the possibility of converting a stretch of the Piccadilly Line between Aldwych and Holborn into a deep shelter. The *Mirror* noted that, while they deliberated, 'thousands of Londoners again took the matter into their own hands last night and flocked to the tubes for shelter'. It described the scene at 4.00 pm: 'at every station between Edgware and the Strand families had piled rugs, blankets and pillows for an all-night tenancy'.[14]

From its conservative perspective, the *Daily Telegraph* shared some of the *Mirror*'s concern for the fate of poorer Londoners. On 19 September, it sent its intrepid special correspondent Leonard Marsland Gander (1902–86) on 'an extensive tour of London's public air raid shelters'. Venturing deep into parts of the East End that were unfamiliar to many of the *Telegraph*'s affluent readers, Marsland Gander, made an initial observation that remains a useful corrective to misunderstanding about the scale of demand for shelter in the London Underground. 'People who leave their homes before the nightly raids are only a small fraction of London's millions', he wrote. However, those who did so 'show a strong preference for deep shelters'.[15] There was, he explained, 'a nightly trek from much-bombed areas in Eastern London to Tube and Underground stations and to the strong basements and other big buildings in the West End'. Unfortunately, congestion 'caused by men, women and children sleeping on the platforms is becoming serious'.[16] Passengers using the underground for transport, including many of the *Telegraph*'s readers who commuted to work in the City of London, were finding it difficult to board and disembark from trains. The government had not forbidden use of the underground network. Indeed, as Ian McLaine explains, the Ministry of Information noted Londoners' 'characteristically stubborn refusal . . . to be deterred by unconvincing official requests not to shelter in underground stations' and Ministers 'wisely decided not to insist on closing the stations to shelterers'.[17] The *Daily Telegraph* observed tartly that official dithering on the topic had 'caused a large increase in the nightly migration'.[18]

The *Telegraph* was not unsympathetic to the refugees from the East End, however. Marsland Gander explained that the use of underground stations was not the only question facing ministers. In many poor districts of the capital, mothers were taking their children to sleep in recently dug trenches 'which may be safe but are uncomfortable

Figure 7.1 A mother and child sleep in a trench shelter in London during the Blitz, November 1940.

and insanitary'. They had been built to protect against short air raids, not persistent heavy night bombing. Surface shelters were shunned almost entirely, and many residents of the East End were 'turned away nightly' from the large basement shelter constructed 35 feet under the Dickins & Jones department store on Regent Street, which Marsland Gander also visited. This had room for 700 people and included a canteen to provide refreshments.

If Dickins & Jones refused admission because its shelter was full, other fine buildings in the wealthy West End were guilty of worse. A stunt carried out by the *Sunday Pictorial* in September 1940 illustrates the depth of concern that, even under intense bombing, Britain remained a society deeply divided by rigid class distinctions. The *Pictorial*'s news desk had picked up powerful indications that 'poor people seeking urgent shelter' were not welcome in shelters created for the wealthy.[19] Readers reported being turned away from London's grand hotels during raids. So, the newspaper sent its intrepid and usually stylish war correspondent, Bernard Gray, to find out more. He did not go in his normal attire. Nor did he go alone. Accompanied by his friend, Sue, Mr Gray wore 'a pair of old flannel trousers, a "mac" borrowed from a respectable working-class friend of mine and a 2s. 11d. scarf in place of a collar and tie'. Sue 'spread her hair about a bit just as one would expect from a working woman who had been harassed by bombs'.[20] His report, described as 'an investigation', told a revealing story.

In September 1940, a government notice appeared on walls throughout Britain advising on conduct during raids. Gray reported its advice to always: 'Open your door to passers-by. They need shelter too.' He noted that 'most people are only too willing to obey the government's request. But not, apparently, the big hotels in London.'[21]

Bernard Gray was familiar with Claridge's, the luxury hotel on Brook Street in London's expensive Mayfair. Normally, when visiting for a drink or to meet a contact, he would be smartly dressed and welcomed with a polite 'Yes, Sir?' or 'This way, Sir'. Now, he and Sue had set out to discover 'the kind of reception that ordinary working people get if they call and ask for shelter at the luxury hotels to escape falling bombs'. He acknowledged that they did not look like typical Claridge's clients, but 'There was nothing very terrifying about either of us. And we'd both taken care to look absolutely clean.' Their cleanliness made no difference.

Bombs had started to fall, but they did not get beyond the sandbags protecting the main entrance to Claridge's. The moment Gray put his hand on the door, a porter emerged and 'his voice was chilly'. The porter said: 'Yes?' Gray replied: 'Can we go into your shelter until it becomes a little quieter? My friend is terribly frightened.' Bernard Gray records that he and Sue felt subject to very critical scrutiny and the porter was certainly unmoved. 'Sorry', he replied, 'Ours is a private shelter. There is a public shelter up the road.' The reporter persisted, explaining that his friend was truly scared and that the raid appeared to be getting heavier. By now, an incessant barrage of anti-aircraft fire was firing at enemy bombers overhead. The porter remained obdurate, but he did offer an explanation: 'I should get badly pulled over the coals if I let you in. I can't. It isn't allowed. It's a shelter for residents.'[22]

The *Sunday Pictorial* investigative duo's evening was not over. Next, they tried the nearby and equally prestigious Berkeley Hotel. Here, an air raid warden was standing in front of the revolving door. Gray suspected he was a hotel employee. His conduct reinforced Gray's suspicion. Before they could cross the threshold, he stepped forward and announced: 'There's a public shelter in Devonshire House, Stratton Street. Go there.' Now Gray pleaded their case. He asked the warden to seek the night porter's consent for them to enter and, when the man turned to ask, Bernard and Sue forced the issue by following him through the door into the hotel reception. Gray lit a cigarette and was immediately told that he could not smoke. Under the gaze of silent hotel residents, Bernard Gray was quietly furious. He reported: 'I've smoked there before and given the man tips.' Now he could do nothing to obtain access. Despite his pleas, night porter and warden moved rapidly to protect the sensibilities of their established clientele. Gray describes them moving in swift unity 'like a screen' between the Berkeley's startled guests and the intruding proletarians. They demanded that the intruders go to the public shelter. Insisting it was not far distant, they offered to 'show [them] the way'.

Finally, the intrepid couple tried the Ritz, grandest of all London's luxury hotels. By now, the anti-aircraft barrage was tremendous and their need for shelter obvious. Sue ran across the road to the colonnaded passage that runs along the front of the Ritz. Immediately, a porter appeared and ordered them to go to a public shelter. As they turned to leave, a bomb fell nearby and Bernard Gray 'threw Sue on the floor against the Ritz wall, covered her head with my hands and we waited'. The bomb exploded too far away to cause them any harm. Gray's report recorded: 'We, refused shelter like any other people dressed like us would be, might have been killed on the doorstep of safety.'

This was not impartial reporting. The *Sunday Pictorial* sent Bernard Gray and his friend Sue to secure evidence of its suspicion that ordinary Londoners, many of them its readers, did not have equal access to luxury air raid shelters. Gray tailored his words to maximize the drama of his experience. He acknowledged that the hotels were not legally obliged to admit them. Nevertheless, his account allowed the *Sunday Pictorial* to make its point. Class equality was a myth not a reality. Rank snobbery was thriving, and class difference was easily and instantly identified. The pair's disguises guaranteed their exclusion from shelters in luxury hotels. At least some clients of Claridge's, the Berkeley and the Ritz really would have been appalled to have their havens invaded by members of the working class. This was stunt journalism designed to make an ideological point. It made the case well that poor Londoners faced discrimination, but not as emphatically as an eyewitness account of suffering in East London's Canning Town compiled more than a week earlier by Peter Ritchie Calder of the *Daily Herald*.

Ritchie Calder knew Canning Town. In the first months of the war, he had written a series of articles about the social conditions facing un-evacuated children there for the TUC-controlled Labour-supporting *Daily Herald*.[23] Dedicated readers were already familiar with his affectionate descriptions of the working-class children he described as the 'Dead End Kids' and the intense struggles of their poor, hard-working parents. Now, as the East End bore the brunt of Luftwaffe attacks, aimed at its concentrated agglomeration of docks and manufacturing industry, he returned to discover how his old stamping ground was faring. At a refugee centre located in what censorship did not permit the *Daily Herald* to identify as South Hallsville School, on Sunday, 8 September,

Ritchie Calder found many families who had only just been rescued from their bombed-out houses waiting anxiously for motor coaches. Local officials promised that these would soon come to convey them to safe refuge in evacuation homes away from the danger. However, the buses did not come, and Calder stayed on to observe at first-hand how the Luftwaffe bombed the East End. His observation of German aircrew following the Thames to the East End docklands helped him to a stark conclusion. The school was on an approach path. German bombers were turning directly above it. Bombs had already fallen perilously close; and he would later describe the likelihood of a direct hit as 'not a premonition' but 'a calculable certainty'.[24]

In fact, a high explosive bomb did score a direct hit on South Hallsville School shortly after 3.00 am on the morning of Tuesday, 10 September 1940. By that time, 600 refugees from Canning Town had been sheltering there since Sunday, 8 September, waiting with increasing anxiety for the coaches that never came. On that Tuesday morning, Calder returned to the school by taxi to see 'a gaping bomb crater' where the refugee centre had stood. He wrote that the crater had become the grave of 'whole families from wrecked homes in the worst raided areas in East London'. They had been 'left by neglect to die in a bombed refugee centre'. His own 'Dead End Kids' were among them. So were disabled children and the 'coloured children' of black British merchant seamen.[25] Calder reflected bitterly that he would never forget them or 'those old women, those pathetic young mothers nursing their babies as they sat on their baggage waiting on Sunday for the coaches that never came'. He recalled that they had been 'desperate to get away from the raids which they knew would follow and from the bombs which would, with merciless certainty, drop on that corner again'. He had watched women and children 'besiege' the officials in charge of the refugee centre, offering to walk to their place of evacuation if only they would tell them where it was. 'But the harassed officials knew no answer other than the offer of a cup of tea'.[26] Calder watched at the edge of the colossal bomb crater with 'more than a hundred men working in it, trying to find the bodies. With ropes around them they were descending into the crater. A big crane was lifting wreckage. They were finding victims.'[27]

Ritchie Calder asked the town clerk who was responsible for the coaches never arriving. The clerk refused to answer. The mayor of Canning Town told the *Daily Herald* man, 'I wish I knew. We have been badgered about from pillar to post.' Calder concluded: 'Official blundering left these people to Hitler's bombs – bombs that were practically certain to fall. This tragedy demands an immediate reorganization of the control and arrangements for receiving the people of the bombed areas.'[28] He revealed that a social worker had described many schools being used as emergency reception centres as 'death traps', full of 'children huddled together with practically no blankets' and 'women huddled in anguish over the children already bombed out of their homes'. Calder's chilling account earned space on both the front and back pages of this severely restricted six-page edition of the *Daily Herald*.

Night bombing of London's East End made shelter policy the focus of serious class-based controversy. In the mainstream press, the *Daily Herald*, *Daily Mirror* and *Sunday Pictorial* did most to advertise injustice and the plight of London's poorest residents.

Figure 7.2 A female Fire Guard using a stirrup pump on the roof of a building in London, 1941.

However, Juliet Gardiner points out that the Communist *Daily Worker* was most forthright in its criticism. The title, wholly owned by the Communist Party of Great Britain, loyal to the Nazi-Soviet non-aggression pact and committed to a policy of revolutionary defeatism, described Sir John Anderson's stubborn commitment to surface shelters as 'calculated class policy'. For the *Daily Worker*, the absence of deep shelters for the poor was a consequence of 'determination not to provide protection because profit is placed before human lives'. It proclaimed: 'the bankruptcy of the government's shelter policy is plain for all to see ... safe in their own luxury shelters the ruling class must be forced to give way'.[29]

The Communist title advanced its policy in detail in a leader column headlined: 'Shelters, Shelters, Shelters'. Published just ten days after the first major raids of

7 September, this pungent editorial declared that: 'For the people of Britain there is nothing more urgent and vital than the building of bomb-proof shelters. It over-weighs every other consideration.' Reminding readers that it had been advocating a policy of shelter construction for two years, the *Daily Worker* used the words of Sir Alexander Rouse, chief technical adviser to the Home Office, to demonstrate what it believed to be deliberate, cynical and deplorable neglect of the working class. Rouse had said: 'If we provide deep bomb-proof shelters for the whole nation, so that people have complete protection, they are going to go underground. Then we would lose the war. We cannot expect as civilians to have more protection than our soldiers and sailors.' His words, declared the *Worker*, revealed the existence of 'a policy of class discrimination dressed up with patriotic frills'. Having made plain its stance, the Communist title indulged its hostility to the mainstream daily newspapers of left and right. They, it declared were inhibited in their treatment of shelter policy by a 'gentleman's agreement with the Ministry of Information that the shelter question shall not be raised'.[30] There was informal pressure to dampen controversy but, on this topic, it had not inspired obedience, despite the close informal links between press and state that existed in September 1940. Nevertheless, despite its tiny circulation, the *Daily Worker*'s blunt ideological zeal put pressure on the mainstream Labour titles to speak up for working-class voters.

The government sought urgently to calm the controversy. On 28 September, *The Economist* explained that a new shelter policy was emerging. Most Britons were continuing to 'look for safety in air raids to their own houses and private shelters'. However, in the heavily bombed areas 'a sense of insecurity has spread among an appreciable minority which is more detrimental to ordinary life and livelihood than the dangers of overcrowding'. In recognition of this the government's plans had changed: 'The use of Underground stations as shelters has been recognised and regulated. . . . More large brick and concrete shelters are being built. Sanitary equipment and water supplies are to be provided and bunks for sleeping are to be installed.' *The Economist* offered a stern reminder that those who had Anderson shelters should continue to use them. There was no question, however, that, by voting with their feet, East Enders had drawn attention to injustice and demonstrated their refusal to accept it.[31]

If the home secretary was now displaying flexibility, his response had come too late to disguise the reality that he had not handled his responsibilities with unimpeachable efficiency. On 3 October, a parliamentary correspondent for *The Times* reported strong rumours that 'some changes in the Government are imminent'.[32] Sir John Anderson and Herbert Morrison were identified as ministers likely to be moved. Guy Eden, political correspondent of the *Daily Express*, had heard the same lobby briefing. He told readers that the expectation at Westminster was that: 'Mr Morrison will move from the Ministry of Supply to the Home Office where he will succeed Sir John Anderson as Minister for Home Security.'[33] The following day's editions had the full story. The War Cabinet was to increase to eight members with the inclusion of Labour's Ernest Bevin, Minister of Labour and National Service, and Kingsley Wood, the Conservative Chancellor of the Exchequer. *The Times* hesitated to criticize Sir John Anderson directly: 'The way in which the civil defence services have helped to sustain the country in the ordeal' reflected well on the outgoing home secretary who would now move to replace the ailing Neville Chamberlain as lord president of the council. This also gave Wood the compensation of membership of the expanded War Cabinet. Criticism was implicit in the establishment title's fulsome welcome for Herbert Morrison though. *The Times* observed that: 'The recent intensive bombing of London has led to special problems that have provoked much criticism relating to the Government's shelter policy.'[34] Responsibility for putting this right would now fall to Mr Morrison. The *Daily Mail* congratulated Mr Churchill on the changes to his government. He had 'been inspired by one purpose only – to strengthen the war effort'. It was not convinced that expanding the size of the war cabinet would assist this effort. In previous wars 'a smaller body' had 'proved to be a compact, workable and efficient committee to exercise supreme direction'. Nevertheless, despite Morrison's socialist ideals, the *Daily Mail* was enthusiastic about his promotion. He was, it declared, 'the right man in the right place. The people have faith in him.'[35] A leader in the *Daily Telegraph* confirmed that the right-of-centre press lacked great sympathy for Sir John Anderson. He had bequeathed to his successor 'many difficult problems' but the *Telegraph* had confidence in the new home secretary's abilities: 'The considerable reputation which Mr Morrison made in London's municipal affairs has been enhanced by the effective energy he has shown in his few months at the Ministry of Supply. The kind of work which lies before him in the expansion of civil defence is such as his understanding of great cities well qualifies him to perform.'[36] For the *Daily Express*, closest of all to the government by virtue of its proprietor, Lord Beaverbrook's service as minister for aircraft production, Mr Churchill was to be commended for running his Cabinet according to the 'rules of the great captains of industry'. The prime minister ignored entirely any ideological division between Conservatives and Labour. He was wise enough to appoint experts who would get the job done. Mr Morrison explained the *Express*'s leader column, 'is a man of the people who knows all about handling the great masses of people'. His new job would be 'full of snags and difficulties' but Mr Morrison would overcome them, 'for he is a man of the people and his instinct and energy are devoted to their welfare. He understands them.'[37] Lord Beaverbrook might have written the column himself. In 1949, he would tell the Royal Commission on the Press that he ran his newspapers 'purely for the purpose of making propaganda and with no other motive'.[38] His editors understood his position and were free to write the propaganda themselves.

If this welcome for a Labour loyalist reflected Conservative reluctance to criticize the national coalition at a moment of crisis, the *Daily Mirror* demonstrated some restraint from its position on the left. On occasion, rather than voice its own criticism, it deployed opinions published in American newspapers. One example explained: 'Authoritative circles frankly admit that a month's "Blitz" has confronted Britain with some staggering problems.' These 'sources' were, in fact, William McGaffin, a London-based correspondent for the Associated Press news agency. His account revealed that homelessness caused by bombing and the absence of safe, comfortable shelters were major problems in the British capital. The *Mirror* quoted his report that: 'Many people are without gas or sanitary facilities. Many have developed air-raid nerves.' It rejoiced in the American's conclusion that a 'new shelter policy is expected from dynamic socialist Mr Herbert Morrison, named Home Secretary after Sir John Anderson made a bust of it'.[39]

Writing shortly after the events in his wartime book, *The Lesson of London*, Ritchie Calder argued that the early experience of intense bombing 'certainly demanded the immediate replacement of Sir John Anderson'.[40] In Calder's assessment, the machinery of civil defence Anderson had designed had delivered effective firefighting and Air Raid Patrol (ARP) services. However, 'Its greatest fault was that it was de-humanized. It made no provision whatever for the biggest and most difficult human problem of all – the homeless. It conceived air-raid shelters purely as a matter of engineering stresses and actuarial calculations of comparative risks, without regard for comfort, health, or, above all, the psychological factors.'[41]

Within days of his appointment, the desperate shortage of public shelters persuaded the new home secretary to 'acquire immediately all available accommodation such as basements'.[42] Ten days later, Morrison wrote to every local authority in a bid 'to speed up the construction and equipment' of public shelters. He told councillors, 'the Government would reimburse the whole cost of future contracts for the construction and equipment of shelters, provided that reasonable economy is practised'.[43]

Demands for Retaliation

Early in the relentless campaign that saw London experience fifty-seven consecutive nights of bombing, the *Daily Mail* detected a clear appetite for retaliation. On 24 September, the *Mail* explained that the number of letters it received from readers had grown dramatically since bombing began. The average number received daily had been more than doubled 'by the addition of hundreds demanding ruthless reprisals on German cities for the air attack on London. Many correspondents blame the Air Minister, Sir Archibald Sinclair for not adopting this policy.'[44] The *Mail* responded with an editorial in which it reflected that: 'Letters from angry readers demanding reprisals for hideous bombing of London's citizens are pouring into the *Daily Mail* and every other newspaper office.'[45] The editorial writer continued: 'Everywhere the same cry is heard – reprisals, reprisals, reprisals. The demand cannot be simply ignored.' However, the voice of cautious, middle-class conservatism was concerned about the morality of bombing civilians. Persuaded by the German claim that Luftwaffe air crews were aiming for military targets in London and that any civilian casualties resulted from unintended collateral damage, it argued: 'So, it comes to this: under the German conception of total warfare the city itself is the "military objective" and if the bombs fall on the people – well, that is just too bad for the people.' Britain, it explained, was aiming its bombs at 'Germany's military nerve system'. Germany's approach was to attack 'Britain's civilian nerve system'. So, if Hitler wanted a total war, the British government should give him what he asked for: 'It is no use trying to meet an all-in wrestler with tactics based on the Queensberry Rules.' However, the *Mail* remained determined to maintain moral superiority. 'Germany might be warned through the medium of neutral Switzerland that if the bombing of so-called

Figure 7.3 A British airman is amongst a group of civilians crowded around the window of a shop in Holborn, London, to look at a map illustrating how the RAF is striking back at Germany during 1940.

"military objectives" in London does not cease, similar targets in Berlin will be destroyed by the RAF.' It insisted that Britain now had the right to 'attack similar objectives in the most thickly populated areas' of German cities.[46]

The *Daily Express* preferred to convey the impression that the RAF was already conducting such raids and with great success. Early in October, an *Express* correspondent in neutral Stockholm reported that: 'RAF bombing of Berlin has been so fierce and so accurate that the Germans have been forced to admit that military objectives have been hit.' Close reading reveals that this was little more than wishful thinking, based on interpretation of the German authorities' decision to maintain summer time throughout the winter because 'putting the clocks back would have allowed the RAF to hit Berlin earlier in the evening'.[47]

To offer a thoughtful perspective on bombing and being bombed, the *Sunday Pictorial* deployed a column by David Lloyd George (1863–1945), the liberal statesman who had served as prime minister between 1916 and 1922. Now father of the House of Commons, the 77-year-old assured readers that the RAF's attacks on Germany were now 'more numerous and destructive than ever before'.[48] He also drew a familiar distinction. British bombers were attacking 'harbours and estuaries where barges and motor-boats are assembling to carry the invading army across'. They were also attacking 'factories and oil tanks'. These were legitimate military targets. He feared that the bombing of capital cities was descending into a cycle of 'revenge and reprisal' and he worried about the consequences. Lloyd George assured readers that during the First World War 'troops were never kept in the line for more than a few days at a time. They were then withdrawn to areas where they enjoyed comparative repose.' Many *Sunday Pictorial* readers had harsher memories of trench warfare, but the father of the House was setting up a contrast. Now, civilians enjoyed no breaks. They were facing 'harrowing experiences' and faced an 'incessant sense of fear, fright and strain'. The Cabinet must make sure that 'every man, woman and child will have a safe refuge at hand in which they know they are secure from murderous raids'. Plentiful shelters were required, and he was glad that ministers 'have at last been roused to an understanding of the importance of this long-neglected duty'.[49]

The Provincial Blitz

Ministers did understand the fragility of brick surface shelters. However, these were the only air raid shelters available in towns and cities from Lerwick to Penzance and the Luftwaffe's 'murderous raids' soon expanded to attack cities beyond London. The Coventry Blitz on the night of 14 November 1940 was among the most concentrated of these provincial attacks. Deploying a new technique of guidance by twin radio signals that intersected over their target, Luftwaffe pathfinders first bombarded the city centre with incendiary devices. The fires these started marked the target for the bombers that followed. Over the next ten hours, these dropped hundreds of tons of high explosive bombs on the vulnerable city. The medieval centre of Coventry was destroyed utterly. Nearly one in three homes were rendered uninhabitable. Railway lines through the city were blocked by rubble. Telephone lines collapsed. Hilde Marchant of the *Daily Express* was among the first journalists allowed through the official cordon imposed around Coventry. Her essay appeared on the front page on Saturday, 16 November. The banner headline offered unambiguous evidence of the *Express*'s patriotic determination to maintain morale and inspire resistance. 'A Very Gallant City', it declared. Beneath it ran the sub-head, 'Stricken, but [it] Keeps Its Courage and Sanity'. Beneath that was an additional sub-head, alerting readers to one of the everyday British heroes to whom the star columnist would introduce them: 'The wonderful story of Mrs Smith, who served tea through it all'.[50] Marchant's first paragraph emphasized the editorial line. 'Amid the black horror of the Nazi attack on Coventry', she wrote, 'two things stand out – the great courage of the people and the devotion of the A.R.P. workers who were only stopped by death.' She spoke to the mayor, Alderman J.A. Moseley, who insisted that Coventry would not be evacuated: 'Of course not. We Stay.' Only then did Hilde Marchant provide the eloquent pen portrait of the stricken city which began on the front page and turned to finish on the back of the newspaper: 'The shopping centre of Coventry is one choking mass of ruins, fire and people who, by some miracle, have emerged alive. They walk through this skeleton of the city centre with faces stained black, breathing the smoke of their homes, trying to find their families and friends.' She described the Auxiliary Fire

Service (AFS) men who had fought the flames: 'The AFS were covered in dirt, were soaking wet, and their eyes were barely open from fatigue and smoke.' Among them, 'There was one woman, whose name is really Mrs Smith, who had been on duty all through the raid, handing out cups of tea from a mobile canteen.'[51] The star columnist concluded:

> But it is useless to try to find heroes in this city. Everyone from the children to the chief constable and mayor has been a hero. The stained glass of the cathedral hangs in tatters in the few windows that are there. The shops, the houses have gone. The sight of Coventry is beyond any words. It is time now for our deepest and most inspired anger. The whole of Coventry cries: BOMB BACK AND BOMB HARD.[52]

Accompanying Marchant's work across three columns in the centre of the front page was a picture of the cathedral 'ruined not by time but by one night's vicious bombing' as the caption explained. It added, 'Coventry is known as the City of the Three Spires, the Cathedral of St Michael, possessing one of them, was a fine building in the perpendicular style, dating from 1373–94.'[53]

The *Daily Mail* correspondent in Coventry was William Hall. He found 'a picture of hideous destruction',[54] but his tone was as fervently patriotic as Marchant's. Two days after the raid, Hall described the evacuation from Coventry of children under five and their mothers: 'Today in this brave city where defiant Union Jacks flutter from reeling, twisted lamp posts, I saw them going.... And as their transport moved off, they cried "We'll soon be back".'[55]

Nonetheless, uplifting tales of stoicism and patriotic determination to carry on could not disguise the death toll. Five hundred and fifty-four people died in Coventry that night. A further 865 suffered serious injury. In these grim facts the *Daily Worker* spotted political opportunity. It did not hesitate to highlight failures of civil defence in an industrial city with a swollen wartime population of 250,000. 'Now', it declared, 'in a single direct raid, one in every 250 of them has been killed or wounded because there was not sufficient protection for the people.' It reminded readers that it had campaigned for 'deep shelters for the people of such places'.[56] Promoting relentlessly its depiction of the war as a conflict between two equally unpleasant regimes, the *Daily Worker* asserted that British bombing of Hamburg had caused casualties 'even higher than the British official estimate of the casualties in Coventry'. It added that eyewitness accounts 'show the fate of that city not only as a warning, but as an urgent call to action by workers everywhere to secure proper protection, proper evacuation schemes and proper compensation payments'. It scorned Herbert Morrison's insistence that local response to the raids had demonstrated the efficiency of regional administration. Rather, the Communist title declared:

> thousands of people have been forced to trek across country and sleep in ditches, only one mobile canteen was available immediately after the disaster, huge queues

had to line up even for bread, the water system broke down altogether, even before the raid was over, and the brick surface shelters proved totally incapable of standing up to the intensive bombardment.[57]

On the mainstream left of the wartime coalition, the *Daily Mirror* took care to display sympathy for its readers. It explained that a thousand people had been killed or injured in the raid that 'began at dusk on Thursday and ended at dawn'. It described how 'Pathetic streams of men, women and children were trekking to the safety of the countryside last night … and Mothers pushed perambulators filled with household goods, their babies lying on top.'[58] Nevertheless, a powerful editorial emphasized that this had been a raid to rank alongside 'the severest of those directed against London'. The *Mirror* regretted the loss of life but insisted that those who had died had not done so in vain: 'These people have given their lives for the cause. They have not flinched from the trial common to all civilian population of this country.' The people of Coventry had behaved 'With a courage matching that of the bravest men who have fought for us in wars when civilians were not, as now in the firing line.'[59] The *Sunday Pictorial* noted the 'cruel ferocity' of the German bombardment. It recognized that Coventry was 'grimly battle-scarred' and that 'a thousand of its citizens lick their wounds', but it insisted that this was 'no dark blow of fate'. On the contrary, 'It was an honour and an inspiration, as Coventry, city of steel has so proudly proved.' Tomorrow, it confidently declared, 'its workers will go back to the factories with renewed zeal and with redoubled energy. They will work as never before to turn out the aeroplanes that will avenge that night of murder.' Coventry had learned the same lesson as London. Other towns would learn it soon, but the *Sunday Pictorial* expressed faith in its readers: 'You may read with horror the story of Coventry's ordeal, but, if your turn comes, you will take it just as nobly as did the brave hearts of that fine city.'[60] The Ministry of Information could be pleased with its work. The mass-market titles were playing the right tunes.

The quality broadsheets were predictably less gushing but no less willing to praise Coventry and bolster morale. A leader in *The Times* pointed out that an important relaxation of normal censorship had allowed journalists to identify Coventry as the victim of the raid: 'The Government have wisely concealed neither the name of the city attacked nor the gravity – from the humanitarian point of view – of the damage caused.' It was certain that Coventry 'will not flinch any more than London and other cities that bear the honourable scars of resistance to barbarism'. *The Times* reported the German claim that the bombing had occurred in reprisal for the RAF's raid on Munich and recommended that Coventry take its own revenge by 'minimizing interruption in the production of those things which the skill of her workpeople has made famous.'[61] The *Manchester Guardian* also emphasized Coventry's industrial prowess. The city had suffered badly 'but it would take many more nights to cripple it as a centre for war production or to drive its population to despair'. Coventry was 'a town given over to the progressive light industries' and a valuable source of 'electrical apparatus and rayon and aircraft'.[62]

For the *Daily Worker*, the only reasonable conclusion was that 'it is a matter of life and death for the people themselves to insist upon bomb-proof shelters'.[63] Its correspondent in Coventry was Peter Kerrigan, a graduate of the Lenin School in Moscow, now working as the Communist Party of Great Britain's industrial organizer. During the Spanish Civil War, Kerrigan had served as political commissar for the English-speaking volunteers in the International Brigades. He had experienced fighting in the battles at Lopera and Jarama, and on the River Ebro. He explained: 'I have been in the bomb-devastated cities and villages of Spain, but nowhere have I seen such sights as in Coventry.' From that personal introduction, Kerrigan moved immediately to advance the party line: 'There was no proper air raid shelter in the whole of Coventry, neither for the factory workers nor for the rest of the population. . . . As for the brick surface shelters, I saw how they had been split in half, bashed in, or completely demolished.'[64]

The raid on Coventry was matched in its ferocity by savage attacks on the Clydeside burgh of Clydebank, adjacent to Glasgow, on the nights of 13 and 14 March 1941. The *Daily Express* offered vivid reports from what censorship required it to call Clydeside not Clydebank. A reporter described 'a pilgrimage of lorries and carts' leaving the town 'piled with furniture with women and children perched on top.'[65] Angus Calder reminds us that the ferocity of the raids on this small town left only seven of Clydebank's 12,000 homes undamaged. In two nights of bombing, '35,000 of its 47,000 inhabitants were made homeless.'[66] The *Daily Express* reporter took care to personalize his account of heroism and suffering. He told the story of Mrs Margaret Johnston, an ambulance worker, who was sent to a building where bombs had injured people. She and her colleague, William Patrick, got most of the injured into their ambulance when bombs began to fall around them: 'One exploded just in front of the ambulance as Mrs Johnston was tending a patient. The ambulance roof was torn off and a piece of debris hit the patient.' The bomb made a crater which the damaged ambulance could not cross. So, amid intense bombing and a retaliatory barrage of anti-aircraft guns, Margaret Johnston and William Patrick carried each of their patients across the crater and transferred them to an undamaged ambulance.[67]

The *Daily Mirror* drew readers' attention to German propaganda boasts that the Clydebank raids 'put Coventry in the shade'. The nature of housing in the town compounded the gravity of the attacks: 'Rescue workers had a heavy task dealing with shattered tenement property where people were buried.'[68] Many Clydebank residents had remained in their homes. Shelter provision in the town consisted of the despised brick surface shelters and, even worse, 'strutted closes', which Calder accurately describes as 'often no more than the roughly protected entrance passage to a block' into which residents could crowd when bombs fell.[69] There were no deep shelters but, in their coverage of the Clydebank Blitz, newspapers did not foreground the shelter issue. A tendency to concentrate on morale-boosting accounts of endurance and understate the extent of the devastation is apparent in several newspaper accounts. The *Daily Telegraph* drew attention to an Air Ministry statement that 'the casualties though serious, were not thought to be heavy'. It reported that 'several fires were started, but they were fought with determination and all were extinguished or brought under control by the early hours of the morning.'[70] *The Times* asserted that: 'Considering the weight and duration of the attack the number of casualties and the damage done was remarkably light.' It advised that: 'The temper of the people of Clydeside was magnificent and the ARP and civil defence personnel responded nobly to all demands.'[71] The *Daily Mail* hinted at one reason for acute official sensitivity about the Clydebank raids. It reported that: 'Many Clydeside apprentices who are on strike offered their services today as firemen, rescue workers or messengers to help in the clearing up of the wreckage caused by the raid on Clydeside last night.' It noted that Sir Patrick Dollan, lord provost of Glasgow, had advised them that the best thing they could do to 'help Clydeside and their country was by getting back to work immediately'.[72] Such opaque reporting failed to reveal the whole truth about the strike.

The Clydeside Apprentices' strike was a significant manifestation of worker power, supported by the Communist Party. Not only did it coincide with the Clydebank Blitz, the strike posed a direct threat to munitions production. Sandy Hobbs notes that working conditions in the engineering industries were harsh and that 'there was little conciliatory in employers' treatment of workers'.[73] Had the *Daily Worker*'s dedicated Scottish edition been available in Clydebank, Glasgow and the neighbouring industrial towns of Paisley, Renfrew and Dumbarton, it would certainly have backed the strikers. It had been launched only months earlier in November 1940 with the avowed intent to promote the Communist cause and the policy of revolutionary defeatism. Publication of its first edition was marked by a leader carried in both the English and Scottish titles. Headlined, 'Making History', this proclaimed its significance as a voice in Scottish politics.[74] However, by the time of the Clydebank Blitz, the Communist daily was not available. It had been banned on 21 January 1941, ostensibly on the grounds that its depiction of the war was damaging the morale of the British people.

Coverage of the Blitz united titles of left and right, popular and elite, in opposition to stubborn and inflexible bureaucracy. Motivated by a shared desire for fairness, though not always by a clear consensus about what it might mean, they put under acute pressure a home secretary who had failed to consider the human dimension. However, as soon as John Anderson, a National Independent MP, was replaced by Labour's Herbert Morrison, newspapers combined to portray Morrison's appointment as an excellent way to reinforce the war effort. From the meticulous eyewitness reporting of the *Daily Telegraph* and the *Daily Herald* to the *Sunday Pictorial*'s assertive stunt journalism via carefully judged human interest story-telling in the *Daily Mail* and *Daily Express,* newspapers responded nimbly to the novel challenge posed by bombing. Their readers were in the front line: they must mobilize protest and promote social empathy. As government tried to respond to civilian needs, the mainstream newspapers united in support of the war effort. Only the *Daily Worker* displayed persistent and venomous hostility to the National government and accused it of putting profit before the lives of the British people. It would face the consequences when the new Labour home secretary acted to protect his party's sectarian interest against challenge from the Communist left.

CHAPTER 8
MORALE, INTIMIDATION AND CENSORSHIP

Home Intelligence reports from August 1940, before heavy bombing began, suggest little concern existed in government about public morale. There had been few civilian casualties and scant thought had been given as to how morale might be maintained if conditions deteriorated. This they duly did with the advent of intensive bombing on 7 September. Now crude pre-war theories about popular vulnerability to mass panic re-emerged. Acceptance of them was apparent in Sir John Anderson's conviction that large crowds gathered underground in tube stations were a dangerous idea.

Responsibility for public morale lay with the Ministry of Information, but precisely what this meant was unclear to the eclectic crew of wartime recruits from literary, creative and professional life who, together with career civil servants, staffed the ministry. Ian McLaine notes that they had 'no precedents to follow' and were obliged 'to improvise and learn from the immediate circumstances quite as fully as the public were forced to readjust their lives to conditions of unremitting danger, discomfort and anxiety'.[1]

Highly literate members of that public offered mixed responses to the coming of the first raids. On Sunday, 8 September, Phyllis Warner, a resident of Tavistock Square in London's expensive Bloomsbury district, recorded in her diary: 'Last night was a night of horror, a hell on earth.' She described the sound of an approaching bomb as 'an appalling shriek like a train whistle growing nearer and nearer, and then a sickening crash reverberating through the earth'.[2] In Hampstead, Eileen Alexander appeared more irritated than alarmed. Her diary for 8 September records 'another disturbed night on the drawing-room sofa' and notes blithely that 'Bernard, Jean and I were nearly blown out of the window by gun-fire from Primrose Hill – but we had a pleasant afternoon in Spite of All'. Eileen's friends stayed for dinner and afterwards 'we all went up to Mrs Seidler's room and watched the glow from the fires at the docks'.[3]

Now, McLaine explains, officials in the Ministry of Information sifted 'anxiously through the intelligence reports hoping to perceive signs that the public were not unduly affected by sustained bombardment'.[4] Such signs were discernible. Panic was rare and courage widespread. Though bombing engendered intense grumbling, determination to keep calm and carry on, or 'see it through'[5] in the words of one Home Intelligence report, was the norm. However, as we have seen, perceptions of class injustice, notably in access to safe air raid shelters, did provoke real grievance; and this, newspapers – particularly those of the left – advertised. Most of them spoke truth to power in the hope that they could make their readers' lives a little safer and more comfortable. Their approach brought pressure to bear on the government.

Reporting the Second World War

'Subversive Articles'

Herbert Morrison had occupied the office of home secretary and minister for home security for just three days when, on 7 October 1940, the prime minister confronted the War Cabinet with his demand for action against newspapers that published 'subversive articles'. Winston Churchill was referring not to the *Daily Worker*, but to the *Daily Mirror* and the *Sunday Pictorial*. The *Daily Herald* was diligent in defence of its readers, as Peter Ritchie Calder's passionate reporting demonstrates. However, it could, when necessary, be held in check by the direct proprietorial influence of its TUC-appointed directors, particularly now that Labour was fully represented in the War Cabinet. Indeed, the challenge posed by Calder's angry defence of his 'Dead End Kids' and their families ended in the summer of 1941 when the government made him an offer he could not refuse. Following a conversation with Clement Attlee, who made it plain that he had no choice, Calder left journalism to join the Political Warfare Executive.[6]

The *Mirror* and the *Pictorial* were harder to manage. These commercial left-of-centre titles had no single dominant shareholder and this ownership model made them harder to intimidate. Each was proudly and overtly hostile to the Conservative Party and, when they added blunt criticism of policy to partisanship, Winston Churchill grew impatient to suppress them. On this occasion, he concentrated his fire on the editorial column that had appeared in the *Sunday Pictorial* on 29 September 1940. The article merits close attention, not least because his angry reaction confirms Churchill's sensitivity to criticism, even from admirers.

The subject of the offending column was the failure of a joint British and Free French taskforce to capture the strategic port of Dakar in French West Africa (now Senegal). General Charles de Gaulle, the Free French leader whom Churchill had made welcome in London, believed he could persuade the substantial French forces in Dakar to abandon Marshal Pétain's Vichy regime and join the Allied cause. In fact, French naval, air and infantry forces in Dakar remained solidly loyal to Vichy and fought back fiercely against the taskforce. De Gaulle's failure to persuade his fellow countrymen to change sides damaged his standing and reflected poorly on Churchill. The loss of British Swordfish aircraft and damage to the Royal Navy's battleships HMS *Resolution* and HMS *Barham* compounded the government's embarrassment.

The *Sunday Pictorial* was scathing. Its declared that: 'De Gaulle's charade at Dakar bears that stamp of asinine incompetence of which it seems Mr Chamberlain's Government did not enjoy a monopoly.' The operation was a farce that should never have been staged: 'In the days of Chamberlain, the defeat at Dakar would have evoked profound resentment.' Now, 'in the days of Mr Churchill', it was 'none the less intolerable'. The *Pictorial* considered it 'a tragedy' that 'so brilliant a premiership should ever be marred by such avoidable episodes'. Mr Churchill should 'dispense with the Old Failures and Old Blunderers'. The prime minister had to remove those responsible. The editorial concluded in block capitals: 'FOR GOD'S SAKE LET US HAVE NO MORE DAKARS'.[7]

Under its pugnacious editor until 1940, Hugh Cudlipp (1913–98), the *Sunday Pictorial* had developed a habit of praising the prime minister, while deploring the attitudes and actions of those he liked and defended. Following Cudlipp's enlistment in the army, his wartime replacement Stuart Campbell (1908–66), a dedicated opponent of social injustice, maintained Cudlipp's bold editorial stance. In a previous leader at the beginning of September, the *Pictorial* had reminded readers that it had faced accusations of 'preaching "Bloody Revolution" when we wisely remarked that Chamberlain would have to go'. It also insisted that: 'Winston Churchill was the only man to lead the nation in war.'[8] Then it praised the socialist views of H.G. Wells and J.B. Priestley. The former had penned sharp criticism of the army's high command. Priestley had declared the 'ruling and official classes … incapable of dealing adequately with the world'. Declaring these two prominent voices in public life 'friends' of the *Sunday Pictorial* and its readers, the newspaper concluded: 'The age of the crusty colonels, the stinted Tories and all the enemies of progress within our midst is doomed. … The glorious day of deliverance will quickly be at hand.'[9]

Next, in its edition of 7 October, the *Daily Mirror* added its own criticisms and the prime minister spotted opportunity. The *Mirror*'s ire was focused on Labour members of the War Cabinet, notably Clement Attlee and Ernest Bevin, whom it described as 'Academic Attlee and Blunt Bevin'. It wondered whether they were 'doing enough – or doing anything – to secure that this should be a People's War'; whether it was a war 'fought for the people by the people'; and whether 'there is not far too much of the old, privileged gangster spirit at its old game of cajoling the workers while it fights for the few'.[10] The *Daily Mirror* fretted that: 'Labour men seem to be getting so pally with the others.' Of course, they must work with Conservative colleagues, but this collaboration should extend to war work only. It should not extend to 'bouquets with compliments'. The *Mirror* worried that Lord Beaverbrook had appointed himself 'Minister of Bouquets' and was handing out lavish compliments in a bid to seduce Labour colleagues. It was adamant that Labour ministers should not be distracted. They should concentrate on persuading the Government to adopt left-wing policies.[11] The *Mirror* believed it knew its working-class readers better than any politician. Hugh Cudlipp explains that the *Daily Mirror*, edited by his colleague Cecil Thomas (1883–1959), 'spoke in the language of the serving men and thus became their mouthpiece'.[12] Cudlipp believed that: 'No daily journal was in a better position to register the people's pulse-beat, reflect their aspirations and misgivings, and make articulate their elation or censure on the progress of the war.'[13]

Acutely sensitive to persistent and pointed criticism of his own class and party, Churchill was incensed. The following day, 8 October, Cecil Harmsworth King (1901–87), chairman of Daily Mirror Newspapers and Sunday Pictorial Newspapers, noted in his personal diary that Churchill had made an angry speech in the House of Commons that afternoon. First, the prime minister denounced criticism of Sir John Anderson, whom he had just reshuffled, as coming from 'ignorant and spiteful quarters'. Turning to the failed mission to Dakar, Churchill 'described the tone of "certain organs of the press" as "so vicious and malignant" that it would be almost indecent if applied to the enemy'. King concluded: 'It rather sounds as if this were aimed at our two papers.'[14]

It was, and Churchill saw only opportunity in the newspapers' additional censure of his Labour colleagues. He hoped they might prove equally sensitive. The prime minister ignored the *Pictorial*'s praise for his personal qualities and the *Mirror*'s willingness to treat him as a good Conservative. He told his cabinet colleagues that these newspapers were guilty of deploying 'language of an insulting nature to the Government.... It was not right that anyone bearing his heavy responsibilities should have to submit to attacks of this nature upon his Government.' Indeed, it was 'intolerable'.[15] Though willing to serve alongside democratic socialists, Churchill's ideological hostility to socialism was intact. It would never waver.

Turning the Screw

Unsurprisingly, in a cabinet that now included Ernest Bevin as minister of labour and national service and no longer included Neville Chamberlain, his colleagues were not easily cajoled into supporting their prime minister's desire to restrain the popular left-wing press. The attorney general reminded colleagues that Defence Regulation 2D only permitted the home secretary to stop publication of a newspaper if it published 'matter which, in his opinion, was calculated to foment opposition to the successful prosecution of the war'. Lord Beaverbrook, minister for aircraft production and proprietor of the *Daily Express*, intervened to propose a less draconian solution. He suggested that an approach to the Newspaper Proprietors' Association (NPA) might persuade the unruly socialist titles to adopt a more supportive tone. Beaverbrook said the NPA had 'considerable disciplinary powers'. Crucially, it would 'realise as strongly as the War Cabinet the disadvantage of action being taken by the Government to suppress a newspaper and would wish to avoid recourse to this procedure'.

Lord Beaverbrook's intervention reflected his commitment to press freedom, but it also rolled the pitch for his Labour colleagues. The new home secretary was certainly not keen to use his quasi-judicial powers against the newspapers: 'He said that the War Cabinet would appreciate that he was new to this matter' and claimed, less plausibly, that 'he had not followed the line adopted by these two newspapers'. He believed an important principle was involved and he asked for 'time to consider the matter'. Churchill concluded the meeting by declaring that, if their proprietors did not bring them to heel, 'the War Cabinet must decide definitely that they were prepared to take action against the newspapers if necessary'.[16] Thus warned, Morrison moved fast. His weapon was a memorandum circulated to the War Cabinet the following day.

The home secretary acknowledged that the *Daily Mirror* and *Sunday Pictorial* published 'much vituperative criticism of members of the Government and much carping at features of the Government's policy'. However, there was much in them 'which is calculated to promote a war spirit'. They seemed to be 'clearly anxious for the defeat of Hitlerism'.[17] Morrison quoted that morning's leader in the *Daily Mirror*: 'Bad as our "pluto-democratic" world may be, it is at least better than the slavery that would suppress all independent action and thought in the devilish way of life commended by the Nazi fanatics'.[18] Acknowledging that the *Mirror* and *Pictorial* had been responsible for 'strong attacks on Ministers and attacks on Generals',[19] Morrison questioned whether parliament and the British public would support any ban on such criticism. He identified a distinction 'between constructive criticism of which the intention is to call attention to errors with a view to securing the better prosecution of the war, and persistent destructive criticism which is calculated to create a spirit of uneasiness and mistrust'.[20] Hard to ignore is the hint that the prime minister himself had, until recently, been a fountain of constructive criticism. Next, Herbert Morrison appealed to a 'tradition of the British people that they still remain obedient to the constituted authorities while retaining their liberty to ridicule and denounce the individuals who are actually in authority'.[21] He doubted that the threat to the realm was sufficient to justify a measure as extreme as a ban on two mass circulation newspapers and concluded with an argument that, from his Labour Party perspective, combined principle with an element of sectarian political advantage: if the *Daily Mirror* and *Sunday Pictorial* were to be banned, must the Cabinet not also 'take similar action against the *Daily Worker*, which has sought in every way (without indulging in direct anti-war propaganda) to impede the war effort, for example, by misrepresenting the Government's shelter policy'.[22]

The home secretary reminded his ministerial colleagues that the *Daily Worker* had also 'misrepresented the scheme for the evacuation of children overseas'.[23] However, he was not persuaded that there was a proper case for deploying his legal powers against the *Daily Mirror* and the *Sunday Pictorial*. Regulation 2D had been introduced 'at a time of acute emergency' and subject to agreement that any further restriction on 'liberty of expression' should be preceded by 'further consultations'.[24] He supported Beaverbrook's suggestion that the War Cabinet should seek help from the NPA. Morrison was clear that this approach should be subtle and made 'in the nature of a friendly appeal, on the basis that we are confident the press is anxious to assist in the war effort and should not be in the nature of a threat'. There was, he warned, a risk that a threat of action under the defence regulations 'might suggest to the representatives of the press that the Government are contemplating interference with their legitimate freedom'.[25]

Esmond Harmsworth (1898–1978), son of Harold Harmsworth, the founder of the *Daily Mail*, was now chairman of its owner, Associated Newspapers, and of the Newspaper Proprietors' Association. On Friday, 11 October, he was required to lead an NPA deputation to meet Clement Attlee. Accompanied by Lord Camrose, owner of the *Daily Telegraph* and *Financial Times*, and Lord Southwood, chairman of Odham's Press which published the *Daily Herald* and the *Sunday People*, Harmsworth arrived to find both Attlee and Lord Beaverbrook waiting for them. Cudlipp tells us that Attlee informed his visitors that the Cabinet had discussed the *Daily Mirror* and *Sunday Pictorial* and had concluded that 'if criticisms of the "irresponsible kind" inserted in our papers were to continue, the Government would introduce legislation making censorship of news and views compulsory'.[26] Richard Toye describes Attlee's words as 'A schoolmasterly telling-off',[27] but the NPA deputation were appalled and immediately briefed Cecil King and Guy Bartholomew, senior directors of the *Daily Mirror* and *Sunday Pictorial*. King and Bartholomew went in search of Clement Attlee with the intention of finding out precisely what the government was threatening. They were led through a maze of corridors to a Whitehall air raid shelter in which the leader of the Labour party was seated on a bunk reading the *New Statesman*. Attlee explained that the Cabinet had asked him to deal with the newspapers. He said he spoke for the whole government. Ministers believed that the *Mirror* and *Pictorial* 'showed a subversive influence, which at a critical time like this might endanger the nation's war effort'.[28]

Despite this show of strength by the most senior Labour member of the War Cabinet, however, the government was not entirely united on the issue. Herbert Morrison was not ready to abandon the distinction between security censorship and policy censorship on which the freedom of the press had been secured in June 1940. The home secretary was playing for time. By focusing attention on the hostility of the *Daily Worker*, he revealed Labour's fear of being outflanked from the left and identified a useful scapegoat. Morrison understood that the Communist newspaper did not criticize in order to advance the war effort. The *Daily Worker* was the primary propaganda weapon of an organization without political sovereignty which routinely obeyed oscillating orders from Moscow.[29] Throughout the raids on London, and with growing fervour as these spread to the industrial towns of the English midlands, the north of England and Scotland, the Communist Party of Great Britain used the *Daily Worker* to advance the Comintern's decree that this was an imperialist war. Good Marxists should oppose it by adopting Karl Liebknecht's First World War dictum that 'the main enemy is in your own country' and advancing a policy of 'revolutionary defeatism'. Among the CPGB's favoured slogans in the winter of 1940/41 was 'workers will turn war into civil war'.[30]

We have seen how the *Daily Worker* distinguished itself from the Labour-supporting titles by depicting failures in shelter policy as the product of calculated class malice. Worse, from the British government's perspective, it treated British and German bombing raids as morally equivalent. In the winter of 1940/41, the *Daily Worker* engaged actively in the CPGB's campaign to undermine public morale and cripple the war effort. This was an ominous time. Invasion and defeat remained live possibilities; enemy aliens were interned; British fascists imprisoned; and 'Fifth Columnists' suspected. In January 1941, night-time temperatures frequently fell below zero, freezing the water in firemen's hoses as they fought the consequences of German bombing, which was intense. The casualty toll for the month was 922 dead and 1,927 seriously injured. The Lend-Lease agreement with America would come into effect in March, but it did not deliver its first consignment of food to Britain until the last day of May. The diet available in early 1941 was the worst of the war. In January the meat ration was cut from two shillings and twopence per week to one shilling and twopence.[31] The CPGB and its daily newspaper exploited misery to promote 'a People's peace, won by the working people of all countries, and based on the right of all peoples to determine their own destiny'.

The People's Convention

The CPGB's efforts peaked in preparation for the party's most high-profile public event of the Second World War. This was the so-called People's Convention which, on Sunday, 12 January 1941, united 2,234 delegates from every part of the United Kingdom in

London's Royal Hotel and Holborn Hall.[32] The Convention was carefully camouflaged. In reality a wholly-owned CPGB project, it concealed the CPGB's ownership and masqueraded as a progressive gathering of the left. The *Manchester Guardian* described it expertly as a carefully manipulated agent of communist propaganda into which 'many excellent but gullible people have been enticed'.[33] Writing shortly after the war, Douglas Hyde, a disenchanted former member of the CPGB, who had worked to organize the Convention, explained that: 'By the time it took place the Blitz on London was at its height and, despite the stiffening of public morale that came with the great hardships caused by bombing, we detected a certain war-weariness on which we could work. And where it did not exist, we set about trying to create it.'[34]

Banning the *Daily Worker*

The home secretary was watching the CPGB and its newspaper carefully and with growing indignation. He had resisted the prime minister's efforts to shut down the Labour-supporting *Daily Mirror* and *Sunday Pictorial*, but his eloquent defence of a free press did not extend to defending a newspaper that was working assiduously to undermine the war effort – and, in doing so, seeking to convert Labour party members to its cause. As we have seen, the *Daily Worker* seized with alacrity the opportunity to advertise the horror and misery brought about by the German raid on Coventry. Now it was recruiting actively for the People's Convention and gaining some traction among workers in factories doing vital war work.

So, on 23 December 1940, Herbert Morrison presented to the War Cabinet a memorandum suggesting the suppression of the *Daily Worker*. Morrison began by reminding his colleagues that they had previously considered banning the newspaper in July. On that occasion his predecessor, Sir John Anderson had sent a 'preliminary warning'. In it, Anderson reminded the *Daily Worker* of his power to suppress a newspaper via Defence Regulation 2D and expressed the hope that 'the paper would be so conducted in future that it would not be necessary to take action under this Regulation'. Morrison noted that the warning had brought about a brief 'modification of the tone of the paper', but its policy had not changed and 'recent issues, generally speaking, have been as bad as those which preceded the warning'.[35] Next, he set out the case for suppression.

Morrison argued that the *Daily Worker* misrepresented the war as 'between rival capitalist or imperialist powers'. It depicted the struggle against Nazism as an unnecessary conflict 'waged by the "capitalists" for the purpose of securing benefit for themselves and robbing the workers of such rights and privileges as they have been able to obtain under peacetime conditions'. The newspaper sought to persuade its readers that 'the "governing class" are entirely callous to the sufferings of the poorer people under war conditions'.[36] Although by doing so it may have assisted his rise to the office he now occupied, the home secretary was most concerned about the *Daily Worker*'s portrayal of shelter policy. It 'maintained that the Government is deliberately refraining from providing proper (deep or bomb proof) shelters for the workers'. It depicted the government as 'indifferent to sufferings and hardships of the "people"'. It had represented the CORB scheme as 'a scheme for providing safety for the families of the well-to-do'. Food policy was shown as 'full of inequalities and designed to ensure that any shortage of food shall be felt by the poor people only'.[37]

Herbert Morrison singled out individual editions of the *Daily Worker* as particularly injurious to the national cause. Among these was the newspaper's leader column of Monday, 28 October 1940. This strident example of Communist ideology had declared that the inevitable outcome of the war would be 'the massacre of the civilian population and the destruction of the big cities'. Borrowing snidely from the prime minister, it had proclaimed that continuing to fight meant only 'blood, sweat, toil and tears for the British people'. In conclusion, it declared: 'In Britain has come the call for a People's Government and a People's Peace.' It reminded readers that 'a great movement has been set in motion for the People's Convention in January. This is our alternative to the imperialist blood and tears.'[38]

Morrison drew his fellow ministers' attention to a headline, describing Birmingham after attack by the Luftwaffe as a 'Monument to Government Callousness'. He noted the newspaper's relentless pessimism about Britain's capacity to sustain the war effort and its predictions that the Germans would soon deploy poison gas against civilians.[39] The home secretary protested that the *Daily Worker* sought to make its predictions come true. It 'seizes every opportunity to give prominence to wage disputes and to emphasise the right to strike'. Determined to persuade its readers that the United States would not ride to Britain's rescue, it gave prominence to 'any news about opposition in the United States to the co-operation of the United States Government with the Allied Cause'. It insisted that American capitalists were determined to extend the war 'in order that they may make more profits'.[40]

Herbert Morrison acknowledged that the *Daily Worker*'s propaganda tried always to 'avoid language which can be made the basis for a charge of incitement to violence'. Nevertheless, it repeatedly reminded its readers that workers in the Soviet Union had achieved their freedom through armed revolution. It encouraged them to believe that German workers might soon bring down Hitler and install a revolutionary government. It implied that they should take similar action. The Communist Party aspired to undermine popular morale and its efforts were set to intensify as the strain on the British people grew greater. It had not had great success yet, but it was focusing its recruitment efforts in important factories. The home secretary believed the *Daily Worker* was preparing to provoke 'the maximum of ill-feeling if and when circumstances become more difficult'.[41]

Having made the case for the prosecution, Morrison acknowledged that there was no evidence of public demand for a ban. He recognized too that, following the War Cabinet's recent approach to the NPA, newspapers were now very sensitive to threats against freedom of expression. Furthermore, there was a risk that any ban might be perceived in the United States as 'a striking departure from the traditional British policy of preserving the liberty of the Press'. Britain might be accused of 'fighting for nationalistic gains rather than for principles of liberty'.[42]

Morrison made a pointed comparison between the Government's tolerance of the Communist Party and its active suppression of Oswald Mosley's British Union of Fascists. He recognized that, if the government chose to suppress the *Daily Worker*, it would inevitably be asked why it should not also suppress the CPGB and intern the party's leaders. He did not believe such steps would be justifiable unless the Communists attempted to 'frustrate the war effort by sabotage or by refusal to handle munitions'. One additional step was necessary, however. For the sake of consistency, any ban on publication should extend to the *Week*. This Morrison described as a hand-printed 'sheet published by Claud Cockburn, alias Frank Pitcairn, one of the principal journalists of the *Daily Worker*'. The *Week* promoted all the arguments made in the daily Communist title but in language designed for an educated readership.[43] The home secretary believed there was a case for banning both titles. He invited his colleagues to decide whether suppression was in the interests of the war effort and if this was the right moment to impose a ban.[44]

Why did Herbert Morrison fear and dislike the *Daily Worker* sufficiently to suggest a ban? Circulation of the title constituted less than one per cent of national daily newspaper sales in 1940.[45] Part of the answer is that the number of readers is only one measure of a newspaper's influence. Also important is who reads it and how instrumentally. The *Daily Worker* was read by trade union officials in key factories, not least in the industrial midlands and the shipyards, steelworks and coalmines of Scotland's west coast. It was no accident that the CPGB had launched a Scottish edition only weeks earlier. Moreover, in pursuit of its strategy of revolutionary defeatism, the *Daily Worker* also aspired to exploit divisions in the Labour Party. These were particularly acute between grassroots anti-war opinion and the pro-war leadership. Memories of resistance to war in 1914 remained potent among Labour activists. Six Labour MPs had declared themselves opposed to hostilities in September 1939. In November of that year a further 22 MPs supported a manifesto demanding an immediate armistice and more than 70 constituency labour parties supported it.[46] Whether they worked in factories or studied in universities, the CPGB hoped to persuade members of Labour's anti-war left to join its cause. Morrison, a visceral anti-communist, was protecting Labour's flank against a newspaper that had demonstrated not only ideological zeal but also an occasionally acute talent for astute criticism of the mainstream press.

The Cabinet voted to suppress the Communist titles on 27 December 1940. No minister, Labour, Conservative or Liberal dissented. Now, before their decision was implemented, the success of the People's Convention brought a fresh perspective. Opening the Convention on Sunday, 12 January 1941, Harry Adams, district organizer of the Amalgamated Union of Building Trade Workers, stuck fast to the pretence that this was not a CPGB event. It was a meeting of progressives united by idealism. 'Our Convention', Adams declared, 'has brought together representatives of many organisations of the Labour movement and of the widest sections of the people.'[47] Many of the delegates were Communists or fellow travellers, but there were less ideologically predisposed folk among them. Angus Calder notes that Mass Observation found delegates who disagreed with parts of the Convention's programme, 'some even remarked that it was a pity it was so left-wing'.[48] Other observers were less easily fooled. Juliet Gardiner recalls that one

Home Intelligence report described the assorted youth organizations, shelter committees and tenants' associations represented at the Convention as 'Left-wing psychopaths'.[49] Celia Fremlin, a Mass Observer who had resigned as a member of the CPGB in response to the Nazi-Soviet Pact, attended the Convention and reported that delegates were 'very predominantly' middle class. A handful of 'student and intellectual types' were also present.[50]

The CPGB's masters in Moscow did nothing to disguise their support. Each of the Soviet Union's flagship national newspapers, *Pravda* and *Izvestia*, devoted half a page to TASS agency coverage in praise of the delegates. TASS described them as 'the best representatives of the English nation, ready to carry on the struggle against reactionaries within the country and with external enemies'.[51]

Ministers were even more dismayed to learn that broadcasts from German-controlled radio stations in occupied Europe also expressed approval for delegates' conduct. They recognized that the Convention's core programme advanced policies intended to 'cripple the war effort' and 'weaken public morale'.[52] Meanwhile, the left-wing press gave the Convention extensive publicity. The *Manchester Guardian* explained that it was 'a carefully manipulated agent of communist propaganda'.[53] The *Daily Herald* condemned it as an effort 'to exploit for partisan purposes the life-and-death struggle in which the British nation is now engaged'.[54] Maurice Webb, political correspondent of the *Daily Herald*, attended the Convention for his newspaper and thought it 'as clever a piece of political exploitation as I have yet encountered'.[55] A subsequent editorial confirmed the *Daily Herald*'s unswerving loyalty to Labour and TUC policy. The Convention was nothing less than 'a people's Reichstag'. It was 'a reckless political stunt' organized by communists who could not 'make the slightest claim to being interested in government of the people for the people by the people'. The CPGB 'pretended as Hitler pretends about his Reichstag that the delegates were fully representative of public opinion'. However, they did not allow delegates who dissented in any way from the party line to express their own opinions.[56]

The *Daily Mirror* was not condemnatory. It warned that the Communists were determined to 'weaken the will of the people to resist by drawing attention to legitimate popular grievances that all decent people sympathise with'. It recognized that adherence to Convention policy would lead to 'civil war and chaos at the very moment when the Germans are massed along the Channel ports'. However, its correspondent among the delegates acknowledged that 'at least ninety per cent of those men and women brought from every part of these islands were honest-to-god British citizens, with no more wish to see Hitler victorious than you or I have'. They had come from factories, coalfields, railway yards and offices all over Britain to air their grievances. Why were such decent folk attending a Communist-controlled event? The *Mirror* correspondent's explanation was highlighted in bold type: '[T]hey have too many grievances the Government leaves unanswered. They expected the Labour Ministers in Government to be their champions. They are disappointed in them. Labour Ministers behave like pale imitations of Tory Ministers. So the people feel themselves leaderless. They are beginning to turn to the Communist Party.' The *Daily Mirror* called on the government to 'deal drastically with the food profiteer'. It should also nationalize the railways and coal mines and 'bring scrupulous fair play into the handling of rationing, wages and shelter provision'.[57] In supporting the Convention's demands for improved living standards and better protection against air raids, the *Daily Mirror* highlighted the relevance of Communist social and economic policy to its working-class readers. It asserted that the Convention spoke for the people more effectively than Labour ministers on core social and economic questions. Its reporting was independent of Labour Party and TUC Policy. It exploited the issues raised at the People's Convention to put pressure on the leadership of the Parliamentary Labour Party.

Such sympathy bordering on admiration from a Labour-supporting newspaper was not enough to balance a generally hostile press. It did, however, advertise the potential influence of Communist ideas beyond the meagre ranks of the CPGB. On Monday, 13 January 1941, the Cabinet decided to implement Herbert Morrison's proposal that the *Daily Worker* should be suppressed. They brought publication to an end on Tuesday, 21 January, following a meeting between the home secretary and the NPA. During this encounter Morrison secured sufficient support and understanding to be confident that his action would not be widely condemned. The following morning's editions illustrate the extent of his success.

The *Daily Telegraph*'s leader opined that the ban 'may raise a certain amount of controversy but must be judged right on any full consideration of the facts'. It recognized that 'freedom of opinion and discussion are at the foundation of democratic institutions'. However, the *Daily Worker* was an 'organ of Communism' that 'existed not to serve British but alien ends by the systematic publication of matter intended to prevent the nation's survival'. It published 'propaganda as hostile to this country as that of Goebbels'. The *Telegraph* concluded by reminding its readers that, if the banned title had tried to subvert Hitler's government, 'it would not merely have been suppressed. Those responsible for its publication would most likely have been beheaded.'[58]

The Times offered a straight, factual account of the ban in which it explained the process applied under Regulation 2D.[59] Its parliamentary correspondent added that the home secretary was expected to 'make it clear that there is no wish to suppress genuine criticism in newspapers, but that while grievances ought to be ventilated, they should not be exaggerated or invented'.[60] The *Daily Mail* condemned the *Daily Worker* as a 'subversive, defeatist sheet'.[61] It also offered evidence of a gesture of Communist defiance. While Scotland Yard detectives kept an all-night watch on the *Daily Worker*'s printing presses, 'a typewritten edition of the paper was brought into the office of the *Daily Mail* at 3 a.m.'. This samizdat *Daily Worker* called on British workers to mount 'protests against the order'.[62] Only the *Daily Mirror*'s leader column offered true defiance. It was not persuaded that the *Daily Worker* or the *Week* (which it referred to as 'the Squeak') had 'much influence in the country'. The question for the home secretary and his ministerial colleagues was 'whether a dead *Daily Worker* will not have much greater influence than one allowed to go on living in a moribund condition of prolonged tedium. In other words, is not Mr Morrison making martyrs? And are not martyrs magnificent advertising for any cause?' The *Mirror* insisted that 'all suppression of opinion, as distinct from falsified fact, is dangerous'. It warned that: 'This is a dangerous precedent.'[63]

The following day, Willie Gallacher MP (Communist, West Fife) questioned the home secretary angrily on the floor of the House of Commons. Herbert Morrison insisted that press freedom was so valuable that it should be preserved even when it was abused. However, the *Daily Worker* was guilty of much more than abusing freedom. It was determined to 'weaken the will of the people' and bring about 'the downfall of democratic and constitutional government'.[64]

The House of Commons debated the ban more fully on 28 January 1941 on a motion tabled by Aneurin Bevan MP (Labour, Ebbw Vale), unofficial leader of the Labour left. In his opening speech Bevan invited the House to express its contempt for the anti-war propaganda published by the *Daily Worker*. This done, he suggested that public confidence in the government would be undermined if it could be shown that a newspaper 'can be suppressed in a manner which leaves that newspaper no chance of stating its case'. He invited MPs to join him in regretting that the home secretary had proceeded against the *Daily Worker* and the *Week* on the basis of Defence Regulation 2D. This Bevan deplored as the use of emergency powers 'which were justified to the House by the Government on the sole ground that they might be needed in circumstances of direst peril arising out of physical invasion'.[65] Bevan argued that the home secretary should have proceeded via the courts. He also issued a coded warning that he was aware of Clement Attlee's recent meeting with Cecil King and Guy Bartholomew. Bevan told fellow MPs that 'only a few months ago the proprietors of two very important papers with large circulations were informed that the Government was worried about the line they were taking.... They saw a member of the War Cabinet who said that in his view the line taken by the papers was subversive.'[66]

Whether Herbert Morrison heard his Labour colleague's eloquent introduction is not clear. The home secretary did not take his seat on the government front bench until the debate was under way. Once in the chamber, he listened to an angry defence of the *Daily Worker* from the Communist Willie Gallacher. D.N. Pritt MP (Independent Labour, Hammersmith North), the former Labour Party member who had played a leading role in the People's Convention, spoke highly of the *Week*, which he complimented for telling the country 'many things it would otherwise not have known'.[67] Richard Acland, the Liberal member for Barnstaple, lamented perceptively that the ban would have a 'chilling effect' on other newspapers that might now hesitate to publish controversial material for fear that they too might be suppressed.[68] Sir Percy Harris, the Conservative MP for Bethnal Green, South West, described the liberty of the press as 'the life blood of parliamentary government'. Sir Percy questioned whether any MP really liked the powers vested in the home secretary under Regulation 2D. For him, they savoured 'much too much of the Gestapo' and put 'too much power in the hands of a Minister'.[69] He invited the home secretary to show 'why he found it necessary to use this more autocratic but quicker procedure'.[70]

In defence of the ban, Herbert Morrison ignored many of his critics' substantial arguments and insisted that the government had shown 'amazing patience'. His speech exposed his resentment of the *Daily Worker*'s persistent campaign for better air raid shelters. This he characterized as 'one of the most contemptible and dangerous things which the Communist party has done'. Morrison asked the House how the *Daily Worker* and the Communist politicians behind it had responded when the humble homes of working Britons were destroyed by bombs. His answer was: 'They go to these brave people who are suffering domestic disaster and family misery, and they say: "All of it was utterly unnecessary and need not be. It is because a cruel capitalist Government want to make profit for the profiteers and to further Imperialistic ends. All your suffering is without necessity and without purpose." Could there be anything more cruel and more cynical than deliberately to say that to the people at that time?'[71] The home secretary reinforced his point by quoting the words of a print worker who had been in the *Daily Worker*'s machine room when the police arrived to close the title. This man, whom Morrison identified as an authentic voice of the British working class, told the police he had been expecting them to arrive for 'some time'. He added: 'I am just here to earn a living and do not agree with the politics of those bastards upstairs.' The CPGB was more than capable of censoring opinion, he explained. Indeed, the Communists' ruthless censorship of dissent 'beats the Home Office hollow'.[72]

Aaron Goldman explains that the *Daily Worker* attracted some support from non-communists beyond the legislature. H.G. Wells and George Bernard Shaw advertised their hostility to the ban. The Archbishop of Canterbury, Hewlett Johnson, widely known as the 'Red Dean' for his extreme left-wing sympathies, offered his support for the newspaper. The National Council for Civil Liberties (NCCL) made common cause with the National Union of Journalists (NUJ) to demand the repeal of Regulation 2D and so deny the home secretary the power to ban newspapers without making his case in court.[73] However, such organizations had little hold on popular opinion. There was no great tide of public sympathy for the *Daily Worker*. Next, as Nye Bevan had suspected, ministers would turn their ire back against the *Daily Mirror* and *Sunday Pictorial*. Their colossal readerships did matter.

Pressure Switches onto the *Daily Mirror*

Correspondence between the prime minister and Cecil King reveals the depth of Churchill's resentment of the two popular left-wing papers. He instructed his private secretary to write to King to complain bitterly about the work of *Daily Mirror* columnist William Neil Connor, who published under the pen name, Cassandra. Connor was a superb and immensely versatile writer who had honed his talents as an advertising copywriter. His Cassandra column could 'purr or bark, nuzzle or bite, canter or gallop, soothe or repel'.[74] He had launched a 'Gutskrieg' against wealthy diners eating lavish meals in restaurants while *Mirror* readers struggled with meagre rations. He had identified the home secretary as 'the well-known chief censor'.[75] Now, Kathleen Hill, personal private secretary to the prime minister, informed Cassandra's employer that Winston Churchill considered it 'a pity that so able a writer should show himself so dominated by malevolence'.[76] She enclosed two cuttings containing criticisms of five ministers. A lively correspondence ensued in which King defended his columnist as hard-hitting but not malevolent. Churchill replied that the *Daily Mirror* and *Sunday Pictorial* showed 'a spirit of hatred and malice against the government'. Their attitude was worse than 'anything I have ever seen in English journalism'.[77] The prime minister accused both newspapers of depicting ministers as feeble and incompetent. He believed they exploited popular grievances for commercial gain, attacked the army's disciplinary procedures and sought to prise apart the Labour and Conservative wings of the coalition. A less combative newspaper group might have been cowed by such sharp warnings from the prime minister and the leader of his coalition ally. The *Daily Mirror* and *Sunday Pictorial* were not and their willingness to speak truth to power on behalf of their readers brought them perilously close to closure. The verve and style with which they did it, and the directly personal tone of columnists such as Cassandra, were learned from popular American journalism. Plainly, however, wartime Britain did not have a first amendment to protect its newspapers.

Following the banning of the *Daily Worker*, Churchill kept up an intermittent barrage of criticism against the *Daily Mirror* and *Sunday Pictorial* throughout the spring and summer of 1941. Cecil King and the *Mirror*'s editor, Cecil Thomas, made assorted unsuccessful efforts to mollify him. Churchill's anger peaked at the end of October when he again wrote to Herbert Morrison suggesting that there now existed 'further foundation for the suppression' of the *Sunday Pictorial*. Again, Morrison expressed sympathy and agreed that the newspaper covered politics in an 'offensive tone'. However, the home secretary was not persuaded that it had breached the terms of the defence regulations. He advised against restricting freedom of expression. Even views which were repugnant to the majority of the population should be 'permissible in a country which prides itself on the tradition of freedom of speech'.[78] Herbert Morrison's confidence that Britain should not fight for democracy while banning journalism that criticized and lampooned government was shaken not by Cassandra or any reporter, correspondent or columnist. The publication that persuaded the home secretary that the *Daily Mirror* hated him at least as much as it disliked senior Conservatives was a cartoon.

The Zec Cartoon

Philip Zec (1909–83) of the *Daily Mirror* was a slim, gently balding Jewish socialist of Russian descent, who drew his bold, striking images on cardboard and delivered them to the newspaper by bicycle. He had learned the foundations of his skill at St Martin's School of Art and developed it in the advertising business, before launching his own commercial art agency. Zec did not draw cartoon strips such as his *Mirror* colleague Norman Pett's outstandingly popular Jane. He was a political cartoonist, employed to illustrate the main themes of news stories, columns and leaders. In one cartoon, while Neville Chamberlain was still prime minister, Zec had depicted the old appeaser as a miserable pianist with Adolf Hitler peeping out from beneath the lid of his grand piano. His caption was: 'Don't shoot the pianist, he's doing his best.' In the aftermath of Dunkirk, he drew Hitler as a moth flying around a candle flame with the caption: 'Sure, he's getting closer.'[79] In March 1942, Philip Zec turned his imagination to the Battle of the Atlantic. German U-boat packs were savaging vital supply convoys bringing food and war materials to Britain from the United States. Oil was among the most precious commodities making the perilous crossing, and the tankers in which large supplies were carried were priority targets for German torpedoes. David Edgerton reminds us that, in his history of the war, Winston Churchill made the surprising assertion that: 'The only thing that really frightened me during the war was the U-Boat peril.'[80] This was potent in the early months of 1942. The merchant seamen who crewed the oil and petrol tankers were dying in large numbers and appalling circumstances. Determined to emphasize that fuel imported in the face of such danger should not be wasted, the government had authorized a one penny increase in the price of petrol. Zec, who often worked in the office alongside William Connor (Cassandra), habitually discussed his drawings and their captions with the star columnist. Connor was impressed when Zec showed him his latest drawing – a torpedoed sailor clinging to a raft in a furious, black sea. It depicted the appalling risks involved in running the gauntlet of the U-boat packs and the stark fate that awaited those who were unlucky. Zec's proposed caption read: 'Petrol is Dearer Now.' Cassandra admired the picture, but he thought his friend needed a stronger caption. He told Zec, 'You need to pinpoint and dramatise the extra penny charge.'[81] The drawing was published on 6 March above a caption that declared: 'The Price of Petrol has been increased by one penny – official.'

The artist's intention was explicitly patriotic. Brave men were sacrificing their lives to bring fuel to the country. Every gallon imported was bought at a savagely high price. Zec hoped to advertise the courage and suffering of the merchant seamen and warn consumers not to waste a drop. *Mirror* readers got the message: shortages and rising prices were the consequences of total war. Sacrifices were necessary and others were suffering more intensely. The home secretary did not interpret it as the artist intended. Morrison was convinced that it meant seamen were squandering their lives pointlessly. He believed it was a wicked cartoon that 'meant that the seaman struggling on the raft at sea – alone, almost exhausted – was risking his life in order that somebody might get additional profits'.[82] His colleague Ernest Bevin, minister of labour, agreed with him. The lord chancellor, the Liberal politician Lord Simon, declared the drawing cruel, deplorable and horrible. Churchill believed the *Mirror* had been warned sternly and repeatedly. It should now be shut down.

Curran and Seaton note that the prime minister was feeling vulnerable and desperate for military victories that might bolster his reputation.[83] Richard Toye recalls that, during a conversation over lunch with W.P. Crozier, editor of the *Manchester Guardian*, Churchill was 'very hot and strong' about the *Daily Mirror*. The prime minister explained that he wanted to 'flatten them out'.[84] Winston Churchill certainly hoped that draconian action against the *Daily Mirror* might serve as a warning to every British newspaper and persuade the press to back the war effort less critically. In Cabinet, on 9 March 1942, Churchill demanded immediate suppression of the *Daily Mirror*. Ten days later, Guy Bartholomew and Cecil Thomas were ordered to attend the Home Office for a meeting with the home secretary. Herbert Morrison produced a dossier of *Mirror* journalism. His first exhibit was Zec's cartoon. He told the *Mirror* duo that it was 'Worthy of Goebbels at his best' and plainly intended to persuade seamen not to go to sea to generate profits for oil companies. Turning to Cecil Thomas, he said that: 'Only a very unpatriotic Editor could pass that for publication.' Then, addressing Guy Bartholomew, Morrison declared that only someone with 'a diseased mind could be responsible for *Daily Mirror* policy'. He reminded them that he had already banned the *Daily Worker* and that it would remain banned for a long time. The government had warned the *Daily Mirror* repeatedly and was not going to waste its breath on further warnings. Morrison said: 'We shall act with a speed that will surprise you.'[85] Christopher Andrew, official historian of MI5, notes that Morrison's fury over the Zec cartoon was so intense that he may have asked the security service to investigate it.[86] This would have been a remarkable use of MI5 resources in wartime.

The Labour and Conservative wings of Mr Churchill's coalition were now united in hostility to the *Daily Mirror*, and Herbert Morrison went straight from his meeting to the House of Commons. Here William Patrick Spens, the Conservative MP for Ashford in Kent, had been primed to ask him a private notice question. Spens inquired whether the home secretary had seen Zec's cartoon which he deplored as a 'suggestion that seamen are risking their lives in order that bigger profits may be made'. It was 'calculated to discourage seamen and readers of all classes from serving the country in its time of need' and 'conducive to defeatism'. Could Mr Morrison act 'to prevent a newspaper from publishing irresponsible matter likely to influence public opinion in a manner prejudicial to the efficient prosecution of the war?'[87]

Herbert Morrison replied with all guns blazing. Britain's free press had a right and a duty to offer reasonable criticism, but the *Mirror* was guilty of 'general, violent denunciation. manifestly tending to undermine the Army and depress the whole population'. He added a new interpretation of Defence Regulation 2D, insisting that it applied not only to incitements to refrain from helping the war effort, but also to 'publication of matter which foments opposition to the war effort, by poisoning the springs of national loyalty, and by creating a spirit of despair and defeatism'.[88] The 'fact that such matter may not deliberately and wilfully desire to hinder the success of the Allied cause' did not make the *Mirror*'s journalism any less dangerous. The only test was the effect the words 'may be expected to produce on the minds of others'.[89] Morrison's conveniently expanded definition relied on subjective judgement and MPs recognized its significance immediately.

Manny Shinwell, the Labour MP for Seaham in County Durham, warned that the country was 'in danger of having the right of public opinion impinged upon'.[90] He explained that the cartoon was not an attack on ministers, it was a simple warning against 'waste of petrol'.[91] Sir Percy Harris asked whether Morrison realized that the House of Commons 'attaches vital importance to the freedom of the press'.[92] Seymour Cocks, the Labour MP for Broxtowe, was a former journalist. He mocked his colleague with the taunt that: 'You must not criticise the Government now.'[93] Morrison had tested the parliamentary water and found it less than entirely welcoming. The following day's press coverage was hostile. *The Times* reminded the home secretary that Regulation 2D gave him a very specific power to suppress a publication that 'was calculated to foment opposition to the successful prosecution of the war'. Ministers were 'apt to take the headier flights of the press too seriously'. If they chose to press ahead with a ban, parliament would be entitled to prevent them. *The Times* leader concluded with a warning that 'yesterday's reminder to one newspaper will in no way deter the rest from the discharge of their duty'.[94] The *Daily Mirror* was not banned, but neither was the home secretary's spite sated. Cassandra was conscripted into the army a few days later along with another critical journalist, Frank Owen, of the *Evening Standard*.

CHAPTER 9
BRITAIN AND RUSSIA: 'ONE TOUCH OF HITLER MAKES THE WHOLE WORLD KIN'

The War Cabinet found the *Daily Worker* intolerable because it promoted the USSR's policy of non-aggression towards Nazi Germany and systematically opposed the war effort. But, if senior ministers understood the Communist Party of Great Britain, they struggled to comprehend its chief sponsor. Indeed, between the outbreak of war and the German invasion of Russia in June 1941, Britain's changing attitude towards the USSR was underpinned by incomprehension often barely distinguishable from ignorance. The Foreign Office had no Russian specialists and nobody who spoke Russian fluently. When Britain and the USSR became allies, the Foreign Office and the Ministry of Information would work to banish fear of Bolshevism by offering a selective depiction of the USSR. This approach was adopted by newspapers of left and right. The result was not so much bowdlerized as misleading. The ruthless Stalinist state at war was portrayed as a haven for artists, musicians and brilliant scientists. The impression was conveyed that it had abandoned the idea of global revolution and was now tolerant of small business. If political repression still existed, it was as an antidote to Nazi aggression not a tool of red terror. This, however, was not the starting point. As appeasement staggered to failure, the British government regarded the regime in Moscow with no more affection than its counterpart in Berlin.

In 1938, Sir Alexander Cadogan, permanent undersecretary at the Foreign Office, characterized Nazi Germany and Communist Russia as the 'mumps and measles'[1] of Europe. The Foreign Office's aversion to Stalinism was shared in Cabinet and, even as his efforts to tame Hitler faltered, Neville Chamberlain remained reluctant to befriend the USSR. Following the Munich Agreement in 1938, which Stalin condemned, a peace front consisting of Britain, France and the USSR appeared hard to create. Ostensibly inconceivable was reconciliation between Nazi Germany and Communist Russia that would give Hitler free rein to launch war in the west. But just such an agreement was signed in Moscow on 23 August 1939 by Vyacheslav Molotov, the Soviet minister of foreign affairs, and Joachim von Ribbentrop, his German counterpart.

Unlike their foreign ministers, Joseph Stalin and Adolf Hitler would never meet but, until June 1941, they collaborated in a pact that astounded the world. Among the consequences of this Nazi-Soviet non-aggression pact was that the official relationship between Britain and the USSR would change utterly during the Second World War. The extent of the volte-face was captured by Winston Churchill's observation on Germany's invasion of the Soviet Union in June 1941 that, 'If Hitler invaded Hell, I would make at least a favourable reference to the Devil in the House of Commons.'[2] A similar transformation occurred in the depiction of the USSR and Russians in British newspapers. Newspapers which had deplored Joseph Stalin as a paranoid savage guilty of crimes against humanity shifted to portray him as an avuncular uncle leading a nation of humble heroes. In his biography of George Orwell, D.J. Taylor notes that the great writer 'could think of no better example of the age's moral and emotional shallowness than the fact that the country's previous differences with Soviet Russia had apparently been forgotten overnight'.[3]

Molotov-Ribbentrop Pact and Invasion of Poland

Plainly a prelude to German invasion of Poland, the Molotov-Ribbentrop pact came as a colossal shock to British newspapers and, most of all, to those that had worked hardest to promote appeasement. The *Daily Express*, zealously committed to its proprietor's insistence that war was thoroughly undesirable, utterly unnecessary and entirely avoidable, advertised its confusion in its edition of 24 August 1939. On its front page the *Express* carried a late news item from Reuters news agency in Moscow confirming that a pact had been signed.[4] Inside, an extended editorial – written before the news arrived – suggested that the proprietor's optimism had endured until the last moment. It advised that peace was 'within the grasp of all men of good will' and speculated that the meeting between Molotov and Ribbentrop must fail because: 'Stalin mistrusts Hitler as much as Hitler mistrusts Stalin.' Anyway, the *Express* reassured its readers, 'While Ribbentrop is outside Germany it is impossible for Germany to take any step that leads to war.' Wise counsel could and should prevail. Hitler must be persuaded that, 'if he overthrows world peace, he overthrows himself'.[5] This wishful thinking was reinforced by a despatch from Italy explaining that 'the almost complete lack of war preparations in Rome' had 'caused hopes of a settlement of the German Polish dispute'. The *Express* noted that Mussolini was encouraging the Polish government to enter into 'direct eleventh-hour negotiations with Germany'.[6]

The *Daily Mail* published a special late edition, including a report from its correspondent in Berlin, conveying German confirmation of the news from Moscow.[7] An editorial warned that Russia must be 'counted out of the Peace front'. However, like its popular conservative rival, the *Mail* sought to bolster morale. It believed deterrence might yet persuade Hitler not to fight. The 'darkness falling over Europe' was relieved by the alliance between Britain and France. The 'two most powerful nations of the Old World' had declared that they would 'meet force with superior force if any attempt is made to destroy another great free democracy in Poland'. Peace could still be preserved because 'Hitler has heard Britain's resolve. He knows what we have said and that we mean it.'[8] The *Daily Mail* did not try to explain how Britain, with no troops on the continent of Europe, could prevent a German invasion of Poland.

The leader writers' positive gloss on the Molotov-Ribbentrop pact could not survive. Hitler invaded Poland and Britain declared war. Any hope that this might be a limited conflict ended on 17 September when Russian forces entered Poland from the east. Now, from left and right, the *Daily Mirror* and *Daily Mail* responded with editorials under exactly the same title: 'Betrayal'. The *Mirror* described Germany and Russia as 'two vultures' united by 'murderous greed'.⁹ For the *Mail*, Poland had been 'stabbed in the back by Russia', while fighting desperately and courageously against Germany. It was too much to hope that the Poles could continue their resistance, but Britain would fight on 'for the independence of Poland and the destruction of tyranny'.¹⁰ The *Daily Express* also published editorial comment: Poland had fought 'a magnificent battle' but her resistance could not continue. From the west, Hitler was eating into her heart. In the east, 'Stalin's teeth' were 'set in her flank'.¹¹

Newspaper cartoonists relished the opportunity. Roger Moorhouse describes 'the apparent absurdity of Stalin's new-found friendship with Hitler' as 'a boon' for artists such as Bert Thomas and David Low.¹² In Lord Beaverbrook's London *Evening Standard*, Thomas depicted Nazi Germany as a gorilla and the Soviet Union as a bear. David Low captured brilliantly Poland's agony in another cartoon for the *Evening Standard* on 20 September. This portrayed Stalin and Hitler meeting amidst the debris of war. At their feet lay prostrate Poland. The dictators doff their caps to each other. 'The scum of the earth, I believe', says Hitler. Stalin replies, 'The bloody assassin of the workers, I presume.'¹³ Low's imagined dialogue captures eloquently an opinion widespread in Britain and

Figure 9.1 David Low, 'The Scum of the Earth, I Presume', *London Evening Standard*, 20 September 1939. Low's cartoon lampoons the cynical alliance between Nazi Adolf Hitler and Communist Josef Stalin.

Figure 9.2 Philip Zec, 'German Murderer and Russian Body Snatcher', *Daily Mirror*, 20 September 1939. Zec's cartoon condemns the division of Poland between Hitler's Germany and Stalin's Soviet Union.

informed by British newspaper coverage: the pact between Germany and Russia was a cynical arrangement between ideological enemies. In the *Daily Mirror*, Philip Zec focused on the grotesque ideological somersault performed in Moscow and captured perfectly Stalin's brutal opportunism. Zec depicted two soldiers, one German, one Russian, standing over Poland's open grave. Each grasps a bloodied knife. The 'German Murderer' says, 'It's all right – he's dead now.' The 'Russian Body Snatcher' replies, 'Then I shall rob the corpse – fearlessly.'[14]

In the 1930s, admiration for the Soviet Union had endured on the British left. Now, it was shattered except amongst members of the Communist Party of Great Britain and in its newspaper, the *Daily Worker*. Beyond these useful fools, the view expressed in *The Times* in the immediate aftermath of the Russian invasion of eastern Poland captured the national mood:

Only those can be disappointed who clung to the ingenuous belief that Russia was to be distinguished from her Nazi neighbour, despite the identity of their institutions and political idiom.... The Germans certainly knew better when they judged that the self-denying objects of a peace front would prove pallid and uninviting beside the offer of two Polish provinces at no immediate cost.[15]

Given the nature of the assailants, *The Times* believed Britain should have known that: 'Germany was to do the murder and Russia was to share the estate.' It was a 'black crime', and the Polish cause would now 'glow in the heart of every civilized man and woman'. A line had been drawn 'between civilization and the jungle'.[16]

In Whitehall, anxious debate centred around whether Britain was now obliged to declare war on the Soviet Union. Sir Lancelot Oliphant, undersecretary of state at the Foreign Office, told the Cabinet an attack on Poland by the USSR had not been envisaged in the Anglo-Polish agreement of August 1939 which referred only to an attack by a 'European power'. The Foreign Office advised that both parties understood this to mean Germany.[17] This allowed Viscount Halifax to cool fevered brows. The foreign secretary explained that there was no obligation to take up arms against Russia. Chamberlain argued for a statement condemning Soviet aggression but was persuaded not to issue one unless the French government insisted on it.[18] Winston Churchill took the view that the Soviet invasion of Poland would oblige the Germans to keep large forces in the east to guard against possible Russian betrayal. This might work to the advantage of Britain and France. He favoured renewal of British diplomatic relations with Russia and suspected that Hitler must, eventually, turn against the Soviet Union. The first lord of the Admiralty believed Britain should continue to sell rubber, tin, copper and non-essential machine tools to the USSR under the terms of the 1936 Anglo-Soviet trade agreement. Such pragmatism was wise: Britain urgently needed supplies of timber in return. In a broadcast on the BBC, Churchill explained that Stalin was pursuing a 'cold policy of self-interest'.[19]

Soviet Invasion of Finland

Pressure to take a more hostile approach to the USSR mounted when the Red Army invaded Finland on 30 November 1939. This aggression provoked popular fury against Russia and Russians. As details of the fighting reached London, the *Sunday Pictorial* carried a front-page editorial written by the editor himself. Beneath a banner headline denouncing 'This Red Butcher' and a picture of Stalin, Hugh Cudlipp wrote that: 'something in us all, tonight, has snapped ... our very faith in humanity and in the future. For in all these miserable and morbid years of international anarchy, oppression and massacre, there has been no act so bloody, so hellish as this rape of Finland.'[20] Inside, the newspaper reported 'a dramatic Finnish counter-attack' towards the northern port city of Petsamo as refugees fled in their thousands. Wire reports from Helsinki told how Russian fighter planes 'skimmed over roads and machine-gunned civilians'. The *Sunday Pictorial* highlighted the fate of children whose 'little bodies lie broken' before 'Stalin's invading hordes'.[21] The following day's edition of the *Daily Mirror* also carried editorial comment, describing Stalin as a paranoid and cowardly bully.[22]

An editorial in *The Times* lambasted Russia's bid to reconquer land that Lenin had been obliged to surrender as 'another demonstration that, in the eyes of the despotisms of Central and Eastern Europe, a small nation possesses no rights save those it can assert by force of its own arms or those of its friends'.[23] Finland soon had many friends in Britain. Newspaper reporting of the Winter War would help to enlist them. It depicted Russia as a vile aggressor served by an incompetent army abysmally led and equipped. One lonely and striking exception, published on 1 December 1939, was a column in *Tribune* by the zealous socialist Labour MP, Stafford Cripps. This defended the Red Army's invasion of Finland.[24] A month later, in the first week of January 1940, Finnish resistance remained stubborn. Now Scrutator, pen name of the expert foreign, political and military columnist, Herbert Sidebotham (1872–1940), put the case against Russia in the *Sunday Times*. Russian troops in Finland were 'ill-shod and thinly clad'. Their 'wretched equipment' raised the suspicion that 'corruption is as bad in revolutionary Russia as it was under the old regime'. Stalin's most recent purge of the Red Army had stripped 'all the men of ability from the Russian higher command'. Scrutator admired the Finnish armed forces. He was sure Hitler had noticed the incompetence of their Russian enemies.[25]

Newspaper sympathy for Finland produced a range of editorial coverage extending from analysis to hagiography, virtually all of it hostile to Russia. *The Economist* explained that even 'The Kremlin will not expect anyone outside Russia apart from fools and fanatics to respect the facade with which they have sought to cover their aggression.'[26] The *Daily Mail* offered hagiography about Baron Carl Gustav Emil Mannerheim, commander-in-chief of the Finnish defence forces. His daughter, Baroness Anastasie Mannerheim, wrote a gushing profile of her father. He had led the anti-communist forces to victory in the Finnish civil war of 1918 and thus 'liberated his people from tyranny'. Now, she was proud that he had been 'again called upon in his old age to take the sword against an ancient enemy'.[27] The *Daily Mirror* sought to persuade the Chamberlain government to offer Finland assistance 'more powerful than that extended to Poland last September'.[28]

The romantic appeal of a small nation fighting insurmountable odds appealed to the best war correspondents. They duly descended on Finland from as far afield as the United States. Their copy brought evidence of Russian savagery to breakfast tables in London and New York. Virginia Cowles, the intrepid American correspondent working for the *Sunday Times*, described the Hotel Kämp in Helsinki 'overflowing with a noisy conglomeration' including 'journalists and photographers of a dozen different nationalities'.[29] The Finnish authorities had admitted them in the expectation that they would convey the horror of Russian aggression. In Britain, such accounts helped persuade ministers to send practical aid. Twelve Hurricane fighter aircraft were sent to Finland, but without RAF pilots. Instead, Britain trained Finnish pilots to fly them in combat. It also sent expert mechanics to maintain the aeroplanes. Enthusiasm for gallant Finland's struggle and the suffering of her people also persuaded men to volunteer for service in an International Volunteer Force. This was intended to fight with the Finns against the Red Army. However, the Chamberlain government remained timid. Concerned that helping Finland might provoke hostilities with the Soviet Union, it imposed restraints on the recruitment of volunteers. They were required to be militarily effective so as not to damage Britain's reputation. They had to travel as individuals or in small groups and obtain valid Swedish or Norwegian visas. Just days before Finland agreed peace terms, on 7 March the *Daily Telegraph* explained that men remained keen to volunteer against the Reds. Many were turning up at the Finnish Aid Bureau in London. There, Lord Davies, a former battalion commander of the Royal Welch Fusiliers had just returned from Helsinki where he had been 'impressed with the morale and discipline of the Finnish Army'.[30] Two days later the *Daily Mail* reported that some of the volunteers had already arrived in Finland.[31]

They were too late. On 12 March 1940 a Finnish delegation to the Soviet capital signed the Treaty of Moscow. Finland surrendered a large area of its south-eastern territory and leased the peninsula of Hanko to the Soviet Union for thirty years. For the *Daily Mail*, W.F. Martin, its special correspondent in the Finnish capital, reported that the people of Helsinki were 'in grim mood'. A silence had fallen over the city and a 'fresh mantle of snow' contributed to the subdued atmosphere that had descended as Finns learned of the peace talks in Moscow.[32] In London, the newspaper's diplomatic correspondent recorded that the 'onerous terms imposed on the Finnish delegates in Moscow' had come as a shock to all parties in the House of Commons. MPs were additionally aggrieved by reports that Finland's delegates in Moscow had been guarded throughout the talks by OGPU agents who had 'controlled their activities'.[33] The *Daily Mirror* revealed that Finnish parliamentarians were similarly appalled and had debated the Russian peace terms in a stormy, secret session.[34] *The Times* offered extensive coverage, including that Moscow Radio had interrupted a concert at 3.00 am to announce the signing of the peace treaty.[35] Recognizing its conservative readers' commitment to the Finnish cause, the *Daily Telegraph* dedicated space on its front page to details of the treaty. It explained that hostilities would cease at noon and that Finland had agreed not to maintain any warships, submarines or warplanes in the North Atlantic.[36] The *Daily Express* gave most of its broadsheet front page to the news. 'Armistice at Noon Today, Says Moscow' was its banner headline. This was accompanied by a strapline emphasizing Stalin's desire for a propaganda victory to compensate for the military embarrassment his forces had suffered in fighting the Finns. It read: 'Stalin claims "I've got nearly all I fought for"'.[37] A single column on the same page revealed that 'a high British Army Officer' had spent time in Finland making preparations for 'possible British action'. A British Expeditionary Force had been readied and specially trained for fighting 'in ice-bound Finland'.[38] A colour piece at the bottom of the page revealed that Stalin had joined the final talks with the Finnish delegation. Giving up his traditional pipe to chain-smoke cigarettes, the Russian leader wore 'his familiar loose fitting white jacket'. When agreement was reached, he whispered something to the Finnish negotiator, Dr Juho Kusto Paasikivi.[39] The *Daily Express* offered no hint as to what Stalin had said.

Operation Barbarossa

Between the end of the Winter War and the German invasion of Russia on 22 June 1941, the British press occasionally turned a watchful eye on Russia. *The Times*, famous for its analysis of international affairs, displayed acuity in an editorial on 3 July 1940 while German troops stood poised to invade Britain. Hitler's intention in achieving the German-Soviet Pact had been 'to immobilize Soviet Russia while he disposed of France and Britain'. However, while Stalin hoped to gain from non-belligerency, he had 'no desire to see Germany dominant in Eastern Europe'. Russia's recently completed occupation of the Baltic states and two Romanian provinces was intended 'to keep Germany and her Axis partners at a safe and respectful distance'.[40] *The Times* predicted that Hitler remained determined to subjugate Russia. He had said as much in *Mein Kampf*. This was prescient. On Sunday, 22 June 1941, Germany invaded the Soviet Union with massed infantry, artillery and armour, heavily supported by the Luftwaffe. Striking in the extensive newspaper coverage that greeted this momentous change in the progress of the war is the absence of any great sense of surprise.

In the *Daily Express*, a banner headline declared 'Red Cities Blitzed, Reds Bomb Back'. The story below described four million men 'locked' on a battlefront extending 'from the Arctic to the Black Sea'.[41] A single-column piece beside the lead story reported that in the Russian capital, wooden buildings were 'feverishly torn down' as a precaution against attack with incendiary bombs.[42] A second sidebar explained that Winston Churchill had 'warned Stalin that Hitler would attack him'. Churchill told the House of Commons that he had revealed Hitler's intentions to Stalin. He offered the same information in a radio broadcast to the nation. On each occasion, Churchill concealed the absolute secret, unknown even to most members of his Cabinet, that his knowledge was the product of Ultra intelligence: intercepted German communications decrypted at Bletchley Park. His prescient warning was widely reported. The prime minister also promised 'all possible aid' to the Soviet Union.[43]

The Times complained that Germany's action was launched despite the non-aggression pact that Russia had 'conscientiously kept in every detail'. Such betrayal was 'without example in the history of civilized nations'.[44] A report by its diplomatic correspondent on 24 June reflects the very rapid adaptation to circumstance then taking place. He reported intense conversation between diplomats in national capitals. Governments 'almost everywhere were quickly readjusting or reversing their policies in the face of Hitler's attack'. Churchill had offered British support to the Soviet Union before he could discuss the issue with the governments of the British dominions. Now, they had all confirmed that they would collaborate. 'One touch of Hitler makes the whole world kin', opined *The Times* man. He explained that the Soviet Union had sweetened the deal by promising that it would pay for all goods and services provided by Britain. The *Daily Telegraph*, sensitive to its readers' loathing of communism, advised that the House of Commons had applauded the foreign secretary, Anthony Eden, when Eden explained 'Britain's intention to take a severely practical view and support Russia as an enemy of Germany'. The *Telegraph* also emphasized that the prime minister had warned Stalin that a German attack was imminent. It added that Anthony Eden had summoned the Soviet ambassador to the United Kingdom and told him that Britain had reliable information that: 'Hitler was going to attack Russia from behind the smoke screen of his non-aggression pact.'[45] *The Times* expressed wry amusement that the Communist Party of Great Britain would now support the government. It reported a speech by CPGB leader Harry Pollitt in which he swore that his party would now make 'every effort to ensure that no obstacle stood in the way of the common victory of the British and Soviet peoples'.[46]

From the left, the *Daily Herald* seized the opportunity to settle old scores in an extended editorial. By pouncing on Russia, Hitler had shattered any 'timorous hopes of appeasers everywhere'. It hoped that 'diminishing sect' was now doomed to extinction.[47] *Daily Herald* diplomatic correspondent William Ewer explained that Hitler had commanded his armies to do precisely what he had sworn not to do. However, they should find nothing surprising in his decision: 'It is Hitler's way to preface assault by perjury.'[48] The *Daily Mirror* gave prominence to Joseph Goebbels' proclamation on Berlin Radio that 'capitalism and Jewry were out to encircle and destroy Germany'. Hitler, it explained, claimed he had no choice but to fight the Soviet Union because Britain refused 'to abandon her hopes of mobilizing a European coalition including the Balkans and Russia against Germany'.[49] That coalition was close now and, in a separate piece, the *Mirror* reported a prediction made by the Soviet minister of foreign affairs, Vyacheslav Molotov, that 'Napoleon was beaten and met his doom' in Russia and the same fate would

Figure 9.3 A huge crowd gathered outside the British Museum to hear Harry Pollitt, General Secretary of the Communist Party of Great Britain, make a speech about aid to Russia, 1941.

"*I can eat anything!*"

Figure 9.4 Philip Zec, Hitler: 'I can eat anything', *Daily Mirror*, 24 June 1941. Zec's cartoon marks the beginning of Operation Barbarossa, the German invasion of Russia.

befall 'the arrogant Hitler'.[50] The *Manchester Guardian*'s diplomatic correspondent was equally optimistic. He believed that the Russians were fully prepared to defend themselves. Russian policy towards Germany had been 'almost unbelievably stupid' but the Kremlin had never made the mistake of trusting Hitler.[51]

The irony is that, in a life characterized by acute and paranoid mistrust, the only man in whom Stalin did invest trust was Adolf Hitler. The Soviet leader reacted to rumours of impending war by issuing a statement to TASS, the official Soviet news agency, insisting that they were 'completely without foundation'.[52] Shown a report from an NKVD spy inside the German air ministry confirming that orders to attack the Soviet Union had been issued, Stalin reacted furiously. 'Tell the source to fuck his mother', he wrote, insisting the NKVD man was really 'a disinformer'. When General Zhukov, deputy minister of defence, sought consent to bring the Red Army to a state of 'full military readiness', the Soviet leader insisted that 'Germany on her own will never fight Russia'. He told Zhukov: 'If you're going to provoke the Germans on the frontier by moving troops there without our permission, then heads will roll, mark my words.' When the German invasion began and Zhukov sought permission for the Red Army to retaliate, Stalin said: 'This is a German provocation. Do not open fire or the situation will escalate.'[53]

The British press had depicted Stalin accurately as a paranoid, bullying butcher, guilty of oppression and massacre. His Soviet Union was a vile aggressor and its army cruel and incompetent. Now, however, such criticism of the Russian leader and the USSR in British newspapers diminished in quantity and venom. In a thoughtful leader, *The Times* lamented that Stalin had allowed Hitler to manoeuvre him out of the reasonably favourable position the Soviet Union had occupied in the summer of 1939. The trap should have been easy to avoid given Hitler's longstanding and clearly expressed ambitions to conquer Russia. It concluded that Stalin, 'though not an unsophisticated politician', had not been able to conceive of the 'blatant treachery' that allowed Hitler to agree a non-aggression pact and then invade.[54] The *Daily Mail* retained a sense of the Russian leader's true personality. It commissioned George Knupffer, described as one of Britain's 'best informed Russian political commentators', to assess Russia's chances of defeating the Nazi invaders. Knupffer, a dedicated anti-communist, explained that Stalin ruled 'by means of a totalitarian terror'. Liberty did not exist in Russia and there was 'not a trace of the rights of citizens'. Millions had starved to death in the country and many were still suffering. Hitler had grounds to believe that he had invaded a country 'which has been very ill and is still in its convalescence'. He conceded, grudgingly, that Britain must help the Russian people to make their country 'a fatal burden to Germany'.[55] The *Daily Herald* summarized the position admirably. The only way to restore order and principle to the world was to defeat Hitler. Evidence of Russian armed strength was 'scanty' and Britons should avoid 'extravagant optimism'. Every Briton should do their 'utmost for victory at every moment of the working day'.[56] In the *Daily Mirror*, Philip Zec preferred to advertise the enormity of the task facing Hitler's armies. He depicted a tiny Führer beneath a huge apple, labelled 'USSR', screaming 'I can eat anything'.[57]

A Second Front

During the winter of 1941/42, the Red Army began to demonstrate that it could mount the type of defence Zec had predicted. As it demonstrated growing effectiveness in combat, Sir Alexander Cadogan argued that: 'We should realise, by retrospect, that our staff have throughout underestimated Russian strength to a highly misleading degree.'[58] In referring to 'our staff', Cadogan was describing the pessimistic assessment of Russian armed prowess by British service departments. In the *Daily Mail*, Sir Basil Liddell Hart (1895–1970), the military historian, theorist and author, raised hackles by arguing that Russian defence was 'remarkable in its tenacity' and 'must have disappointed German expectations'. The First World War veteran outlined the tactic of 'elastic defence' and explained that Hitler's armies had failed to 'cut off and annihilate' Soviet divisions to 'anything like the extent' predicted in Nazi propaganda. Despite the savagery and speed of the German attack, Russian defence was 'being maintained to a remarkable extent'.[59] Hart's view had merit. Despite the loss of vast territories, Russia prevented the capture of Moscow. In the Foreign Office, concern emerged that Russia might defeat the Germans before Britain had any troops on European soil. British forces had suffered grave setbacks against the Germans in the Middle East and against the Japanese in Singapore. Evidence of Russian resilience risked highlighting Britain's relative frailty. Anthony Eden feared that, if Russia pushed the Germans back, it would emerge as a European superpower. In such circumstances Britain would need amicable relations with the USSR to prevent Stalin making a fresh deal with Hitler.[60]

Early 1942 saw the emergence of rumours that stubborn Russian defence and German overstretch had brought about secret peace talks between the Soviet Union and Germany. The Foreign Office was quick to characterize these claims as German propaganda and *The Times* was briefed to pour cold water over them. It duly published an extended editorial describing how Russian forces were taking maximum advantage of the winter weather to press and harry the German invaders. The Red Army was making increasingly heavy thrusts and its efforts had strategic intent. The voice of the British establishment declared that: 'The initiative lies in Russian hands and the Germans are being put to all sorts of shifts in order to maintain their ground.'[61] Saying nice things about the Soviet Union was easy, particularly with the support of *The Times*, which was still regarded by allies and enemies alike as a guide to British policy. However, the foreign secretary knew that warm words were unlikely to be sufficient.

In March 1942 Anthony Eden wrote that the Russians 'suspect that we are interested in co-operation with themselves solely to the extent that such collaboration will keep them fighting hard against Germany, while in their view we are not pulling our weight in the war'.[62] Britain was struggling to meet its commitments to supply the Soviet Union with munitions and raw materials. More ominously, Britain was not remotely ready to open the second front in western Europe that Stalin persistently demanded. This demand reflected more than the Russians' earnest desire to force Germany to relocate forces. It advertised Stalin's fear that the Western powers would reach a separate peace accord with Hitler.

The Anglo-Soviet treaty negotiated amidst intense secrecy in London in May 1942 by Winston Churchill, Anthony Eden and Vyacheslav Molotov was designed to reassure the Russian leader. It committed Britain and the Soviet Union to supporting each other and bound them not to enter negotiations with Germany without consulting the other in advance. The foreign secretary did not reveal it in the House of Commons until 11 June, by which time Molotov had flown from London to Washington DC and back again. Reporting of the treaty offers a vivid example of the close control government could exercise over newspapers in their treatment of high policy. On such occasions, censorship was not the primary tool. The key information was the exclusive property of minsters and their senior advisers. Newspapers could access it only via official sources. Self-censorship came into play too. Those who followed the official lines most closely, and promoted them most enthusiastically to their readers, might be trusted with a little more precious information.

The *Manchester Guardian* reported that the 'mutual aid pact' included 'full understanding on the urgent tasks of creating a second front in Europe this year'.[63] Appealing directly to the pro-Russian sympathies of its large socialist readership, the *Daily Herald* rejoiced at the signing of the pact. An editorial argued that it proved Britain and Russia were now partners, not only in 'the stern task of winning the war' but also in mutual pursuit of a better world when the fighting ended. However, the *Herald* also emphasized the need for a second front in Europe if the new spirit of Anglo-Soviet friendship was to be sustained. It was 'an essential condition of victory' and must happen at 'the earliest practical moment'.[64] The *Daily Mirror*'s treatment of the news was typically bold and direct. Its front page carried the banner headline 'A Second Front in 1942'. Its political correspondent reported that a crowded House of Commons had cheered repeatedly the news that Britain and Russia were now committed to mutual assistance.[65] Beside the main story appeared a separate piece filed by Reuters from Washington DC. This revealed that President Roosevelt's administration was thrilled by the agreement. It added that the implication was that the US government would not let 'shipping difficulties' stand in the way of the promised second front. This was the closest the *Mirror* came to discussing the blunt reality that there were not yet American forces in Britain that could launch landings in occupied Europe. An additional sentence revealed that the Anglo-American solution, at least in the short term, would be to deploy air power. The *Mirror* explained that 'forthcoming big raids by British and American forces will constitute the preliminary action'.[66]

The *Daily Mail* offered its conservative readers a gushing paean to the apparent emergence of love and understanding between the Kremlin and Whitehall. An editorial declared that the treaty gave 'formal sanction to a comradeship in arms that has been sealed in blood'. The promised second front and agreement that Anglo-Soviet collaboration should continue after the war were both to be welcomed. Only in conclusion did the *Mail* offer a soupçon of scepticism. 'Let us hope', opined the leader, 'that the suspicions which marred relations in the past will be permanently removed.'[67] The *Daily Telegraph* revealed the political journey it had made. It too gave the treaty front-page billing.[68] Inside appeared an editorial written to encourage its readers to embrace the USSR. By their extreme suffering 'under the abomination of Nazism', the Russian people had made Britons proud 'that we can assist with our utmost efforts'. Anglo-Soviet friendship would be met in Britain with 'good will and firm resolution'. The *Telegraph* dared to hope that the long-term nature of the treaty meant that Europe could now look forward to 'a period of greater security than it has known for a hundred years'.[69] The *Times* began by waxing almost as lyrical as a schoolgirl with a crush, but more ponderously. The treaty was an 'event of historical importance'. Mr Molotov's visit to the United Kingdom marked 'a capital contribution to the realization of that vast conception of common planning among the United Nations which is necessary both to win the war and build the peace after the war'. However, hints of realism appeared with reference to the second front. Soviet Russia would have to 'sustain the full brunt' of Hitler's military power for some time to come. There was nothing Britain or America could do 'at this moment' to relieve the Red Army of 'the major share of the burden and the glory'. Again,

The Times was briefed to convey a crucial diplomatic message: a second front in Europe would not be possible immediately. Stalin would have to be patient.[70]

The *Daily Express* was offered tailored access that allowed its readers to imagine they had access to diplomatic secrets and a privileged relationship with power. A single-column story by Guy Eden on its front page revealed that, during his time in Britain, Vyacheslav Molotov had travelled under the alias of 'Mr Smith from abroad'. He became 'Mr Brown' when he went to Washington DC.[71] The *Express*'s banner headline was pure boosterism. It declared that there would be a second front in 1942. The story beneath explained that invasion of Europe was an urgent priority.[72] The newspaper's editorial reinforced this message. The treaty was the 'worst blow' for Hitler and readers were invited to feel their pulses quicken at the news that Britain was 'going to relieve the pressure on our Russian comrades'.[73] Lord Beaverbrook had the insider knowledge to know how hard it would be to keep such a promise but the proprietor of the *Daily Express* valued propaganda above truth. A short piece from Moscow helped to explain why. The *Daily Express* reported that cheering crowds in Moscow had greeted news of the treaty which was read out in full in official broadcasts. These gave 'special emphasis' to the Anglo-American commitment to open a second front.[74]

Stalingrad

In the summer of 1942, Stalin and his generals anticipated a renewed attack on their capital. Hitler chose an alternative. Stalingrad on the River Volga was one of the Soviet Union's major industrial centres. It produced artillery for the Red Army. The Volga was an important transport link, providing for the carriage of heavy goods between western and eastern Russia. Adolf Hitler also had a propaganda motive for taking the city: it bore Stalin's name. The German advance towards Stalingrad began on 23 August 1942. Two days later, the *Daily Mail* reflected on the city's strategic significance in a thoughtful leader that emphasized the perilous state of the war. It observed that Leningrad and Moscow might have fallen to the Nazis 'without irreparable injury to the fighting strength of the Russian armed forces'. However, if Stalingrad fell, Germany would be free to withdraw infantry, armour and aircraft from Russia. The threat to Stalingrad was, therefore, a threat to the British Isles. The editorial concluded that a German victory would make Germans 'the masters of the European mainland'. The resources of Europe would be at their disposal. They would turn them against 'their principal and their most hated foe – Great Britain'.[75]

The following morning's edition of the *Daily Mirror* reported that the German advance was within forty miles of Stalingrad and described 'fierce fighting for the crossing of the Don'.[76] This front-page account was accompanied by a photograph of a smiling Winston Churchill seated beside an equally jovial-looking Joseph Stalin. The accompanying caption might have been written by an official in the Ministry of Information that had supplied the image. It read: 'This picture of Stalin, the strong silent man of Russia, and Mr Churchill was taken in the Kremlin during one of their meetings.

It was the first time they had met in their lives.'[77] The meeting had taken place only twelve days earlier. As he departed London to fly to Russia via Gibraltar and Cairo, Clementine Churchill described his mission as a 'visit to the ogre in his den'.[78] Strict security backed by rigid censorship prevented any disclosure by newspapers of her husband's journey until he had returned safely to London. On 26 August, the *Mirror* revealed that German forces were closing in on Stalingrad. Large enemy forces of tanks and infantry had crossed the River Don. A communiqué issued in Moscow suggested that Red Army forces were outnumbered and acknowledged that the situation around the city had 'become more complicated'.[79] The Russians emptied Stalingrad of grain and cattle but they did not evacuate the city's people. Stalin ordered every Russian who could do so to fight in defence of the city that bore his name. He believed the presence of civilians would inspire a stronger will to resist. By the third week of September, *The Times* leader could tell its readers that they were witnessing a 'resistance rivalling the majestic defence of Verdun' by the French in the First World War. It noted that on this occasion it was not achieved by 'a ring of long prepared forts' but by the people of Stalingrad who bravely 'dispute each step of the enemy's advance'. The column advised that Germany sought absolute victory in the east in order to turn its forces against Britain and America. The valour of the people of Stalingrad continued to 'delay that achievement'.[80] The *Daily Mail* dedicated its leader column to Stalingrad on 22 September. It noted that German propaganda now insisted that the people of the besieged city were still fighting only because they were 'too brutish to understand' that they had lost the battle and that further bloodshed was useless. This, the *Mail* opined, was contemptible nonsense. In fact the entire military situation had been transformed by the Russians' heroic defence: 'The longer Stalingrad holds, the further must recede German hopes of a decisive victory.'[81] A *Daily Telegraph* leader the following day described devastating bombardment of Stalingrad by the Luftwaffe and German artillery. It noted 'desperate hand-to-hand fighting' and appalling slaughter in the battle for the city. However, the once bitter critic of Soviet Russia now believed that every drop of blood shed was justified because failure to capture Stalingrad would leave the German position in the east 'dangerously unstable'. The *Telegraph* explained that newspapers in Nazi Germany were reflecting on the harshness of the fighting and the stress imposed on exhausted German officers and men. It reflected that, 'as the Autumn comes down' German prospects at Stalingrad were not good and wondered what would happen when winter arrived.[82] The *Manchester Guardian* wondered too. In a colourful account from a Reuters correspondent, the provincial broadsheet reported that the Germans had now learned that Stalingrad was 'an infinitely tougher prospect than they expected'. It praised the fighting skills of 'ordinary workmen with just a cartridge belt slung across their overalls'. An efficient guerrilla Home Guard was giving Moscow's disciplined professional army valuable support. Stalingrad was holding strong and 'Very soon all the trenches, anti-tank obstacles and wire entanglements will be white with snow.'[83] The *Daily Mirror* spotted what Stalin wanted in return for the colossal sacrifices his forces were making: that second front in the west. Conscious, as always, of its readers' interests, the *Mirror* reported food minister Lord Woolton's warning that a second front would require fast ships to transport troops and equipment 'and fast ships are meat ships'. The minister added that, 'we cannot pursue a more and more vigorous war and still keep up the same standard of living'. The *Mirror*'s headline on the story made its point crystal clear. It read: 'Second Front Will Cost You Food Cuts'.[84]

The problem facing Winston Churchill and Franklin D. Roosevelt was that the risks inherent in Anglo-American landings on the soil of occupied Europe extended well beyond dietary restrictions. Allied commanders feared immense losses in men and equipment and urged caution. However, if Britain could not yet offer the military engagement Russia demanded, it could exercise every element of soft power at its disposal. So, as Russia first stemmed and then forced back the Wehrmacht in 1942 and 1943, every effort was made to flatter Stalin and the country he led. Among the first great beneficiaries of this flattery was the *Daily Worker*. Having closed it down in January 1941, Herbert Morrison rescinded his ban on 26 August 1942. The *Daily Herald*, which probably had most to fear from the revival of the Communist Party's daily newspaper, reported its revival on its front page. The *Herald* noted that, in lifting his prohibition, the home secretary wrote to the CPGB indicating that he would re-impose it if the *Worker* returned to its old ways. Systematic publication of 'matter calculated to foment opposition to the prosecution of the war to a successful issue' remained illegal.[85] In the same edition, William Rust, editor of the *Daily Worker*, celebrated the decision as 'a victory for national unity at a perilous moment in the fight against fascism'. Liberated from the intellectual and moral encumbrance of revolutionary defeatism, Rust could also reveal that German bombers had destroyed his newspaper's presses. Alternative arrangements were in place but it would not be possible to resume publication until 7 September.[86] The revived *Daily Worker* had a print run of 120,000 copies per day. Angus Calder estimates that, in the new atmosphere of friendship for the USSR, it 'was probably seen by half a million people daily'.[87] The home secretary's new tolerance for the Communist title was a sign of the times. Soon, distinguished regiments of the British Army taught their musicians to play fanfares glorifying Stalin. Martin Kitchen notes that 'John Gielgud appeared at the Albert Hall as the "voice of Radio Moscow"'.[88] In February 1943, the *Manchester Guardian* risked a hint of scepticism about such uncritical flattery, noting that the Seatonian Prize 'is awarded annually at Cambridge University for a poem on a sacred subject. This year's subject is "Holy Russia"'.[89] Whether Cambridge had really succumbed to the appetite for uncritical worship of the Soviet Union is not entirely clear. The *Sunday Times* simply reported that Cambridge had identified as the best poem in English on a sacred subject a composition entitled 'Holy Russia'.[90]

February 1943 saw Russian victory at Stalingrad. *The Times* reported President Roosevelt's message of congratulations to his Russian counterpart. It was a 'brilliant victory' in an 'epic battle'. The Red Army's achievement had 'forever honoured your name'.[91] In the *Daily Mail*, a thoughtful editorial captured the strategic significance. Despite colossal loss of life and military equipment, Hitler had achieved only negative results. His invasion of Russia was exhausting Germany's formidable strength in 'futile aggression against a great and courageous people'. The *Mail* surmised presciently that history might well conclude that Hitler 'broke the back of his Greater Reich in Russia'.[92] In the *Daily Mirror*, Bill Greig also reflected on the consequences of Stalingrad for

Germany. Perhaps, he speculated, the military catastrophe might provoke instability in Berlin. Greig detected evidence that Reich propaganda minister Josef Goebbels was 'preparing the ground so that friend Hitler gets all the blame'.[93] The *Daily Herald* emblazoned across its front page the news that a Nazi army had been encircled and wiped out at Voronezh with 5,000 men killed and 13,000 taken prisoner. On the Kharkov front, the Red Army was 'pouring forward' on a front 180 miles wide.[94] A down-page column reported that throughout Germany there had been 'a day of dirges for Stalingrad'.[95] The *Daily Express* updated its front page at 2.00 am to report that advancing Russian forces had forced their way between German bridgeheads. The Red Army was now only twenty miles from the Sea of Azov.[96] Under the caption, 'The Girl Behind the Tommy-Gun', a front-page picture depicted a smiling female Russian soldier standing guard over German prisoners of war. The story beneath explained that 'the handsome Russian girl' was relieving a Red Army man to do 'more important work at the front'.[97] Inside the *Daily Express* Sidney Strube's cartoon depicted his proprietor, Lord Beaverbrook, now serving in Cabinet as minister for war production, overseeing the export of British warplanes in crates labelled 'More Aid for Russia'. Beside the beaming Beaverbrook, Strube drew John Bull carrying a bouquet of newspapers bearing headlines including 'To Russia with Admiration', 'Marvellous', 'Wonderful' and 'Brilliant'.[98] An editorial in *The Times* captured the nagging tension beneath the euphoria. The Red Army's sweeping advances were sustained by faith that 'they will not be left much longer to bear so great a part of the burden alone'. As Russia's allies, Britain and the United States had a duty to compel the Germans to fight on several fronts simultaneously. The forces to engage in such battles were already assembled, noted the leader writer. Unfortunately, there was a residual challenge: how to get them onto French soil. Until it was resolved, *The Times* concluded that war on a second front could be waged 'with aircraft over Lorient and Cologne'.[99]

* * *

In their treatment of the Russian war effort, British newspapers achieved a level of collective compliance with government policy that exceeded even the support many had offered for appeasement. Conservative titles embraced the USSR, its people and leader with an enthusiasm that almost matched the zealous promotion offered by the left and liberal press. *The Times* functioned as a willing presenter of War Cabinet strategy and benefited once again from detailed briefing. Its readers could rely on it to offer knowledge from the inside track. Government press management was as successful as it had been during the Battle of Britain. The press pulled together in the national interest to such an extent that the devoutly conservative *Daily Telegraph* found itself singing from the same hymn book as the *Daily Worker*. These ideological enemies risked little by agreeing that the USSR deserved British thanks, support and admiration. Each could be certain that few of their readers read the other. That they abandoned their critical faculties so completely reflects both sincere gratitude for Russian sacrifice and awareness of the huge contribution Russia was making to the defeat of Nazi Germany. That Russia was fighting a desperate war of national survival and required American and British aid did not provoke serious criticism of Stalin and his regime even from the acerbic tongues at the

Daily Mirror and *Sunday Pictorial*. British newspaper opinion was too easily persuaded to portray the Soviet Union as a flawless saviour of mankind. Around the United Kingdom civic dignitaries would sing the 'Internationale' and stage pageants in celebration of the Red Army. And *The Times* was right. The Royal Air Force and the United States Army Air Force would make sustained and increasingly heavy attacks on Germany and military targets in occupied Europe between February 1943 and the D-Day landings in June 1944. Persuading Stalin that an Anglo-American air campaign was an adequate substitute for early invasion by ground forces would prove a great deal harder.

CHAPTER 10
THE BEVERIDGE REPORT: BANISHING WANT FROM CRADLE TO GRAVE

The colossal sacrifices made by the men and women of the Red Army awoke great sympathy for the Russian people and revived Britons' curiosity about the social and economic system under which they lived, fought and died. However, the most radical example of social policy to emerge in the UK during the war was Sir William Beveridge's December 1942 report on Social Insurance and Allied Services. This was more a highly progressive product of consensus than revolutionary thinking. However, this would not prevent it being depicted as dangerously left-wing by some traditional Conservatives.

Britain's pre-war mix of old-age pensions, unemployment insurance and health insurance came nowhere near to achieving comprehensive coverage. There was broad agreement on the left and centre of politics that something better was needed. This emerging political consensus was supercharged by the wartime civil servants David Marquand describes as the 'philosopher princes': brilliant young graduate men – and a few women – inspired by the exigencies of war to believe that the state could solve colossal problems.[1] President Franklin Roosevelt of the United States and Winston Churchill had agreed broad principles for the organization of post-war civilisation in the Atlantic Charter of August 1941. These included enhanced labour standards and social security. Sir William Beveridge 'learned the meaning of poverty and saw the consequences of unemployment'[2] when, as a young graduate, he worked as a researcher at Toynbee Hall in the East End of London. Between 1919 and 1937 he had been director of the London School of Economics. Now a civil servant, he began the work of enhancing both employment and social security as the chairman of an interdepartmental committee of civil servants, the Social Insurance Committee.

To hard-working people on meagre incomes, the prospect of real post-war change was enticing and, in the early winter of 1942, expectation grew that Beveridge would produce something more than a dry proposal for reform of social insurance. His report was eagerly anticipated by the *Daily Mirror* and *Sunday Pictorial*. Indeed, so determined were both titles to secure a better future for their readers that they suspected dark forces of conspiring to prevent publication and discussion of Beveridge's proposals. The author was a man of great intellect, unmatched by tact, and with a fondness for publicity. Naively, or foolishly, he spoke to a *Daily Telegraph* reporter on 12 November and the journalist presented the fruits of their conversation as 'an exclusive interview'.[3] The manner of its reporting suggests it was really a detailed briefing that Beveridge wanted to place in the public domain but for which he preferred not to take responsibility.

The *Telegraph*'s account explained that Beveridge had revealed that his 'long-awaited report on Britain's social insurance' would be published on or about 26 November. (The specificity of this date explains subsequent suspicion and controversy when it was not published until 1 December.) Then, Beveridge made two points which the *Telegraph* reporter found 'striking'. The manner in which these were reported is revealing. None of Beveridge's words appear in quotes. This is significant because the *Telegraph* man had excellent shorthand skills. He could have quoted his source directly, had he secured Beveridge's consent. Instead, he presented what Beveridge said without direct attribution. His account was intriguing and plausible. Sir William Beveridge explained that his report would 'take us halfway to Moscow'. It would not do so because Beveridge had been converted to Socialism but because: 'We must go halfway unless we want to be landed there altogether.' The great economist declared that 'a completely new system' was required to avoid political extremism, not a 'mere adjustment of the economic system'. Britain had failed in the last war 'because the people were not interested in what happened afterwards'. This time, he insisted, they were.[4]

Sir William's willingness to brief journalists extended beyond the staff of the *Daily Telegraph*. On 17 November, *The Times* lent its voice to the cause of cautious progress. Its parliamentary correspondent reported that Sir William's report would be in ministers' hands 'within a day or two'. He explained that it would be 'a State paper of outstanding importance' and would bring government and Parliament 'face to face' with problems in which 'the whole country is deeply interested'. The correspondent reported expectations that it would become 'the principal topic of domestic politics in the immediate future'.[5] Later the same day, William Brown, the Independent MP for Rugby, used an oral question in the House of Commons to ask when the report of the Beveridge committee would be available for discussion. The lord privy seal, Sir Stafford Cripps, for the Government, indicated that he expected it to be published at the end of the month. Sir John Mellor (1893–1986), the Conservative MP for Tamworth in Warwickshire, intervened to ask whether Cripps was aware that 'Sir William Beveridge has stated that his Report takes us half-way to Moscow?' Sir John wondered whether the government agreed with that opinion.[6] The lord privy seal claimed not to be aware of what Sir William had said. Provoked to anger by the exchanges on the floor of the House, Sir William immediately wrote to the *Daily Telegraph*. His letter was published on 18 November. Referring to the Moscow claim, Beveridge wrote: 'I never made that statement or any other statement about the contents of my report to your representative.'[7] It was a peculiar denial that obliquely confirmed that Beveridge had spoken to the *Telegraph* reporter even if the reporter had interpreted his words. In fact, the argument appears plausible. Real reform would be necessary to defend against the growing appeal of political radicalism made additionally popular by the Red Army's bravery.

The *Daily Mirror* of 18 November carried a front-page report confirming that Sir William Beveridge had completed his report, which was in the hands of the government. It hoped that the public would have access to it 'within the next ten days'. It predicted that MPs would request a full debate on the contents and 'there is no doubt that it will be granted'.[8] Two days later, the mood was less optimistic. Columnist Bill Greig lamented that the date of publication was slipping 'back and back' and that many MPs had identified 'a strong desire' that there should be no discussion of it during the debate on the King's Speech setting out the government's priorities. Greig feared that there was 'little hope' of a full debate on the proposals before the end of the year.[9] Reinforcing its columnist's concern, the *Mirror* reported that Tom Driberg, newly elected MP for Maldon and a former Communist sitting as an independent, feared 'powerful interests' were 'trying to prejudge and sabotage the Beveridge Report'. Driberg thought Beveridge had been fooled into giving the interview with the *Telegraph*. He accused the Conservative title of deploying 'a stratagem to entrap' him.[10]

By the end of the week, the *Daily Mirror* – ever watchful on behalf of its readers – was deeply frustrated that Beveridge's work was not already in the public domain. It feared that even to speak about fundamental reform of Britain's social and economic system risked splitting Labour ministers from their Conservative partners. A leader expressed concern that the coalition was too 'determined to be polite to itself'. It urged the Labour leadership to accept that the report must be discussed in public and insisted: 'It cannot be indefinitely pigeon-holed on the excuse that it might disturb the national unity – or equanimity – of those who see Moscow in any proposal for social reform.'[11] Plainly, the *Mirror* was making excellent use of its sources in the Labour Party. The *Sunday Pictorial* added to the pressure initiated by its daily counterpart. In a front-page news story, it welcomed speculation that Herbert Morrison was to be promoted to the War Cabinet. The Sunday title recognized that Morrison was unpopular on Labour's Socialist left, but he was among the few members of the government who had openly discussed 'the need for a new social system after the war'. The *Pictorial* believed membership of the Cabinet's inner circle would allow Herbert Morrison to promote the Beveridge Report among key decision makers. This, it gloated, 'would not amuse the Tories'.[12] Inside the *Pictorial* appeared a report of a four-point declaration made in London by Sir William Beveridge and designed to divert attention from his dispute with the *Daily Telegraph*. Sir William's prescription for post-war harmony included full employment and a system of national planning for industrial production. Central organization of the civil service would be required to manage the 'extension of state activity in the economic sphere'.[13]

As the nation awaited publication of his report, the *Daily Telegraph* was as worried about Beveridge's work as the popular left-wing titles were excited. It noted that Sir William was conscious of the need to balance the 'benefits of private enterprise at private risk' with the necessity of post-war economic planning. It reported without comment his corrective pledge that: 'I do not want a Soviet system applied to this country.'[14] Above all, the *Telegraph* advised the government to take its time and think very hard about Beveridge's proposals. It predicted that they would be 'highly technical' and recommended 'considerable examination' in advance of any firm decisions.[15] If the *Daily Telegraph* reflected astutely the financial interests of Conservative readers and advertisers employed in the private sector, *The Times* was equally adroit in recognizing that the establishment for which it spoke included many in senior echelons of the civil service, local government and the universities. *The Times* offered an extended news report of the speech to the Fabian Society, in which Sir William had outlined his vision of full employment while insisting that he could offer no hint about the content of his forthcoming report.[16] This was accompanied by the first of two editorials on Beveridge's proposals that would appear in *The Times* in the week before they were published.

In the first, it congratulated Sir William for recognizing that preventing unemployment after the war should be a top priority. It acknowledged with regret that collective memory of the aftermath of the First World War meant that 'the fear of being unemployed is the greatest anxiety of most people today'. Preventing fresh unemployment would require answers to fundamental questions about the appropriate balance between private and public sectors. *The Times* celebrated Sir William's comment to the Fabians that private enterprise was 'not anarchy'. Rather it was 'a system ruled by competition . . . a good ship that has brought us far'. However, an exclusively private system would not deliver fast enough 'the changes that will be needed'. These, *The Times* explained included converting war industries to peacetime production, expanding British exports to pay for imported food and raw materials and maintaining elements of the wartime system that had limited conflict between capital and labour.[17]

The second *Times* editorial appeared under the headline, 'Obligations of Victory'. It predicted that peace would bring urgent demands for 'freedom from want'. Radical measures would be essential. The coalition should resist its instinct to avoid discussion of controversial topics in domestic politics and start to plan now for a new post-war social and economic order. An important lesson must be learned from the failure of 1919: '[T]he powerful impulse towards social progress and administrative reform' must not on this occasion be 'forgotten and dissipated'. If ministers could not now agree the need for post-war reform they would 'discredit and destroy both the coalition and the parties composing it'. *The Times* feared that the removal from the War Cabinet of Labour's radical Sir Stafford Cripps and his replacement by the moderate Herbert Morrison might 'betoken a disinclination on the part of the Government to concern themselves with issues of social policy'. This would be a grave error. Commitments to full employment and social change now would 'infuse fresh enthusiasm into the war effort'. The coalition must have a social policy as well as a military policy.[18]

The Times would be proven right. The Beveridge Report was a wartime sensation. The aloof, irascible Sir William Beveridge became an unlikely popular hero. His marriage to his assistant, the 66-year-old economist Jessy Mair OBE, a graduate of the University of St Andrews with 'a great record of public service' and a 'first-class brain'[19] was widely celebrated. When the full text of *Social Insurance and Allied Services* was published on Tuesday, 1 December 1942, popular newspapers gave it huge publicity. The following morning's edition of the *Daily Mirror* carried the banner headline, 'Banish Want from Cradle to Grave Plan'. The story beneath explained that Sir William described his plan as a revolution under which 'every citizen willing to serve according to his powers has at all times an income sufficient to meet his responsibilities'.[20] Inside, with great design skill, the *Mirror* explained and depicted 'What the Plan Does for Everyone'. A poster-style depiction of the major aspects of the Beveridge Report showed readers, 'How to Be Born, Bred and Buried by Beveridge'. Beside a pair of wedding bells, it explained, 'On marriage there's a lump sum of £10'. A depiction of a pram accompanied description of a 'lump sum of £4' for becoming a mother. The *Mirror* was thrilled by the proposals for health care. Beside a picture of a doctor in surgical whites, it reported that: 'In case of illness, there's medical, dental and hospital treatment to be had by all.' It was equally pleased that provision extended to retirement. At the bottom of the page appeared a picture of an old man smoking a pipe and an old woman knitting. Each was comfortably seated in an armchair. 'And there's a happy old age for Darby and Joan on retirement', explained the *Mirror*. It noted that the retirement age for men would be 65, while women would receive their pension at 60.[21] On page seven, the *Mirror* provided a handy guide 'The Beveridge Plan at a Glance'. This consisted of a grid, detailing the benefits available to a family of man, wife and two children and contrasting the new plan with the meagre support under existing schemes. The improvement in each category was clear and substantial.[22] The *Daily Mirror*'s exhaustive and meticulous coverage was completed by a column by Sir William Beveridge himself. The great man explained that: 'Growing general prosperity and rising wages' meant Britain could afford his plan. Indeed, abolition of want had been 'easily within the economic resources of the community' before the war. The fact that 'want' had not already been abolished was 'a needless scandal'. Beveridge added optimistically that his proposals 'raise no issues of political principle or party'. Indeed, it was now essential that 'a plan for freedom from want' should be 'ready when the war ends'. For that to happen, 'it must be prepared during the war'.[23] Sir William heartily recommended immediate legislation to prepare for implementation.

The *Daily Herald* shared the *Mirror*'s enthusiasm for the Beveridge Report but not its American-inspired flair for page design. It welcomed the report on its front page and rejoiced at the prospect of economic security and health care for all. The *Herald* was also delighted by the promise of a £2 per week minimum income, even if a worker was sick or jobless. However, its news story shared space on the front page with an account of Allied military success against the Luftwaffe in Tunisia.[24] Creativity came on the inside pages and in words not pictures. Reporter Hugh Pilcher devised an imaginary working-class family, the Johnsons, and depicted their post-war life 'in Beveridge Britain'. Social security made a very welcome difference to their finances, but the new health service was the icing on the cake. Pilcher depicted father, Bill Johnson, a skilled worker in a motor factory, leaving work to hurry home by bicycle to look after his pregnant wife, Mary. In fact, Pilcher explained, Bill need not have worried. The new 'state health service' was looking after Mary Johnson and providing all the health care and nutritious food she needed to prepare for her baby's arrival.[25]

That a degree of political consensus might be achievable was evident in the *Daily Mail*'s enthusiasm for Sir William Beveridge and his report. In common with its Labour-supporting rivals, the popular Conservative title rejoiced in his decision to marry Mrs Mair, the widow of his cousin, David Beveridge Mair. Keen as ever on human detail, it noted that Mrs Mair had a married son, two married daughters and a third daughter, Dr Lucy Mair, 'a lecturer at Oxford'.[26] On the eve of the report's publication, the *Mail* reported that Sir William would speak to the nation 'after the news at 9.25 tomorrow night'.[27] This casual reference to 'the news' confirms that by 1942 the BBC's main evening news bulletin, broadcast nightly at 9.00 pm, constituted an unmissable appointment to listen for millions of Britons. On publication, the *Daily Mail* offered comprehensive coverage focusing, as so often, on the advantages afforded to women. It described the Beveridge scheme as 'a plan to insure us all from cradle to grave with shilling benefits for threepenny premiums'. Housewives would have a new status conveyed by 'generous pensions, maternity benefits, widows' benefits and separation pensions'. The cost of this would be borne jointly by citizens, employers and government.[28] The *Mail*'s enthusiasm was confirmed in an extended editorial. Beveridge's proposals would 'create a world sensation – even in a world at war'. Nothing comparable had 'ever been attempted in any country'. The report marked 'a big step forward in the march of human progress'. Beveridge would 'not only assure to the British people that freedom from want that is the third of President Roosevelt's four freedoms', he would also lay the foundations for a better life post-war. There would be debate about specific points, but Beveridge's report was 'one of the most remarkable state documents of our time' and an 'astonishing achievement'. The country must work together to make sure it was affordable.[29] This welcome was accompanied by a detailed guide to how much each reader would be likely to pay and how much they would receive in return with particular focus on benefits for 'wives, widows and spinsters'.[30] The *Daily Mail* carried a drawing by its star cartoonist, Illingworth (Leslie Gilbert Illingworth, 1902–79). He depicted a British soldier raising a foaming jug of beer with 'social security' written on the head. The caption was 'Here's to the brave new world, O rare and refreshing Beveridge'.[31] The welcome was not yet complete. True to its philosophy of understanding news through the lens of personality, the *Daily Mail* also offered a detailed profile of Sir William Beveridge. He was amongst the most 'romantic, whimsical, human men in Britain'. Nobody had made a greater difference to British lives and yet 'no great man has been so little known'. Readers learned that he had invented labour exchanges, devised the first system of unemployment insurance and given Britain old-age pensions.[32]

Intriguingly, amidst the chorus of praise, the *Daily Mail* did not abandon its critical faculties. In a coherent analysis of medical provision under the Beveridge Plan, the newspaper identified a problem that would torment Aneurin Bevan when, as secretary of state for health in the post-war Labour government, he worked to create the NHS. What would happen to doctors if free medical treatment was provided for all? The *Mail* wondered whether private practice would be abolished. If so, would doctors be compensated? Sir William Beveridge's answer was intriguing. He admitted that he did not know. Doctors 'might be paid salaries, they might be paid on a panel system or they might be paid on a mixture of the two'. It was somebody else's job to look into this complex challenge: 'Doctors and medical health services were not ready to deal with the question. I believe it is the next thing to be tackled.'[33]

The Times handed down its verdict in another extended editorial. Since President Roosevelt identified his four freedoms nearly two years earlier, it reflected, the phrase 'freedom from want' had expressed a vague aspiration. Beveridge's work had transformed it into a realistic and 'plainly realizable project'. It deserved national effort and commitment. Sir William Beveridge and his committee had 'put the nation deeply in their debt, not merely for a confident assurance that the poor need not always be with us, but for masterly exposition of the ways and means whereby the fact and the fear of involuntary poverty can be abolished altogether'.[34] *The Times* considered Beveridge's report imaginative and remarkable. Crucially, it reassured its readers that it did not require any departure in principle from 'policies and methods which have characterized British social services during the last half century'. Drawing a line back to the Liberal leader Sir Henry Campbell-Bannerman (1836–1908) and the Liberal government he led between 1905 and 1908, *The Times* greeted Beveridge's proposals as a prescription for a 'British revolution'. The experience of the past and the value of Britain's tested institutions would play their part in implementing these reforms. They would bring order, consistency and efficiency to social services. In many ways, they represented a tidying up of an uncoordinated aspect of British domestic policy. This was not Marxism. It was British good sense which proved 'the power of democracy to answer the imperious needs of a new age'.[35]

The *Manchester Guardian*'s treatment was thoughtful. It welcomed Beveridge's proposals as 'A British Revolution' and agreed that they should be implemented as a comprehensive package.[36] It offered detail of the benefits and services that would be made available.[37] However, the Liberal title also wondered whether Beveridge's critics were simply biding their time. A political correspondent reported from Westminster that the report had received a more flattering reception than any he could remember. Indeed, British newspapers had offered 'nearly a unanimous welcome'.[38] The correspondent found that many Conservative MPs welcomed Beveridge's proposals. He quoted Captain Somerset de Chair (1911–95), the Conservative MP for South West Norfolk and a wounded veteran of recent fighting in Syria. The *Manchester Guardian* portrayed de Chair as 'representative of the progressive young Conservative' wing of his party. This was credible both politically and socially. De Chair had voted against Chamberlain in the Norway debate of 1940. He had served bravely as an intelligence officer in the senior regiment of the Household Cavalry. Now he declared the Beveridge Report 'what we young Conservatives have always demanded: a square deal for the working man within the existing social and economic framework instead of some Utopia on the further side of an economic torrent'.[39] Beveridge's depiction of his proposals as a necessary alternative to Marxism plainly appealed to its target audience. The regional broadsheet also noted that it had made its mark on opinion in the United States. A correspondent reported that the *New York Times* had devoted 4,000 words to coverage of the Beveridge Report. Other American newspapers had published 'long analyses'.[40] In the *New York Herald Tribune*, William Shirer had described it as 'a revolutionary document'.[41] The *Manchester Guardian* was equally pleased to note that listeners in Nazi-occupied Europe would be told all about Britain's progressive ambitions. From dawn on 3 December, the BBC would transmit in twenty-two languages the story of how 'Britain, even in the midst of war is grappling with social problems.'[42] Nonetheless, the *Manchester Guardian*'s antennae were sensitive enough to pick up real opposition too. A spokesman for Manchester's powerful Cotton Spinners' and Manufacturers' Association explained that placing the burden of workmen's compensation on industry was 'quite inequitable'. Beveridge's proposals would create unacceptable costs and price UK exports out of international markets. Sir Edward Mountain, chairman of the Eagle Star Insurance company was equally blunt. Any infringement on the role of private insurance would have very serious consequences.[43]

The Economist had ample time to reflect before it greeted Beveridge with an editorial. It was represented at the press conference in the University of London's Macmillan Hall at which, on the evening of 2 December, Sir William Beveridge, plainly enjoying the attention, offered confident and detailed answers to reporters' questions. Photographers' flashbulbs popped and sparkled as if at a Hollywood first night but, while *The Economist* was impressed, it was not enraptured. Sober, analytical and clear headed, it recognized the remarkable ambition behind a scheme designed to meet 'all the contingencies of life and livelihood'. However, *The Economist* understood what newspapers of left and right had not. This was not really the insurance plan the popular newspapers had depicted. Payments in would not meet the full cost of payments out. Instead, Beveridge had designed 'a tax plan by which specific levies, supplemented from general taxation, will be earmarked for the specific purpose of securing a national minimum income' for all. It would only be sustainable if Britain's economy recovered quickly from war, national income was maintained and mass unemployment prevented. Beveridge's scheme took for granted that there would be post-war 'world cooperation in world economic policies'. *The Economist* warned that Beveridge knew there would have to be 'heavy expenditure from the national exchequer'. It concluded that inflation would 'surely wreck' his plans and worried that his assumption of only 25 per cent price increases between 1938 and 1945 might prove optimistic. It worried too that guaranteed minimum incomes might 'lessen the incentive' to work hard and seek promotion. Had Sir William offered sufficient safeguards against the 'growth of a class of drones' with no ambition to rise above drone status? *The Economist* recognized in Sir William Beveridge a brilliant technocrat, but it suspected that he lacked passion. It contrasted his cool, technical approach with the passionate condemnation of poverty and squalor offered by the novelist Charles Dickens. It believed the true test of the Beveridge Report would be whether it could 'inspire regardless of vested interests a nationwide determination to set right what was so plainly wrong'. *The Economist* recognized that, if social security was really possible, a growing economy would be necessary to achieve it. Now government must make prompt decisions to 'ensure that whatever else the war may bring, social security and economic progress shall march together'.[44]

The Beveridge Report was an instant best-seller. Beyond the detailed coverage in newspapers, His Majesty's Stationery Office sold more than 100,000 copies of the complete report. An abridged version would sell more than half a million copies. Within 24 hours of publication, a random sample of public opinion by Mass Observation found that 88 per cent of those questioned thought the government should adopt Beveridge's proposals.[45] However, official caution was already apparent. Juliet Gardiner explains that the Army Bureau of Current Affairs prepared a pamphlet summarizing the Beveridge proposals for British troops at home and abroad. Printed to coincide with publication, these were hastily withdrawn on the orders of the War Office.[46] Government would not immediately commit to implementation. The Treasury was gravely concerned that the bill for imported fuel, arms and ammunition would bankrupt Britain and appalled by the additional expenditure Beveridge proposed. Beyond the ranks of its progressive, younger members, parts of the Conservative Party opposed the plans for social security on principle. Meanwhile, Sir William Beveridge launched a speaking tour of the country, addressing eager audiences in communities large and small and campaigning for acceptance of his report. He spoke in a Britain in which the state had proven its capacity to respond to crisis by organizing evacuation and rationing. Ministers controlled manufacturing and dictated what farmers should grow. They decided whether a man should serve in the armed forces or mine coal to power factories. The belief was abroad that government not only should but certainly could implement what was now universally referred to as the Beveridge Plan.

Nevertheless, the prime minister's first instinct was to prevaricate. Churchill feared that Beveridge's recommendations might create 'false hopes and airy visions of Utopia and Eldorado'.[47] Labour ministers did not put him under immediate pressure to comply with the popular will. Ernest Bevin was initially concerned that Beveridge might be treading on territory the trade unions were accustomed to regarding as theirs alone. Clement Attlee admired Beveridge's proposals, but he displayed no appetite for confrontation with Conservative colleagues and did not argue vigorously for a commitment to implement them. Herbert Morrison did make the case powerfully in his new role as a full member of the War Cabinet, responding to the question, 'Can we afford to do this?', with a sharp, 'Can we afford not to?'[48] The House of Commons did not debate the proposals in detail until a three-day debate between 16 and 18 February 1943. It opened with MPs beseeching Mr Speaker to select an amendment requiring the government 'to set up forthwith the proposed Ministry of Social Security for the purpose of giving effect to the principles of the Report'.[49] Mr Speaker declined and the debate proceeded on the motion tabled by Arthur Greenwood MP (Labour, Wakefield), deputy leader of the Labour Party. Though not formally a government motion, this was certainly designed to assist the government. It invited the House to welcome Sir William Beveridge's report on *Social Insurance and Allied Services* 'as a comprehensive review of the present provisions in this sphere' and 'a valuable aid in determining the lines on which developments and legislation should be pursued as part of the Government's policy of post-war reconstruction'.[50] Greenwood himself described it as nothing more than 'a peg' on which to hang a debate that had already been rehearsed in countless newspaper articles, readers' letters, political speeches and BBC broadcasts. Older, traditional Conservatives urged the government not to make any premature commitment. They hoped time and intense scrutiny could lessen Beveridge's impact. Anyway, they insisted, it would be impossible and irresponsible to commit to such expenditure before post-war economic conditions were known and Britain's performance assessed. The Labour left was adamant that ministers should adopt Beveridge's prescription immediately and begin preparations to implement it.

John McGovern (1887–1968), the devoutly Socialist Labour MP for Glasgow Shettleston, set the tone in the opening exchanges. McGovern alleged that the government and, to his dismay, senior Labour MPs who were formally members of the opposition were colluding in a plot to prevent implementation. McGovern lamented that such behaviour risked 'upsetting democracy in this country'.[51] The Glasgow MP had been alerted by an article and editorial in the previous weekend's edition of the *Sunday*

Pictorial. Editor Stuart Campbell, a determined social reformer who stood in for Hugh Cudlipp during the latter's war service with the Royal Sussex Regiment, had seized on Arthur Greenwood's parliamentary motion to accuse the Labour Party of colluding to kill the Beveridge Plan. The *Pictorial* did not know whether Greenwood understood the risk or not. It was certain that, if MPs supported his bland text, they would 'slaughter' a plan that served the interests of its readers.[52] The accompanying editorial showed that the *Pictorial*'s determination to speak truth to power was undimmed. It described the Labour leadership as a 'floundering chorus of yes-men' willing to 'sell our children's future in the cause of a sham national unity'.[53] The front-page piece offered additional praise to the small group of Liberal MPs who were determined to oppose Greenwood's meek compromise in the name of full and prompt introduction of real social security.

As the parliamentary debate concluded on Thursday, 18 February, Sir Herbert Williams, the 59-year-old MP for Croydon South, advertised the profound caution of traditional Conservatives. Congratulating the government for refusing to make any firm commitment, he regretted that it had come perilously close. The wise approach was to delay any decision while fighting continued. Until the war was won, ministers could not know what resources would be available, or what costs they would have to meet. The responsible course was to 'refuse to commit ourselves in any shape or form whatever'.[54]

Herbert Morrison, who had been vocal in support of Beveridge, was placed in the invidious position of making the closing speech on behalf of the government. Loyally, he insisted that he and his colleagues took 'a favourable view of the principles of the Beveridge Report'.[55] Morrison also insisted that there would be a comprehensive health service. He described this as 'a very big change to which subject to reservations the Government have committed themselves'.[56] The home secretary concluded by pleading with the House of Commons to solve the problems of want and destitution in a spirit of 'give and take'.[57] He implored MPs not to do anything that might provoke serious political difficulties in the War Cabinet.[58] The Government won by 335 votes to 119, giving it a majority of 216. The revolt in support of a firmer pledge to implement Beveridge's scheme was the biggest of the war. Among those refusing to accept the Government's caution were Arthur Greenwood himself. Labour left-wingers, including Aneurin Bevan, Emmanuel Shinwell and John McGovern, also rebelled. The Liberals were true to their word. Among the Liberal dissenters were David Lloyd George, the former prime minister whose party had begun the creation of a welfare state. His daughter, Megan Lloyd George (1902–66), the Liberal MP for Anglesey, voted alongside her father.

The *Daily Mirror* took the view that Herbert Morrison's adroit defence of the government's position had saved it from greater embarrassment. It believed that as many as 180 MPs might have rebelled had Morrison not spoken as a Socialist and made plain his own admiration for both social security and a national health service. Plainly, the *Mirror* remained cautious of Mr Morrison. Nevertheless, it concluded that the scale of the Labour rebellion meant the crisis was not over.[59] Inside the *Mirror*, columnist Bill Greig explained that the mood of the country had changed. He noted that Sir Kingsley Wood (1881–1943), the Conservative chancellor of the exchequer, had failed utterly to grasp the extent of that change. Sir Kingsley did not recognize the depth of feeling in the country which made the Beveridge Report 'a symbol of a new Britain'.[60] The *Daily Mirror* columnist was right. The government's lack of enthusiasm did precipitate change in public opinion. Conservative support fell, and a new Common Wealth Party emerged to promote the slogan, 'Beveridge in Full Now'. It would eventually win three by-election victories against the Conservatives. The first of these came in Eddisbury, Cheshire, very shortly after the parliamentary debate in April 1943. In March Winston Churchill, who had hitherto stuck resolutely to the insistence that victory was his government's sole war aim, recognized his error. He remained concerned that Britain would end the war too indebted to enact radical social change. Nevertheless, he conceded that the War Cabinet must look 'through the mists of future to the end of the war'. The prime minister promised a plan to care for people's needs from cradle to grave. In November a Ministry of Reconstruction was established to plan for the post-war world.

Newspaper reporting of the Beveridge Plan showcased the freedom wartime newspapers could exercise when liberated from security concerns. In their coverage, conservative titles acknowledged willingly that economic and social reform would be necessary to meet British peoples' needs when the fighting ended. Conservative newspapers insisted that these reforms should not be Marxist in character, but embraced the demand that they should be radical and thorough. On the left and centre, newspapers championed Beveridge's ambitions while challenging directly the caution they identified in senior Labour members of the National Government. Quality right of centre titles offered critical analysis of the costs that would fall on taxpayers. Popular titles of left and right pinpointed the proposals that would bring greatest benefit to their readers. On the right, the *Daily Mail* identified presciently the difficulties the post-war government would encounter in aligning general practitioners with the National Health Service. *The Economist* advertised the distinctive capacity weekly political titles enjoyed to analyse in forensic detail complex problems of implementation. Reporting of the Beveridge Plan was among the most impressive offered by wartime British daily newspaper journalists. Across the spectrum of national titles, creativity was partnered by analytical ambition, social empathy and a sincere desire to mobilize opinion in favour of virtuous ideas. Hesitant politicians were reminded that even supportive titles would hold them to account if they proved unwilling to advance Beveridge's ambitions for a kinder post-war Britain.

The coalition formed when Labour and Liberal politicians joined the government in May 1940 had come into being for the sole purpose of winning the war. It brought with it an outlook from the First World War with which its members were familiar and largely content: party politics and war fighting were not compatible. Normal politics should not resume until victory restored peace. The general election that should have taken place by 1916 was repeatedly postponed and the parliament elected in December 1910 continued to sit until December 1918. When Labour declared its support for war in September 1939, it concluded an electoral truce with the Chamberlain government and the Liberal Party. This stipulated that wartime vacancies in the House of Commons should be filled by a nominee of the party in possession without opposition from the other two. By-elections were contested by pacifist, anti-war and other minority interest candidates but the major parties did not fight each other. Acts of prolongation maintained the parliament elected in November 1935 until July 1945.

In the summer of 1940, amid the threat of German invasion, and the subsequent reality of nightly air raids, and battle in the Atlantic, this consensus held firm and was supported by newspapers. Neither they nor the politicians they scrutinized realized how long the war would last, nor the extent to which it would precipitate mixing of social classes. By 1943, wide-ranging newspaper support for Beveridge's ideals of social security and a national system of health care illustrated awareness of and sympathy for a new approach. Plainly this extended from the centre of the Conservative Party to Labour's hard left and had the Liberal Party's enthusiastic backing. In voicing it and publishing pointed and persistent criticism of politicians who resisted any commitment to implementation, newspapers demonstrated growing confidence in their duty to hold ministers to account. They functioned not as enemies of parliamentary democracy but as the Victorian politicians, who had given them freedom, intended: as a fourth estate determined to keep the other estates honest and accountable.

CHAPTER 11
PECULIAR PROBLEMS: REPORTING THE AMERICANS IN BRITAIN

On 7 December 1941, Japan's surprise attack on the US Navy's Pacific Fleet at Pearl Harbor forced President Roosevelt's hand and removed Congressional opposition to war. Now America had to become a belligerent and Hitler's subsequent declaration of war on the United States ensured that US forces would fight in Europe as well as the Pacific. It was an outcome for which Britons had hoped and prayed, led and encouraged by their prime minister. Winston Churchill set out immediately for Washington DC, and president and prime minister spent Christmas 1941 planning how their alliance would achieve victory. Among the most visible consequences for the British people would be the arrival in Britain of American service personnel. President Roosevelt's initial preference was for an indirect strategy based on strategic bombing of German industry. President and prime minister quickly agreed that US bomber squadrons would launch attacks on Germany from bases in Britain.

The first 4,058 US troops arrived in January 1942 crossing the Atlantic in fast, secret convoys in order to avoid U-boats. The *Daily Express* sent staff reporter Montague Lacey to witness their landing in Belfast. He described 'well trained, well-armed' soldiers whose officers described them as 'all pepped up and roaring to go'.[1] The *Daily Mail*'s special correspondent witnessed 'The Doughboys' arriving 'fighting fit'.[2] On the quayside, hot tea and coffee were waiting for them. The following day, the *Mail* acknowledged that the Americans thought 'the tea was terrible, and we like our coffee about twice as strong'.[3] The *Daily Mirror* previewed their arrival by offering readers a lesson in US Army slang. 'Slum' was the term for army stew, explained John Walters, the *Mirror* correspondent in New York. A 'bomb heaver' was a pretty girl, a complete glamour girl might expect to be referred to as a 'a six and twenty tootsie' and a nurse was 'a ward mama'. But Walters warned that Britons should abandon any delusion they may have picked up from films that Americans always spoke in slang: 'They can speak as well as you do, and they resent any suggestions to the contrary.'[4] When the first Americans arrived, the *Daily Mirror* described the camps of Nissen huts built to house the early arrivals. These, it explained, were 'cities where American food and cigarettes and entertainment will make them feel at home'.[5] By August there were 156,118 American service personnel in the United Kingdom, many of them pilots, crew and ground staff of the US Army Air Corps.[6] David Reynolds explains that Churchill and the Foreign Office hoped that the mixing of GIs and Britons would help to cement 'at the grass-roots level, the "special relationship" that they deemed essential for Britain's future'.[7] The process would not prove straightforward.

From the moment the United States entered the war, American editors were asked to comply with a code of practice that made all news about US forces a matter for army censorship. Sent to the UK in 1941 to study British censorship arrangements, Colonel

Figure 11.1 A US serviceman having tea with the former mayor of Winchester, Mr Edmonds, and his wife and daughter in the garden of their home during 1944.

Homer Case of the US Army proposed a similar arrangement for British newspapers: they should be subject to American military censorship when reporting the activities of US forces in the UK.[8] British objections that American control of the British press would be unacceptable led rapidly to a compromise that often amounted to little more than a fig-leaf. Britain's chief press censor, for whom the glass was invariably half full, explained that his censors had strict instructions to comply with any requests made by their American counterparts unless these were 'entirely contrary to our rules'. When incompatibility was identified, a face-saving compromise was invariably agreed. It usually met American needs. In Rear Admiral Thompson's words, 'Here again, British editors deserve the highest praise for they were often asked to suppress news – such as the details of a disturbance between negro troops and local inhabitants in a public house – which had no security significance whatever.'[9] Censorship would soon provoke tension and restrict debate, but the initial reaction of newspapers and their readers was curiosity.

Beyond a small elite of very wealthy Britons, 17 per cent of whom had travelled across the Atlantic, only about six per cent of His Majesty's subjects had ever visited the United States. A poll conducted in the summer of 1942 indicated that 65 per cent of the population did not 'know any Americans personally'.[10] Many Britons' preconceptions about the new arrivals were shaped by images they had seen in popular Hollywood films – and, of course, glittering images of American men, as depicted by stars such as James Stewart, Cary Grant and Clark Gable, told nothing approaching the whole story. The GIs, whose presence George Orwell would describe as an 'occupation', came from small towns, farms and cities. They included rich and poor, professional soldiers and draftees, the religiously devout and the boisterously irreverent. Many were black conscripts serving in an army that, like the United States but not Britain, was itself racially segregated. Sex, race and segregation would attract the interest of British newspapers, but coverage would be neither easy nor comprehensive.

Discrepancies in style and disposable income were instantly apparent. American soldiers arrived from a land in which rationing of petrol did not begin until December 1942. The food rationing that followed was modest compared with the stringent controls in force in the UK. The separate national experiences of war were not only marked by Britain's harsh experience of German bombing and missile attacks. Britain grew poorer in wartime while America grew wealthier. In the United States, consumer purchases of goods and services increased by twelve per cent between 1939 and 1944. In Britain, they fell by almost twice as much. To their British hosts, bombed, hungry and short of new clothes, ordinary Americans appeared very prosperous. Moreover, GIs were much better paid than their British counterparts. Figures set out by the chancellor of the exchequer, Sir Kingsley Wood, in July 1942 convey the scale of the discrepancy. A newly recruited American private earned a basic monthly wage of $50. All those serving in Britain received a twenty per cent bonus for overseas service giving a total income of $60 per month. A GI was accommodated and fed at his Government's expense, so most of this income was disposable. He could spend $2 per day which translated to ten shillings sterling. His British counterpart had a disposable income of three shillings per day if unmarried or two shillings and sixpence if married.[11]

Captain Alec Cunningham-Reid (1895–1977), the Conservative MP for St Marylebone in London, captured some of the consequences in an adjournment debate in the House of Commons on 10 February 1942. 'The British private often finds himself in a humiliating position when he meets soldiers from other countries', the former First World War flying ace told the House: 'In the part of the world where I live the ordinary British private will not go into a pub if privates from other countries are there.'[12] The GIs also had very smart uniforms which made it hard to distinguish between officers and other ranks. They spoke like the heroes, cowboys and gangsters in the Hollywood movies. On their bases they had access to luxuries such as chocolate, cigarettes and nylon stockings. And, unlike their predecessors who had fought in the First World War, these

Americans were not simply using Britain as a transit camp on their way to a frontline in continental Europe. Britain was the frontline and many of them would be based here for the duration of the war.[13] Approximately three million American soldiers and airmen spent time in the UK between January 1942 and December 1945. Their free-spending ways and relaxed social style made them attractive to British women and resented by British men. Differences between British and American approaches to the administration of justice would compound the problem.

The British tradition was that a soldier, even in wartime, remained liable to prosecution in ordinary courts for breaches of the criminal law. Initially, the wartime coalition insisted that American soldiers accused of criminal offences in the United Kingdom should face British justice. However, in the United States, such procedures were suspended in wartime. Article 74 of the US Articles of War gave American armed forces exclusive jurisdiction over their officers and men. Now, the US government insisted that members of its armed forces in Britain should be subject to US military justice. If a GI was arrested by the British police, he should be handed over to a US court martial, not prosecuted in an English or Scottish court. The British government regarded this as a direct threat to its sovereignty. The Allied Forces Act 1940 allowed visiting friendly forces to operate their own military law for offences committed on base or against fellow servicemen. It insisted that British courts must have jurisdiction when Americans were accused of offences against Britons or British law. Britain was reluctant to concede that America should have extraterritorial jurisdiction over its military personnel. President Roosevelt's administration was equally adamant that American opinion would not tolerate the punishment of American servicemen by foreign courts. Reynolds notes that the salience of the issue was tested early when two American volunteers in the Canadian Army were accused of robbing a British driver at gunpoint. Convicted in an English court, they were sentenced to six months' hard labour. One faced additional corporal punishment by whipping. John Gilbert Winant (1889–1947), US ambassador to the United Kingdom, was furious. He approached Herbert Morrison to insist that American servicemen would be outraged if a comrade were subjected to flogging. The home secretary agreed to prevent the whipping. The ambassador accepted that he should keep his intervention private to avoid alienating opinion at Westminster.[14]

Brisk correspondence between Britain's foreign secretary, Anthony Eden (1897–1977), and Ambassador Winant followed. As an ally, the United States was simply too valuable to alienate. So, despite concern about hostile reaction from press and public, Eden grudgingly agreed that ministers would urgently introduce in Parliament a United States of America (Visiting Forces) Bill. This would reserve to American courts martial sitting in the United Kingdom exclusive jurisdiction over serving American military personnel. *The Times*, *Daily Telegraph* and *Manchester Guardian* recorded evidence of opposition. The *Telegraph* reported that, during the Bill's second reading in the House of Lords, the lord chancellor, Viscount Simon (1873–1954), acknowledged that this was 'a most unusual proposal'. It could only be tolerated in wartime and because the alliance with America was so valuable.[15] The *Manchester Guardian* offered a detailed account of the second reading in the House of Commons. Here MPs objected to the Government's decision to complete parliamentary scrutiny in a single day. Clement Davies MP (Liberal, Montgomery) described it as a hasty fait accompli. Major Lyons (Conservative, Leicester East) said he had heard no argument that justified the measure or the 'haste with which it had been introduced'.[16]

James, Baron Atkin (1867–1944), a retired judge with extensive experience in the King's Bench of the High Court and the Court of Appeal, wrote to *The Times*. He conceded that the United States deserved special treatment but he raised an issue that would encourage newspapers to subject exterritorial jurisdiction to intense scrutiny: the treatment of sexual offences against British women by American soldiers. Atkin sought assurance that 'equal crimes will receive equal punishment in the visiting courts'. In particular, he wished to be assured 'that sexual offences are treated in the same way; that the age of consent does not differ unfavourably to our girls and that indecent assault means the same thing'.[17] In the second week of August, Arthur Goodhart (1891–1978), American-born professor of jurisprudence at the University of Oxford, responded to Baron Atkin's plea. Goodhart explained that, under the American Articles of War that would be applied in court martial trials for rape, the prescribed punishment was 'death or imprisonment for life, while the English penalty is less drastic'. Goodhart expressed confidence that British concerns were caused by misunderstanding and would soon disappear.[18] On the same page, *The Times* reported that the first American court martial on British soil was underway. It was alleged that the accused 'forcibly and feloniously against her will did have carnal knowledge of a girl stated to be sixteen'.[19]

The alleged rapist was Travis P. Hammond of Keltys, Texas, a divorced 25-year-old private in the US Army Air Corps. The *Daily Mirror* reported that Hammond told the court he and another American private had met two girls at the YMCA. After 'various drinks', they went into an air raid shelter. Here, defence counsel Captain Lester Pritchard told the jury of eleven serving officers, 'whatever took place between him and his companion was with her consent'.[20] The *Daily Mail* revealed that the incident had occurred on 17 July 1942, several weeks before Britain granted the United States extraterritorial jurisdiction. Private Hammond had been arrested by a British police officer. British detectives were questioning him in the guard room of his air force base, when Hammond asked for a 'fatherly talk' with his superior officer. Immediately, the police were asked to leave the guard room and the conversation between Travis Hammond and his superior took place in private. The officer concerned was about to tell the court what Private Hammond said, when the presiding law officer ruled that details of the conversation were not admissible 'as Hammond had not been warned'. The *Mail* explained that, under US law, such 'father and son' conversations between a private soldier and his senior officer were considered a right.[21] Both a British Home Office pathologist and a British detective inspector of police gave evidence to the court martial. The detective was pressed by Hammond's defence counsel on whether the police had warned the accused that rape was a capital offence under US law. The police officer replied pointedly that he had not brought the charge. 'As to penalties', he explained 'he is an American soldier, not a British subject'.[22]

The sensitivity of the case, and the care taken to ensure that it appeared fair, emerge clearly from the newspaper coverage. The officers serving on the court martial together with the accused were taken to inspect the air raid shelter where the alleged rape took place. A *Daily Mirror* reporter accompanied them. His account reveals that Private Hammond gazed silently at the floor for a minute, said nothing, then 'swung on his heel and came outside'. A picture portrayed Colonel Martin Towner, president of the court martial, examining the floor of the shelter for evidence. The court heard that, at the time of his arrest, Hammond's face was visibly scratched. He said that, on leaving the shelter, the young woman had slapped him hard. He said she had then helped him to wipe the scratches. The court heard that Hammond told the guards who held him after his arrest that he was 'too drunk to remember what he was doing'. He also said that he feared he would be 'shot at sunrise', but 'guessed he had it coming to him'. The *Mirror* described how the 'girl concerned in the case' sat in a room adjoining the court, 'playing interminable games of patience while her mother hovered in the background'.[23]

The first American court martial to be held in Britain concluded after four days. Private Hammond was found not guilty after a secret ballot conducted in a closed session.[24] Close reading of the testimony published in British newspapers conveys the possibility that the severity of the sentence required under US law persuaded the jury to acquit, despite the evidence. Deployment of the ultimate penalty was not long delayed, however. In December 1942, a US court martial did sentence a soldier to death. Private First Class Sammie Mickles was a 23-year-old black GI from Citronelle, Alabama, convicted of the murder of Jan Ciapciak, a Polish seaman. The crime took place in Glasgow where the court also sat. *The Times* reported the 'first sentence of death by hanging by a United States court martial in the United Kingdom'.[25]

Acts of violence committed by American servicemen against other men were routinely reported in British daily newspapers, but they rarely merited extensive coverage. Allegations that American soldiers had harmed British women secured more editorial space. In May 1943, the *Daily Mirror* drew attention to the trial of US Private Arthur Arseneaux, who accused his British girlfriend of betraying him and assaulted her outside a dance hall in the English midlands. An English Dunkirk veteran, Victor John Chapman went to the young woman's assistance. Arseneaux retaliated by stabbing Chapman twice. Convicted of assault, the American was dishonourably discharged and sentenced to five years' hard labour.[26] In October 1943 the trial by court martial of Private Lee A. Davis of Temple, Texas, attracted extensive coverage in popular newspapers of the left and the right. Davis was accused of the murder of nineteen-year-old Cynthia June Lay, who worked as a hospital cook. He was further accused of the rape at gunpoint of her friend, Muriel Joyce Rosaline Fawden, aged twenty-two, a clerk in the same hospital.

June Lay was found dead on a road at Savernake, Wiltshire. She had two bullet wounds in her head. The *Daily Mail* offered a detailed account of a written statement offered by the accused and read to the court martial on the opening day of his trial. It was essentially a confession. Davis did not deny the offences. He admitted guilt and threw himself on the mercy of the court. In the statement he said he had taken his rifle and gone into town. There he had consumed beer, wine and whisky, which he referred to as 'scotch'. Along with other soldiers, he had added aspirin to some of his beer. After his drinking session, he encountered two young women. Davis testified that: 'I spoke to them and asked where they were going, and they told me. I told them to wait and go over in the forest. They did not and I told them I was going to shoot.' Private Davis said that he pulled the trigger 'two or three times and one girl fell and the other ran. I did not know I had shot her because I was pretty intoxicated.' He said that he then went into the woods with the other girl. At this point his evidence became less precise. He said: 'I know I have committed a crime and should be punished for it, but I did not mean to kill anyone. All I ask of you all is, will you spare my life?' The *Mail* reported that Davis had written to Muriel Fawden while she was in hospital recovering from her ordeal. He pleaded for her forgiveness and asked her to pray for him.[27] Following this initial testimony, the court martial was adjourned for eighteen days to allow Miss Fawden sufficient time to recover to give evidence in person. This she did on 26 October. The newspapers sent reporters to court to hear her.

The Times offered a succinct and decorous account of Muriel Fawden's story. Private Davis told her: 'Either you do what I want you to do or you die. I am going to count to ten.' He started to count and, 'as she did not want to die, she had no option but to give in to him'.[28] The *Daily Mirror* gave ample room for colour and detail. It reported that Miss Fawden 'gave her evidence in a low, educated voice'. She explained that an American soldier had approached her and June Lay and asked where they were going. They replied that they were going to the hospital and proceeded on their way. A few moments later, Muriel Fawden heard a voice behind them say: 'Stand still or I'll shoot.' Where *The Times* had chosen brevity, the *Mirror* judged that its readers would want much more. It described the moment of shock when the young women turned on the road and saw a soldier pointing a rifle at them. He ordered them into the bushes. They told him they could not go because the bushes were strewn with barbed wire. They were trying desperately to stall and to remain in a public area where rescuers might see them. Both of the women faced Private Davis and walked backwards. Then, Muriel Fawden explained, they began to run. She told the court martial: 'I heard shots. I was in front and June behind. I looked around and she was still running. I heard more shots. June screamed and fell over in the road.' The *Daily Mirror* described what followed. Davis ordered Muriel Fawden to go through the barbed wire and take her coat off. He stood over her holding his rifle and told her that, if she did not do as she was told, he would shoot her. Fawden told the court martial that she had no choice but to follow his instructions. The *Mirror* did not describe the assault, but it is plain that Davis raped her. Afterwards, he told her that he would not release her until the morning. Muriel Fawden was frightened for her life. Davis told her he had thirty rounds of ammunition and threatened to shoot her instantly if she tried to escape. She recalled that she could see torches in the woods and realized that a search party was trying to find her. She asked Davis whether he was a Christian and he began to calm down. She walked away, expecting at any moment to be shot in the back. When she could no longer see Private Davis, she began to run and, on seeing torch beams close by, she shouted: 'Help!'[29] Muriel Fawden was rescued. Although she took time to recover from her ordeal, the evidence she gave before the court martial was clear and compelling. She made a powerful impression not only on the newspaper reporters but on the military jury too. Private Lee A. Davis was found guilty of murdering June Lay and assaulting Muriel Fawden. He was sentenced to death by hanging on 26 October 1943.[30]

A confrontation that threatened to embarrass the US Army greatly occurred in a normally quiet Cornish market town on 26 September 1943. The national newspapers were alerted to it by a bald statement issued by General Eisenhower's US headquarters in the first week of October. The *Daily Mail* reported on its front page a 'street gun battle' during which civilians living around a quiet square were 'startled by shouting and the sound of guns'. It explained that American soldiers had left their base armed and come into town 'bent on trouble'. Bullet holes were found in the windows of houses. Senior American officers visited the town the following morning and many photographs were taken of an immobilized jeep at the scene.[31] The *Daily Express* added that two American military policemen had been wounded in the fracas, 'one seriously in the side'.[32] The *Manchester Guardian* described briefly a 'shooting affray with United States Army military policemen' and twenty-one American soldiers arrested.[33] The *Daily Telegraph* said residents living around the 'usually quiet square of a Cornish town' had been startled by 'chattering of guns and the sound of shooting'.[34] When the immediate needs of security censorship had been satisfied, the location would be identified as Launceston. The *Daily Mirror* obeyed the law and called the scene of the fighting 'a quiet Cornish market town', but it commissioned a reporter to obtain details on the streets of Launceston. This allowed the *Mirror* to include significant detail absent from the American press statement. Revolver shots had echoed across the main square shattering windows and forcing civilians to dive for cover. One local witness explained that nothing as exciting has happened in the town since 'the days of the smugglers'. The British police left the scene and allowed men of the American Provost Corps to deal with it.[35] Crucially, the *Mirror* reported that this had been an armed confrontation between black soldiers and white soldiers.

The American authorities were determined to disguise the racial causes of the events in Launceston. Evidence of acute tension between black and white soldiers in America's segregated Army would raise awkward political questions in the United Kingdom. In the United States such fighting had the potential to make front-page news across the country and provoke fury in Congress. Fourteen of the GIs arrested in Launceston were charged with mutiny and shooting with intent to murder two US Army police sergeants and other people in the town square. All of those charged were black soldiers. The court martial convened in the Palace Avenue police court in Paignton, Devon on 15 October 1943. Reporters were allowed to attend and the *Manchester Guardian* was among the titles that provided coverage of the proceedings. The liberal broadsheet reported the testimony of a British police sergeant who had been on duty in Launceston on the night of Sunday, 26 September. He said that he had heard a disagreement in a public house shortly before the shooting during which one GI had asked whether others would 'stick together against the whites'. Two American military policemen testified. Sergeant Neilson explained that, along with comrades, he had found himself surrounded by a crowd of soldiers. He said that they were not ordered to put up their hands but most of the men had done so and he had raised his. Neilson's fellow military policeman, Sergeant R.

Simmonds, appeared on crutches. Simmonds testified that he had taken cover behind a parked jeep but was hit in both legs. He recalled seeing 'about three guns'. A local hotel worker, Mr Tom Gosset, recalled that, after the shooting 'a Negro soldier ran into the hotel with a knife'. Mr Gosset also saw another man with a rifle concealed under his coat.[36] In subsequent coverage, the *Manchester Guardian* added an account of an incident that may have provoked the shooting. It reported that 'eighteen coloured soldiers entered the lounge' of the public house at which they had been drinking in the public bar. They were told that they could not be served 'in that part of the house'. The *Guardian* added that 'the men had been restricted to camp for eight weeks'.[37]

Unsurprisingly, the *Daily Mirror* was also represented in court. It described a group of nine American military policemen in the market square at Launceston surrounded by a crowd of 'coloured American soldiers'. The *Mirror* believed the soldiers responsible for shooting were members of a larger group of black GIs who had been drinking in the pubs of Launceston before agreeing 'between them to stand against white soldiers'. Determined to add the human colour that made its journalism additionally attractive, it described the chaos in Launceston when the shooting started: 'Women started screaming – there were WAAFs [Women's Auxiliary Air Force personnel] and Land Army girls in the square.' Captain F. Scott, a military policeman, testified that he heard 'a volley of firing' and, after a lull, 'a second volley'. Scott said about thirty-five men were involved. Many had fled down one of three exit roads from the square before they could be apprehended.[38] The *Sunday Pictorial* set out the case for the defence. It explained that the accused had been confined to barracks while awaiting the delivery of 'proper walking-out dress'. They had grown frustrated when it did not arrive and so broke out of camp and went to a dance in Launceston. Military police ordered them to leave the dance hall – almost certainly on the segregationist grounds routinely enforced by the US military to prevent black and white soldiers enjoying the same social activities or spaces. An altercation in a pub followed, after which, some of the excluded GIs went back to base, secured a tommy gun and rifles and marched back to the square. There they opened fire on a military jeep.[39] The accused were all serving in the 581st Ordnance Ammunition Company based on former farmland at Pennygillam, a mile south-west of Launceston.[40] Giving evidence to the court martial on behalf of the prosecution, Captain Richard P. Scott of the 115th US Infantry described the base at Pennygillam as 'a coloured camp'.[41] The court martial transcript confirms that this description was used throughout the trial. All fourteen prisoners pleaded not guilty to each of the ten charges against them. As proceedings began, the president of the court martial, Lieutenant Colonel Raymond E. Zickel, addressed the journalists present and issued a demand: 'No reference will be made to the race or colour of the accused or any parties who are witnesses of the proceedings.' Kate Werran explains that one of the British journalists present pointed out immediately that the demand was futile: '"It has already been announced in the newspapers that the accused are coloured", he explained.'[42] Britain's left-wing newspapers would make every effort to identify and draw attention to all evidence of discrimination on the grounds of race.

The *Daily Herald* sent a staff reporter, Murray Edwards, to cover the trial. His account was among the most detailed and revealing. All the court officials, judge, jury and counsel were white and 'colt automatics stuck of out of their belts'.[43] The accused must, certainly, have been acutely aware that they faced dire consequences including death if convicted. Despite the gravity of their plight, each revealed that he had no legal representative of his own. The case for the defence would be made by court-appointed defence counsel in the form of two US Army captains, Defence Counsel John A. Philbin and Assistant Defence Counsel Alvin E. Ottum. They opened proceedings by exercising their right to a 'no cause' challenge against one member of the jury. A Major Dierdoff was thus excused any further involvement. For the *Daily Herald*, Murray Edwards noted that the major 'left smiling, his part over in ten minutes'.[44]

The sentence for mutiny was death by hanging. The accused were on trial for their lives, but their demeanour resonated with bravado and insolent defiance. Edwards described how one of the accused 'unconcernedly read wild western magazines throughout the day.... All of them chewed gum.' As the prosecuting counsel outlined the case against them, the accused 'whispered freely among themselves. Some of them sat with their tunics unbuttoned.'[45] Murray Edwards explained the basis of their defence. All the prisoners denied that they had taken part in the shooting. They said they ran away as soon as it started. The court martial transcript was expertly recorded by a 21-year-old Briton from Torquay, Miss Joyce Packe, one of six British women hired as an official court reporter for the American courts martial.[46] Packe's transcript suggests that the men on trial had objective grounds for optimism. The prosecution case was not convincing. Key witnesses failed to identify any of the fourteen accused as individuals they had seen in Launceston Square when shots were fired. They could do no more than confirm that all of those who had fired shots were black soldiers and that all the men in the dock were also black. Defence counsel exposed evidence that signed confessions had been written in formal legal language that the accused would not have used spontaneously. At least one confession was deemed to have been read and understood by an illiterate. That shots had been fired was beyond doubt. Precisely who had fired them was not clear.

The *Daily Mirror* offered a flavour of the mood in court as the jury of nine white US Army officers considered their verdicts. It was a time-consuming exercise, and the GIs did their best to feign insouciance. They 'sat back and lit cigarettes'. Some borrowed newspapers from the journalists covering their trial. One soldier passed around pictures of his girlfriend. The *Mirror*'s reporter noted that 'wagers were made on what the verdicts would be'.[47] Readers were denied the answer. After nine hours of deliberation and with the press seats full of reporters determined to relay the verdicts to readers in Britain and the United States, the court president, Lieutenant Colonel Zickel, declared that the court had directed 'that the findings and sentence be not announced'.[48] Conservative British newspapers would report that the jury chose not to announce their findings.[49] This bland formulation was designed to hide a more complex and sensitive truth. The racial divisions and sharp injustices revealed in Launceston and confirmed at the court martial were too sensitive for government and their censors on both sides of the Atlantic. Now, the distinction between security censorship and policy censorship was breached and the partial freedom under which British newspapers were obliged to operate achieved suppression of any further detail about an inconvenient and embarrassing story. Even the accused left court without knowing their fate. For the *Daily Herald*, Murray Edwards reported that 'Only the Deputy Judge Advocate' knew what the verdicts were and 'until he himself confirms the findings none of the men will know'. Edwards described the defendants whispering 'excitedly among themselves as they were ushered back by armed police into the covered lorry that brought them to court'.[50] After three days of court drama, much of it recorded in British newspapers despite the court martial's efforts to suppress evidence of racial tension, the men accused of mutiny filed out of court under armed guard. A band played in the street as they were loaded into the waiting US Army truck. A photograph at the bottom of the *Daily Herald*'s front page captured all fourteen defendants walking towards it.[51] Several Britons who witnessed the proceedings assumed that the defendants had been sentenced to death and taken away to be hanged behind prison walls. Shepton Mallet Prison in Somerset, commandeered by the US Army, was used for hangings and seventy American military personnel were executed in the European Theatre of Operations (ETO) during the Second World War. This, however, was not the fate of those found guilty of mutiny at Launceston. All fourteen were convicted. Eleven were sentenced to fifteen years of hard labour. Three soldiers considered by the court martial to be the ringleaders were each sentenced to twenty years of gruelling hard labour. These were Sergeants Henry Austin and Rupert Hughes and Private Clifford Barrett.[52] Extraterritorial jurisdiction combined with an unmodernised nineteenth-century code of military justice achieved both secrecy and harshness. The *Daily Mirror*, *Daily Herald* and *Manchester Guardian* tried to expose the issues at stake including the racial segregation and injustice that polluted the American armed forces. They did not, however, focus with any acuity on the origins or causes of these challenges. Nor did they make any systematic argument against racism or segregation. Their reporting was curtailed by censorship and official silence.

The trial in May 1944 of a black American soldier for the alleged rape of a woman in Combe Down on the outskirts of Bath would inspire the *Daily Mirror* to a more determined effort to secure justice. The case involved the wife of a lorry driver who claimed she had been raped at knifepoint by Corporal Leroy Henry of St Louis, Missouri. Henry was a thirty-year-old truck driver based in England pending the invasion of France. At about midnight on 5 May 1944 he knocked on the bedroom window of Mrs Irene Maude Lilley. In her account to the police, Mrs Lilley claimed that Henry said he was lost. He asked whether she or her husband could help him to find the way back to his base. Irene Lilley agreed to help and went down the road with Henry ostensibly to show him the way to the station. When she did not return immediately, Mr Lilley left the house to search for her. He found her beside the road in a ditch. She claimed Henry had raped her. He was detained when the police car taking her to hospital passed him on the road and Mrs Lilley identified him as her assailant.[53] David Reynolds explains that Leroy Henry was tried and found guilty at a general court martial convened at Knook Camp in Wiltshire on 25 May.

In December 1943, General Jacob Devers, the clever, eloquent and ambitious military bureaucrat then commanding American forces in the ETO, had made an important change to court martial procedure. Henceforth, at any prosecution of a black GI one member of the court must be a black officer. At Leroy Henry's trial, a black first lieutenant joined the twelve-man court. The other eleven members were white, with only one exception all were senior in rank to the black officer. Colonel Devers' innovation did Leroy Henry no good. His signed confession admitting rape at knifepoint was placed before the court and all twelve jurors found him guilty. He was sentenced to be hanged by the neck until dead.[54]

Evidence that the conviction was less than secure appeared in the *Daily Mirror* on 30 May 1944. In an incomplete but detailed report of proceedings at the court martial, the *Mirror* revealed that Leroy Henry had only signed the confession after he had been without food for twenty-four hours. Two American military police investigators 'admitted they had made him stand to attention for forty-five minutes during questioning'. A police surgeon testified that Mrs Lilley bore 'no visible signs of a woman who had offered physical resistance'. Henry told the court he had paid Mrs Lilley for sex on two previous occasions. He said: 'I made a date with her and she told me where I had to knock.'[55] David Reynolds completes the detail. The GI said he had first met Mrs Lilley at a pub on 27 April. On that occasion they had sex in a field and he paid her £1. On 3 May they met again and again Leroy Henry paid Irene Lilley £1 for sex. They met at the pub again on 5 May and she told him to knock on her window later. He did and she went with him to the field where they again had sex. This time, however, Irene Lilley demanded that he give her £2. He refused and she threatened to cause him trouble.[56] The *Daily Mirror* reported that Leroy Henry's defence counsel described Lilley's evidence as 'hard to credit'. His client had no previous convictions and Henry's comrades offered evidence that the accused did not own a knife and they had never seen him carrying one. At the *Mirror*'s headquarters in London's Holborn Circus, editor Cecil Thomas and his chief leader writer, Richard Jennings, now had the bit between their teeth. On 2 June the *Mirror* published a thoughtful, balanced, intriguing editorial entitled 'Clemency'. This revealed that the newspaper had received 'a large number of letters' expressing unease about the death sentence against a 'coloured American soldier' convicted of rape. Leroy Henry was not identified by name, but the *Mirror* insisted that its readers did not approve of this man 'having to pay the extreme penalty'. The *Mirror* reflected judiciously, but not entirely accurately, that extraterritorial justice had worked very well so far. American military discipline had been maintained. American courts martial were demonstrating their 'determination to protect our womenfolk'. However, while the verdict was unanimous and the *Mirror* claimed not to question it, there were 'certain points in it which would have inspired an element of reasonable doubt in the minds of a British jury'. Given that the offence was against a British woman on British sovereign territory, the leader writer believed 'popular sentiment would be much appeased', if, on this occasion, justice could be tempered with mercy. In conclusion, the *Daily Mirror* raised the racial issue. In the United States, 'which has a colour problem peculiar to herself, clemency might not be possible'. In the United Kingdom, it ventured to hope, 'it may not be impossible as an act of grace to take a different view'.

The *Mirror*'s intensely cautious balance of praise and special pleading reflects in part the bruising legacy of its recent confrontations with Winston Churchill and Herbert

Morrison. However, this was not simply a whipped dog returning to slink around its master's ankles in the hope of modest reward. The editorial reflects the acute sensitivities created by the American presence in the United Kingdom. Essential to victory and simultaneously a forewarning of Britain's diminished status, the power and prosperity of the United States was now a colossal physical presence. The confidence that underpinned the Hollywood glamour was vivid. So, too, was the acute racial fissure in American society, a division that, in 1944, the British Empire had still kept largely remote from home shores. But, if the *Daily Mirror* was walking on eggshells, its approach was nevertheless highly successful. Its coverage provoked angry protests. On the day the *Mirror*'s editorial was published, two hundred citizens of Combe Down submitted a petition. It reflected their view that Mrs Lilley was an unreliable witness with a record of promiscuity and a particular fondness for black GIs. Six days later, General Eisenhower, now commander of US forces in the ETO, received a second petition signed by the mayor of Bath and more than thirty thousand local residents.[57]

The controversy soon crossed the Atlantic. On 7 June, Thurgood Marshall, founding head of the National Association for the Advancement of Coloured People (NAACP) Legal Defense and Educational Fund, asked General Eisenhower for a stay of execution. On 9 June, *Tribune* advanced the campaign for justice by publishing lengthy extracts of the court martial transcript. These included Leroy Henry's claim that he had been forced to confess and Mrs Lilley's implausible explanation of her decision to join him on the street outside her home. In the United States, the mass-circulation *Time* magazine brought the case to the attention of its readers by publishing a summary of the *Daily Mirror*'s account. Now the legal process moved swiftly to avert a diplomatic embarrassment. The assistant staff judge advocate for the ETO was Captain Frederick J. Bertolet. His review of the court martial proceedings and the guilty verdict concluded that Leroy Henry's confession had not been voluntary. Indeed, Bertolet advised that the convict had been held without food and that he was 'an ignorant soldier' with minimal formal education. He was not persuaded that Henry had understood what he was signing. Nor did he believe that Henry understood the seriousness of the crime of which he was accused, or the penalties permitted under American military law. The assistant staff judge advocate was luminously unconvinced by Mrs Lilley's 'remarkable conduct' in leaving her home with the visiting GI at midnight. For Bertolet, this decision 'cast doubt on her credibility'.[58]

General Eisenhower did not wait to receive Bertolet's opinion before commuting the death sentence. The *Daily Mirror* was able to report on 16 June the General's response, following his receipt of a petition containing 32,000 signatures from the London office of the League of Coloured Peoples. Eisenhower replied immediately that the American authorities would never approve the death penalty unless there were 'circumstances of the most aggravated nature'. In this case, he had been advised that there might be 'many mitigating factors'. He was confident that a formal review of the case would certainly 'result in the amelioration of the sentence'.[59] His decision was widely reported in the British press. *The Times* offered an account that reflected its willingness to respect without demur American sensitivity on the issue of race. It carried the press statement issued by General Eisenhower's HQ. The General had disapproved the finding of guilty.[60] Lord Beaverbrook's *Daily Express* was a little more expansive. It summarized the case and Eisenhower's decision to overturn the verdict. Scrupulously neutral in tone, the *Express*'s version did include necessary explanation: it added the detail that, though Leroy Henry had signed a confession, he had not been aware of what he was signing.[61] The *Manchester Guardian* explained that General Eisenhower had 'disapproved the finding of guilty in the sentence of death imposed on Technician Fifth Grade Leroy Henry (30) by a court martial on May 25, 1944, because of insufficient evidence'. It added that a petition for reprieve was signed by '33,000 people in the Bath area'.[62] The initial account in *The Times* conveyed the impression that Leroy Henry had been spared the death penalty but that a reconvened court martial would impose an alternative sentence. It subsequently reported that he had been 'returned to duty'.[63] The *Daily Mirror* offered the important additional detail that American military justice had concluded that there was 'insufficient evidence to support the conviction or to warrant a retrial'.[64] Leroy Henry was free and could return to duty. His comrades were already fighting in the Normandy bocage.

Having meekly conceded extraterritorial jurisdiction after only token resistance, the British government was also anxious that newspapers should do nothing to offend the Americans. Formally, the Visiting Forces Act allowed the press to report the trials of GIs in Britain. However, George Orwell put it well when he wrote in *Tribune* in December 1943 that it was apparently Britain's 'fixed policy . . . not to criticise our allies' and lamented that the newspapers 'barely reported' the concession of extraterritorial jurisdiction. He was certainly right that they 'refrained from commenting on it'. He warned that Britain's 'official soft-soaping policy does us no good in America, while in this country it allows dangerous resentments to fester just below the surface'.[65] On the issue of race, American commanders wanted to stray beyond security censorship and achieve policy censorship. Admiral Thompson's bland bromides about 'a disturbance between negro troops and local inhabitants in a public house' glossed over the more serious issues that arose from segregation and the resentment it fostered among black GIs. That American objectives were usually achieved via self-censorship did not reduce the pressure brought to bear. Newspapers of the right and centre chose not to examine the issues of segregation and discrimination. Those on the left were hampered in their ability to do so by the Americans' careful restriction of access to information. Reynolds explains that, in October 1942, American officers in the ETO expressed concern about the 'growing number of racial incidents in which British civilians were taking the side of the black GIs'.[66] Indeed, as George Orwell also noted in his 3 December 1943 'As I Please' column for *Tribune*, 'The general consensus of opinion seems to be that the only American soldiers with decent manners are the Negroes.' It went beyond manners. Britons, particularly those at the lower end of the social scale, did welcome the presence of black GIs and condemn intolerance and discrimination against them. However, a distinction was drawn between 'civil rights and sexual wrongs'. David Reynolds notes that an overview of Home Intelligence reports for August to December 1942 found that Britons were 'characteristically against discrimination, though association between [black] troops and British girls' met with disapproval.[67] Mary Louise Roberts argues that such prejudices 'led to the prosecution of Leroy Henry for a crime he most likely did not commit'.[68] In this context, the *Daily Mirror*'s defence of Henry was brave and principled. It compelled the US Army to reconsider Henry's conviction through the prism of evidence rather than blind prejudice. It also infuriated Colonel Jock Lawrence, public relations officer for the ETO. He complained that the '*Daily Mirror* and certain other newspapers of that nature, constantly make us look as if we are some uncivilized nation, having come here to invade them, rape their women etc.' Like Herbert Morrison before him, Lawrence believed such newspapers 'do more harm than Goebles [sic] himself'. The American military police wanted British newspapers to 'accept censorship in rape cases'.[69] This request was denied but in November 1944 the ETO decreed that crime statistics shared with British officials should make no distinction between white and black soldiers in case such details reached Parliament or the dreaded press.

It is beyond irony that the USA, so proud to proclaim its first amendment rights, applied pressure to suppress reporting that might embarrass its government and armed forces. Equally depressing is that the British government, which was equally proud to fight in the name of democracy, willingly imposed its allies' censorious instincts. British newspapers were determined to report sex offence by US servicemen because they knew that their readers would consume such journalism with relish. However, the left and liberal newspapers went beyond prurience to emphasize the consequences of racial discrimination in American military justice. In pursuing stories of racial injustice in American court martials, the *Daily Mirror* and *Daily Herald* took particular risks to investigate and publicize complex controversies in the public interest. In this work they were ably assisted by *Tribune*. The distinctive role of such weekly political titles was also apparent in *The Economist's* response to the Beveridge Plan. Such weekly journalism would play an important part when controversy arose over the RAF's bombing of German cities.

CHAPTER 12
'BOMB BACK AND BOMB HARD': ALLIED BOMBING OF GERMANY

In Britain, enthusiasm for the bombing of German cities emerged first in response to the Blitz. Attacks by the Luftwaffe on London and provincial cities such as Coventry, Clydebank and Southampton inspired popular belief that, if Britain was 'taking it', then Germany should take it at least as hard, if not harder. As we have seen (Chapter 7), the *Daily Mail* called for retaliatory raids in the final week of September 1940 and understood that cities might be treated as 'military objectives'. Initially, many newspaper readers hoped that RAF raids would inflict on German civilians enough misery and disruption to persuade their government to cease attacks on British towns and cities. Britons took pride in the belief that they were fighting a just war, but Brett Holman shows that they were 'ultimately willing to accept the need to wage total war'. He adds that the bombing of civilian populations in Germany 'was not merely acquiesced to by British civilians: it was desired and demanded'.[1]

'Moonlight Sonata', as the Luftwaffe codenamed its devastating attack on Coventry in November 1940, helped to cement that view. It provoked shrill demands for retaliation. Mark Connelly demonstrates that newspapers' demands for reprisals intensified in the spring of 1941 as German bombing of Britain became less intense.[2] A *Daily Telegraph* editorial in March celebrated Winston Churchill's assurance that in 1941 the RAF would 'turn the scale of bombing, weight for weight, in our favour'.[3] The *Telegraph* rejoiced that command of the air would give Britain 'fire to scourge the foe, steel to smite and death to drive him down an unreturning way'. The words are from Swinburne's poem, 'An Autumn Vision'.[4] When the RAF attacked Berlin in September 1941, the *Daily Mirror* expressed its approval in a less poetic voice. It was overjoyed that the German capital had taken 'its biggest bashing of the war' and gleeful that its people 'promptly began to squeal'. It was amused to hear Goebbels deploying what it termed 'sob stuff about poor little Germany being cruelly bombed by the big, bad RAF'. However, always aware of its readership among servicemen and their families, the *Mirror* also noted soberly that twenty bombers had failed to make the 600-mile journey home from Berlin.[5]

The *Daily Mail* was equally pleased about the Berlin raid, and it was not content to rely on official British briefings alone. It brought its readers eyewitness testimony from the German capital written by a neutral American correspondent. The front page proudly promoted a special '*Mail despatch*', dateline 'Berlin, Monday (via New York)'. This described how Berliners had gone to work 'shaken, subdued and weary' after the 'most terrifying RAF raid since the war began'. Interviews with Berliners revealed that they 'shook with fright'. Hitler's capital had been 'rocked by explosions' that caused great fires and 'a hellish chorus' of retaliatory anti-aircraft fire. The *Mail* noted that German radio had launched a campaign to boost morale. One broadcast explained that soldiers fighting for the fatherland on the

Eastern Front 'must know that their families at home are not breaking under the strain'.[6] The *Daily Express* also made use of testimony available in neutral countries. Following raids on Cologne in July 1941, its reporter, Henry Buckley, filed a colourful account from Lisbon. Buckley reported that Germany's cities were producing accounts of 'war factories being hit, well-known buildings, shopping and business centres being smashed'. He revealed that a chalked message on the base of an equestrian statue of Kaiser Wilhelm II, had called for the last German emperor to return and 'deliver the German people' from Hitler. Hundreds of people had seen it before the police could wash it off. The *Express* gleefully described its correspondent's account as 'the news you have been wanting to read – how the face of Germany is showing the scars of the daily increasing blows with which the RAF is repaying the punishment Britain's cities so resolutely withstood'.[7]

Intriguingly, Lord Beaverbrook himself was unconvinced that British bombing could defeat Germany. His biographer recounts that Beaverbrook 'believed in a defensive strategy' until the United States could be drawn into the war. Beaverbrook was not persuaded that strategic bombing could win the war and, as minister for aircraft production, he prioritized the RAF's need for fast fighters.[8] Later, in February 1942, he insisted that any achievements of Britain's growing bomber force were 'in no way commensurate with its potentialities' or 'with the man-hours and materials expended on its expansion, nor with the losses it has sustained'. Beaverbrook concluded that bombing Germany would 'yield no decisive results within any measurable period of time' and should 'no longer be regarded as of primary importance'.[9] This was his lordship's personal opinion, but as proprietor of the *Daily Express* he had too acute a sense of his readers' priorities to put his flagship newspaper at odds with their enthusiasm for the RAF's campaign. Beaverbrook's stance is instructive. A newspaper baron depends on the support of his readers. If they are offended by the tone or content of his title, they may stop buying it. Any notion that proprietors dictate public taste must be understood within this context. They may decide what readers read about. Their influence over what those readers think is less certain. For all his bombast, Beaverbrook grasped this. To leverage the power of mass circulation in his political life, he had to maintain that circulation. This denied him the option of confronting popular opinion on the issue of bombing Germany.

Others did question the purpose and morality of area bombing and such criticism was never entirely extinguished. It emerged in the letters' pages of national newspapers and made a first high-profile appearance in April 1941. Then, the Australian-born, British classical scholar, Gilbert Murray (1856–1957) and his Irish friend, the playwright, George Bernard Shaw (1856-1950) wrote to *The Times* to demand an end to the bombing of cities. Murray and Shaw were provoked by a British threat to bomb Rome but their suggestion went beyond the protection of one city. They proposed a negotiated deal with Germany to end all raids on cities. Such attacks could not achieve militarily valuable results. They were simply killing British and German civilians.[10] Though naive, Murray and Shaw came close to pinpointing the reality that bombing was woefully random and imprecise. Connelly notes that the film, *Target for Tonight*, produced by the Crown Film Unit and directed by the Scottish documentary maker Harry Watt (1906–87), offered a compelling rebuke to such criticism. Watt's film was commissioned to convince viewers that raids were meticulously planned with targets chosen following diligent intelligence gathering and photographic reconnaissance. Its message reiterated the contents of an Air Ministry memorandum that explained 'everything is done according to a long term and carefully prepared plan. The one word that can never be applied to British bombing is haphazard. Every bomb has its mark worked out for it perhaps weeks in advance.'[11] The carefully constructed crew of 'F for Freddie', a Vickers Wellington bomber, were the stars. Cast to represent the class and national diversity of Bomber Command, this contained three English airmen, a Scot, a Canadian and an Australian. They fly a mission to bomb an oil storage facility in the Freiburg region of Germany. Their first four bombs fall short, but the final one hits the target, and it is set ablaze. The radio operator is wounded in the leg and one of the Wellington's engines is hit by flak. Squadron Leader Dixon, played by a real RAF officer, brings the plane home safely despite the damage and a fog-blanketed airfield.

Connelly demonstrates that, far from being an accurate depiction of an RAF raid on Germany, *Target for Tonight* was 'more like wish fulfilment'. It depicted British airmen achieving what they dearly wanted to achieve, not what they were actually capable of.[12] This was expert propaganda masquerading as documentary, but press reaction was rapturous. *The Times* acknowledged that this was the war depicted as Britons would wish to see it depicted. Nevertheless, it was a powerful corrective to any impression that raids were haphazard affairs. The RAF did not set off 'with vague orders to bomb Germany'. Every aspect of a raid was planned in advance. The reviewer concluded that *Target for Tonight* was 'a record set down in something more than cinematic shorthand, and an inspiring record'.[13] Inspiring was about as cautious as the coverage got. For the *Daily Mail*'s Seton Margrave this was 'the best air war film I have ever seen'. For security reasons, a few details had been changed but 'what is shown is the real thing and the result is incomparably the greatest picture ever made of the war in the air'. All who saw it would be filled with pride and gratitude for the RAF.[14] The *Daily Telegraph*'s film correspondent adored it too and did not doubt that it was authentic. The cameraman had repeatedly risked his life over Germany and 'It is proof of the power of truth that the result is more exciting than the most lavish spectacle from a studio.'[15] Reginald Whitley, film critic of the *Daily Mirror*, was similarly enchanted. *Target for Tonight* was 'A big thrill for picturegoers' and 'a wonderful piece of work' that depicted a real RAF raid from start to finish.[16] Bomber Command reinforced its impact with a polished and highly professional official history of the campaign, *The Air Ministry Account of Bomber Command's Offensive Against the Axis, September 1939 – July 1941*.[17] This made a few timely and judicious concessions to plausible criticisms. Early accuracy had left something to be desired. Although raids always had important military or economic targets, larger areas were subjected to bombardment. This – and the repeated insistence that German civilians were not deliberately targeted – was published at a time when nothing approaching accuracy was realistically achievable.

In fact, precision was almost unachievable and the big lie about American and British bombing of Germany between 1942 and 1945 was that it was directed primarily at military targets. The areas bombed were almost always city centres or suburbs densely populated by civilians. These target zones may or may not contain industry. By the end of the war in Europe, the RAF had smashed Germany's railways and destroyed many factories, but it had not destroyed Germany's capacity to make weapons. It had also killed more than half a million German non-combatants and wrecked 3.37 million houses.[18] For Bomber Command, this was deliberate but officially unstated policy. Air Chief Marshal Sir Arthur 'Bomber' Harris knew that true precision bombing was beyond the competence of his heavy bombers and their brave, vulnerable crews. His strategy of area bombing saw Bomber Command launch huge 1,000-bomber raids against cities including Cologne, Essen, Bremen and Hamburg.

Hamburg

The biggest of the early raids attacked Germany's second city, the northern shipbuilding port of Hamburg on the River Elbe. In July 1943, the growing combined might of the United States Army Air Force (USAAF) and RAF was turned against Hamburg. Round-the-clock bombing achieved apocalyptic consequences. Firestorm turned the city into a furnace. Temperatures exceeded 800 degrees centigrade. Masonry, heated as if in a brick kiln, glowed dull red. Metal bent. Wood, fabric and flesh burned. Fire crews were completely overwhelmed. The attack was codenamed Operation Gomorrah, after the biblical city destroyed by God's wrath in the form of fire and brimstone. Newspapers, briefed by the dynamic, efficient and publicity-hungry Air Ministry, enthused about the devastation and barely deviated from the official line. A *Daily Telegraph* editorial welcomed a punishing Allied air offensive against Germany that had been promised and was now being delivered with 'paralysing effect'. It was greatly impressed that 5,000 tons of bombs had been dropped on Hamburg's 'docks, stores and factories'. It reminded its readers that Hamburg shipyards were responsible for U-boat construction. The *Telegraph* did not mention civilian casualties but it noted that 'symptoms of local paralysis' had appeared. Bombing would continue relentlessly and it would 'destroy the will and the power to fight'.[19] *The Times* also penned a leader which appeared two days further into the series of raids against Hamburg. By this stage, more than 7,000 tons of bombs had fallen on the city. *Times* readers learned that Allied bombing had now reached an unprecedented peak of intensity. Hamburg, one of Germany's 'principal shipbuilding centres' was facing a campaign designed to achieve 'the destruction of the industrial equipment and communications of the Reich'. The leader writer acknowledged that bombing alone could not defeat Germany. However, he stuck firm to the Air Ministry line that there could be 'no doubt of the contribution strategic bombing has made' to the combined assaults by Russia, Britain and America.[20]

Massacre by Bombing?

Popular opinion remained supportive of the raids, despite casualties among RAF crews that would see 55,573 airmen killed.[21] However, on the fringes of public opinion, a sustained campaign against Bomber Command's approach was led from May 1942 by the Bombing Restriction Committee, initially launched in August 1941 as the Committee for the Abolition of Night Bombing.[22] Leading members included the Labour MP for Ipswich, Richard Stokes (1897–1957), George Bell (1883–1958), bishop of Chichester, Corder Catchpool (1883–1952), a Quaker, First World War conscientious objector and member of the Peace Pledge Union, and Vera Brittain (1893–1970), an eloquent feminist and pacifist who had served as a Voluntary Aid Detachment nurse during the First World War. In early 1944, Brittain published for the committee, *Seed of Chaos*,[23] a pungent denunciation of Allied bombing policy. Reprinted in the United States as *Massacre by Bombing*,[24] her powerful polemic offered eyewitness accounts of the consequences of RAF raids extracted from neutral Swiss and Swedish newspaper reports and from German sources. An extract from the Stockholm newspaper, *Aftonbladet*, quoted a Danish consular official who had survived the Hamburg raids. He said: 'Hamburg has ceased to exist. I can only tell you what I saw with my own eyes – district after district razed to the ground. When you drive through Hamburg you drive through corpses. They are all over the streets and even in the treetops.'[25] Brittain quoted extensively from an account of firestorm in Hamburg written by the editor of *Baseler Nachrichten* (*Basel News*). He described tens of thousands of German civilians in bomb shelters 'suffocated, charred and reduced to ashes'.[26] Contemplating British newspaper reports of an RAF raid on Remscheid on the night of 30–31 July 1943, Brittain conjured her own vision of 'frantic children pinned beneath the burning wreckage, screaming to their trapped mothers for help as the uncontrollable fires come nearer.'[27] Another account, from the Swiss, *St Gallen Tagblatt*, described the aftermath of devastating raids on Berlin: 'It was nerve shattering to see women, demented after the raids, crying continuously for their lost children, or wandering speechless through the streets with dead babies in their arms.'[28] Brittain concluded that area bombing invited vicious reprisal attacks and caused 'moral deterioration which displays itself in a loss of sensitivity and callous indifference to suffering'.[29]

Vera Brittain's stance attracted some support and respect from the *Manchester Guardian* which afforded space on its letters page to members of the Bombing Restriction Committee.[30] The socialist weekly *New Statesman and Nation* had made a principled case against bombing civilians as early as 1941. It argued that the effect of German bombing of Britain had 'unquestionably been to unite the British people in a far tougher determination to resist' and concluded that 'civilian bombing is a waste of pilots and bombs'.[31] By 1944, the *New Statesman and Nation* was less certain in its criticism. It recognized that 'the magnitude and efficacy' of the RAF's work was impressive but insisted that the legitimacy of area bombing could only be confirmed if 'the war can be as good as won by bombardment from the air'.[32]

In *Tribune*, the weekly newspaper founded in 1937 by two Socialist Labour MPs, literary editor George Orwell condemned Brittain. Her talk of limiting or humanizing war was 'sheer humbug'. Orwell asked why it was 'worse to kill civilians than soldiers?' Reminding *Tribune*'s readers that the fascist states had started the war, Orwell advised that: 'It is probably somewhat better to kill a cross section of the population than to kill only the young men.' Those who opposed the killing of German women were guilty of 'sheer sentimentality'. He thought child casualties were probably exaggerated. The combined circulation was insignificant but these titles were read by opinion formers. Indeed, their status as intelligent titles for thoughtful people made weekly political magazines valuable. Left free to publish and debate dissenting ideas, they helped to burnish Britain's democratic credentials in wartime. *Tribune*'s letters pages suggest that many readers found Orwell's stance perverse, but it may have been more damaging than Vera Brittain's overt hostility to bombing. Orwell advertised the plain truth that ministers were determined to conceal. The RAF was not killing civilians by accident: this was policy.[33]

Deliberate Terror Bombing?

Arthur Harris never wavered in his commitment to the campaign of destruction, but he recognized quickly that claiming precision strikes against military targets while bombing cities indiscriminately risked moral jeopardy. Accordingly, he pleaded with the prime minister and his air minister, Sir Archibald Sinclair, to acknowledge plainly that these attacks involved the deliberate murder of civilians. In October 1943, Harris wrote to Sinclair imploring that the tactics used by British and American bombers be 'unambiguously and publicly stated. That aim is the destruction of German cities, the killing of German workers and the disruption of civilised community life throughout Germany.' Harris asked, in particular, that the air minister tell the British public that the killing of German civilians by RAF Lancaster bombers was not a 'by-product of attempts to hit factories'. Rather, it was among 'the accepted and intended aims of our bombing policy'.[34] Arthur Harris had developed his policy of area bombing specifically to kill and de-house German workers. He chose to identify any enemy civilian engaged in economic activity as a contributor to the Nazi war effort. Harris understood this meant the deliberate and systematic killing of women, children and old men. Ministers knew it too, but they were determined to disguise the brutal truth. They used a series of euphemisms to describe area bombing raids. These included 'blanketing an industrial district', 'neutralising the target' and 'softening up the area'.[35] The British government was acutely anxious about this aspect of Bomber Command policy. Ministers worried that it offered the Germans a propaganda tool that might allow them to attack Britain's moral credibility.[36] The additional problem was that candour risked provoking serious disagreement with Britain's American allies.

The USAAF policy of bombing in daylight, while British raiders bombed at night, produced casualty rates among air crew even more devastating than those endured by the RAF. Nevertheless, the Americans maintained the fiction that their approach allowed them to conduct precision bombing. In all their public comments, commanders of the US Strategic Air Forces in Europe insisted that American bomber crews were aiming at military targets and hitting them. This was untrue. US Eighth Air Force crews attacking Germany during the winter of 1944–45 dropped 42 per cent of their bombs more than five miles off-target. The average circular error for those that fell within the five-mile radius was 2.48 miles.[37] Still, the US public was led to believe that no American boys were engaged in the murder of German civilians. To admit that the RAF was killing them in great numbers would have undermined the message. Archibald Sinclair stuck to the official line. He repeated it even after Howard Cowan, an Associated Press war correspondent based at the Supreme Headquarters of the Allied Expeditionary Force (SHAEF) in Europe, reported that the Allies were now engaged in deliberate 'terror bombing'. Cowan wrote that Allied air commanders had made a 'long-awaited decision' to use the tactic against 'the great German population centres'. He noted that recent raids on residential areas of Berlin, Dresden, Chemnitz and Cottbus were all examples. More were planned to create confusion and sap German morale. Howard Cowan described this as 'a ruthless expedient to hasten Hitler's doom'. His report, first published in Washington DC by the *Sunday Star* newspaper, appeared following the devastating Dresden raids in February 1945.[38]

Dresden

Today, the destruction of Dresden is widely perceived as a moral crime that served no military purpose. Dresden and Coventry are twin cities. Children are taught that Dresden was not producing German armaments and that it was not a major industrial centre. This alone should alert the perceptive reader to a flaw in any depiction of the two cities as equally deserving of concentrated bombardment. Coventry was certainly a major manufacturing centre. In attacking it, the Luftwaffe identified a location responsible for important war work. The RAF and USAAF attacked Dresden because, having got his second front, Stalin now sought further pressure on Germany to support the accelerating offensive that had brought the Red Army to within fifty miles of Berlin. Biddle confirms that Churchill took a close interest in the RAF's capacity to support the Russians. He encouraged Archibald Sinclair to ensure retreating German forces were blasted from the air and asked whether Germany's large cities should not now 'be considered especially attractive targets'. The prime minister's apparent enthusiasm for raids on cities persuaded the Air Ministry to identify Dresden as a priority target.[39]

At the Yalta Conference, which concluded just two days before the Dresden raids began, Churchill and Roosevelt agreed to Sir Arthur Harris's proposal for a spectacular attack on eastern Germany. Harris believed a massive demonstration of Allied air power might shatter German morale and hasten the end of the war. The combined weight of British and American heavy bombers might have been turned on Leipzig or Chemnitz, but conditions favoured Dresden. The historic city in eastern Germany, affectionately referred to as 'the Florence of the Elbe', had not previously been a target for bombing. Now Operation Thunderclap began on the night of 13–14 February 1945. The initial raid involved 796 RAF Lancaster bombers guided by four fast Mosquito pathfinders. The Lancasters carried 1,478 tons of high explosive and 1,182 tons of incendiary bombs. The following day, 200 American bombers added 950 tons of high-explosive bombs and 290 tons of incendiaries. Connelly writes that: 'For the RAF it was the most effective fire-raising raid since Hamburg.'[40] Calder describes area bombing that had 'proceeded to the point of manifest insanity'.[41]

The Dresden raid was incomparably more destructive than anything the Germans had attempted against British cities. In scale it was similar to the Hamburg raid of 1943, but there was much less resistance from German fighters and many fewer Allied casualties. The RAF lost only six planes in its initial assault on Dresden. The impact was devastating. Some German military personnel were killed but most of those who died were women, children and men too old for military service. The charred remains of the dead were cremated in batches of 500 on open-air funeral pyres. Howard Cowan's description of it as 'terror bombing' emerged from a press conference given at SHAEF on 16 February 1945 by RAF Air Commodore Colin McKay Grierson, assistant chief of staff (intelligence) at SHAEF. Among Grierson's objectives was to explain how area attacks on German cities hampered the enemy's logistics and administration. He told the assembled correspondents that 'employment of the heavies against the centre of population' had occurred only after 'a lot of thought' and 'careful consideration'. Grierson was asked whether the intention was 'to cause confusion among the refugees or to blast communications carrying military supplies?' He replied that the raid aimed 'to stop movements in all directions if possible – movement of everything'. The clear implication was that killing civilians was part of the plan and Cowan grasped it instantly. His report was widely published in the United States where official fury could not overcome the constitutional guarantee of press freedom. British newspapers did not report Grierson's comments. Instead, newspapers swallowed the Air Ministry briefing whole and expressed enthusiasm for the Dresden raid. 'Dresden is a Mass of Flame' proclaimed the front-page headline in the *Daily Mirror*. The story below parroted Bomber Command's propaganda. Dresden was a 'great German industrial and rail centre'. The RAF's overnight raids had been 'highly concentrated and successful'. Returning pilots reported that they could still see the fires burning when they were 200 miles away 'as factories and supply dumps blazed'. As the RAF planes returned to their bases, a '300-mile stream' of American heavy bombers escorted by 900 fighters had continued the attack. German raid warnings were unrelenting.[42] The *Mirror*'s competitor and ideological soulmate the *Daily Herald* was similarly enthralled by the awesome power deployed against Dresden. Describing 'the greatest air offensive of the war', it gloated that the RAF had dropped '650,000 incendiaries on Dresden in one raid'. The Reich had never before 'suffered such a scourging of her cities, troop concentrations and supply lines'.[43] In the following morning's edition, the *Herald* reported that the raids were part of a 'non-stop Blitz to aid the Russians'. From Moscow, *Daily Herald* correspondent John Evans reported that General Ivan Konev's tanks had taken advantage of the raids to race twenty-five miles up the Silesian motorway. The Red Army was now just forty-three miles from Dresden.[44]

The *Daily Express* described Dresden as the Nazi regime's 'substitute capital'. It noted German claims that art treasures and beautiful buildings had been lost and countered with the truth according to Bomber Command: Dresden was a major contributor to the

German war effort. It had been used 'to pump German troops into counter attacks' against Marshall Zhukov's army.[45] The following morning the *Express* carried a piece from its correspondent in neutral Stockholm describing coverage of the raid in Berlin newspapers. They described 'one of the most concentrated bombings of any German city'. The Germans had invented a new word to describe it: atomization. The *Daily Express* man explained that this meant the entire city had been 'blown to smithereens'.[46]

Without referring to any criticism, although it was certainly aware of Howard Cowan's report, an editorial in *The Times* addressed the purpose of this furious onslaught from the air. This it did by posing a question: Why had Germany failed to organize any counter-offensive on the Eastern Front, despite its evident strategic need for one? The leader writer offered two possible explanations. Either the Nazi regime was short of fuel, or its military communications were failing. In fact, he explained, both were true, and this was because of the 'unprecedented fury' unleashed by the RAF and USAAF. This had 'fallen upon Germany continuously by day and night'. Dresden had suffered accordingly, and readers could rest assured that the bombing would not stop. The war against Germany, *The Times* declared, 'is and will be in increasing measure an affair of combined operations to the end'.[47] The *Sunday Times* did refer directly to terror bombing. It published on its front page a Reuters agency report filed from Allied Supreme Headquarters in Paris. This revealed that SHAEF had 'denied reports that Allied air chiefs have decided to adopt deliberate terror bombing of German centres of population'. The piece insisted there had been no change in Allied policy in the air or on the ground. This was 'to destroy German armed force and secure unconditional surrender'. The Dresden raid was 'designed to cripple communications and prevent the shuttling of troops between the Eastern and Western fronts. . . . The fact that the city was crowded with refugees at the time of the attack was a coincidence.'[48]

Sir Arthur Harris died in 1984. Since his death, the bombing of Dresden has come to be regarded as nothing less than a British war crime and a crime against humanity. Some critics have sought to suggest that it was seen as such at the time. In fact, as we have seen, the British public was broadly supportive of area bombing but did not have the full consequences of raids drawn vividly to its attention. Meticulous management of photography ensured newspapers did not depict the real impact of raids such as those on Hamburg and Dresden. Editors were fed a range of dramatic pictures showing aircraft production, aircraft in flight and brave bomber crews. Selected images of the destruction these aircraft could inflict were shared, but they depicted damaged buildings, not dead human beings. The Air Ministry and Ministry of Information shared dramatic aerial images that promoted Bomber Command's prowess and obscured evidence of its consequences for human life. Tom Allbeson explains that these departments 'provided attention grabbing photographs which effectively screened from public view the impact of total war'.[49] New public relations skills pioneered during the Battle of Britain were applied and refined in the depiction of Bomber Command's campaign of area bombardment. Newspapers carried extensive detail about the RAF's work. They told heroic tales about distinctive missions.

Reporting the Second World War

The Dambusters and Perfect Bombing

One of the clearest examples appeared in coverage of 617 Squadron's raid on the Möhne, Eder and Sorpe dams on the night of 16–17 May 1943. The Dambusters Raid used Barnes Wallis's innovative bouncing bomb to achieve the inventor's ambition to target a major piece of German civil engineering. It was, in fact, a very temporary victory. The dams were soon repaired, and the raid was so costly in men and materiel that the RAF did not return to attack those completing the repairs. Nor did Bomber Command make any further use of the new weapon. At the end of the war, unused bouncing bombs were simply dumped.[50] These inconvenient caveats did not emerge until long after the war. Many Britons still understand the Dambusters Raid through the prism of Michael Anderson's 1955 film starring Richard Todd as Wing Commander Guy Gibson and Michael Redgrave as Barnes Wallis. The newspaper coverage achieved in 1943 certainly helped to prime audiences for the poignant blend of triumph tempered by regret that the film inspires.

Operation Chastise, as the Dambusters Raid was codenamed, was a big hit in newspapers on both sides of the Atlantic. The *New York Times* reported: 'RAF Blasts 2 Big Dams in Reich' and 'Ruhr Power Cut, Traffic Halted as Floods Cause Death and Ruin'.[51] At home, the Air Ministry's dedicated and innovative team of specialists in the developing field of public relations achieved a clean sweep in popular and broadsheet newspapers. The front page of the *Daily Mirror* proclaimed: 'Torrent Rages Along Ruhr – Huns Get a Flood Blitz'. The headline was accompanied by dramatic images of the Möhne dam before and after the raid. Beneath, the *Mirror* described 'hundreds of square miles of devastation' in Germany's 'most vital and densely populated industrial area'. The RAF's attack had been 'staggering'. Also included was a colourful account of Wing Commander Guy Gibson's outstanding and selfless courage. The *Daily Mirror* reported that Gibson drew enemy fire to allow fellow Lancaster crews to press their own attacks. Only one aspect of the report diverged from the heroic narrative generations of Britons have learned since. The *Mirror* did not mention bouncing bombs. Their existence was a complete secret. It explained that after Gibson had 'dropped his mines', he flew up and down alongside the Möhne dam to attract 'the fire of the light A.A. [anti-aircraft] guns on it'.[52]

Lord Beaverbrook knew about Barnes Wallis's imaginative designs. In the summer of 1940, Wallis had proposed a six-engine 'High Altitude Stratosphere Bomber'. Vickers, the company that employed Wallis, backed his project, named it the 'Victory Bomber' and sought Beaverbrook's support from the minister for aircraft production. The idea of a precision bomber capable of hitting coal mines, oilfields and hydro-electric dams appealed to Beaverbrook. Later, Barnes Wallis said of the newspaper baron, 'I always knew if I went to see him about what seemed to be some outsize or absurd idea at least he would be responsive and push it.' When the Victory Bomber project was abandoned in 1942, Lord Beaverbrook supported Wallis's plan for the bouncing bomb.[53] When it demolished the Ruhr dams, his flagship title maintained the fiction that the RAF had dropped 'sea mines'. Having disguised the secret weapon, the *Daily Express* gave its achievement a warm welcome. The headline across all eight columns of its front page on 18 May 1943 was: 'Floods Roar Down Ruhr Valley'. It described waterspouts shooting 1,000 feet into the night sky as Lancaster bombers swooped in to press the attack. When the first dam collapsed, torrents of water devastated war industries and destroyed railways, bridges and power stations.[54] The story was accompanied by a large picture depicting the breached Möhne dam. This was captioned simply: 'The Breach: RAF took this amazing picture yesterday'.[55] Wing Commander Gibson was also pictured on the front page. The 'Dam Buster in Chief' appeared in uniform, smiling and smoking his pipe.[56]

'Floods Pouring Through Ruhr' was the banner headline in the *Daily Mail*. It reported that the mine-wrecked dams had paralysed Germany's industrial heartland and swept away vital infrastructure. A front-page picture caption carried a message central to the Air Ministry's propaganda mission. It described the attack as evidence of the RAF's 'perfect bombing'.[57] A collection of RAF and Air Ministry photographs appeared inside the newspaper. These included a close up of the Möhne dam with the 'Engine House' and 'Power Station', located below it, carefully labelled. It was accompanied by a picture of Guy Gibson being helped into his parachute harness before climbing into the cockpit for take-off.[58] That a photographer was present to take it is testament to the care and attention to detail with which this propaganda campaign was prepared. The *Daily Herald* eulogized in a leader that might have been written by Sir Arthur Harris. Every citizen of the United Nations would be 'awed and uplifted by the latest feat of Britain's Bomber Command'. The RAF had displayed 'a magnificent combination of daring and accuracy' to breach Germany's biggest dams.[59]

The elite titles joined in with more prose calculated to polish Bomber Command's reputation. *The Times* celebrated 'vast damage' to crucial German infrastructure which had dealt the enemy 'a severe blow'. Two-thirds of the water storage capacity of the Ruhr basin had been destroyed. It recognized the RAF's expertise and bravery too. Attacks had been made by specially selected crews that flew as low as 100 feet above the surface of the water 'to plant their mines on the lips of the dams'. Sir Archibald Sinclair, the minister for air, declared the raid 'a trenchant blow for victory'. Sir Arthur Harris told *The Times*: 'We had high hopes, but the immediate results of breaching the dams were far beyond our expectations.'[60] Guy Gibson was identified and praised for his leadership. It would praise him again ten days later when he was awarded the Victoria Cross. Wing Commander Guy Penrose Gibson had led the mission, having 'pressed strongly to be allowed to remain on operations' despite having completed three gruelling tours of duty. *The Times* applauded an inspiring leader who 'personally led the initial attack on the Möhne Dam, descending to within a few feet of the water and taking the full brunt of the anti-aircraft defences'.[61] Like the popular titles, *The Times* would continue to give the Dambusters Raid extensive coverage for two weeks after it took place. It lapped up every detail the Air Ministry and Bomber Command offered and happily published 'reconnaissance photographs' offering 'proof of the accuracy and intensity of the RAF attack'.[62]

The *Manchester Guardian* echoed the consensus, linking the success of the raid to the audacity and courage of its leader and crews. Quoting the citation that had accompanied the award of a bar to his Distinguished Service Order in April 1943, it described Guy Gibson as a 'pilot with contempt for danger'. It added that 'guns appeared out of slots in the wall of the dam' as the wing commander flew alongside it to draw flak away from his comrades. An unidentified flight lieutenant recalled that he had been able to watch the whole process. He saw Gibson drop his weapon with perfect accuracy and 'a spout of water went up 300 feet'. A second Lancaster attacked with equal accuracy, but the dam wall remained intact: 'Then I went in, and we caused a huge explosion up against the dam.' It broke and the flight lieutenant saw a breach about 500 yards wide.[63] The *Manchester Guardian* concluded that the raid was a 'new blow at Ruhr industries'. Power stations and bridges had been swept away.[64]

The *Daily Telegraph* captured the key elements of Bomber Command's preferred narrative on its front page. Here, in a single edition, were devastation, heroism, rigorous secret planning and precision accuracy. Indeed, the Air Ministry's statement was published in full alongside a picture of Guy Gibson.[65] It explained that the 'Lancaster crews knew how much depended on their success. The opportunity might never come again, and it was an opportunity, as they knew, of doing as much damage as could be done by thousands of tons of bombs dropped on many nights running.'[66] In retrospect, this might be read as an admission that area bombing was wasteful and imprecise. In fact, it was a gentle reference to the high price 617 Squadron paid for its heroism. Nineteen Lancaster bombers, each with a crew of seven, flew in the raid. Eight failed to return. Of the 133 skilled airmen who took off from RAF Scampton in Lincolnshire, 53 were killed and three were captured and made prisoners of war. These were among Bomber Command's most effective and experienced crews. Their loss in a single operation is not prominent in any of the immediate reporting of the Dambusters Raid. The *Daily Express* captured the essence of Sir Arthur Harris' white propaganda mission when it quoted his message to the surviving crews: 'Your skill and determination in pressing home the attack will forever be an inspiration to the RAF.'[67]

Connelly notes that Viscount Kemsley's Conservative populist *Daily Sketch* described the floods as a 'terrible, but unavoidable necessity' and *The Spectator* reflected that 'The effects of these bombing attacks on the war as whole cannot be seen immediately.'[68] Such modest quibbles did little to disrupt the chorus of praise that poured forth in newsprint. The newspapers responded to the Dambusters as cheerleaders for the RAF and its heavy bombers. They conveyed the impression that precision was not just possible, but a particular attribute of the service that had already excelled itself in the Battle of Britain. Such reporting set a tone that persisted as evidence of accuracy diminished and casualties mounted in the air and on the ground.

* * *

The Ministry of Information concluded early in the war that the British people were resilient and could deal with bad news. From 1941, it fought the service departments over censorship and argued for a supply of comprehensive news.[69] Obstruction came from the service departments. They had the raw information about military action and they decided what to release.[70] The Air Ministry engaged in public relations with great enthusiasm and considerable expertise, but its objective was to depict success and heroism. It did not encourage sceptical reporting that might hold Bomber Command to account for the sizeable gap that existed between rhetoric about area bombing and the harsh reality.

Newspaper reporting of Bomber Command's long campaign of strategic bombing was largely informed by official briefing. Necessary security ensured that only the RAF knew the details of raids. Until the end of the war brought journalists to Germany, pictures available to newspapers were those supplied by the Air Ministry. Newspapers sought additional independent sources. As we have seen, these frequently came in the form of reports filed from Germany by journalists from neutral countries or translated from the German press by British correspondents in neutral capitals. In the mass-market press, such reports were frequently deployed as confirmation that the RAF's work was disruptive, damaging and effective. Mainstream newspapers declined to represent such evidence in the challenging style adopted by opponents of area bombing such as Vera Brittain. Brief letters to the editor might be published, but overt condemnation of area bombing did not appear on news pages or in commissioned editorial comment.

When discussion of the civilian deaths caused by raids did emerge in public print, it did so in a polemical article by George Orwell published in a small circulation title read by intellectual leaders. For *Tribune,* the weekly title founded in 1937 by Sir Stafford Cripps and George Strauss, wealthy Labour MPs from their party's socialist left, area bombing was a topic on which dissent was worth advertising. Edited by Aneurin Bevan MP with the assistance of John Kimche, a historian and journalist, *Tribune* was keen to promote intelligent controversy. It hired Orwell as its literary editor in the late autumn of 1943 and made vividly apparent to readers its enthusiasm for his work. Issue number 350 sported a bright pink glossy band stapled to the cover boasting 'CONTIBUTIONS BY J.B. PRIESTLEY, GEORGE ORWELL, ETHEL MANN, RHYS DAVIES'.[71] Orwell's subsequent insistence that the RAF was killing German civilians deliberately and that it was right to do so appeared in May 1944. Reviewing Vera Brittain's *Seed of Chaos*[72] the literary editor acknowledged 'an eloquent attack on indiscriminate or "obliteration" bombing' before advising readers that:

> No one in his senses regards bombing, or any other operation of war, with anything but disgust. On the other hand, no decent person cares tuppence for the opinion of posterity. And there is something very distasteful in accepting war as an instrument and at the same time wanting to dodge responsibility for its more obviously barbarous features. Pacifism is a tenable position, provided you are willing to take the consequences, but all talk of limiting or humanising war is sheer humbug.... Why is it worse to kill civilians than soldiers? Heaven knows how many people our blitz on Germany has killed and will kill, but you can be quite certain that it will never come anywhere near the slaughter that has happened on the Russian front.[73]

Orwell's argument dovetailed with *Tribune*'s established view that area bombing was a distraction from Britain's duty to fight an effective ground campaign, but this did not make it universally popular with *Tribune's* readers. They soon made it plain that they were not united in support of the literary editor. Several wrote to contest what they considered to be his relativism and aggression. Typically, rather than retreat Orwell returned to his theme with renewed vigour. The 'parrot cry' against 'killing women and children' was absurd:

> It is probably somewhat better to kill a cross section of the population than to kill only young men. If the figures published by the Germans are true and we have really killed 1,200,000 civilians in our raids, that loss of life has probably harmed the German race somewhat less than a corresponding loss on the Russian front or in Africa and Italy.[74]

In writing explicitly about the killing of civilians by the RAF Orwell revealed a truth Air Ministry staff had worked tirelessly to exclude from newspapers. I will discuss the tolerance of dissent in weekly political titles in my concluding chapter. For now suffice it to say that *Tribune* was not persecuted for publishing a blunt contradiction of the Air Ministry's insistence that any civilian casualties were unintended victims of precision attacks on strategic targets. Indeed, neither Orwell nor *Tribune* faced adverse consequences for publicizing the hitherto unmentioned fact that Bomber Command killed German civilians as a conscious act of policy.

Such killing came at a high price in the lives of aircrew, but David Edgerton makes the telling point that total wartime losses of RAF Bomber Command and British merchant navy personnel 'were each of the same order as those resulting from a single very heavy raid on a German city, say Hamburg (1943) or Dresden (1945)'. And Britain killed between three and six times as many German civilians by bombing as the Germans killed British civilians with bombs or V1 and V2 rockets.[75]

Only in the final days of the war, as the ruins of Dresden still smouldered, did ministers begin to feel queasy about what they had authorized and funded. Their unease was amplified, if not caused, by the first reports of mass civilian casualties in daily newspapers and the re-emergence of Howard Cowan's report that the Allies were subjecting German cities to 'terror bombing'. On 6 March 1945, Richard Stokes MP (Labour, Ipswich), a leading member of the Bombing Restriction Committee, raised in the House of Commons a report of the Dresden raid that had appeared in the previous day's *Manchester Guardian*.[76] Culled from accounts in the German press, this alleged that there had been one million people in the city on the night of the RAF's main assault. It said 600,000 of them were refugees fleeing the Red Army. Stokes quoted an account of 'raging fires which spread irresistibly in the narrow streets and killed a great many from sheer lack of oxygen'. Acknowledging that the German version might contain overstatement, Richard Stokes proceeded to read into the official record Howard Cowan's account for Associated Press. He noted that it had been 'published very widely in America' and that it had originally been 'released by the censor ... for publication in this country'. However, some people had objected and it had been suppressed. Stokes complained that Cowan's story had been 'widely broadcast in America, broadcast on the Paris Radio to Germany, but not communicated to people in this country'.[77] He warned that Britain risked occupying cities in which 'the disease, filth and poverty which will arise, will be almost impossible either to arrest or to overcome'.[78]

Such criticism hit home. On 28 March 1945, Winston Churchill drafted a telegram to the chiefs of staff, in which he wrote: 'It seems to me that the moment has come when the question of bombing German cities simply for the sake of increasing the terror, though under other pretexts, should be reviewed. Otherwise we shall come into control of an utterly ruined land.'[79] The prime minister was persuaded that the chief of air staff, Charles Portal, would not accept such direct criticism. Churchill revised his message and sent instead a personal minute that began: 'It seems to me that the moment has come when the question of the so called "area bombing" of German cities should be reviewed from the point of view of our own interests. If we come into control of an entirely ruined land, there will be a great shortage of accommodation for ourselves and our Allies.'[80] The Labour government that took office in 1945 continued to treat Sir Arthur Harris and Bomber Command with a chilly disdain that had its origins in the final weeks of the wartime coalition. Harris was not elevated to the House of Lords. A memorial to the 55,573 members of Bomber Command who lost their lives during the war was not unveiled until 2012. It stands in London's Green Park.

Newspapers made scant effort to understand or question the military value of the Allied bombing of German cities. The Air Ministry's presentation of the campaign went almost entirely unchallenged. For the service ministry publicists who had won their spurs during the Battle of Britain, this was almost a comparable success. Many of the same tactics were used, notably the selective briefing of tailored detail to individual titles that made national heroes of brave men such as Douglas Bader in 1940 and Guy Gibson in 1943. It took reaction to the Dresden raid to raise hard questions about who the RAF was killing and how beyond the narrow circle of the Bombing Restriction Committee and its sympathizers. Investigation of the fate of Europe's Jewish population began early in the war and newspapers returned to the question repeatedly. On this issue absence of definitive eyewitness evidence, the damaging legacy of First World War atrocity stories, and plain incredulity combined to limit the extent and impact of reporting.

CHAPTER 13
CONCENTRATION CAMPS

British newspapers identified the brutality of Nazi race laws long before the war began. Andrew Sharf identifies examples of such reporting. These include a dramatic picture in the *Daily Herald* in March 1933 of a German Jew being dragged through the street with his head shaved and a placard round his neck.[1] Pre-war headlines alerting British readers to Nazi anti-Semitism in the year Hitler became Chancellor included: 'Boycott of Jews, Lynching Case at Kiel' (*The Times*) and 'Eyewitness Tells of Jew Baiting Tragedies, Nazi Mob Lynch Lawyer' (*Daily Herald*).[2] Sharf describes the *Manchester Guardian*'s early and principled commitment to describing accurately the treatment of European Jews. This coverage included a detailed report about the legal regime established for the concentration camps and an extensive list of offences punishable by death. Such offences included 'talking about politics' and 'collecting true or untrue information about the camps' for transmission abroad.[3] Sharf notes that the newspaper also carried a special report on Dachau in 1935.[4] He notes that Conservative titles, including *The Times* and *Daily Telegraph*, also reported Nazi persecution of the Jews and concludes that, by 1936, 'the press as a whole was fully alive to the violent aspect of anti-Semitism in Germany'.[5] Such pre-war coverage peaked in 1938 as internment and violence mounted in the pogroms that culminated in Kristallnacht. Stephanie Seul offers an important caveat: British journalists were powerfully influenced by their liberal democratic assumptions. They imagined that indignation about anti-Semitism in the liberal democracies and public opinion in Germany must eventually temper Hitler's venom. 'Ultimately', Seul writes, 'the press in liberal democracies was in search of rational explanations for an apparently irrational phenomenon.' Even while reporting fully the impact of Nazi race laws, their understanding of the persecution 'remained preconditioned by liberal thinking'.[6]

Once war began and evidence of the final solution accumulated, Laqueur notes that: 'People could deal with the fate of an individual or a family but not with the fate of millions. The statistics of murder were either disbelieved or dismissed from consciousness.'[7] Such incredulity was amplified by the enduring influence of lurid Allied atrocity propaganda during the First World War. This had left a malign legacy of profound and widespread suspicion about atrocity stories. In July 1941, the Ministry of Information's planning committee issued a memorandum suggesting that, in publicising German brutality, which it actively encouraged, 'A certain amount of horror is needed.' However, it advised that this 'must be used very sparingly and must deal always with treatment of indisputably innocent people. Not with violent political opponents. And not with Jews.'[8] These attitudes would prove slow to shift, particularly because until April 1945 the insurmountable paucity of eyewitness testimony and pictures reduced the impact of such stories and kept them off front pages.

Hitler's Final Solution

The Holocaust may be distinguished from all previous acts of barbarity by the obscene and meticulous precision with which the Nazi state set out to murder the Jews of Europe. Jews were not murdered because of what they thought or did. They were hunted down and killed simply because they were Jewish. In January 1942, Reinhard Heydrich of the SS announced to the Wannsee Conference plans for a 'final solution to the Jewish problem' intended to achieve a 'Jew-free' Reich. In August, Samuel Silverman MP (Labour, Nelson and Colne), chairman of the British section of the World Jewish Conference (WJC) was alerted to the growing horror by a telegram sent to him, via the British consul general in Geneva, by Gerhart Riegner, secretary of the WJC's Geneva section. The Riegner Telegram revealed discussion within Hitler's inner circle of a plan 'according to which all Jews in countries occupied or controlled by Germany' would be deported to the East and 'at one blow exterminated'. Riegner noted that his 'informant is reported to have close connexions with the highest German authorities and his reports are generally reliable'. He asked Silverman to 'Please inform and consult New York'.[9]

Growing awareness of the scale of Nazi persecution of the Jewish people and its obscene ambition appeared in British newspapers in the summer and autumn of 1942. Newspapers including *The Times*, *Daily Mail* and *Evening Standard* reported the World Jewish Congress's belief that a million Jews had already died.[10] In September, the *Manchester Guardian* came close to revealing the true nature of the Holocaust. By collating eyewitness accounts smuggled out of the region of Czechoslovakia then labelled the German Protectorate of Bohemia and Moravia, the *Guardian* identified 'a vast system of organised traffic in human beings'. It reported that 'the fit may survive for as long as they are useful: the aged and unfit may perish at will'.[11] The *Manchester Guardian* described its account as authoritative and 'probably the first to reach the outside world'. The claim was not hyperbolic. The report described how Jewish people in Nazi-occupied territory had had their money confiscated and their personal possessions seized. Each refugee was allowed to pack 100lb of luggage, but the *Guardian*'s special correspondent explained that: 'No luggage of this description has found its way to Terezin.' He described how, between December 1941 and July 1942, 7,000 young Jewish citizens were brought to Terezin as forced labour. Barely surviving on the most meagre rations, they built huts 'which were rapidly filled by Jews brought first from Czechoslovakia and later from Germany and the countries of Western Europe'. Accommodation was 'totally inadequate', sanitation non-existent and the mortality rate high. The report revealed that a group of young single men, ostensibly chosen for their good health and usefulness as labourers had been sent from Terezin to Upper Silesia. Nothing had been heard from them since their departure. The piece concluded ominously that Terezin provided just 'one concrete example' of the fate of the Jews under German rule. It was part of a vast system.[12] Three weeks later the *Manchester Guardian* reported that Hitler had 'reaffirmed his intention to exterminate the Jews of Europe and to encourage anti-Semitic feeling throughout the world'. It estimated that the pre-war Jewish population of European countries now occupied by the Third Reich had been six million. Of these people, it was sure that one million were already dead. Their names could not be listed, but they had been 'shot, hanged, buried alive, burnt or beaten to death in Russia, Poland, the Protectorate and the Balkans'.[13]

In fact, the *Daily Telegraph* had already identified use of the murder weapon now most closely associated with the Holocaust: gas. When the World Jewish Congress met in London in June 1942, the *Telegraph* reported the use of 'travelling gas chambers' to murder 1,000 Polish Jews every day. Noting that complete extermination of the Jewish population of Poland was the Nazis' declared objective, it confirmed that they were well on their way to achieving their appalling ambition. Many Polish Jews had already been forced to dig their own graves before being knifed, machine gunned or killed with hand grenades. Now, however, 'a special van fitted as a gas chamber' had been deployed. It could kill ninety victims at a time.[14] The *Manchester Guardian* returned to the topic in late October 1942 with a leader entitled simply: 'Extermination'. It explained that this meant that: 'Jews are rounded up, deprived of their belongings, packed together in cattle trucks, and transported for many days and nights to Poland.' The Jewish populations of Holland and Belgium had already been deported. French Jews were suffering 'the same brutality' and persecution was beginning in Italy, Hungary and Romania. The residual question was whether the Allies could defeat Germany in time to prevent complete extermination. The *Guardian* was not optimistic. It feared prosecution of German war criminals might be the only achievable form of retribution.[15]

By December 1942 the War Cabinet was confident that Hitler's final solution really was underway. Accordingly, Samuel Silverman asked the foreign secretary, Anthony Eden, to make a statement 'regarding the plan of the German Government to deport all Jews from the occupied countries to Eastern Europe and there put them to death'.[16] Eden told the House of Commons that information received from the Polish government and discussed with the Americans, Russians and other Allied governments confirmed that the Germans were 'now carrying into effect Hitler's oft-repeated intention to exterminate the Jewish people in Europe'. He described Poland as 'the principal Nazi slaughterhouse' and identified the 'appalling horror and brutality' with which: 'The able-bodied are slowly worked to death in labour camps. The infirm are left to die of exposure and starvation or are deliberately massacred in mass executions.' Eden estimated the number of victims at 'many hundreds of thousands of entirely innocent men, women and children'.[17]

The *Daily Express* was the only mass-market title to report the story on its front page. This it achieved by the populist contrivance of personalizing it. Editor Arthur Christiansen introduced news of the Holocaust through the part played by Mr Sampson Cluse, the Labour MP for South Islington. The *Express*'s parliamentary reporter explained that it was Mr Cluse, 'a little man with his little moustache and his grey hair and his gold-rimmed spectacles', who managed to make every member of the House of Commons stand in silence. Making only the third speech of a parliamentary career that began in 1923, Mr Cluse asked the Speaker if 'we might stand in protest against this disgraceful barbarism'. Mr Speaker FitzRoy replied that it would have to be a spontaneous gesture. MPs duly rose to their feet and stood in hushed silence.[18] On an inside page, Lord Beaverbrook's flagship title reported the foreign secretary's statement in detail. It noted that MPs 'listened with grim faces' and cheered only once when Anthony Eden confirmed 'the resolve of the United Nations to exact retribution'.[19] The *Daily Mail* picked out a speech made by James de Rothschild MP (Liberal, Isle of Ely). He thanked Eden for his 'eloquent and just denunciation' of Nazi barbarity. The *Mail* welcomed the dignity MPs had shown by standing in silence to record their sorrow for 'the Jews Germany is slaughtering and their loathing of history's most infamous act'.[20] The *Daily Mirror* welcomed the news that 'Germany's cold-blooded extermination of the Jews' had been broadcast in twenty-three languages over a worldwide radio network from London.[21] *The Times* reported that MPs had been 'moved by the horror of Mr Eden's recital of German atrocities' and by his stern warning that the perpetrators would face retribution.[22] For the *Sunday Pictorial* this was 'The Foulest Crime on Earth' and 'a horror that numbs the mind',[23] but it did not put the enormity on its front page. This was dominated, as so often, by news of victories on the battlefront. Russian forces had made fresh advances between Stalingrad and Rzhev.[24]

The Fate of the Hungarian Jews

In the spring of 1944, the 750,000-strong Hungarian Jewish community was the largest single Jewish community left in Europe. Hungary's alliance with the Axis powers had kept the government of Admiral Miklos Horthy (1868–1957) in office and allowed Hungary to identify its own solution to the 'Jewish problem'. However, by early 1944, the Red Army was advancing rapidly, and the Hungarian government made secret efforts to arrange a separate peace with the Allies. Determined to retain Hungarian support, the Germans seized key strategic locations in Hungary, placed Horthy under house arrest and installed a more compliant government and a German military governor. Before the war, assimilation between Jewish and non-Jewish Hungarians had been successful and inter-marriage quite common. Now, Samuel Silverman again asked the foreign secretary for information about the mass deportation of Jews 'from Hungary to Poland for the purpose of massacre'.[25] Mr Eden replied that he had no definite information about numbers, but there were 'strong indications from various reliable sources that the German and Hungarian authorities have already begun these barbarous deportations'. Many had already been killed and nothing Britain nor its Allies said about post-war punishment of the perpetrators appeared to make any difference. Only a speedy Allied victory could bring to an end the furious persecution of the Jewish people.[26] The *Daily Herald* commended Eden's strong words but warned that nobody could expect them to be effective. The Hungarian government had been aware throughout the war that British public opinion was repelled by the treatment of the Jews. British indignation had produced no result. Even with their German masters in full retreat, the Hungarian puppet politicians showed 'no more regard for British wrath than they showed in the early days of the war'.[27] A leader in *The Times* noted that the Hungarian community was 'marked for extermination'.[28] Mass deportation was already underway and *The Times* identified a key distinction between 'so-called concentration camps' and the death camps of Poland 'which are in fact slaughterhouses'. It emphasized that the Jewish citizens of Hungary were the victims not only of the Nazis but, crucially, of their own authorities too. Hungarian administrators identified and located Hungarian Jews. The police and paramilitaries who herded them onto trains were fellow Hungarians. On this occasion, the *Manchester Guardian* was content to report the exchange in Parliament[29] but the *Daily Telegraph* published a powerful leader. The Hungarian government had 'yielded to German pressure' and begun the systematic round up, deportation and elimination of the last remaining organized Jewish community in Europe: 'Outraged humanity can but strive to rid the earth of this monstrous wickedness.' The only way to stop the butchery was to achieve 'a speedy victory'.[30] Brendan Bracken, minister of information, followed his colleague the foreign secretary's statement in Parliament with a speech at London's Dorchester Hotel. He told his audience that the Germans were 'setting up abattoirs in Europe into which are shepherded thousands of Jews'. It was the 'biggest scandal in the history of human crime'. Bracken insisted that he could not 'exaggerate the brutality of the Germans in Hungary'. He stressed that the Hungarian government was wholly complicit, and that blame attached to the German people and the Wehrmacht general staff too, not just to leading Nazis. He hoped that exemplary punishment would be applied to all who could have prevented the slaughter. The minister for information was delighted that the Russian general most likely to lead the first Red Army soldiers onto German soil was 'a very distinguished Jew'.[31]

The following day after Bracken's speech, British broadsheet newspapers identified Oświęcim (Auschwitz) as a death camp. *The Times* detailed information received by the London-based Polish government-in-exile from its representative in Poland. It described the arrival of hundreds of thousands of Hungarian Jews at Oświęcim. On 15 May, the Germans had deported from Hungary '62 railway carriages filled with Jewish children'. Afterwards, 'six railway trains laden with adult Jews' had followed daily. Most of the deportees had been put to death in the gas chambers. Prior to their deportation they had been told that they would be exchanged for prisoners of war. To discourage panic at home, 'some were compelled to write cheerful letters to their relatives in Hungary'. *The Times* added that Oświęcim's gas chambers could kill 6,000 victims per day. Additional death camps at Treblinka and near Lwów had allowed the Germans to murder two million Polish Jews since 1939.[32] *The Times* had refined and clarified the distinction between concentration camps and those intended explicitly for extermination. The *Daily Telegraph* reported the same basic facts in a single-column story on page three.[33] The *Manchester Guardian* preferred evidence sent from Switzerland by its special correspondent. There, the Ecumenical Refugee Commission in Geneva and the Refugee Relief Committee in Zurich offered testimony that 400,000 Hungarian Jews had already died in Oświęcim or Birkenau. Some had died on route in the squalid, crowded cattle trains. Eastern and northern provinces of Hungary were 'now denuded of Jews'. Between 300,000 and 400,000 more awaited deportation from Budapest and the region around the Hungarian capital.[34]

The popular papers reported some of the details emerging from Hungary and Poland. The *Sunday Pictorial* offered an intriguing illustration of its preference for tales of individual suffering in a story about Oświęcim. It began by revealing that patients who lay ill in the camp 'have been murdered in their beds by the injection of drugs near to the heart'. Only having described this Nazi perversion of medicine did it report that 'from April 1942 to April 1944 between 1,500,000 and 1,750,000 Jews were put to death by gas or other methods' at Oświęcim and Birkenau. It described Oświęcim as housing 15,000 prisoners 'in rows of huts surrounded by electric fencing with machine-gun towers every 500 yards'. The *Daily Mail* offered a short report of Brendan Bracken's speech at the Dorchester. It recorded that he had 'officially confirmed reports of the mass extermination of the Jews in Europe'. It also indicated approval of his insistence that responsibility for it lay not only with Nazis but 'also on the German people and general staff'.[35] The *Daily Express* waited for American comment before putting the extermination of Hungarian Jews on its front page. It reported that US Secretary of State Cordell Hull had received reliable reports from Hungary confirming 'the appalling news of mass killing of the Jews by the Germans and their Hungarian quislings'. The report concluded by mentioning that 'both Mr Eden and Mr Bracken' had condemned the treatment of Hungarian Jews recently'.[36] It preferred to report and celebrate Allied military victories. The market leader did give one new statistic early prominence on its front page though; it was proud to declare that: 'More than 3,000,000 copies of the *Daily Express* are now sold every day'.[37]

Liberation of Auschwitz

Truly detailed reports of obscene barbarity on an unprecedented scale only began to emerge when Allied forces advancing from the east and west reached the concentration camps. The speed of the Russian advance meant that Auschwitz, in which more than one million people were murdered, was liberated on 27 January 1945. When the soldiers of the Red Army fought their way in about 7,000 prisoners remained in the camp. Other surviving inmates had been forced to leave in frozen death marches towards camps in Germany. The liberation of Auschwitz, referred to by its Polish name, Oświęcim, earned relatively brief coverage in British newspapers. No British reporters were accompanying the Red Army, and news from its fighting fronts was controlled in and released through Moscow. *The Times* reported from the Russian capital that soldiers of the Red Army had made important gains in the area around Cracow 'including the capture of Oświęcim, the scene of many German massacres'.[38] The following day's edition of the *Sunday Times* offered more detail. It described the seizure of Oświęcim in Polish Silesia as closing 'one of the blackest chapters in human history'. Many paragraphs into a front-page story that concentrated on the Red Army's advance through Poland, the *Sunday Times* recorded that Oświęcim was among the Gestapo's 'biggest and most terrible concentration camps'. It explained that: 'To Poland's millions of Jews especially, Oświęcim was a name to be dreaded.' Special trains had moved the populations of the ghettos in Warsaw and Lublin to the camp. Very few of those who 'disappeared through the gates ever emerged alive'.[39] The *Manchester Guardian* also focused its attention on the Red Army's rapid progress towards Germany. It found room to mention that: 'Oświęcim, site of the concentration camp which became notorious for the cruelties inflicted on its inmates, was one of the places captured.'[40] Details emerged slowly from the cautious and suspicious Russian military censors but, on 3 February, the *Daily Telegraph* carried a Reuters agency report that began to convey details of the systematized horror perpetrated at Auschwitz. Reuters in Moscow reported Russian investigators' conclusion that, when it was operating at capacity, between five and eight locked trains had arrived at Auschwitz every day from Russia, Poland, France, Yugoslavia and Czechoslovakia. It explained that, on arrival, the prisoners were divided into two categories. Those who were deemed 'fit to work before going to the slaughter' and the old, weak, young and disabled who were killed immediately. The version in the *Daily Telegraph* confirmed that, having initially murdered their victims by shooting, the Germans subsequently 'introduced a mechanised slaughter system including gas chambers'.[41]

Another Reuters report, this time from Athens and published in the *Manchester Guardian* offered an account by a survivor of Auschwitz. Leon Vatis, a 36-year-old Athenian businessman, had been among 20,000 Greek Jews deported to Poland in March 1944. Now, following a 45-day journey by train and on foot, he had made his way home. Mr Vatis explained that barely 300 of his fellow deportees were still alive. He described how anyone in the camp who was no longer able to work was removed to the crematorium on the pretext that they would be disinfected. Naked men, women and children were 'put in an overheated room into which was thrown a special powder producing suffocating gas'. The Germans watched through a spyhole the agonized death struggles of those murdered with Zyklon-B. Some took fifteen minutes to die. Then, Vatis told Reuters, 'the bodies were moved to the ovens for burning'.[42] These reports from camps in eastern Europe were not accompanied by photographs.

Belsen and Buchenwald

As the Red Army liberated concentration camps, British incredulity was slow to fade. Enduring hardship on the home front made it easier to overlook the suffering of others, particularly when their fate felt remote. Only when British and American forces advancing from the west entered Germany did Allied war correspondents begin to offer eyewitness testimony that would promote the death camps to prominence in popular newspapers. However, while such reporting offered drama, it did not offer immediate clarity. A telling example of reporting against a deadline while details were still emerging appeared in the *Daily Mail* the day before British soldiers entered Belsen. Alexander Clifford (1909–52) of the *Daily Mail* had already spent time reporting from the desert war in North Africa. Now Clifford, a serious and thoughtful journalist, encountered Heinrich Himmler's futile efforts to disguise evidence of Nazi atrocities. He reported that an 'exciting series of trips by blindfold emissaries' from the German lines had resulted in agreement between the British and German armies for an ostensibly orderly handover of the Belsen camp in Lower Saxony. Clifford reported that British forces would take control on the basis of 'a detailed plan' for collaboration between British and German forces.

After six days, with the disease-afflicted camp safely transferred to British control, the Germans would be 'escorted back to their own lines'. If this sounded improbable, so was the story told by the German delegation at Himmler's insistence. Alexander Clifford reported their claim that Belsen contained 60,000 prisoners 'partly political and partly criminal'. They did not mention the presence of Jewish prisoners.[43]

Versions of the same story were filed by Christopher Buckley, special correspondent for the *Daily Telegraph*, David Woodward of the *Manchester Guardian* and by *The Times* special correspondent. Each was able to report that the planned truce had failed. Buckley wrote that a German delegation commanded by a Colonel Schmidt approached the British to request a truce to prevent the spread of typhus. The German officer said there were 'between 2,000 and 3,000' cases among the prisoners at Belsen. The Germans were 'not unnaturally disturbed both about the possibilities of typhus spreading eastwards into the Reich and also of criminals breaking out and roaming all over the country'. For the *Manchester Guardian*, David Woodward added that Colonel Schmidt claimed Allied air raids had disrupted all organization in the camp and there was only enough food to feed the prisoners for six days.[44] The *Daily Telegraph* man noted that Schmidt asked the British to assume command of the camp and a radius of one mile around it. To protect their own men against infection, British officers demanded a wider perimeter. Schmidt replied that he was not authorized to change the terms. He would have to refer to Heinrich Himmler, head of the SS. A British brigadier accompanied the German delegation to its HQ where Himmler's office was called. He could not be reached, but his staff declined the British request. The British officer left, and the truce ended.[45] *The Times* offered a little more context. It explained that the 'extraordinary step' had initially been agreed 'because typhus is rampant in the camp, and it is vitally necessary that no prisoners should be allowed out until the infection is checked'. However, Himmler's chief of staff rejected the British terms and 'a very odd interlude in the battle of Germany ended'.[46] All three accounts were informed by the same British briefing. The most plausible explanation for Alexander Clifford's failure to inform *Daily Mail* readers that the truce had failed is that he was working to an earlier deadline than his rivals. This is explained by the *Daily Mail*'s commercial success. It had an audited daily circulation of 1,532,683 and thus began printing earlier than quality broadsheets such as *The Times* which had a circulation of *c*. 200,000.[47]

Soldiers of Britain's Second Army entered Belsen on 15 April 1945. Many Britons heard the abominable scenes within described by Richard Dimbleby for the BBC. His script is an example of journalism as the first draft of history. He took meticulous care to deploy facts and compel understanding, combining humanity, authority and faultless craft to convince listeners that what he told them was entirely true. Despite his outstanding skill, his employer initially refused to broadcast the report. Senior BBC staff did not believe him. They found the scenes he described literally incredible. Richard Dimbleby had to threaten resignation before the BBC relented. His report was transmitted on 19 April. It was heard by an audience of millions and is widely admired to this day. It deserves the respect and admiration that attaches to it. However, newspapers responded to Ed Murrow's account of the American liberation of Buchenwald before anyone heard Dimbleby describe Belsen.

Concentration Camps

Murrow, the CBS radio correspondent who had brought the Blitz to American homes, entered Buchenwald on 12 April, one day after soldiers of America's Sixth Armoured Division reached the camp northwest of Weimar. Shaken by what he had seen and very angry, Murrow chose to delay his report and returned to London, hoping that distance might achieve emotional detachment. CBS transmitted his account on 15 April. The BBC and several newspapers also carried it. Editors hoped Murrow's authority might persuade sceptical listeners and readers that this was not propaganda.[48] The *Daily Mirror* acknowledged that the facts were horrifying, but it expressed surprise that Murrow's 'quiet, unemotional recital . . . seems to have caused a feeling of intense revulsion'. Readers had felt physically sick listening to the news. The *Mirror* told them that the existence of death and torture camps should come as no surprise. Such camps had been the chosen Nazi instrument of political oppression before the war. Now the *Daily Mirror* asked whether it was really 'possible that there is one solitary person in these islands who does not know?' Nevertheless, it acknowledged that 'the full enormity of Hitler's offence against God and man is still not understood in this country'. The *Mirror* advised that 'our sacred duty is to learn the facts. They must never be forgotten.'[49]

Atrocity Pictures

The arrival of journalists at Buchenwald secured the pictures popular newspapers needed to convey the horror. On 19 April 1945, the *Daily Express* published some of the first images to emerge from the liberated camp. Civilians from the town of Weimar were depicted beside a cart piled high with dead bodies. The *Express* described these well-dressed Germans as 'dreading to look at the work their warped masters had done and they, themselves, had tacitly approved'.[50] It depicted a prosperous German citizen walking haughtily past the atrocious evidence with his eyes averted. On a subsequent page, it showed the brick ovens in which the murdered dead were burned. The caption noted evidence that the work had not been finished when American troops entered Buchenwald: 'blackened skeletons were still in position when the doors were opened'.[51] In an editorial, the *Daily Express* explained its decision to publish the pictures. It was the newspaper's 'solemn duty to publish at least some of the photographic evidence . . . of the vileness we are fighting. This is no propaganda. It is blunt, spine-chilling fact.'[52] The *Daily Mirror* filled most of a page with a searing image of a huge pit at Belsen filled with the naked, emaciated bodies of the innocent dead.[53] Beneath it, a column pleaded with readers to understand that all they were reading and seeing was true. The Germans really had done this. Collective guilt must apply.[54] This view was widely debated in newspapers of left and right. *The Times* advised that photographic evidence had destroyed any doubts that 'the low horrors of torture, starvation and induced disease' had murdered tens of thousands of prisoners in Buchenwald and Belsen. Moral perversion had been cultivated in an entire generation of Germans, but how far direct responsibility extended would require full investigation. First, Germany must 'face without self-deception the hideous truth about the present'.[55]

If collective responsibility made a strong debating point, tales of individual evil made better popular journalism, particularly when supported by good pictures. These had to be very powerful to displace news of the Russian advance on Berlin that dominated front pages in the second half of April 1945. The *Sunday Pictorial* identified such an image for its edition of 21 April. Beneath the headline 'Hitler's Beast Women', it portrayed two female Belsen guards in uniform. They appeared well fed and anxious. The *Pictorial* invited readers to 'Look this morning upon the faces of the vilest women history has yet produced'. Describing the duo as murderesses, it reported that they had participated in the 'indescribable horror of Belsen'. The *Sunday Pictorial* declared that they had betrayed 'the sacred human instincts of their sex'. It explained that, alongside their male colleagues, they were forced at bayonet point to bury the bodies of the dead.[56]

Female Nazis provoked particular revulsion in the popular newspapers but male monsters produced powerful newspaper treatment too. The *Daily Express* made full use of its broadsheet front page to combine latest news of the fighting around Berlin with compelling images from the liberated concentration camps. Beneath a banner headline, 'Berlin Ringed by Flames', and beside a story describing desperate fighting for the German capital, it ran a picture of 'The shackled monster of Belsen'. The caption described camp commandant Josef Kramer shuffling across the courtyard of the death camp. His ankles are fettered and he is escorted by a British soldier with a revolver in his hand. The *Express* describes him as 'a typical German brute ... a sadistic, heavy featured Nazi, quite unashamed'.[57] Another front-page picture depicted German lawyers, doctors, storekeepers and labourers sweating as they dug long graves for dead prisoners under the watchful eye of American soldiers.[58]

Contradictions between German culture and German guilt perplexed Christopher Buckley of the *Daily Telegraph*. Buckley had visited Buchenwald and Belsen when he wrote that he was struggling with 'the problem of the German people'. It was not simply that he could not find an adequate explanation for the 'fiendish cruelties and inhuman callousness' that had been discovered. The special correspondent also had difficulty 'reconciling it with the manifest docility and what would appear to be kindness of the ordinary citizens in the Rhineland and Westphalia'. He was mystified to watch burgomasters and regular German soldiers taken on a conducted tour of Belsen. All 'professed their ignorance that anything of the sort had been going on in their country'. Some were indignant. Among the camp guards he could not work out 'whether they feel any sense of shame or whether they regard our present treatment of them, which is not gentle, as just retribution'. Christopher Buckley revealed the intellectual and moral confusion of a highly intelligent liberal exposed to the morally repulsive. He wondered why, if the Germans had wanted the prisoners to die, they had not found quicker more humane ways to murder them. If they hoped to use them to defend Germany, why had they not done so? He despaired that interrogation of the guards produced no satisfactory answers. Not one of them was willing to take responsibility for their crimes.[59]

The *Daily Express* deplored German brutality but it remained aware that Germans too were suffering. On 20 April 1945, its former chief Berlin correspondent, Selkirk Panton, captured by the Germans in Denmark in 1940 and only recently repatriated, filed his first despatch in six years from Leipzig. Panton described a macabre supper party at which the mayor had thanked his senior staff before retiring to his office where he, his wife and eighteen-year-old daughter immediately committed suicide.[60] A reader, describing himself as 'A Jewish Refugee from Nazi Oppression', expressed similar tolerance in a letter to the *Manchester Guardian*. Every German knew that concentration camps existed, he explained, 'but very few knew the exact nature of the atrocities committed there'. He thought that many had guessed quite a lot and that many Germans privately despised the Nazi regime. However, German anti-Nazis also knew that participation in any conspiracy against Hitler would result in them, their families and their friends being subjected to the same atrocities.[61]

Such efforts to portray a nuanced account of German character and experience met with scant sympathy from readers. In the leading titles of left and right, accounts from Belsen and Buchenwald inspired venomous letters. A retired major writing in the *Daily Mirror* suggested that Germans should be castrated: 'Painlessly, humanely, all Germans must be deprived of the power to beget children.' Only when the inventors of Nazism were gone 'will our children die in their beds, not by the violence of war'.[62] Photographs of the concentration camps made emphatic impact. Lena Ransom wrote to the *Mirror* to suggest that pictures of Belsen should be pasted on everyday groceries such as tea, cigarettes and beer throughout Germany. She believed this would have 'a psychological effect'.[63] A young reader explained that, until he had seen the evidence, he had thought that 'there were good and bad Germans'. Having seen the brutal atrocities depicted in his newspaper, he now understood that 'the German nation is completely rotten'. The editor replied: 'Welcome to the fold!'[64] In the *Daily Express*, reader Richard Moorhouse of Watford objected to the depiction of Germans as animals, compared to the people who had run Belsen, wild beasts were tame.[65] Staff Sergeant E.R. Lawrence of the Royal Electrical and Mechanical Engineers wrote to condemn Britons who called for any type of 'kindness to the Hun'. He described watching two German schoolboys playing a game in which they built a tiny scaffold and hanged toy dolls before throwing them into a communal grave. He was appalled so see their mother teach them how to make a hangman's noose.[66]

In the broadsheets, readers' letters identified the pressing need to establish a reliable, authoritative and impartial record of what had happened in the concentration camps. Professor Vivian Hunter Galbraith (1889–1976) of the Institute of Historical Research, University of London, wrote to *The Times* to explain that visits to the camps by delegations of MPs were necessary but not sufficient; 'Trained observers with medical and other scientific qualifications' should also be sent. A complete and impartial record would be required to 'establish the facts beyond all shadow of a doubt, and so remove them from the realm of passion and feeling'.[67] In the *Manchester Guardian*, Dr Fletcher Burden, the prospective Liberal parliamentary candidate for Stalybridge and Hythe, wrote that neutral Swiss or Swedish MPs should be asked to inspect the concentration camps. Their testimony would be valuable if memories faded, or Nazi apologists emerged to claim Allied accounts were prejudiced. There was an urgent need to 'deprive future generations of Germans of a valuable propaganda weapon'. Writing in the same edition, J. Redvers

Batty of Cheadle acknowledged that he had previously 'cast doubt on the accuracy of many of the stories of atrocities attributed to the Germans'. He had hoped no civilized people could sink to such depravity. Now he had received a 'terrible shock' and he had no residual doubts. Newspapers were 'doing the world a service by printing the photographs of the horror and nothing, no matter how shocking, should be left out'.[68]

Inconsistent Coverage

In March 1944, the *Manchester Guardian* penned an editorial following the foreign secretary's declaration that one million Jews in Hungary faced extermination. 'Little now appears in the press about the massacre of the Jews', it lamented, 'but the truth is, as Mr Eden said yesterday, that the extermination goes on with "unexampled horror and intensity"'.[69] The *Guardian* was right, the fate of the Jews was not a consistently high-profile theme in British newspapers between 1939 and 1945. None ignored it entirely, but most chose to highlight events in the fighting war. This contrast between coverage of the kinetic war and the reporting of Jewish suffering was sometimes stark. Only when graphic images and eyewitness accounts of the horror combined to make a powerful impact in the spring of 1945 did news of the final solution briefly dominate the news agenda. It was soon replaced on the front pages by the final battle for Berlin and Hitler's suicide. Concern that the nature of the concentration camps had not been universally understood or believed was detectable in the didactic and occasionally pleading tone adopted in some newspaper coverage. Reporters who visited the camps begged to be believed but struggled to convey the enormity of the crime. The extent to which public scepticism endured is apparent in a soldier's letter published prominently in the *Daily Mail*. He explained that he had been depressed to hear a senior officer's account of a conversation with his barber. The latter had revealed that he found it hard to believe the stories emerging from the concentration camps. Challenged to justify this scepticism, the barber explained that in his London pub 'none of his friends believed a word of the stories from Belsen and Buchenwald'.[70]

Hitler had outlined his ambition in *Mein Kampf*, and the SS newspaper *Das Schwarze Korps* had promised 'the final end of Jewry in Germany' and 'its absolute annihilation' in 1938.[71] However, with the exception of the *Manchester Guardian*, which actively sought to confirm it, British newspapers were initially cautious about declaring the reality of the final solution. W.P. Crozier, the *Manchester Guardian*'s editor between 1932 and 1944, had inherited from his predecessor, C.P. Scott, a commitment to the Zionist cause. He committed to reporting the fate of the Jews and by doing so ensured his readers were prepared for the scale of the horror when it emerged. Other broadsheet newspapers, notably *The Times* and *Daily Telegraph*, followed the growing evidence of genocide and reported it honestly but with less consistent prominence.

Popular titles of left and right reported factually the evidence offered by the Polish government and World Jewish Congress and confirmed in statements by British ministers. However, Britain had not gone to war to protect the Jewish people. The government depicted the struggle, first, as one for national survival and, subsequently, as a defence of democracy against totalitarianism. To many Britons, it was always a fight for the control of territory and the right to live in freedom. When the *Daily Mirror* asked whether there was really anybody in Britain who did not know about the concentration camps, it was certainly protesting too much. The popular titles did too little to make it impossible for their readers to dismiss the reality of genocide. There were many who did not know in the spring of 1945, some because they chose not to dwell upon the horror, others because they were still wary of atrocity propaganda, some too for whom the scale of the evil was literally incredible. The BBC's initial reluctance to broadcast Richard Dimbleby's honest account of Belsen is instructive. Even the most sophisticated readers of newspapers would take time to absorb, process and accept the stark and appalling truth.

CHAPTER 14
VE DAY, GENERAL ELECTION AND ATOMIC BOMBS

The *Daily Mirror*, most successful of Britain's wartime popular titles, celebrated Victory in Europe with a banner headline declaring: 'Public Holiday Today and Tomorrow – Official'.[1] Beneath the text was a picture of an Allied soldier atop the statue of Eros in London's Piccadilly Circus. The caption described him as 'On top of the world'.[2] However, the *Mirror* tempered triumph with realism. A subtitle on its front page declared: 'Massacre Goes On in Prague as War Ends' and the newspaper reported that: 'In a final burst of fiendishness, S.S. troops in Prague last night were firing the last shots of the war on helpless Czech civilians.'[3] Its correspondent, Bill Greig, was afforded additional front-page space to remind readers that VE Day brought an end to 'five years, eight months and four days of the bloodiest war in history'.[4] But candour about the endurance that had brought victory was not the element that did most to attract left-leaning servicemen and made the *Mirror* so popular among Britain's fighting men and their families. This was sex appeal, delivered with a dose of demotic humour, in the form of the cartoon beauty Jane. Artist Norman Pett based Jane on a model, Chrystabel Leighton-Porter. Throughout the war, he depicted her in his daily cartoon strip in the *Mirror* as a beautiful and scantily clad girl-about-town. She became a potent symbol of British cheerfulness; Winston Churchill described her as the country's 'secret weapon'. Jane was certainly the British serviceman's favourite and on VE Day, Pett took the unprecedented step of portraying her entirely naked.

In his VE Day cartoon,[5] Jane first appears in full army uniform seated on a table in a bar. A chiller bucket containing a bottle is behind her. She holds a glass of champagne in her left hand. In her right is the hammer and sickle flag of the USSR – a clear nod towards *Mirror* readers' intense admiration for the Red Army and Socialist ideals. A male solder friend stands in the doorway carrying a Union Jack. Raising her glass, Jane declares, 'Victory at Last, Smiler! I shall soon be out of my uniform now!' In the next frame Jane is mobbed by a group of British squaddies all demanding 'a souvenir' of their favourite pin-up girl. In the final frame, Jane emerges from the crush, naked except for a loosely held, but strategically draped, Union Jack. Smiler jokes, 'You've said it Jane – You've been demobbed already.' In the following day's edition, Jane, still naked except for her flag, is detained by a military officer who insists: '[I] must keep you under arrest until your identity is established.'[6] Wartime popular humour did not conform to our modern concerns about gender stereotypes. Even at the decorous BBC, Mrs Mopp, cleaning lady and star of the immensely popular wartime comedy, ITMA (It's That Man Again), was popularly known for her catchphrase: 'Can I do you now, Sir!'

If cartoon nakedness did not appeal to readers of the popular Conservative *Daily Mail*, its proprietor the 2nd Viscount Rothermere and his low-profile editor Bob Prew

Figure 14.1 Norman Pett's VE Day cartoon for the *Daily Mirror* depicted Jane naked for the first time, 8 May 1945.

certainly understood that pictures gave them an advantage with which radio news could not compete. The *Mail*'s banner headline declared: 'VE Day – It's All Over. All quiet till 9pm then the London crowds went mad in the West End.'[7] The front-page picture depicted huge crowds in Piccadilly Circus. Beneath it appeared the caption: 'The Face of Victory – Daily Mail pictures give you a vivid impression of the great concourse of joy.'[8]

Throughout their reporting on 8 May 1945, newspapers reflected public frustration that the official announcement of the end of hostilities in Europe had been postponed. The surrender of all German forces had been agreed at Reims on 7 May. However, Field-Marshall Keitel, chief of the German High Command, did not sign the instrument of unconditional surrender until shortly before midnight on 8 May. Working throughout the evening of the seventh among the crowds in central London, reporter Guy Ramsey of the *Mail* captured the popular reaction to this delay: 'London, dead from six until nine, suddenly broke into victory life last night. Suddenly, spontaneously, deliriously. The people of London, denied VE Day officially, held their own jubilation.' Ramsey described: 'The sky once lit by the glare of the Blitz' now shining 'red with the victory glow.'[9] Additional images of the crowds dominated pages three and four.

In the VE Day edition of the elite, establishment *Times*, a parliamentary correspondent diligently recorded why 8 May 1945 is recognized to this day as the official end of the war in Europe. Mr Churchill would make 'the official announcement' at 3.00 pm. There would be simultaneous announcements in Washington DC and Moscow.[10] *The Times* reported the previous evening's festivities with restrained and decorous pride:

> Although by 9 o'clock last night the expectation of a victory declaration by the Prime Minister had been dispelled by official warnings of its postponement, civilians and service men and women thronged the road and pavements carrying flags and paper hats. Cheering demonstrators climbed the roofs of buses; the only people the crowds would make way for were lines of shouting, singing girls arm-

in-arm with service men waving flags and yelling at the top of their voices. Cars trying to press through the crowds emerged with dozens of men and women clinging to the bonnets.[11]

After six years of blackouts, the *Times* was thrilled to note that 'Large bonfires ringed London and most public buildings were floodlit.'[12] It also made excellent use of the tool BBC radio could not deploy, filling an entire broadsheet page with a gallery of pictures. This spanned the war from the 'triumphal entry of Hitler's forces into Warsaw' in September 1939, via the Dunkirk evacuation, the Blitz, Tobruk and Stalingrad to D-Day.[13]

For the mass-market Liberal *News Chronicle* (1.3 million daily sales in 1939, 1.6 million in 1948), writer A.J. Cummings went among the London crowds. He noted a spirit of decency and order as well as elation. His impression was that people were experiencing a release from years of strain rather than intense excitement. At the smaller, more graduate-oriented though equally Liberal *Manchester Guardian*, an international flavour was apparent. 'Nations Rejoice at Victory' was the headline on one prominent news story. This recorded that: 'The great bells of St Peter's and those of a hundred other Rome churches rang out in jubilation.' In neutral Switzerland, 'Allied flags were unfurled and crowds jammed the streets of Geneva.' Meanwhile, King Gustav of Sweden had broadcast 'warmest congratulations to Denmark and Norway now that our Nordic neighbours have once again become free and independent nations.'[14] The *Manchester Guardian* paid particular attention to another neutral country, Ireland, where in the capital, Dublin, 'passers-by were surprised to see students at Trinity College hoisting the Union Jack and the Red Flag over the main entrance to the University'. Next, 'the students assembled at the windows and sang "God Save the King" and "Rule Britannia!" amidst an outburst of booing from the crowd'. Police had to be despatched to prevent a violent confrontation between students at the Protestant Unionist Trinity College and the majority Catholic republican population of the Irish capital. The *Manchester Guardian* noted that 'windows were broken'.[15]

Further highlighting the deep divisions apparent in Irish society, the *Guardian* reflected that only days earlier the Taoiseach, Éamon de Valera, had called on Dr Hempel, the German ambassador to express condolences for Hitler following the Führer's suicide on 30 April. This insensitive diplomatic visit provoked questions in the House of Commons where the under-secretary for Dominion affairs, Emrys Evans, explained that His Majesty's government had not considered it necessary to submit a formal protest to the Irish government. Ministers were confident that: 'Mr De Valera can be safely left to realise for himself the universal feeling of indignation which his action has aroused in this country and throughout the United Nations.'[16]

The *Manchester Guardian* also recorded a note of caution that was present throughout Britain's wartime press on VE Day. 'We dare not forget', it reminded readers, 'that war still rages over a quarter of the globe, that British, Americans and Chinese are being wounded or killed every hour of the day and that many of the men who have won this victory in Europe will have again to screw their courage to the sticking point and risk their lives in the Far East.'[17] The King would emphasize this point in his VE Day broadcast to the nation, in which he reminded millions of listeners that: 'In the Far East, we have yet to deal with the Japanese, a determined and cruel foe. To this we shall turn with utmost resolve and all our resources.'[18] Small wonder so many of Britain's fighting men were pleased to be temporarily distracted by Jane's cartoon antics in the *Daily Mirror*.

The 1945 General Election

For the national press, however, a domestic contest would initially take precedence over the war against Japan. Robert Kee reminds us that Churchill had told Parliament in 1944 that it would be appropriate to hold a general election when Germany was defeated.[19] Now, with victory in Europe secure, the prime minister suggested instead that the coalition government he had led since May 1940 should remain in office until the war against Japan was also over. The Labour Party rejected his suggestion. Since the beginning of the year, Arthur Greenwood, Labour's leader in the House of Commons, had been anxious to make it plain that Labour wanted a contest and would fight to win. The poll due in 1940 had been repeatedly postponed via amendments to the Septennial Act of 1716 and Britons had not voted in a general election since 14 November 1935.[20] Now Churchill's deputy, the Labour leader Clement Attlee insisted on a contest, which was duly scheduled for 5 July. A massive logistical effort was launched to ensure that soldiers, sailors and airmen serving overseas could vote by post. This meant that ballots would not be counted until 26 July. During the interregnum, Labour ministers left office and Churchill led a temporary coalition of Conservatives and Liberals.

Despite the wartime popularity of Beveridge's proposals for social security and the dominance of housing as an election issue, Labour did not expect to win. In fact, uncertainty about the outcome was widespread in the weeks between voting and counting. A Gallup poll conducted in November 1944 had produced results that hinted at public support for collaboration of the type that had characterized the wartime coalition. Asked 'What form of Government would you like to see lead Britain in the period following the war?', 35 per cent of respondents had said all-party government, 26 per cent Labour and 12 per cent Conservative.[21] Juliet Gardiner notes that, in June 1945, 'Mass Observation found that 39% of young first-time voters in London were undecided' about which party to vote for.[22] On one question, though, voters appeared to favour the Conservatives. Twenty-four per cent said they would like Winston Churchill to serve as prime minister and almost as many, 21 per cent, indicated a preference for Anthony Eden, the Conservative foreign secretary. Just 7 per cent of those polled preferred Clement Attlee and 2 per cent his colleague Ernest Bevin, minister of labour and national service.

The *Daily Mirror* was adamant that every eligible adult should exercise his or her vote and vigilant on behalf of any service men who might be denied their democratic rights. On Saturday, 21 July, more than two weeks after the main polling day, a headline declared: 'No Vote for These Soldiers'. A correspondent with British forces in Germany reported that 'several soldiers with 21st Army Group, at Hertford, Westphalia, Germany, were still waiting for their ballot papers'. Officials at the barracks polling station feared: 'The papers may have been sent to the wrong address.'[23]

During the three weeks between voting and counting, the *Sunday Pictorial* sent correspondent Denis Myers to Portugal, apparently to remind its readers that the Conservative Party had strange friends. Noting that the government had sent warm thanks to Britain's 'oldest ally' for remaining neutral during the fighting, Myers wrote that 'more than three quarters of the people of Portugal are violently opposed to the regime that has been thrust upon them'. He noted that 'They call it fascism' and pointed out that Hitler, Franco, Mussolini and the Portuguese dictator Antonio Salazar would have been the 'Big Four' if Germany had won.[24] The *Pictorial* did not dare to anticipate a Labour victory, but it was confident that the Conservatives would lose seats and concerned that the Liberals would be prepared to form a new coalition to keep Winston Churchill in office. 'Since it is almost certain that the Tories will not have a working majority', it reported from Westminster, 'they will probably jump at the Liberals' offer'. There was also a rumour that Churchill 'will propose another coalition with the Labour Party'. This, warned the *Pictorial*, 'would require the consent of a Special Labour Party Conference and the abandonment of existing policy'.[25]

The *Sunday Times* offered a front-page picture of Mr Churchill 'taking the salute in the British victory parade in Berlin'. He was accompanied by Field Marshals Bernard Montgomery and Sir Alan Brooke.[26] A news story on the same page explained that Churchill 'will come to London on Wednesday in order to be in the closest touch when the result of the general election is known'.[27] On the following Wednesday, the *Daily Mail* confirmed that the prime minister, foreign secretary and Clement Attlee 'will arrive in London from the Potsdam Conference this evening in readiness for the declaration of the polls'.[28] *The Times* did not speculate about the result, but its reticence did not deter reader Mr George Schuster of Oxford. He wrote that whether the election delivered 'a big majority for Churchill or a small one, or even a minority, the right course in the national interest is clear – to go back to true all-party government. The times are far too serious for ordinary party politics.'[29]

The *Mail* expected to be able to make an assessment of the true state of the parties by late on the afternoon of Thursday, 26 July. As counting began that morning, it reported the mood detected at respective party headquarters the previous evening: 'At Conservative HQ the view was maintained that Mr Churchill was certain of a majority ... even though it might be somewhat shrunken compared with earlier optimistic forecasts.' It added, without comment, 'At Labour HQ, experts were confident that Labour had won at least 100 seats, mostly from the Conservatives and probably more.'[30] The *Daily Mirror*, desperate for a Labour victory, was nevertheless circumspect. 'Today the ballot boxes give up their secret', it reflected but, whatever the complexion of a new government, 'whether it is Conservative, Labour or anything else – it is not to be envied. The tasks ahead are so formidable that they might make any set of Ministers quail.'[31]

A further report in the *Daily Mail* revealed the extent to which newspapers were now working in informal partnership with the BBC. The *Mail* explained that, 'Last results are expected to be known by 7.30 tonight', and added, 'At noon the BBC will give the first of a series of hourly summaries lasting about five minutes. Programmes will be interrupted for any important announcement.'[32] The *Daily Telegraph* advised that counting would begin at 9.00 am and 'so much preliminary work' had already been completed that 'the earliest results may be known within three-quarters of an hour'. The same report also drew readers' attention to the BBC schedule and noted that 'the trend of voting will be clear by midday' and, for those listening to BBC bulletins, 'it may then even be known whether or not the National Government has been returned to power'.[33] Since the launch of BBC radio in 1923, newspapers had fought tooth and nail to restrict its capacity to compete as a news provider. By May 1945, newspaper proprietors had long recognized that the struggle was futile. Now, drawing the public's attention to BBC coverage of the election was simply realistic. Millions of Britons would hear news of Labour's growing landslide in the corporation's hourly bulletins.

Throughout the election, the conservative *Daily Telegraph*, owned by William Berry, 1st Viscount Camrose, and his brother Gomer Berry, 1st Viscount Kemsley, made plain its antipathy to the Labour Party. Editorial policy dictated that it should be referred to as 'the Socialist Party' or simply 'the Socialists'. Reader Mr T.W. Laming of Stroud, Gloucestershire, wrote to the editor, Arthur Watson, to deplore the party's activities: 'It has not been unknown for the Socialist Party to produce in the later stages of an election a flagrant falsehood about their opponents. During the recent campaign the following poster appeared: "Vote Hawkins for Labour. Tories in Power Means War with Russia."' Mr Laming told his fellow *Telegraph* readers: 'It would be charitable to suppose that the Socialist candidate honestly believed that such a statement was either true or would advance the cause of friendly relations with the USSR which his party professes to consider important.'[34] On the morning that counting began, columnist J.L. Garvin, wondered whether a 'leftward swing' in public opinion might have 'swelled both the Socialist and Liberal vote' at Conservative expense. Garvin, who in 1942 had resigned his editorship of *The Observer* rather than obey his proprietor's instructions to criticize Churchill, was clearly worried. A news report revealed that American newspaper correspondents in London were predicting a close result. The *Telegraph* noted the North American Newspaper Alliance's view that 'markets generally would prefer Churchill to win' and feared a Labour victory would mean 'the socialisation of the country'.[35]

By the early evening of Thursday, 26 July, the outcome was clear. Labour had won an outright majority. In fact, Mr Attlee's party had secured 47.8 per cent of the national vote and the Conservatives had managed to retain just 39.8 per cent. In a House of Commons made up of 615 seats, this gave Labour 393 MPs and the Conservatives 213. The Liberals had just twelve seats and Labour had a commanding overall majority. 'A Sweeping Labour Victory' declared *The Times*, 'Mr Churchill's Resignation Accepted by the King – Mr Attlee Asked to Form a Government'.[36]

The *Daily Telegraph* reported the enormity with cold precision: 'The Socialist Party has been returned to power with a working majority for the first time in the history of the country.'[37] The *Telegraph* also recorded that the 'election result was accompanied by a sharp fall in Stock Exchange prices which gathered momentum as the day went on'.[38] Moreover, the Conservative broadsheet knew whom to blame. Its correspondent at British forces headquarters in Germany wrote that: 'Most of the troops believe that the Services vote, as well as the influence of Servicemen on those at home, was the major cause of the move to the left in the election.' He explained that: 'The vast majority of the British troops in the British area of Germany are known to have voted for the Socialist Party. There were cheers and clapping in many messes today when the results came over the radio.'[39]

For the *Daily Herald*, jointly owned since 1929 by Odhams Press Ltd (51 per cent) and the Trades' Union Congress (49 per cent), which retained the right to determine editorial policy, Labour's victory was an event to rejoice. A mass-market newspaper with populist instincts and, by 1945, a daily readership of more than two million, the *Herald* existed to promote the mainstream social democratic instincts of the Labour leadership. Its banner headline on Friday, 27 July ran across all eight columns and declared simply: 'Labour in Power'.[40] Political correspondent Ernest Jay emphasized the new prime minister's humble demeanour. 'In a car driven by his wife', wrote Jay, 'Mr Clement Attlee went to Buckingham Palace last night and accepted the King's invitation to form a Labour Government.'[41] In the right-hand column on the front page, *Herald* reporter W.A.E. Jones conveyed the mood on the streets of the capital in a piece datelined 'London – Midnight'. 'Bonfires are burning in the streets', he explained, 'It is the story all over again of VE Day – the celebration by the rank and file of Britain for the victory of the Labour Party.' In the East End, hammered by bombs during the Blitz, 'the people have come out from their battered houses to signal the Labour Government with fires, fireworks and dancing'.[42]

Celebrations spread well beyond the East End. On the evening of Thursday, 26 July, jubilant Labour supporters had also packed the streets around Central Hall Westminster to celebrate their party's achievement. They cheered rapturously when Harold Laski, their party chairman, proclaimed 'a great victory for Socialism' and promised them 'full friendship with the Soviet Union'. Having sworn that Labour would offer 'no help to either decaying monarchs or obsolete social systems', Laski aimed a gracious jab at Winston Churchill. Referring to a disastrous election broadcast in which Churchill had warned that Socialism in Britain would require 'some form of Gestapo, no doubt very humanely directed in the first instance',[43] Laski asked:

> May I, as the temporary head of the Socialist Gestapo, say that not all of us have been treated with generosity in this election. But on the day his rule as Prime Minister draws to a close, I want in the name of the British Labour Party, to thank Mr Churchill for the great service he has rendered to this nation.'[44]

Clement Attlee, the new prime minister adopted a more cautious tone. Labour faced 'great tasks' and its supporters must not underestimate the scale of the challenge. One immediate objective must take precedence over all others. 'We have first of all to finish the war with Japan', he warned the crowd.[45]

'What a hair-trigger business the world has become' – Atomic Bombs

Nobody who heard Attlee speak expected it to end soon. British and Commonwealth forces had been fighting the Japanese in Burma since December 1941. By August 1945, their casualties amounted to 71,244 killed or wounded.[46] On Okinawa, 325 miles from the Japanese home islands, American forces had lost 10,000 dead in a ferocious 82-day campaign to defeat the Japanese garrison. They had killed 90,000 Japanese in the process. Captain Russell Grenfell, naval correspondent of the *Sunday Times* wrote that: 'The protracted and extremely bitter fighting involved in the capture of Okinawa and the substantial casualties incurred by the attackers convey the obvious warning that the invasion of the Japanese homeland, if and when it comes, may be a very tough and expensive affair.'[47] Just days later, *The Times* correspondent in Washington DC explained that such concerns had shaped the decision to drop an atomic bomb on Hiroshima. 'Until early June', he reported, 'the President and military leaders were in agreement that this weapon should not be used, but a reversal of this High Command policy was made within the last 60 and possibly the last 30 days.' Sources suggested that 'those responsible came to the conclusion that they were justified in using any and all means to bring the war in the Pacific to a close within the shortest possible time'.[48]

This was the consensus in British newspapers, but first they were simply stunned by the technology. The Manhattan Project, whose team of American, British and Canadian scientists had completed the design and assembly of the first atomic bombs at the Los Alamos National Laboratory in New Mexico, was an intensely guarded secret. Beyond a tiny elite of political and military leaders, the weapon that would 'radically alter the military and diplomatic power of the USA'[49] and define the strategic politics of the post-war world was unheard of and unimagined. The *Manchester Guardian*'s first reports of the Hiroshima bomb, dropped on 6 August, concluded that it was the result of 'Immense Co-Operative Effort by Ourselves and US'.[50] A combination of awe at an astonishing scientific achievement and patriotic pride united newspapers of left and right in their editions of 7 August 1945. From New York, the *Daily Mail*'s James Brough informed readers that Japan faced obliteration by 'the mightiest destructive force the world has ever known – unless she surrenders unconditionally in a few days'.[51] A second report described the extreme secrecy that had shrouded the weapon's development. It told how the workers who built it had never seen their final product 'and until today, they did not know what they were doing'.[52] *The Times* took care to explain the 'vast scale' of the project that had made the atomic bomb a reality. The decision to build a bomb had been taken in 1942. However, 'Great Britain at this stage was fully extended in war production, and we could not afford such grave interference with the current weapons programmes on which our warlike operations depended. Moreover, Great Britain was within easy range of German bombers and the risk of raiders from the sea or air could not be ignored.'[53] The *Daily Telegraph* celebrated the British contribution. It ran front-page pictures of the men who had invented the bomb and identified in this category Britons including Sir George Thomson of Imperial College, Sir James Chadwick of Liverpool University, Professors John Cockcroft and Norman Feather of Cambridge University and Professor Mark Oliphant of Birmingham University.[54]

To demonstrate the exceptionally destructive power of their new weapon – and the meticulous care with which they had prepared to use it – the American War Department released details of the test explosion conducted at the USAAF Alamogordo Bombing and Gunnery Range in New Mexico's Jornata del Muerto desert on 16 July 1945. New Mexico had been home since 1943 to the Manhattan Project team of scientists who would develop Little Boy, the uranium device that destroyed Hiroshima, and Fat Man, the plutonium bomb deployed against Nagasaki.[55] Ever loyal to its formula of personalization, the *Daily Mail* identified 'stocky, grey-haired Major General Leslie Richard Groves, of Pasadena, California' as the 'driving force' behind the Manhattan Project. It described how Groves and his colleagues had watched from a shelter ten miles distant as their test bomb was detonated on a metal tower erected at Alamogordo. It quoted extensively from the War Department's description of the test: 'At the appointed time, there was a blinding flash, lighting up the whole area, brighter than the brightest sunlight. Then came a tremendous, sustained roar and a heavy pressure wave which knocked down two men outside the experimental shelter.' The *Mail* reported that the explosion was so powerful that: 'clouds in its path disappeared' and: 'A blind girl near Albuquerque, 120 miles from the scene cried "what's that" when the flash lighted the sky.' The steel tower was 'entirely vaporised'.[56]

The Times, citing the same War Department statement, noted that the test explosion had 'sent a massive cloud billowing into the stratosphere with tremendous power'.[57] On the same page, it outlined the impact of the uranium device on Hiroshima. The explosion was the astonishing product of an 'Anglo-US War Secret of Four Years' Research'. It had produced a yield 'equal to 20,000 Tons of TNT' and brought a 'Rain of Ruin from the Air'. Within *The Times*' coverage appeared a hint as to why moral outrage did not emerge immediately. The US War Department had announced that 'an impenetrable cloud of dust and smoke had covered the target area after the atom bomb had been dropped'. This made 'accurate reports of the damage impossible at present'.[58] Eyewitness accounts of the devastation and the condition of survivors poisoned by radiation did not emerge immediately. The US War Department was determined that they should not.

Concern was not entirely buried, however. Winston Churchill, so recently exiled from Downing Street, recognized immediately that: 'This revelation of the secrets of nature, long mercifully withheld from man, should arouse the most solemn reflections in the mind and conscience of every human capable of comprehension.'[59] The *Manchester Guardian* was proud that Manchester scientists had played a part in devising the bomb.[60] However, it too revealed doubts. A day after news of the attack on Hiroshima, its London correspondent reflected that: 'The most notable thing about the discussion of the bomb here today ... is that hardly anyone mentions the fact that it will shorten the war with Japan. That seems unimportant compared with the fact, so suddenly and appallingly revealed to us, that we have devised a machine that will either end war or end us all.'[61] From Washington DC, *The Times* reported that some Americans too were revealing qualms: 'Some people are jubilant; others are shocked; some are incredulous; and on the lips of many is the word "awful" used in its original sense because they realise ... how terrible it could be in ruthless hands.'[62]

Two days after the bombing, the *Daily Mirror* sought to make sense of the weapon's power by relating it to its readers' own lives. Under the headline: 'Just Suppose It Had Happened Here', it explained, 'More than four square miles of Hiroshima, a city as big as

Leicester, were what Japan calls "literally seared to death" by the atom bomb.' Next it asked: 'Suppose that had happened in London ... or Edinburgh ... or Glasgow'? Then, in a superb example of quality popular journalism, commissioned just twenty-four hours after the first bomb fell, the *Mirror* asked its reporters around the country to supply detailed answers. From Edinburgh it reported that: 'In a square bounded by Bonnington Toll and Comely Bank, Morningside and King Arthur's Seat – there would be nothing but destruction. All historic Edinburgh would have disappeared.' The Glasgow news desk concluded that: 'Devastation would obliterate everything around Sauchiehall Street. Everything from the James the Fifth Bridge up to Port Dundas, across to the University.' In London, 'There would be a swathe of utter destruction from Kensington Church to the Mansion House, as wide as the parks and the West End, from Bayswater Road and Oxford Street, across to Piccadilly and the Strand.' Manchester believed everything between Victoria Station and Old Trafford would be levelled.[63]

On the same day, *The Listener*, a weekly title owned by the BBC, offered a thoughtful perspective. It believed that: 'The feeling that wells uppermost in the hearts of ordinary people on hearing of the atomic bomb is one of practical relief that our side discovered it first.' It hoped that: 'The Japanese government will bow to this new form of force majeure and so spare their people and their country the appalling destruction that otherwise awaits them.' It took pride in the 'selfless and enthusiastic labours of the men of science here, in the United States and in Canada who, working together as a team, have elaborated this discovery'. Their outstanding discovery showed 'what can be done under the compelling hand of war'. Now, 'the prayer of all mankind' must be 'that the maintenance of peace will exercise an equally compelling influence'.[64] The newspapers of 9 August 1945 had first access to official reconnaissance pictures of Hiroshima after the bombing. *The Times* noted that they:

> show clearly that four and one tenth square miles of the city, of a total area of almost seven miles, were completely destroyed by one atomic bomb.... Destroyed is the word used officially but it appears that 'Obliterated' might be a better word. ... The Japanese state that 'most of Hiroshima no longer exists, and blasted corpses too numerous to count litter the ruined city ... practically all living things, human and animal, were literally seared to death by the tremendous heat and pressure engendered by the blast'. Tokyo talks of the 'indescribable destructive power of the bomb', most bodies are so badly battered that men cannot be distinguished from women.[65]

Newspapers believed the new technology would be used to generate cheap energy. For the *Daily Mail* this offered an opportunity to chide the new Socialist government: Labour 'need not waste time nationalising the coal industry, nor the electric or gas industries, since these industries are from now on obsolete'.[66]

The second bomb, dropped on Nagasaki on 9 August, polarized opinion. For the young Communist Dorothy Thompson, writing in *The Observer*, 'The last weapon to be discovered and used awed and frightened its own users. ... If we are no longer fully at war, we are not yet at peace, the mood of mankind has radically altered and the constellation of power has decisively changed for all foreseeable time.'[67] In the *Daily Mirror*, columnist Bernard Buckham acknowledged 'some revulsion of feeling', but concluded, 'There is no moral difference between dropping a small bomb or a large one.'[68] The *Sunday Pictorial*'s headline was: 'The Bomb That Won the War!' It explained: 'Here is the first picture of the atom bomb in action. It was taken three minutes after it had exploded on Nagasaki and wiped out the city. Below you can see the colossal explosion that has been built up and rising 20,000 feet above it is the most awe-inspiring mushroom of smoke.'

The Japanese surrender was not yet signed, but it was clear that the fighting must end. The *Manchester Guardian*'s London correspondent captured the public mood as crowds took to the streets in spontaneous celebration: 'There has not been the single-hearted gaiety of VE Day. This has been to most of us a thoughtful celebration, sobered by thoughts of the fateful task which the discovery of the atomic bomb has laid on us.' He described London 'pausing and thinking, not exuberant'. People wondered how the capital 'would have stood it had the Germans been first with the atomic bombs. What a hair-trigger business the world has become.'[69] Three days later, writing under his pen name, 'Artifex', his colleague Canon Peter Green was close to despair. For him, 'The really appalling news of the atomic bomb' was proof that 'nothing but a great moral and spiritual advance can avert a third war, which must be much nearer than most people suppose possible. And from that civilisation would hardly survive.' He feared that 'centuries of misery and ruin would follow a third world war.'[70]

Britain formally celebrated VJ Day on 15 August 1945. The journalist and broadcaster Robert Kee notes: 'The holiday started slowly, partly because many people were not aware of it until they had set off for work only to find that there was no work to go to.'[71] In the morning, the king and queen drove to Westminster for the state opening of the new, Labour-majority Parliament. Many people watched King George VI arrive to announce the nationalization of the Bank of England and the coal industry. Later, happy crowds gathered in central London and, around the country, people came together to dance and build bonfires.

On 5 September, the *Daily Mail* reported that Japanese doctors in Hiroshima were seeing patients 'dying at the rate of about one hundred daily through delayed action effects of the atomic bomb which they say are similar to an overdose of exposure to X-rays or radium'. Symptoms included 'bleeding of gums, falling hair and ulcers of the throat'.[72] On the same day, the *Mail*'s dominant conservative rival, the *Daily Express*, published a searing account of the devastation of Hiroshima by Australian reporter Wilfred Burchett. Burchett was the first Western journalist to enter Hiroshima. He was shocked by what he saw. Describing his account as 'a warning to the world', Burchett told of a city reduced to 'reddish rubble' and people dying from an unknown 'atomic plague'.[73]

This prompted a response from Lord Cecil, joint president of the League of Nations Union, who warned that Britain would be uniquely vulnerable to future attacks by atomic bombs. He feared that the 'immense aggregations of people in its great cities' would be sitting targets for an aggressor.[74]

The authorized eyewitness account of the Nagasaki bombing, written by William L. Laurence for the *New York Times*, was published a month after the event on 9 September. Laurence had flown with the crew of the Boeing B29 Super Fortress that dropped Fat Man. In awestruck tones, he described 'a giant flash that broke through our arc-welder's lenses and flooded our cabin with intense light'. Airmen in the tail of the plane saw 'a giant ball of fire rise as though from the bowels of the earth'. Laurence watched a pillar of smoke and debris 'like a living totem pole with many grotesque masks grimacing at the earth'. The mushroom cloud was still plainly visible at a distance of 200 miles from the target.[75] Such accounts, though contrasting in tone, would change the tenor of debate.

As 1946 began, a leader in *The Times* reflected that 'both bombs caused immense destruction of property and men's minds were at once preoccupied with the significance of this new and terrible weapon'.[76] In June the *Sunday Times* paid close attention to the findings of an official British mission sent to Hiroshima and Nagasaki to 'make an authoritative study of the damage done' by the two atomic bombs. Among its findings were that a bomb dropped on a city with a population density of approximately 45 residents per acre would kill about 50,000 people: 'Risk of death is approximately 70 per cent at half-a-mile from the centre of the damage and 20 per cent at one mile.'[77] Dr Jacob Bronowski, a British mathematician who had worked during the war to increase the efficiency of Allied bombing, was one of a group of scientists who visited Japan in the summer of 1946 to assess the damage inflicted by the atomic bombs. He wrote about his experience in *The Listener*, describing Hiroshima as 'flat waste of wood-ash'. Its appearance was 'more desolate than that of the bombed European cities'. The atomic bombs had created 'new forms of death'. These included 'exposure to the heat flash of the bomb' and 'its penetrating radio-activity'. Bronowski warned that these also produced 'more terrifying and permanent moral effects'.[78]

Concern about the consequences of atomic warfare emerged more rapidly in newspapers than any about conventional bombing of German or Japanese cities. This had killed more civilians.[79] Within weeks of the bombings, British newspapers had raised questions about how future use of atomic power might be effectively controlled and whether it could be used for peaceful purposes. Japan raised the question of moral culpability. 'This is not war, not even murder, it is pure nihilism', declared its state broadcaster.[80] Such responses begin to explain why, eight decades later, few Germans challenge their nation's war guilt, but many Japanese consider their country a victim as much as a perpetrator of war.

CONCLUSION

The Second World War began only 20 years, nine months and three weeks after the first ended. The conflict of 1914–18, optimistically identified by H.G. Wells as 'the war that will end war',[1] left Britons disillusioned with their newspapers. At its outbreak, national titles hoped to present vivid descriptions of the fighting. They were frustrated. Censorship obstructed the adventurous style of war reporting to which Victorian and Edwardian readers had grown accustomed. The government had no interest in promoting accurate journalism. It wanted journalists to encourage enlistment and maintain home front morale. Many newspapers behaved as patriotic propagandists. They downplayed misery and extolled victory. War reporting promoted the belief that newspapers could not be trusted to tell the truth. Newspaper conduct spawned among surviving members of the Western Front generation a belief that national titles had failed to do their duty and were vulnerable to manipulation. It promoted among military leaders and politicians an understanding that journalists might be exploited in ways that rendered them valuable as agents of state propaganda.[2]

By September 1939, newspaper circulations were burgeoning and competition between national titles was fierce. But, for all their popularity, Britain's daily newspapers were not greatly trusted. They had the resources to provide coverage of national and international affairs. They were also sources of entertainment. However, conservative titles had made no serious attempt to investigate or challenge the failed policy of appeasement. Newspapers of left, right and centre had colluded with ministers to keep Edward VIII's relationship with Wallis Simpson secret from their readers. Yet, despite their failings, daily national newspapers remained the best available source of intelligence about British and international affairs. Their readers did not regard them uncritically, but they were the foundation for conversations at home, at work and in pubs. Mass Observation's *Report on the Press* found that between March 1939 and March 1940, 'there was widespread scepticism of press reports'. However, Britons still believed 'purely factual reporting of events' was possible. Indeed, they wanted more of it.[3]

The press benefited from the absence of effective competition because, when the war began, the national broadcaster was even less trusted. The majority of British households owned a radio, but the BBC of 1939 was a small organization, ponderous in tone and accustomed to working in partnership with government. It had limited reporting resources and was regarded with grave suspicion on the left. Memories of its obedience to ministers during the General Strike of 1926 counted against it. It had done nothing to expose the Royal affair or challenge appeasement. By the summer of 1945, the BBC had grown enormously in scale, reporting resources and quality of output. It had won the British public's respect and affection. Nevertheless, newspapers remained equally popular with their readers.

Newspapers did not offer the people of the United Kingdom a consistently incisive understanding of their world between 1938 and 1945. Arthur Mann's denunciation of appeasement in the *Yorkshire Post* stands out as brave and inspiring, not least for its persistence. But Mann set an example that only a few rivals, notably the *Manchester Guardian* and *Daily Herald*, sought to emulate. Conscious of their failure to offer effective or consistent scrutiny, newspaper editors began to challenge ministers more pointedly during the phoney war. They questioned Neville Chamberlain's military caution and, notably, his treatment of Leslie Hore-Belisha. Controversy concerning the evacuation of children emerged while Chamberlain remained premier. It revealed estrangement and incomprehension between social classes that would be eroded but not extinguished by the unequally shared experience of aerial bombardment. May 1940 saw the formation of a National government resolute in its determination to fight on. Now newspapers of all mainstream political complexions had ministers in office with whom they might expect their readers to agree. Their instinct to challenge power was diluted.

Dunkirk saw the British press united in morale-boosting celebration of the 'miracle of deliverance'. It did not prompt newspapers to interrogate the morale, equipment and leadership of the British Expeditionary Force. During the Battle of Britain, titles of all complexions celebrated the RAF's prowess and welcomed tailored Air Ministry briefings that helped each to tell the same stories of heroism in terms that would engage their readers. This moment of extreme national peril set a pattern in relations between the Air Ministry and newspapers that would insulate the RAF from critical scrutiny until the very end of the war.

Nonetheless, even while promoting patriotic fervour in the years when Britain stood alone, newspapers did, on occasion, perform their duty to democracy by enabling informed debate and controversy. In this, too, the newspapers established a practice that would endure. They recognized that an overwhelming majority of their readers supported the war effort. Indeed, conscription to the armed forces meant many had direct interest in the wellbeing of those fighting it. Henceforth, editors challenged government on topics of direct relevance to their readers' daily lives, rarely on military tactics or points of abstract moral principle. Thus, newspaper investigation of social injustice in policies for evacuation and the provision of air raid shelters placed ministers under direct pressure. Editorial scrutiny by elite and popular titles contributed to the replacement of John Anderson as home secretary. It alerted his successor to the power of popular journalism.

Later, newspapers took close and persistent interest in the Beveridge Report before and after publication. Titles on the left paid little heed to any divisions support for social security might generate in the national coalition. Instead, they sought promises that Beveridge's proposals would be implemented. The *Daily Telegraph* urged caution, but other titles of the centre and right did not disguise their sympathy. They recognized the Beveridge Report's value to their readers and characterized Sir William's proposals as a quintessentially British solution to genuine injustice. For the *Daily Mail* and *Daily Express*, Beveridge offered a practical response to ambitions for a fairer post-war world. For the *Times*, it was a remarkable triumph of British ingenuity that could equip the country for a new social and economic era and enhance the war effort.

Conclusion

Such diligence did not extend to newspaper scrutiny of the fate of Europe's Jewish people. This was intermittent and only occasionally high-profile. A sophisticated reader who yearned to know what was happening to the Jewish population of Nazi-occupied territories might discover much chilling detail in the elite titles. By 1943, attentive readers of the *Daily Herald*, *Manchester Guardian*, *The Times* and *Daily Telegraph* could certainly piece together the emerging horror of what we now know as the Holocaust. The *Manchester Guardian* maintained its attention to the issue throughout the war but, while its commitment was real, it did not always give the fate of the Jewish people prominence. The popular titles reported and condemned on occasion. Indeed, the *Daily Express* made the Holocaust front-page news before the first concentration camp was liberated. But, until the camps were photographed, coverage in the popular press was neither prominent nor consistent. Newspapers were not reluctant to believe the depth of Nazi depravity. They did not indulge the doubts that persuaded BBC editors to delay broadcast of Richard Dimbleby's account of conditions in Belsen. However, although it was accurate and chilling, coverage in the British press lacked the prominence and persistence that might have compelled better understanding.

Unanimous condemnation of the Nazi/Soviet non-aggression pact and its consequences turned almost seamlessly into reverence for the Russian people when Hitler launched Operation Barbarossa. Popular journalism promoted a wholly deluded version of Josef Stalin and a Panglossian view of Russian armed forces. The Russians were fighting the Germans across a colossal front. There was no appetite for scrutiny of a brave ally and government discouraged it. Reluctance to campaign on issues of principle that might offend another vital ally characterized reporting of the American presence in Britain. Elite and popular titles displayed concern about mistreatment of British women by American soldiers. They shone light on miscarriages of justice against black GIs at American courts martial. They did not systematically or persistently question why US forces were segregated. Nor did they challenge directly the government's meek surrender of legal jurisdiction over American soldiers stationed in the UK. Britain's largely informal press censorship was expanded to avoid offending the US government and newspapers did little to contest this expansion. By 1941, the Newspaper Proprietors' Association understood the extent to which ministers resented harsh criticism. Editors chose their targets. They did not always provide investigation, scrutiny and analysis. In this war for democracy, they always treated victory as the most important objective.

Plainly newspaper reporting had to be selective because paper shortage was acute. In 1938 newspapers and magazines had routinely consumed more than 20,000 tons of newsprint in a week. At the point of greatest shortage in February 1943, only 4,320 tons were available. Pagination duly suffered and the popular national dailies were reduced from pre-war editions of sixteen to 24 pages to six, or, at worst, four pages. Elite titles including *The Times*, *Daily Telegraph* and *Manchester Guardian* retained eight- or ten-page editions only by strictly limiting their own circulations.[4] Newspapers were also starved of talent. They lost many of their best editors, reporters and columnists to the armed forces. Of the 9,000 newspaper journalists employed in Britain in 1939, more than

3,000 were serving as soldiers, sailors or airmen by late 1943. Many others had left their employers to work for service departments.[5] Some joined the BBC.[6]

Vital information relating to the conduct of the war on land, at sea and in the air was controlled by the armed services and the Ministry of Information. In much of their coverage of the fighting, newspapers had only official sources of information. Often their choice was limited to whether to convey or not what they were told by the MoI and the service departments. However, on some topics considered here greater investigation and analysis of evidence would have been achievable. The area bombing of Germany is a clear example. The Air Ministry's portrayal of RAF raids as precisely aimed at military and industrial targets, and the suppression of photographs depicting their impact on residential districts, should not have posed an insurmountable challenge. Nor should the determined efforts of Brendan Bracken, the minister of information between July 1941 and the end of the war, to promote the achievements of the RAF's pilots and crews. Neutral Swiss and Swedish reporters worked in Germany during the war. Their accounts of civilian casualties were accessible and the Bombing Restriction Committee used them. Intriguingly, these accounts resembled some that British newspapers had obtained from their own reporters in British cities bombed by the Luftwaffe. They demonstrated that British bombs were killing women, children and old men. Objective scrutiny might have revealed that RAF raids had not shattered the German will to resist. And, although these were much heavier than German raids on British targets, newspapers knew enough to question whether area bombing could destroy German morale. British cities including London, Southampton and Liverpool had proved they could 'take it'. Neither popular nor elite daily titles asked whether, perhaps, the Germans could take it too. Instead, they accepted claims of precision bombing which even propaganda photographs of mass raids rendered implausible. RAF crews on night raids over Germany faced grave risks from night fighters and anti-aircraft guns. The damage they inflicted was achieved at great cost in British lives. Editors concluded that criticism of raids might be perceived as criticism of the brave men who carried them out. Their largely uncritical support for Bomber Command's ruthless raids against German population centres contrasts with their early concern about the atomic bomb attacks on Hiroshima and Nagasaki. Meanwhile, newspaper depictions of the contribution made by British science to the Manhattan Project offered only modest challenge to American exceptionalism.

My study finds newspapers struggling alongside their readers to adapt to the challenge of total war. They did not abandon their fourth estate principles, but they compromised them in what they perceived to be the national interest. They were encouraged to do so by a combination of political pressure, sensitivity to their readers' opinions, and their own eagerness to secure access to information available only from the Ministry of Information and the service ministries. The Second World War was a just war and a war for national survival. Readers were anxious for hope and reassurance and, as the war proceeded, increasingly also for evidence that victory might bring better homes, health care and secure employment.

Britons were increasingly aware of the BBC as a reliable source of news and information. They sought from their newspapers detail, analysis and entertainment, colour and opinion that the BBC did not supply. Crucially, they relied upon their newspapers to challenge government in a way that the BBC would not. Newspapers adapted to their new role. Their pre-war hostility towards the national broadcaster had persuaded the postmaster general that the broadcaster should not produce news. By the end of the war, colossal audiences often consisting of half the adult population listened to the main 9.00 pm radio news bulletin. 'War Report', the radio sequence programme launched to coincide with the D-Day landings in Normandy, brought eyewitness accounts of the fighting into homes in the UK and abroad.[7] The BBC was now popular among their readers, and newspapers embraced it as a partner in the national conversation. They began to advertise BBC services to their readers. They adapted their content in recognition that they would rarely be first with the news. Pictures became additionally valuable. These the BBC could not broadcast and newspapers learned to make optimum use of their advantage. Star columnists and correspondents, cartoons and distinctive editorial opinions emphasized their affinity with their particular community of readers. That their circulations grew alongside expansion of the BBC's audience suggests that the new partnership served both readers' interests and the newspapers' commercial ambitions.

Although they are not the focus of this study, my reading of wartime editions of weekly political titles such as *Tribune*, the *New Statesman and Nation*, the *Spectator*, *The Listener* and *The Economist* suggests that they sometimes questioned orthodoxy and challenged policy more diligently than national daily titles. Purchased by a range of intelligent opinion formers that extended from the left of the Parliamentary Labour Party to the right of the Conservative Party, their readers included civil servants, diplomats, lawyers, university academics, teachers, trade unionists, churchmen and industrialists. Ministers tolerated the circulation of critical ideas amongst such people. When distributed to local intellectual leaders the weekly political titles served as useful safety valves. *Tribune*'s treatment of the bombing campaign offers a compelling example of this approach in action. Officials who worked assiduously to exclude unpalatable accounts of the campaign from mass circulation newspapers treated occasional examples of intelligent dissent in *Tribune* as a way of burnishing Britain's democratic credentials. Its editor, Aneurin Bevan, sat in the House of Commons and exemplified the British tradition of loyal opposition. Space might be granted in his newspaper for intelligent and provocative debate, provided it did not provoke industrial unrest. *The Economist* offered meticulous analysis of the costs involved in implementing the Beveridge Plan. *The Listener* thought deeply about the atomic bomb. The government could afford to tolerate such journalism as evidence that Britain was a true democracy in which opinion was not censored.[8]

Wartime newspapers were not tame agents of propaganda. These mass-market, commercial products remained conscious that they played a role as servants of Britain's representative democratic settlement. With that settlement strengthened by truly universal suffrage following the Representation of the People Act of 1928, they recognized that their objective in wartime must be to inform, entertain and defend the electorate. In their treatment of issues affecting hearth and home, the bread and butter of British politics, newspapers performed admirably and consistently. They offered descriptions of state management and planning that challenged injustice, lambasted incompetence and praised progress. Their approach contributed to the Labour Party's success in the 1945 general election.

Britain's politicians certainly regarded newspapers, not the BBC as the country's most effective influencers of political opinion.[9] A study of the 1945 general election attempted to assess their influence. R.B. McCallum and Alison Readman's account concluded that Labour-supporting newspapers achieved a national circulation of about six million copies during the campaign. Churchill's Conservatives were backed by titles which sold about 6.8 million copies.[10] Labour's victory may suggest that Labour voters were less likely to read newspapers than their Conservative counterparts. It is also likely that some readers of the *Daily Express* and *Daily Mail* resisted their newspapers' political advice. However, Labour's unprecedented parliamentary majority was not enough to placate Herbert Morrison. He carried his obsession with newspaper bias into office as lord president of the council and leader of the House of Commons. Ernest Bevin, now foreign secretary, also perceived a threat from newspapers, particularly those owned by Lord Beaverbrook. So, when left-wing members of the National Union of Journalists (NUJ), several of them Beaverbrook employees, beseeched Clement Attlee to establish a Royal Commission on the Press, the prime minister agreed. The commission was appointed by Royal Warrant on 14 April 1947 under the chairmanship of the Scottish philosopher and ethicist, Sir William David Ross (1877–1971), Provost of Oriel College Oxford.

The terms on which Sir William and his commissioners went about their work reflected the concerns of the NUJ and the left of the parliamentary Labour Party. They were invited to proceed: 'With the object of furthering the free expression of opinion through the Press and the greatest practicable accuracy in the presentation of news, to inquire into the control, management and ownership of the newspaper and periodical Press and news-agencies including the financial structure and the monopolistic tendencies in control and to make recommendations thereon'.[11] Conservative newspaper barons were alarmed. Lord Beaverbrook concluded that the commission was 'one of the Government Agencies in the persecution of newspapers'. He predicted 'Sorrow, sorrow ever more' and decided that his best course of action would be to 'bow my head in misery'.[12] James Gomer Berry, Lord Kemsley, was persuaded that his best defence against a government that regarded him as a ferocious opponent was to establish in his newspaper empire a professional training scheme, the Kemsley Editorial Training Plan.[13] Professional training of reporters would prove to be an excellent idea, but these wealthy conservative proprietors need not have worried.

The commission reported on 13 June 1949. To the dismay of the left, it found scant evidence to support the allegations made by those David Marquand defines as 'democratic collectivists', people who believe that democratic election offers them a mandate to impose their will.[14] Newspapers survived scrutiny and emerged almost entirely unscathed. The commission found that neither government nor advertiser influence compromised the performance of the press. Newspapers presented a wide range of opinion and there were no grounds to believe that a sensible reader should be misled by their reporting. Indeed, the British press was free of corruption, eminently readable and 'inferior to none in the world'.[15] Crucially, there was no case for state regulation of newspapers and little to support the NUJ's assertion that there had been 'a progressive decline in the calibre of editors and in the quality of British journalism'.[16]

The commissioners did offer a condescending view of the popular press. They lauded *The Times* and *Daily Telegraph* while criticizing popular titles for offering too much that was designed to entertain their readers. They hoped to encourage a better balance between quality and popular appeal. The only enduring consequence for journalism emerged from the Royal Commission's recommendation that a General Council of the Press should be established. This was to be a self-regulating professional body 'which would derive its authority from the press itself and not from statute'. It was invited to censure 'undesirable types of journalistic conduct' and 'build up a code of conduct in accordance with the highest professional standards'.[17] This resulted in the creation in 1951 of the National Council for the Training of Journalists (NCTJ).[18] Seventy years later, this admirable organization continues to oversee the education of trainee journalists. The NCTJ offers rigorous, formal qualifications that ensure high standards of professionalism and ethical conduct. In 1962, the General Council would become the Press Council, the newspaper industry's first self-regulatory body. The Royal Commission's refusal to curtail press freedom suggested that Britain's newspapers ended the war in robust health. My analysis of their content largely confirms that conclusion.

Wartime newspaper were much more than the trivial playthings of millionaire proprietors. They could and did challenge government on topics about which their readers cared deeply. Popular and elite titles spoke truth to power sometimes and ministers resented their candour. Plainly, however, they also saw themselves as the government's partners in the national effort to defeat Hitler and defend democracy. And in these dual roles they operated at all times in alliance with their readers. They could not thrive by ramming down readers' throats attitudes and opinions inimical to their interests. Winning the war and the interests of their readers were their joint priorities. In wartime this made the space given to entertainment in popular titles, which the Royal Commission found offensive, genuinely valuable.

Readers working long hours and eating diets rigidly limited by rationing required levity and humour to maintain their spirits. German bombing and fear for the lives of loved ones only intensified this need. The BBC was obliged to learn that humour was important. It introduced radio shows such as ITMA to meet that need. Newspapers should not be criticized for responding to the same appetites. Indeed, had they not done so, the hard news, comment and analysis which appeared in popular and broadsheet titles would not have reached as many readers. We cannot know precisely how many Britons bought a newspaper primarily to look at cartoons, read lifestyle tips or horoscopes or enjoy gossip. We do know that, having bought one, they acquired a title that also brought them essential news and commentary. This title was then shared with their family. Wartime newspapers served democracy and gave it meaning. Their circulation grew in response and continued growing until the mid-1950s when television offered new and daunting competition.

NOTES

Introduction

1. Mass Observation Archive (MOA), 'Report on the Press', File Report (FR) 126 (May 1940), Section 3, p. 1.
2. Ibid.
3. Ibid.
4. Juliet Gardiner, *Wartime: Britain 1939–1945* (London: Headline, 2004), p. 170.
5. Action on Smoking and Health, *ASH Fact Sheet: Smoking Statistics: Who Smokes and How Much* (2016), p. 1, available online at http://ash.org.uk/wp-content/uploads/2016/06/Smoking-Statistics-Who-Smokes-and-How-Much.pdf
6. Angus Calder, *The People's War*, 12th edn (London: Pimlico, 2008), p. 504.
7. Adrian Bingham, *Family Newspapers?: Sex, Private Life and the British Popular Press 1918–1978* (Oxford: Oxford University Press, 2009), p. 6.
8. Ibid., p. 478.
9. Guy Hodgson, 'Propaganda Sheets: Trust in the Press Declined during the Second World War, as Did Its Influence', *History Today* (December 2015), available online at https://www.historytoday.com/propaganda-sheets
10. James Curran and Jean Seaton, *Power without Responsibility: Press, Broadcasting and the Internet in Britain*, 7th edn (London: Routledge, 2010), p. 120.
11. Hodgson, 'Propaganda Sheets'.
12. I.C.B. Dear and M.R.D. Foot (eds), *The Oxford Companion to World War II* (Oxford: Oxford University Press, 2001), p. 712.
13. Patrick Blackett, *Studies of War: Nuclear and Conventional,* (Edinburgh: Oliver & Boyd, 1962), p. 103.
14. Richard Overy, 'Constructing Space for Dissent in War: The Bombing Restriction Committee, 1941–1945', *The English Historical Review* 131, no. 560 (June 2016), pp. 596–622.
15. James Curran and Jean Seaton, *Power without Responsibility: Press, Broadcasting and New Media in Britain*, 6th edn (London: Routledge, 2003), p. 139.
16. George Boyce, 'The Fourth Estate: The Reappraisal of a Concept', in G. Boyce, J. Curran and P. Wingate (eds), *Newspaper History: From the 17th Century to the Present Day* (London: Constable, 1978), pp. 19–40.
17. James Curran, 'Narratives of Media History Revisited', in M. Bailey (ed.), *Narrating Media History* (Oxford: Routledge, 2009), pp. 1–21.
18. Brian Leveson, 'The Freedom of the Press and Democracy', in B. Leveson, *The Leveson Inquiry: The Report into the Culture, Practices and Ethics of the Press* (London: HMSO, 2012), Vol. 1, Part B, Chapter 2, para. 2.19, p. 61.
19. Mark Hampton, 'Renewing the Liberal Tradition', in M. Bailey (ed.), *Narrating Media History* (Oxford: Routledge, 2009), pp. 26–35.

Notes to pp. 4–10

20. Adrian Bingham, 'Ignoring the First Draft of History', *Media History* 18, nos 3–4 (2012), pp. 311–26.
21. Bingham, *Family Newspapers?*, p. 6.
22. David Thorburn, 'James W. Carey, 1934–2006' (2011), http://web.mit.edu/comm-forum/legacy/forums/carey_memoriam2.htm
23. Michael Schudson, *Why Democracies Need an Unlovable Press* (Cambridge: Polity Press, 2009).
24. Philip Knightley, *The First Casualty: The War Correspondent as Hero and Myth-Maker from the Crimea to Iraq* (London: John Hopkins University Press, 2004).
25. Richard Collier, *The Warcos: The War Correspondents of World War Two* (London: Weidenfeld & Nicolson, 1989).
26. Virginia Cowles, *Looking for Trouble* (London: Faber & Faber, 2010 [1941]).
27. Clare Hollingsworth, *The Three Week's War in Poland* (London: Duckworth, 1940).
28. Hilde Marchant, *Women and Children Last* (London: Gollancz, 1941).
29. Alan Moorhead, *The Desert War* (London: Aurum Press, 2009).

Chapter 1

1. Thomas Paine, *Rights of Man* (Mineola, NY: Dover Publications, 1999).
2. Kate Campbell, 'W.E. Gladstone, W.T. Stead, Matthew Arnold and a New Journalism: Cultural Politics in the 1880s', *Victorian Politics Review* 36, no. 1 (2003), 20–40.
3. Nils Bejerot, 'The Six-Day War in Stockholm', *New Scientist* 61, no. 886 (1974), 486–87. See also N. deFabrique et al., 'Understanding Stockholm Syndrome', *FBI Law Enforcement Bulletin* 76, no. 7 (2007), p. 10.
4. Harold Lasswell, *Propaganda Technique in the World War* (Eastford, CT: Martino Fine Books, 2013), p. 195.
5. Philip Gibbs, *Adventures in Journalism* (London: W. Heinemann, 1923), p. 253.
6. Niall Ferguson, *The Pity of War* (London: Allen Lane, 1998), p. 238.
7. Malcolm Brown (ed.), *The Wipers Times: The Complete Series of the Famous Wartime Trench Newspaper* (St Albans: Little Books, 2006).
8. Matthew Farish, 'Modern Witnesses: Foreign Correspondents, Geopolitical Vision, and the First World War', *Transactions of the Institute of British Geographers* 26, no. 3 (2001), pp. 273–87.
9. Sarah Lonsdale, 'A Golden Interlude: Journalists in Early Twentieth Century British Literature', *Parliamentary Affairs* 64, no. 2 (2011), pp. 326–40.

Chapter 2

1. Duff Cooper, *Old Men Forget: The Autobiography of Duff Cooper (Viscount Norwich)* (London: Rupert Hart-Davis, 1953), p. 175.
2. M.M. Knappen, 'The Abdication of Edward VIII', *Journal of Modern History* 10, no. 2 (1938), pp. 242–50.
3. G.M. Young, *Stanley Baldwin* (London: Rupert Hart-Davis, 1952), p. 234.

4. Richard Cockett, *Twilight of Truth: Chamberlain, Appeasement and the Manipulation of the Press* (London: Weidenfeld and Nicolson, 1989), p. 2.
5. Mick Temple, *The British Press* (Maidenhead: McGraw-Hill, 2008), p. 141.
6. *Time*, 'Great Britain: The Crown', Vol. 28, no. 14 (5 October 1936), pp. 18–19.
7. *Time*, 'Education: Nomination', Vol. 28, no. 20 (16 November 1936), p. 85.
8. Dennis Griffiths, *Fleet Street: Five Hundred Years of the Press* (London: The British Library, 2006), p. 21.
9. *Time*, 'Foreign News: World's Greatest Romance', Vol. 28, no. 20 (16 November 1936), p. 31.
10. Dennis Griffiths, *A Century of Journalism 1900–2000* (Oxford: Coranto Press, 2012), p. 21.
11. A.J.P. Taylor, *Beaverbrook* (London: Hamish Hamilton, 1972).
12. J. Lincoln White, *The Abdication of Edward VIII* (London: George Routledge & Sons, 1937), p. 96.
13. Cecil King, *Strictly Personal, Some Memoirs of Cecil H. King* (London: Weidenfeld & Nicolson, 1969), p. 107.
14. *The Times*, 'King and Monarchy', 3 December 1936, p. 15.
15. *Hansard*, HC Debates, Vol. 318, cols 1611–12, 4 December 1936.
16. Fred Siebert, 'The Press and the British Constitutional Crisis', *Public Opinion Quarterly* 1, no. 4 (1937), p. 124.
17. George Orwell, 'As I Please', *Tribune*, no. 393, 7 July 1944, p. 12.
18. Siebert, 'The Press and the British Constitutional Crisis', p. 121.
19. *Time*, 'Foreign News: World's Greatest Romance', Vol. 28, no. 20 (16 November 1936), p. 31.
20. *Literary Digest*, 'Queenly Enigma: What Will Mrs Simpson and King Edward Do? Asks Wondering World', 7 November 1936, p. 11.
21. *The Times*, 'A Lull', 9 December 1936, p. 15.
22. Ibid.
23. Ibid.
24. Ibid.
25. Martin Pugh, *State and Society: A Social and Political History of Britain 1870–1997* (London: Arnold, 1999), p. 217.
26. Jerry Brookshire, *Clement Attlee* (Manchester: Manchester University Press, 1995), p. 16.
27. A.J.P. Taylor, *English History 1914–1945* (Oxford: Oxford University Press, 1990), p. 383.
28. Martin Gilbert and Richard Gott, *The Appeasers* (London: Orion, 2000), p. 41.
29. Cockett, *Twilight of Truth*, p. 186.
30. Sir Nevile Henderson, *Failure of a Mission: Berlin 1937–39* (London: Hodder & Stoughton, 1940), p. 115.
31. Cited in Guy Hodgson, 'Sir Nevile Henderson, Appeasement and the Press', *Journalism Studies* 8, no. 2 (2007), pp. 320–34.
32. Colin Seymour-Ure, *Prime Ministers and the Media: Issues of Power and Control* (Oxford: Blackwell, 2003), p. 128.
33. Ibid., p. 181.
34. James Margach, *The Abuse of Power: The War between Downing Street and the Media from Lloyd George to Callaghan* (London: W.H. Allen, 1978), p. 129.
35. Ibid.

Notes to pp. 19–25

36. *The Times*, 'Munich and After', 3 October 1938, p. 13.
37. Ibid.
38. *Daily Express*, 'Make this "Cheerful Monday"', 3 October 1938, p. 1.
39. *Daily Express*, 'British Defensive Strength', 3 October 1938, p. 10.
40. Ibid.
41. *Yorkshire Post*, 'A Momentous Debate', 4 October 1938, p. 10.
42. *Daily Mail*, 'On Guard', 4 October 1938, p. 10.
43. Ibid.
44. *Yorkshire Post*, 'Twenty Years After', 11 November 1938, p. 10.
45. *Daily Mirror*, 'The King Thanks You', 3 October 1938, p. 1.
46. *Daily Mirror*, 'Hitler's Visit to His New Empire', 3 October 1938, p. 1.
47. *Daily Mirror*, 'March On', 4 October 1938, p. 11.
48. Ibid.
49. Daniel Hucker, *Public Opinion and the End of Appeasement in Britain and France* (Farnham: Ashgate, 2011), p. 29.
50. *Manchester Guardian*, 'For Our Time?', 3 October 1938, p. 8.
51. Ibid.
52. *Manchester Guardian*, 'Looking Forward', 7 October 1938, p. 10.
53. *The Times*, 'The Tragedy of Guernica. Town Destroyed in Air Attack. Eye Witness's Account', 28 April 1937, p. 17.
54. Ian Youngs, 'Picasso's Guernica in a Car Showroom', 15 February 2012, available online at https://www.bbc.co.uk/news/entertainment-arts-16927120
55. *Hansard*, HL Debates, Vol. 107, col. 424, 13 December 1937.
56. Gardiner, *Wartime: Britain 1939–1945*, p. 17.
57. BBC, 'The Transcript of Neville Chamberlain's Declaration of War', BBC Archive Written Document (1939), available online at http://romanohistory.pbworks.com/w/file/fetch/73728956/British%20Declare%20War%20on%20Germany.pdf
58. Sian Nicholas, '"There Will Be No War": The *Daily Express* and the Approach of War, 1938–39', in D. Welch and J. Fox (eds), *Justifying War: Propaganda, Politics and the Modern Age* (London, Palgrave Macmillan, 2012), pp. 200–17.
59. Cockett, *Twilight of Truth*, p. 1.
60. MOA, 'Report on the Press', Section 4, p. 1.
61. Tim Luckhurst, 'War Correspondents', in *1914–1918 Online: International Encyclopedia of the First World War*, ed. by Ute Daniel, Peter Gatrell, Oliver Janz, Heather Jones, Jennifer Keene, Alan Kramer and Bill Nasson, issued by Freie Universität Berlin (2016).
62. MOA, 'Report on the Press', Section 4, p. 2.

Chapter 3

1. Adam Matthew Publications, *Popular Newspapers during World War II* (Marlborough: Adam Matthew Publications, 1993), p. 7.

2. Adam Matthew Publications, *The (Sex) Bomb that Won the War* (2018), available online at https://www.amdigital.co.uk/about/blog/item/the-sex-bomb-that-won-the-war
3. George Perry and Alan Aldridge, *The Penguin Book of Comics* (London: Penguin, 1967).
4. Gardiner, *Wartime: Britain 1939–1945*, p. 146.
5. Jay McInerney, *Bright Lights, Big City* (London: Jonathan Cape, 1985), p. 11.
6. Adam Matthew Publications, *Popular Newspapers during World War II*, p. 7.
7. *Daily Mirror*, 'Britain's First Day of War: Churchill Is New Navy Chief', 4 September 1939, p. 1.
8. Ibid., 'Petrol Will Be Rationed', 4 September 1939, p. 1.
9. *Daily Mail*, 'Submarine Sinks Liner, 160 Americans Aboard', 6 am Special Edition, 4 September 1939, p. 1.
10. Ibid., 'Premier Broadcasts to German People this Morning', 6 am Special Edition, 4 September 1939, p. 1.
11. George P. Thompson, *Blue Pencil Admiral: The Inside Story of the Press Censorship* (London: Sampson Low, Marston & Co., 1947), p. 2.
12. Ibid., p. 3.
13. Ibid.
14. Ibid., p. 7.
15. Ibid., p. 23.
16. Ibid., p. 24.
17. Ibid., p. 12.
18. Ibid.
19. Tom Harrison, *Living Through the Blitz* (London: Faber & Faber, 2010), pp. 19–30.
20. Cited in ibid., p. 22.
21. Cited in ibid., p. 25.
22. Cited in ibid., p. 25.
23. Cited in ibid., p. 24.
24. Cited in ibid., p. 24.
25. *Daily Express*, 'Evacuation Today', 1 September 1939, p. 1.
26. Ibid., 'Three Million People Begin to Leave Their Homes Today in History's Greatest Exodus', 1 September 1939, p. 5.
27. *Daily Mirror*, 'Evacuation of 3,000,000: The Plans', 1 September 1939, p. 4.
28. Ibid., 'A Good Time Will Be Had by All', 1 September 1939, p. 3.
29. Ibid., 1 September 1939, p. 2.
30. *Daily Express*, 'Village Plans Its Welcome', 1 September 1939, p. 5.
31. *The Times*, 'Evacuation To-day', 1 September 1939, p. 11.
32. *The Times*, 'A Childless City', 5 September 1939, p. 9.
33. Ibid.
34. Gardiner, *Wartime: Britain 1939–1945*, p. 34.
35. *The Times*, 'After the Dispersal', 15 September 1939, p. 9.
36. *Daily Worker*, 'Evacuation: The Way to Make it Work' by Charlotte Haldane, 16 September 1939, p. 3.

Notes to pp. 33–39

37. *Daily Express*, 'Mothers Are Evacuation Problem Number 1', 15 September 1939, p. 5.
38. *Manchester Guardian*, 'Right Child in Right Place: Difficulties Experienced in Reception Area', 9 October 1939, p. 8.
39. Ibid.
40. Calder, *The People's War*, p. 75.
41. Cited in Keith Feiling, *The Life of Neville Chamberlain* (London: Macmillan & Co., 1946), p. 434.
42. A.J. Trythall, 'The Downfall of Leslie Hore-Belisha', *Journal of Contemporary History* 16, no. 3 (1981), pp. 391–411.
43. Cited in ibid., p. 391.
44. *Daily Mirror*, 'Hore-Belisha Resigns', 6 January 1940, p. 1.
45. *Daily Mirror*, 'Bombshell!', 6 January 1940, p. 7.
46. *Manchester Guardian*, 'War Minister's Departure: A Surprising Affair with No Explanation Given', 6 January 1940, p. 9.
47. Ibid., 'Mr Hore-Belisha "Amazed"', 6 January 1940, p. 9.
48. Ibid., 'Questions in the Press – War Office Change – This Morning's Comments', 6 January 1940, p. 9.
49. Ibid.
50. Ibid., 'Questions in the Press – War Office Change – This Morning's Comments', 6 January 1940, p. 9.
51. Ibid.
52. Ibid.
53. Ibid.
54. Brian Bond (ed.), *Chief of Staff: The Diaries of Lieutenant-General Sir Henry Pownall: Volume One 1933–1940* (London: Leo Cooper, 1972), p. 203.
55. Trythall, 'The Downfall of Leslie Hore-Belisha'.
56. Iain Macleod, *Neville Chamberlain* (London: Frederick Muller, 1961), p. 284.
57. Cockett, *Twilight of Truth*, pp. 169–70.
58. Tim Luckhurst, '"It Is Thrown Against Me that I Have a Castle": A Portrait of Newspaper Coverage of the Central Southwark By-election, February 1940', *Journalism Studies* 13, no.1 (2012), pp. 107–23.
59. Calder, *The People's War*, p. 58.
60. MOA, By-elections 1937–47, Topic Collection (TC) 46/3/A.
61. Christopher Andrew, *The Defence of the Realm: The Authorized History of MI5* (London: Allen Lane, 2009), pp. 263–65.
62. Paul Addison, 'By-elections of the Second World War', in Chris Cook and John Ramsden (eds), *By-elections in British Politics* (London: Macmillan, 1973), pp. 165–97.
63. *London Evening Standard*, 13 February 1940.
64. MOA, By-elections 1937–47, TC 46/3/Gb.
65. Ibid.
66. William Barkley, 'Mrs Van der Elst Wants to End Misery but Mr Martin is Most Likely to Win', *Daily Express*, 10 February 1940, p. 5.

67. Paul Addison, *The Road to 1945: British Politics and the Second World War* (London: Cape, 1975), pp 137–40.
68. Knightley, *The First Casualty*, pp. 246–47.
69. MOA, By-elections 1937–1947, TC 46/3/Ca.
70. Ibid., TC 46/3/Bc.
71. Ibid., TC 46/3/Ga.
72. Arthur Greenwood, 'Get This Straight', *Daily Herald*, 15 January 1940.
73. *Daily Herald*, 'Report of Speech by Clement Attlee', 16 January 1940.
74. *Daily Worker*, 'Labour Students Vote Against the War', 4 January 1940, p. 1.
75. Ibid., 'Ex-Mayor Supports Anti-war Candidate', 4 January 1940, p. 2.
76. *Daily Worker*, 'Searson for Southwark', 6 January 1940.
77. *Daily Herald*, 25 January 1940.
78. MOA, By-elections 1937–1947, TC 46/3/A.
79. Ibid., TC 46/3/C.
80. *The Times*, 'Polling Today in Southwark', 10 February 1940.
81. *Manchester Guardian*, 'Today's Poll at Southwark', 10 February 1940.
82. *London Evening Standard*, 'Polling Day Fixed', 25 January 1940.
83. *London Evening Standard*, 13 February 1940.

Chapter 4

1. *Daily Mirror*, 'Cassandra', 5 April 1940, p. 6.
2. Ibid., 'Premier 10 Times Sure of Victory', 5 April 1940, p. 4.
3. *Daily Express*, 'Ten Times as Sure of Victory Now', 5 April 1940, p. 4.
4. Olivia Cockett, *Love and War in London: The Mass Observation Wartime Diary of Olivia Cockett*, ed. Robert Malcolmson (Stroud: The History Press, 2008), p. 81.
5. *Daily Mail*, 'To Force Britain to Her Knees', 10 April 1940, p. 1.
6. Ibid., 'Big Battle off Coast of Norway, Reported "Heavy German Losses: Bremen Sunk"', 10 April 1940, p. 1.
7. Ibid.
8. *The Times*, 'A New Phase of the War', 10 April 1940, p. 9.
9. Ibid., 'Aggression without Limit', 10 April 1940, p. 9.
10. *Daily Mirror*, 'Nephew of Churchill Held', 10 April 1940, p. 1.
11. Ibid., 'Cassandra', 10 April 1940, p. 6.
12. Cited in Nicholas Shakespeare, *Six Minutes in May: How Churchill Unexpectedly Became Prime Minister* (London: Vintage, 2017), p. 67.
13. Ibid.
14. Ibid.
15. *The Times*, 'Conduct of War in Norway', 8 May 1940, p. 3.
16. Ibid., 'Mr Chamberlain's Case', 8 May 1940, p. 7.

Notes to pp. 45–50

17. Ibid.
18. Ibid.
19. John Evelyn Wrench, *Geoffrey Dawson and Our Times* (London: Hutchinson, 1955), p. 408.
20. Ibid., p. 366.
21. Ibid.
22. *The Times*, 'A Warning and An Opportunity', 6 May 1940, p. 7.
23. Ibid.
24. *Daily Mirror*, 'Who Held Back Navy? Admiral Hero Asks', 8 May 1940, p. 1.
25. *Hansard*, HC Debates, Vol. 360, cols 1150–51, 7 May 1940.
26. *Daily Mirror*, 'In Name of God, Go, Premier Told', 8 May 1940, p. 1.
27. Ibid., 'How Much Longer?', 8 May 1940, p. 7.
28. Philip Zec, 'Gid-Up!', *Daily Mirror*, 8 May 1940, p. 7.
29. Wilson Broadbent, political correspondent, 'Churchill to Answer Keyes', *Daily Mail*, 8 May 1940, p. 1.
30. Ibid.
31. Ibid.
32. Ibid.
33. *Daily Express*, 'I Offered to Take Trondheim – I Implored Them but They Would Not Let Me Go', 8 May 1940, p. 1.
34. Ibid., '50 Years in the Navy', 8 May 1940, p. 1.
35. Ibid., 'Debate Severely Damages Government's Prestige', 8 May 1940, p. 1.
36. Ibid., 'Amery to Premier: Get Out!', 8 May 1940, p. 1.
37. Ibid., 'Opinion', 8 May 1940, p. 4.
38. Strube, 'Winston's New Job', *Daily Express*, 8 May 1940, p. 4.
39. Shakespeare, *Six Minutes in May*.
40. Ibid., p. 307.
41. Richard Toye, *Winston Churchill: A Life in the News* (Oxford: Oxford University Press, 2020), p. 178.
42. Ibid., p. 179.
43. *The Times*, 'Mr Chamberlain Resigns', 11 May 1940, p. 7.
44. Ibid.
45. *Daily Express*, 'British Troops Pour through Belgium', 11 May 1940, p. 1.
46. Ibid., 'Churchill Is Premier', 11 May 1940.
47. Ibid., 'The Man All Germans Hate', 11 May 1940, p.1
48. *Manchester Guardian*, 'Mr Churchill Premier, Mr Chamberlain Staying in War Cabinet', 11 May 1940, p. 7.
49. Ibid., 'Mr Churchill's Ministry', 11 May 1940, p. 9.
50. *The Observer*, 'Mr Churchill as Premier, Crisis and After – Wanted, A Great Government', 12 May 1940, p. 6.
51. Ibid.
52. *Sunday Times*, 'Unity', 12 May 1940, p. 6.

53. Ibid.
54. Toye, *Winston Churchill*, p. 182.
55. *Daily Worker*, 'Communist Party on War and Government Crisis – No Man, Woman or Child Is Safe', 11 May 1940, p. 1.
56. *Daily Worker*, 'Attlee and Greenwood Ask for Support of Conference', 13 May 1940, p. 1.
57. Julian Jackson, *The Fall of France: The Nazi Invasion of 1940* (Oxford: Oxford University Press, 2003).
58. Neil Hanson, *Priestley's Wars* (Bradford: Great Northern Books, 2008), p.203
59. *Manchester Guardian*, 'The Miracle of the B.E.F.'s Return', 1 June 1940, p. 7.
60. *Daily Mirror*, 'BLOODY MARVELLOUS!', 1 June 1940, p. 7.
61. Ibid.
62. Ibid.
63. Philip Zec, 'This Way, Chum!', *Daily Mirror*, 1 June 1940, p. 7.
64. *The Times*, 'Lord Gort's Return', 3 June 1940, p. 7.
65. *The Times*, 'Anabasis', 4 June 1940, p. 7.
66. *The Times*, 'A Miracle of Deliverance', 5 June 1940, p. 7.
67. *Daily Mail*, 'Will Italy Fight', 8 June 1940, p. 4.
68. *Daily Mail*, 'Help for France', 4 June 1940, p. 4.
69. The National Archives W P (G) (40) 145, 'War Cabinet Memorandum, Title: Compulsory Censorship. Author: Duff Cooper.', section 4, p. 2.
70. Ibid., section 5, p. 3.
71. Ibid.
72. Ibid., section 1, p. 1.
73. Aaron L. Goldman, 'Press Freedom in Britain during World War II', *Journalism History* 22, no. 4 (1997), pp. 146–55.
74. *Daily Worker*, 'New Law Penalises Opinion', 11 May 1940, p. 1.
75. *The Times*, 'Censorship of the Press', 22 July 1940, p. 4.
76. Ibid., 'Freedom of the Press', 22 July 1940, p. 2.
77. Ibid.
78. *Manchester Guardian*, 'Censorship of the Press: Voluntary Still, Tighter Control Rejected', 22 July 1940, p. 5.
79. *The Economist*, 'Eyes Open', Vol. 138, no. 5053 (29 June 1940), p. 1107.

Chapter 5

1. Angus Calder, *The Myth of the Blitz* (London: Pimlico, 1991), p. 1.
2. Ibid., p. 2.
3. Jessica Mann, *Out of Harm's Way: The Wartime Evacuation of Children from Britain* (London: Headline Books, 2005), p. 2.
4. Ibid., p. 36.

Notes to pp. 58–62

5. Henry Channon, *Chips: The Dairies of Sir Henry Channon* (London: Weidenfeld & Nicolson, 1967), p. 259.
6. Ibid.
7. Mann, *Out of Harm's Way*, p. 55.
8. Statement to the nation after a bomb hit Buckingham Palace on 13 September 1940, cited in William Shawcross, *Queen Elizabeth The Queen Mother: The Official Biography* (London: Penguin Random House, 2010).
9. *The Times*, 'Emigration of Children', 29 June 1940, p. 7.
10. The National Archives CAB 65/7/65
11. Mann, *Out of Harm's Way*, p. 59.
12. *Hansard*, HC Debates, Vol. 362, col. 699, 2 July 1940.
13. Ibid., col. 706.
14. Stuart Hylton, *Reporting the Blitz: News from the Home Front Communities* (Stroud: The History Press, 2012), p. 73.
15. *Daily Express*, 'Radio Is So Wonderful, Nice Kind Nazis, Please Save Us: Take Our City', 14 September 1939, p. 3
16. William Joyce, 'Germany Calling', broadcast of 6 June 1940, available online at https://www.iwm.org.uk/collections/item/object/80024329
17. *Hansard*, HC Debates, Vol. 362, col. 713, 2 July 1940.
18. Ibid., col. 747.
19. *The Times*, 'Sending Children to Dominions: Limited Scheme Being Considered', 1 June 1940, p. 3.
20. J.B. Priestley, *Postscript*, 16 June 1940, reproduced in Hanson, *Priestley's Wars*, pp. 207–9.
21. Ibid., p. 208.
22. Ibid., pp. 208–9.
23. Paul Addison and Jeremy Crang (eds), *Listening to Britain: Home Intelligence Reports on Britain's Finest Hour, May to September 1940* (London: Vintage Books, 2011), p. xi.
24. Ibid., p. 124.
25. Ibid., p. 125.
26. Ibid., p. 126.
27. Ibid., p. 127.
28. Ibid., p. 160.
29. *Daily Express*, 'To Go – or Not to Go? The Rich Go First', 3 July 1940, p. 4.
30. *Daily Mirror*, 'Let Children into America', 8 July 1940, p. 2.
31. *Daily Mirror*, 'Refugee Limit Dropped', 15 July 1940, p. 7.
32. *Manchester Guardian*, 'Children for Dominions', 20 June 1940, p. 4.
33. *Manchester Guardian*, 'Children for the Dominions – Parents Told that They "Must Weight the Risks" and Decide', 24 June 1940, p. 10.
34. Ibid.
35. *Manchester Guardian*, 'Sending Children Overseas', 25 June 1940, p. 2.
36. *Manchester Guardian*, 'Children for Overseas, Graduates' Offers', 4 July 1940, p. 3.

Notes to pp. 62–67

37. Carol Dyhouse, 'The British Federation of University Women and the Status of Women in Universities, 1907–1939', *Women's History Review* 4, no. 4 (1995), pp. 465–85.
38. *Manchester Guardian*, 'Letters to the Editor', 'Sending Children Overseas: The Military Reasons', 27 June 1940, p. 10.
39. *Daily Mail*, 'Children Sail Free to Safety', 20 June 1940, p. 5.
40. Adrian Bingham, 'The Woman's Realm: The *Daily Mail* and Female Readers', Daily Mail Historical Archive 1896–2004 (©Gale, a Cengage Co., 2013)
41. *Daily Mail*, 'Look at It in This Way, Mrs Smith, Says Ann Temple', 3 July 1940, p. 4.
42. *Hansard*, HC Debates, Vol. 363, cols 338–66, 17 July 1940.
43. Ibid., cols 394–95, 18 July 1940.
44. *Daily Worker*, 'MPs Denounce Class Evacuation', 18 July 1940, p. 1.
45. Addison and Crang, *Listening to Britain*, p. 183.
46. Barbara Bech, account of the sinking of the SS *City of Benares* (2015), available online at: https://www.liverpoolmuseums.org.uk/maritime-museum/city-of-benares
47. *Hansard*, HC Debates, Vol. 365, cols 476–77, 10 October 1940.
48. Ian Kershaw, *Fateful Choices: Ten Decisions that Changed the World, 1940–41* (London: Penguin, 2008), p. 11.

Chapter 6

1. *Hansard*, HC Debates, Vol. 364, col. 1167, 20 August 1940.
2. Calder, *The People's War*, p. 502.
3. *Daily Mirror*, 'RAF's Battle Score 37', 11 July 1940, p. 1.
4. *Daily Express*, '37 German Raiders Down – Three Spitfires Attack Fifty, and Win', 11 July 1940, p. 1.
5. *Yorkshire Post*, '14 Nazi Planes Down, 23 Badly Damaged – RAF Pilots' Best Day', 11 July 1940, p. 1.
6. *Daily Telegraph*, 'RAF Put 37 Raiders out of Action – 14 Shot Down: Others Unable to Get Home', 11 July 1940, p. 1.
7. *Daily Mail*, 'RAF Win Big Air Victory off Kent Coast – 14 Germans Shot Down, 23 Crippled in Battle', 11 July 1940, p. 1.
8. *The Times*, 'Air Defence Cadets', 11 July 1940, p. 2.
9. Richard Norton-Taylor, 'Months Before War, Rothermere Said Hitler's Work Was Superhuman', *The Guardian*, 1 April 2005, available online at: https://www.theguardian.com/media/2005/apr/01/pressandpublishing.secondworldwar
10. Adrian Addison, *Mail Men: The Unauthorised Story of the Daily Mail* (London: Atlantic, 2017), p. 99.
11. Ibid., p. 107.
12. *Daily Mail*, 'Legless Pilot Dances', 15 July 1940, p. 3.
13. *The Times*, 'Legless RAF Pilot's Achievement – Grit and Determination', 15 July 1940, p. 2.
14. *Daily Mirror*, 'Greatest Hero of Them All', 15 July 1940, p. 1.

15. *Manchester Guardian,* 'Our London Correspondence', 15 July 1940, p.4
16. *Daily Telegraph,* 'Identity of Legless Pilot – Leads Canadian Squadron', 15 July 1940, p. 5.
17. *Daily Mail,* 'Collie Knox visits the RAF Nursery', 17 July 1940, p. 2.
18. Calder, *The Myth of the Blitz*, p. 212.
19. Mollie Painter-Downes, *London War Notes 1939–1945* (New York: Farrar, Strauss and Giroux, 1971), p. 60.
20. Calder, *The Myth of the Blitz*, p. 210.
21. *New York Times,* 'Coalition Meets British Problem', 19 May 1940, p. 70.
22. *New York Times,* 'On British Shake-Up, Author Says Only Democracy Can Win War Dull Ruling Class Has Nearly Lost', 8 September 1940, p. 43.
23. Philip Seib, *Broadcasts from the Blitz: How Edward R. Murrow Helped Lead America into War* (Dulles, VA: Potomac Books, 2006), p. 55.
24. Ibid.
25. Ibid., p. 52.
26. H.R. Pratt Boorman, *Hell's Corner 1940: Kent Becomes the Battlefield of Britain* (Maidstone: Kent Messenger, 1940), p. 7.
27. Calder, *The Myth of the Blitz*, p. 215.
28. Robert W. Desmond, *Tides of War: World News Reporting 1940-1945* (Iowa City: University of Iowa Press, 1984), p. 104.
29. Philip Nel, 'Said a Bird in the Midst of a Blitz: How World War II Created Dr Seuss', *Mosaic* 34, no.2 (2001), pp. 65–85.
30. Ibid.
31. Paul Milkman, *PM: A New Deal in Journalism* (New Brunswick, NJ: Rutgers University Press, 1997), p. 60.
32. Ben Robertson, *I Saw England* (New York: A.A. Knopf, 1941), p. 79.
33. Collier, *The Warcos*, p. 48.
34. Ibid., pp. 48–49.
35. Cowles, *Looking for Trouble*, p. 417.
36. Collier, *The Warcos*, p. 48.
37. Ibid., p. 49.
38. Nicholas Cull, cited in Calder, *The Myth of the Blitz*, p. 212.
39. Royal Airforces Association, *History of the Battle of Britain*, available online at: https://www.rafmuseum.org.uk/research/online-exhibitions/history-of-the-battle-of-britain/
40. *Daily Mail,* 'Greatest Day for RAF – 350 Came, Only 175 Returned', 16 September 1940, p. 1.
41. Ibid.
42. *Daily Mail,* 'St Paul's Is Saved by Six Heroes', 16 September 1940, p. 1.
43. *The Times,* 'New Enemy Tactics', 16 September 1940, p. 2.
44. *Daily Mirror,* 'London Oil Fires – Nazis', 17 September 1940, p. 2.
45. *Daily Mirror,* '80, Tried to Fight Bombs', 20 September 1940, p. 6.
46. *Daily Mirror,* 'Folly Cost 3 Lives in Hunt for Souvenirs', 17 September 1940, p. 6.

Chapter 7

1. Calder, *The Myth of the Blitz*, p. 120.
2. Cockett, *Love and War in London*, p. 150.
3. Eileen Alexander, *Love in the Blitz: The Greatest Lost Love Letters of the Second World War*, ed. David McGowan and David Crane (London: Harper Collins, 2020), p.89.
4. Ibid, p. 89.
5. Seib, *Broadcasts from the Blitz*, p. 75.
6. *The Times*, 'Theft of Air Raid Shelters', 9 August 1940, p. 9.
7. Gardiner, *Wartime: Britain 1939–1945*, p. 372.
8. *Daily Mirror*, 'Homeless Find Refuge in the Underground', 14 September 1940, p. 7.
9. *Daily Mail*, 'Deeper Raid Shelter Is Rejected', 17 September 1940, p. 1.
10. Ibid.
11. Ibid.
12. *The Times*, 'Use of Public Shelters', 17 September 1940, p. 2.
13. *Daily Mirror*, 'If I were OC London', 21 September 1940, p. 4.
14. *Daily Mirror*, 'Tube May Be Made Shelter', 21 September 1940, p. 1.
15. *Daily Telegraph*, 'Refugees Prefer Tubes to Shelters', 20 September 1940, p. 5.
16. Ibid.
17. Ian McLaine, *Ministry of Morale: Home Front Morale and the Ministry of Information in World War II* (London: George Allen & Unwin, 1979), p. 111.
18. *Daily Telegraph*, 'Refugees Prefer Tubes to Shelters', 20 September 1940, p. 5.
19. *Sunday Pictorial*, 'Rich Hotels Turn People Away during Air Raids', 22 September 1940, p. 4.
20. Ibid.
21. Ibid.
22. Ibid.
23. Ritchie Calder, *The Lesson of London* (London: Searchlight Books, Secker & Warburg, 1941), p. 17.
24. Ibid., p. 18.
25. Ritchie Calder, 'This Must Not Happen Again', *Daily Herald*, 11 September 1940, p. 1.
26. Calder, *The Lesson of London*, p. 18.
27. Calder, 'This Must Not Happen Again'.
28. Ibid.
29. Cited in Gardiner, *Wartime: Britain 1939–1945*, p. 376.
30. *Daily Worker*, 'Shelters, Shelters, Shelters', 17 September 1940, p. 4.
31. *The Economist*, 'New Shelter Policy?', 28 September 1940, Vol. 139, no. 5066, p. 395.
32. *The Times*, 'Impending Cabinet Changes', 3 October 1940, p. 4.
33. Guy Eden, 'Chamberlain to Go: Cabinet Shuffle: Morrison to Home Office', *Daily Express*, 3 October 1940, p. 1.
34. *The Times*, 'Reconstruction of the Government', 4 October 1940, p. 4.
35. *Daily Mail*, 'Eight in the Team', 4 October 1940, p. 2.

36. *Daily Telegraph*, 'New Blood in the Ministry', 4 October 1940, p. 4.
37. *Daily Express*, 'Opinion', 4 October 1940, p. 4.
38. Cited in Ian Jack, 'Leveson Isn't Unprecedented. The Same Issues Came up 60 Years Ago', *Guardian*, 22 June 2012, available online at: https://www.theguardian.com/commentisfree/2012/jun/22/do-failings-of-newspapers-matter
39. *Daily Mirror*, 'Big Task Follows Air Blitz', 7 October 1940, p. 11.
40. Calder, *The Lesson of London*, p. 77.
41. Ibid., p. 78.
42. *The Times*, 'Raid Shelters', 11 October 1940, p. 4.
43. *The Times*, 'Cost of Air Raid Shelters', 21 October 1940, p. 2.
44. *Daily Mail*, 'It's Your Opinion – Postbag Analysis', 24 September 1940, p. 3.
45. Ibid., 'A Call for Clear Thinking', 24 September 1940, p. 2.
46. Ibid.
47. *Daily Express*, 'Military Damage in Berlin', 3 October 1940, p. 1.
48. David Lloyd George, 'Britain Could Defy the Nazi Bombers for Ever', *Sunday Pictorial*, 29 September 1940, p. 9.
49. Ibid.
50. Hilde Marchant, 'A Very Gallant City', *Daily Express*, 16 November 1940, p. 1.
51. Hilde Marchant, 'Mrs Smith Hands Out Cups of Tea as Bombs Come Down', *Daily Express*, 16 November 1940, p. 6.
52. Ibid.
53. *Daily Express*, 'Coventry Cathedral in the Centre of the City', picture caption, 16 November 1940, p. 1.
54. *Daily Mail*, 'Coventry – Britain's Rotterdam', 16 November 1940, p. 6.
55. William Hall, 'Every Coventry Child in Safety Today', *Daily Mail*, 18 November 1940, p. 3.
56. *Daily Worker*, '1000 Casualties in Reprisal Raid on Coventry', 16 November 1940, p. 1.
57. Ibid.
58. *Daily Mirror*, 'Coventry Raiders Return', 16 November 1940, p. 1.
59. Ibid., 'Coventry's Ordeal', 16 November 1940, p. 5.
60. *Sunday Pictorial*, 'The Great Example', 17 November 1940, p. 6.
61. *The Times*, 'A Martyred City', 16 November 1940, p. 5.
62. *Manchester Guardian*, 'Coventry', 16 November 1940, p. 6.
63. *Daily Worker*, 'Fiercer Air War Breaks Out After Coventry Raid', 18 November 1940, p. 1.
64. Peter Kerrigan, 'Coventry a Shambles', *Daily Worker*, 18 November 1940, p. 1.
65. *Daily Express*, 'Woman Carries Injured from Bombed Ambulance', 15 March 1941, p. 5.
66. Calder, *The People's War*, p. 210.
67. *Daily Express*, 'Woman Carries Injured from Bombed Ambulance', 15 March 1941, p. 5.
68. *Daily Mirror*, 'Blitz over Clyde', 15 March 1941, p. 3.
69. Calder, *The People's War*, p. 210.
70. *Daily Telegraph*, 'Heavy Raids on Ports', 15 March 1941, p. 5.
71. *The Times*, 'First Big Raid on Clydeside', 15 March 1941, p. 2.

72. *Daily Mail*, 'Raiders May End Strike', 15 March 1941, p. 6.
73. Sandy Hobbs, *Clyde Apprentices' Strikes* (1988), available online at: http://www.workerscity.org/workers_city/sandy_hobbs.html
74. *Daily Worker*, 'Making History', 16 November 1940, p. 4.

Chapter 8

1. McLaine, *Ministry of Morale*, p. 109.
2. Cited in Cockett, *Love and War in London*, p. 165.
3. Alexander, *Love in the Blitz*, p. 103.
4. McLaine, *Ministry of Morale*, p. 109.
5. Cited in ibid.
6. Fiona Rudd, 'An Unpublished Biography of Peter Ritchie Calder', available online at: https://digital.nls.uk/propaganda/calder/calder_biography.pdf
7. *Sunday Pictorial*, 'Another Blunder', 29 September 1940, p. 6.
8. *Sunday Pictorial*, 'Friends', 8 September 1940, p. 8.
9. Ibid.
10. *Daily Mirror*, 'A People's War', 7 October 1940, p. 5.
11. Ibid.
12. Hugh Cudlipp, *Publish and be Damned! The Astonishing Story of the Daily Mirror* (London: Andrew Dakers Ltd, 1953), p. 143.
13. Ibid., p. 136.
14. Cited in ibid., p. 149.
15. The National Archives, CAB 65/9 WM 267 (40), 7 October 1940.
16. Ibid.
17. The National Archives, CAB 66/12 WP 402 (40), 'Memorandum. Type: Subversive Newspaper Propaganda. Author: Herbert Morrison', 8 October 1940, para. 2.
18. *Daily Mirror*, 'We Can Rebuild', 8 October 1940, p. 5.
19. The National Archives CAB 66/12 WP 402 (40), 8 October 1940, para. 3.
20. Ibid., para. 4.
21. Ibid., para. 5.
22. Ibid., para. 6.
23. Ibid.
24. Ibid., para. 8.
25. Ibid., para. 7.
26. Cudlipp, *Publish and Be Damned!*, pp. 150–51.
27. Toye, *Winston Churchill*, p. 185.
28. Ibid., p. 152.
29. John McIlroy and Alan Campbell, 'Histories of the British Communist Party: A User's Guide', *Labour History Review* 68, no. 1 (2003), pp. 33–59.

Notes to pp. 96–101

30. David Childs, 'The British Communist Party and the War, 1939–41: Old Slogans Revived', *Journal of Contemporary History* 12, no. 2 (1977), pp. 237–53.
31. Calder, *The People's War*, p. 231.
32. Tim Luckhurst, 'Excellent but Gullible People: The Press and the People's Convention', *Journalism Studies* 14, no. 1 (2013), pp. 62–77.
33. *Manchester Guardian*, 'Labour and "People's Convention"', 22 January 1941, p. 6.
34. Douglas Hyde, *I Believed* (London: The Reprint Society, 1952), p. 70.
35. The National Archives, CAB 66/14 WP (40) 482, 'Memorandum. Title: The "Daily Worker". Author: Herbert Morrison', 23 December 1940, para. 1.
36. Ibid., para. 3.
37. Ibid.
38. *Daily Worker*, 'There is No Morality', 28 October 1940, p. 4.
39. The National Archives, CAB 66/14 WP (40) 482, 'Memorandum. Title: The "Daily Worker". Author: Herbert Morrison', 23 December 1940, para. 3.
40. Ibid., para. 3.
41. Ibid., para. 4.
42. Ibid., para. 5.
43. Ibid., para. 7.
44. Ibid., para. 8.
45. Curran and Seaton, *Power without Responsibility: Press, Broadcasting and New Media in Britain*, p. 57.
46. Tim Luckhurst, 'It Is Thrown Against Me that I Have a Castle'.
47. National Committee of the People's Convention, *The People Speak: Official Report of the People's Convention* (London: National Committee of the People's Convention, 1941).
48. Calder, *The People's War*, pp. 245–46.
49. Gardiner, *Wartime: Britain 1939–1945*, p. 298.
50. Ibid.
51. *Manchester Guardian*, 'People's Convention, Moscow Papers Give It Half a Page', 17 January 1940, p. 7.
52. Hyde, *I Believed*, pp. 92–93.
53. *Manchester Guardian*, 'The Communists', 20 December 1940, p. 4.
54. *Daily Herald*, 'Obstruction', 11 January 1941, p. 2.
55. *Daily Herald*, 'Maurice Webb Goes to the People's Convention', 13 January 1941, p. 5.
56. *Daily Herald*, 'The People's Reichstag', 14 January 1941, p. 2.
57. *Daily Mirror*, 'This Is a Cloak for Defeatism', 13 January 1941, p. 12.
58. *Daily Telegraph*, 'Freedom & Licence', 22 January 1941, p. 4.
59. *The Times*, 'Daily Worker Suppressed', 22 January 1941, p. 4.
60. Ibid., 'Speedy Action Taken', 22 January 1941, p. 4.
61. *Daily Mail*, 'Good Riddance', 22 January 1941, p. 2.
62. Ibid., 'The Daily Worker Defies Ban', 22 January 1941, p. 1.
63. *Daily Mirror*, 'Making Martyrs', 22 January 1941, p. 5.

Notes to pp. 102–109

64. *The Times*, 'Attempt to Weaken War Effort', 23 January 1941, p. 4.
65. *Hansard*, HC Debates, Vol. 368, col. 465, 28 January 1941.
66. Cudlipp, *Publish and Be Damned!*, p. 154.
67. *Hansard*, HC Debates, Vol. 368, col. 508, 28 January 1941.
68. Ibid., col. 486.
69. Ibid., col. 506.
70. Ibid., col. 507.
71. Ibid., cols 520–21.
72. Ibid., col. 522.
73. Goldman, 'Press Freedom in Britain during World War II'.
74. Cudlipp, *Publish and Be Damned!*, p. 133.
75. Calder, *The People's War*, p. 288.
76. Cudlipp, *Publish and Be Damned!*, p. 162.
77. Ibid., p. 163.
78. Goldman, 'Press Freedom in Britain during World War II'.
79. Cudlipp, *Publish and Be Damned!*, p. 173.
80. David Edgerton, *Britain's War Machine: Weapons, Resources and Experts in the Second World War* (London: Penguin Books, 2012), p. 158.
81. Cudlipp, *Publish and Be Damned!*, p. 175.
82. Ibid., p. 176.
83. Curran and Seaton, *Power without Responsibility: Press, Broadcasting and New Media in Britain*, p. 60.
84. Toye, *Winston Churchill*, p. 201.
85. Cudlipp, *Publish and Be Damned!*, p. 180.
86. Andrew: *The Defence of the Realm*, p. 289.
87. *Hansard*, HC Debates, Vol. 378, col. 1665, 19 March 1942.
88. Ibid., col. 1666.
89. Ibid., col. 1667.
90. Ibid.
91. Ibid., col. 1668.
92. Ibid.
93. Ibid., col. 1669.
94. *The Times*, 'Regulation 2D', 20 March 1942, p. 5.

Chapter 9

1. Cited in Donald Lammers, 'Fascism, Communism, and the Foreign Office, 1937–39', *Journal of Contemporary History* 6, no. 3 (1971), pp. 66–86, p. 83.
2. Churchill College Cambridge, 'Sir Winston Churchill: A Biography', available online at: chu.cam.ac.uk/archives/collections/churchill-papers/churchill-biography

Notes to pp. 110–115

3. D.J. Taylor, *Orwell: The Life* (London: Vintage, 2004), p. 302.
4. *Daily Express*, 'Pact Signed', 24 August 1939, p. 1.
5. *Daily Express*, 'Opinion', 24 August 1939, p. 10.
6. Alan Moorehead, 'Rome Moves for Peace', *Daily Express*, 24 August 1939, p. 1.
7. *Daily Mail*, 'Soviet-German Pact Signed: 2 am Announcement', 24 August 1939, p. 1.
8. Ibid., 'The Pact Signed', 24 August 1939, p. 8.
9. *Daily Mirror*, 'Betrayal', 18 September 1939, p. 7.
10. *Daily Mail*, 'Betrayal', 18 September 1939, p. 6.
11. *Daily Express*, 'Opinion', 18 September 1939, p. 6.
12. Roger Moorhouse, *The Devils' Alliance: Hitler's Pact with Stalin, 1939–41* (London, Vintage, 2016), p. 146.
13. Ibid., p. 147.
14. *Daily Mirror*, Zec cartoon, 20 September 1939, p. 7.
15. *The Times*, 'Stalin Shows His Hand', 18 September 1939, p. 7.
16. Ibid.
17. Martin Kitchen, *British Policy Towards the Soviet Union during the Second World War* (New York: St. Martin's Press, 1986), p. 1.
18. Moorhouse, *The Devils' Alliance*, p. 148.
19. Kitchen, *British Policy Towards the Soviet Union during the Second World War*, p. 2.
20. *Sunday Pictorial*, 'This Red Butcher', 3 December 1939, p. 1.
21. Ibid., 'Finns Fight Reds with Fire', 3 December 1939, p. 2.
22. *Daily Mirror*, 'Hitler and Stalin', 4 December 1939, p. 9.
23. *The Times*, 'The Invasion of Finland', 1 December 1939, p. 9.
24. Cited in Kitchen, *British Policy Towards the Soviet Union during the Second World War*, p. 16.
25. Scrutator, 'Our Debt to the Finns', *Sunday Times*, 7 January 1940, p. 8.
26. *The Economist*, 'Russia and the League', 23 December 1939, Vol. 137, no. 5026, p. 459.
27. Baroness Anastasie Mannerheim, 'My Father, Field-Marshall Baron Carl Gustav Emil Mannerheim', *Daily Mail*, 30 January 1940, p. 6.
28. *Daily Mirror*, 'New Moves', 3 January 1940, p. 7.
29. Cowles, *Looking for Trouble*, p. 300.
30. *Daily Telegraph*, 'Working for Finland', 7 March 1940, p. 6.
31. *Daily Mail*, 'British Volunteers in Finland', 9 March 1940, p. 2.
32. W.F. Martin, 'Helsinki in Grim Mood', *Daily Mail*, 13 March 1940, p. 1.
33. *Daily Mail*, 'Terms Signed under Duress', 13 March 1940, p. 1.
34. *Daily Mirror*, 'Reds Say Peace Is Signed', 13 March 1940, p. 1.
35. *The Times*, 'Cease Fire at Noon Today', 13 March 1940, p. 8.
36. *Daily Telegraph*, 'Peace Pact Signed in Moscow', 13 March 1940, p. 1.
37. *Daily Express*, 'Armistice at Noon Today, Says Moscow', 13 March 1940, p. 1.
38. Guy Eden, 'BEF for Finland Still Stands', *Daily Express*, 13 March 1940, p. 1.
39. *Daily Express*, '"Friendly" Stalin in Drama of the Kremlin', 13 March 1940, p. 1.

40. *The Times*, 'The Balkan Cauldron', 3 July 1940, p. 5.
41. *Daily Express*, 'Red Cities Blitzed, Reds Bomb Back', 23 June 1941, p. 1.
42. *Daily Express*, 'Moscow Rips Down Wooden Houses', 23 June 1941, p. 1.
43. *Daily Express*, 'All Aid for the Soviet Union', 23 June 1941, p. 1.
44. *The Times*, 'How Russia Was Told', 23 June 1941, p. 3.
45. *Daily Telegraph*, 'Help for Russia to Be on a Mutual Basis', 25 June 1941, p. 3.
46. *The Times*, 'Communists to Support Government', 27 June 1941, p. 2.
47. *Daily Herald*, 'Full Speed Ahead', 23 June 1941, p. 2.
48. W.N. Ewer, 'The War this Morning – Appeasement Fails Again', *Daily Herald*, 23 June 1941, p. 2.
49. *Daily Mirror*, 'Britain, Russia in Plot, Say Huns', 23 June 1941, p. 3.
50. *Daily Mirror*, 'Fate of Napoleon', 23 June 1941, p. 3.
51. *Manchester Guardian*, 'Russia Told of Our View', 23 June 1941, p. 5.
52. Moorhouse, *The Devils' Alliance*, p. 256.
53. Ibid., pp. 257–62.
54. *The Times*, 'The Consistency of Hitler', 24 June 1941, p. 5.
55. George Knupffer, 'Will the Russian People Follow Stalin to the End?', *Daily Mail*, 24 June 1941, p. 2.
56. *Daily Herald*, 'To the Government and to the Workers', 24 June 1941, p. 2.
57. Philip Zec, cartoon, *Daily Mirror*, 24 June 1941, p. 4.
58. Kitchen, *British Policy Towards the Soviet Union during the Second World War*, p. 117.
59. *Daily Mail*, 'Crimea: Hitler's Armies Threaten the Black Sea Fleet, Liddell Hart Sums Up', 4 November 1941, p. 2.
60. Kitchen, *British Policy Towards the Soviet Union during the Second World War*, p. 117.
61. *The Times*, 'The Russian Advance', 3 March 1942, p.5
62. Kitchen, *British Policy Towards the Soviet Union during the Second World War*, p. 119.
63. *Manchester Guardian*, 'Treaty of Alliance with Russia', 12 June 1942, p. 5.
64. *Daily Herald*, 'Partners', 12 June 1942, p. 2.
65. *Daily Mirror*, 'A Second Front in 1942', 12 June 1942, p. 1.
66. Ibid., 'Second Front Thrills US', 12 June 1942, p. 1.
67. *Daily Mail*, 'The New Alliance', 12 June 1942, p. 2.
68. *Daily Telegraph*, 'Britain and Russia Sign 20-Years Pact', 12 June 1942, p. 1.
69. Ibid., 'Alliance with Russia', 12 June 1942, p. 2.
70. *The Times*, 'The Treaty', 12 June 1942, p. 5.
71. Guy Eden, 'Mr Smith Came to London', *Daily Express*, 12 June 1942, p. 2.
72. *Daily Express*, 'Britain, U.S.A. and Russia Agree on Second Front this Year', 12 June 1942, p. 1.
73. Ibid., 'Urgency, Speed, Courage', 12 June 1942, p. 2.
74. Ibid., 'Cheering Crowds in Moscow', 12 June 1942, p. 2.
75. *Daily Mail*, 'Safe Home', 25 August 1942, p. 2.
76. *Daily Mirror*, 'Stalingrad: Hun Spearhead Is 40 Miles Off', 24 August 1942, p. 1.

Notes to pp. 123–129

77. Ibid., 'Picture of Churchill and Stalin', 24 August 1942, p. 1.
78. Martin Gilbert, *Road to Victory: Winston S. Churchill 1941-1945* (London: Heineman, 1989)
79. *Daily Mirror*, 'Stalingrad Now Is Battle Area – Moscow', 26 August 1942, p. 8.
80. *The Times*, 'The Siege of Stalingrad', 19 September 1942, p. 5.
81. *Daily Mail*, 'The Volga Verdun', 22 September 1942, p. 2.
82. *Daily Telegraph*, 'It Is Sept. 23', 23 September 1942, p. 4.
83. *Manchester Guardian*, 'Stalingrad's Home Guard: Valuable Part in the Struggle', 26 September, p. 4.
84. *Daily Mirror*, 'Second Front Will Cost You Food Cuts', 25 September 1942, p. 5.
85. *Daily Herald*, 'Ban Lifted from *Daily Worker*', 27 August 1942, p. 1.
86. Ibid., 'Victory for Unity', 27 August 1942, p. 1.
87. Calder, *The People's War*, p. 349.
88. Kitchen, *British Policy Towards the Soviet Union during the Second World War*, p. 158.
89. *Manchester Guardian*, 'Our London Correspondence', 9 February 1943, p. 4.
90. *Sunday Times*, 'The Universities', 7 February 1943, p. 7.
91. *The Times*, 'The Epic Battle for Stalingrad', 5 February 1943, p. 4.
92. *Daily Mail*, 'The Might of Russia', 5 February 1943, p. 2.
93. Bill Greig, 'Poor Adolf', *Daily Mirror*, 5 February 1943, p. 2.
94. *Daily Herald*, 'Another Encircled Nazi Force Is Wiped Out', 5 February 1943, p. 1.
95. Ibid., 'Germany Has a Day of Dirges for Stalingrad', 5 February 1943, p. 1.
96. *Daily Express*, 'Russian Army 20 Miles from Sea of Azov', 5 February 1943, p. 1.
97. Ibid., 'Her Job Is Bringing in the Germans', 5 February 1943, p. 1.
98. Sidney Strube, cartoon, *Daily Express*, 5 February 1943, p. 2.
99. *The Times*, 'The Tide Flows On', 5 February 1943, p. 5.

Chapter 10

1. David Marquand, *Britain Since 1918: The Strange Career of British Democracy* (London: Orion Books, 2009), p. 106.
2. Gardiner, *Wartime: Britain 1939–1945*, p. 581.
3. *Daily Telegraph*, 'Beveridge Plan Public Soon', 13 November 1942, p. 5.
4. Ibid.
5. *The Times*, 'Future of Social Service', 17 November 1942, p. 2.
6. *Hansard*, HC Debates, Vol. 385, cols 187–88, 17 November 1942.
7. W.H. Beveridge, letter to the editor, *Daily Telegraph*, 'Beveridge Report', 18 November 1942, p. 4.
8. *Daily Mirror*, 'The Beveridge Report Ready', 18 November 1942, p. 1.
9. Bill Greig, 'Inequality', *Daily Mirror*, 20 November 1942, p. 2.
10. *Daily Mirror*, 'Beveridge Report "Sabotage"', 20 November 1942, p. 2.

11. *Daily Mirror*, 'Beveridge Mystery', 21 November 1942, p. 2.
12. *Sunday Pictorial*, 'Morrison Going Up', 22 November 1942, p. 1.
13. *Sunday Pictorial*, 'He Talks Sense', 22 November 1942, p. 3.
14. *Daily Telegraph*, 'Post-War Plan for Workers', 23 November 1942, p. 3.
15. *Daily Telegraph*, 'Beveridge Plan', 26 November 1942, p. 1.
16. *The Times*, 'Employment after the War', 23 November 1942, p. 2.
17. Ibid., 'Freedom from Idleness', 23 November 1942, p. 5.
18. *The Times*, 'Obligations of Victory', 26 November 1942, p. 5.
19. *Daily Mirror*, 'Beveridge to Wed Assistant Aged 66', 28 November 1942, p. 4.
20. *Daily Mirror*, 'Banish Want from Cradle to Grave Plan – All Pay, All Benefit', 2 December 1942, p. 1.
21. Ibid., 'What the Plan Does for Everyone – How to Be Born, Bred and Buried by Beveridge', 2 December 1942, p. 5.
22. Ibid., 'The Beveridge Plan at a Glance', 2 December 1942, p. 7.
23. Sir William Beveridge, 'Social Security for All', *Daily Mirror*, 2 December 1942, p. 4.
24. *Daily Herald*, 'Beveridge Plans Security Against Want Every Day of Their Lives for Every Man, Woman and Child', 2 December 1942, p. 1.
25. *Daily Herald*, 'Life in Beveridge Britain', 3 December 1942, p. 3.
26. *Daily Mail*, 'Sir William Beveridge to Marry', 28 November 1942, p. 3.
27. *Daily Mail*, 'Beveridge on Radio', 1 December 1942, p. 4.
28. *Daily Mail*, '£2 a Week for All – New Status for Housewives', 2 December 1942, p. 1.
29. Ibid., 'The Plan', 2 December 1942, p. 2.
30. George Murray, '£2 a Week for Everyone – A New Deal for Wives, Widows and Spinsters', *Daily Mail*, 2 December 1942, p. 2.
31. Leslie Illingworth, cartoon, 'Here's to the brave new world', *Daily Mail*, 2 December 1942, p. 2.
32. *Daily Mail*, 'Report on Beveridge', 2 December 1942, p. 3.
33. Ibid., 'Beveridge Plan Problems – Future of Doctors Still to Be Settled', 2 December 1942, p. 3.
34. *The Times*, 'Freedom from Want', 2 December 1942, p. 5.
35. Ibid.
36. *Manchester Guardian*, 'A British Revolution: No Case for Patching', 3 December 1942, p. 6.
37. *Manchester Guardian*, 'Social Security for All', 2 December 1942, p. 5.
38. *Manchester Guardian*, 'The Social Security Plan: Flattering Reception: Critics Holding Back?', 3 December 1942, p. 5.
39. Ibid.
40. *Manchester Guardian*, 'American Interest', 3 December 1942, p. 5.
41. *Manchester Guardian*, 'Revolutionary: An American Comment', 2 December 1942, p. 5.
42. Ibid., 'Telling Occupied Europe', 2 December 1942, p. 5.
43. *Manchester Guardian*, 'Beveridge Plan Comments', 3 December 1942, p. 2.
44. *The Economist*, 'Social Priorities', 5 December 1942, Issue 5180, p. 689.
45. Gardiner, *Wartime: Britain 1939–1945*, p. 582.
46. Ibid.

Notes to pp. 135–143

47. Richard Toye, *Winston Churchill: A Life in the News*, p. 210
48. Ibid., p. 584.
49. *Hansard*, HC Debates, Vol. 386, col. 1596, 16 February 1943.
50. Ibid., col. 1616.
51. Ibid., col. 1615.
52. *Sunday Pictorial*, 'Why Was He in this Plot?', 14 February 1943, p. 1.
53. *Sunday Pictorial*, 'Beware', 14 February 1943, p. 4.
54. *Hansard*, HC Debates, Vol. 386, col. 2021, 18 February 1943.
55. Ibid., c. 2032.
56. Ibid., c. 2040.
57. Ibid., c. 2049.
58. Ibid., c. 2050.
59. *Daily Mirror*, 'Beveridge Vote Has Killed Labour Support of Government', 19 February 1943, p. 1.
60. Ibid., 'Pathetic', 19 February 1943, p. 2.

Chapter 11

1. Montague Lacey, 'U.S. Army Lands in Ulster', *Daily Express*, 27 January 1942, p. 1.
2. *Daily Mail*, 'You Will Fight in Europe', 27 January 1942, p. 1.
3. *Daily Mail*, 'They Salute Our Officers', 28 January 1942, p. 3.
4. John Walters, 'Your First Lesson in U.S. Soldier Slang', *Daily Mirror*, 9 January 1942, p. 2.
5. *Daily Mirror*, 'Yanks Are Over: U.S. Infantry in N. Ireland', 27 January 1942, p. 1.
6. David Reynolds, *Rich Relations: The American Occupation of Britain, 1942-1945* (New York: Random House, 1994), p. 99.
7. Ibid., p. xxix.
8. Thompson, *Blue Pencil Admiral*, p. 121.
9. Ibid., p. 124.
10. Reynolds, *Rich Relations*, p. 37.
11. Ibid., p. 152.
12. *Hansard*, HC Debates, Vol. 377, col. 1473, 10 February 1942.
13. Reynolds, *Rich Relations*, pp. 4–5.
14. Ibid., p. 146.
15. *Daily Telegraph*, 'Scourging the Reich', 30 July 1942, p. 3.
16. *Manchester Guardian*, 'Offences by U.S. Service Men: Protest Against Hasty Passage of Military Courts Bill', 5 August 1942, p. 8.
17. James, Baron Atkin, letter to the editor, *The Times*, 'Americans and the Law', 3 August 1942, p. 5.
18. Arthur Goodhart, letter to the editor, *The Times*, 'American Principles and Practice', 11 August 1942, p. 2.
19. *The Times*, 'American Courts Martial', 11 August 1942, p. 2.

Notes to pp. 143–150

20. *Daily Mirror*, 'U.S. Court Visits', 13 August 1942, p. 5.
21. *Daily Mail*, 'Fatherly Talk Is a Right', 12 August 1942, p. 3.
22. Ibid.
23. *Daily Mirror*, 'US Court Visits', 13 August 1942, p. 5.
24. *Daily Telegraph*, 'Court-Martial Acquittal', 15 August 1942, p. 3.
25. *The Times*, 'U.S. Soldier Sentenced to Death', 5 January 1943, p. 2.
26. *Daily Mirror*, 'Rat Stabbed Her Rescuer', 1 May 1943, p. 2.
27. *Daily Mail*, 'U.S. Soldier Wrote to Girl, Court Told', 8 October 1943, p.3
28. *The Times*, 'U.S. Soldier Sentenced to Death', 27 October 1943, p. 2.
29. *Daily Mirror*, 'I Stalled. I Didn't Want to Die', 27 October 1943, p. 2.
30. *The Times*, 'U.S. Soldier Sentenced to Death', 27 October 1943, p. 2.
31. *Daily Mail*, 'Soldiers in Street Gun Battle', 5 October 1943, p. 1.
32. *Daily Express*, 'Shots Fired in Town, Soldiers Held', 5 October 1943, p. 4.
33. *Manchester Guardian*, 'Shooting Affray', 5 October 1943, p. 6.
34. *Daily Telegraph*, '21 US Troops Arrested – Shooting Affray in Cornwall', 5 October 1943, p. 5.
35. *Daily Mirror*, 'US Men in Wild West Fight', 5 October 1943, p. 1.
36. *Manchester Guardian*, '14 US Soldiers on Mutiny Charge – Shots in Market Square', 16 October 1943, p. 7.
37. *Manchester Guardian*, 'Mutiny Charge: Trial of US Soldiers', 18 October 1943, p. 6.
38. *Daily Mirror*, '"Mutiny" Shots: 14 Charged', 16 October 1943, p. 4.
39. *Sunday Pictorial*, 'Dance, Pub and then Court-Martial', 17 October 1943, p. 2.
40. Kate Werran, *An American Uprising in Second World War England: Mutiny in the Duchy* (Barnsley: Pen & Sword History, 2020), p. 8.
41. Ibid., p. 10.
42. Ibid., p. 8.
43. Murray Edwards, 'A Briton at the Court of the Yankees', *Daily Herald*, 16 October 1943, pp. 1 and 4.
44. Ibid.
45. Ibid.
46. Werran, *An American Uprising in Second World War England*, p. 6.
47. *Daily Mirror*, 'Accused Soldiers Bet on Verdicts as Rioting Case Ends', 18 October 1943, p. 8.
48. Werran, *An American Uprising in Second World War England*, p. 173.
49. *The Times*, 'News in Brief', 18 June 1943, p. 2.
50. Murray Edwards, 'Soldiers Do Not Know Their Fate', *Daily Herald*, 18 October 1943, p. 3.
51. *Daily Herald*, 'Secret Verdict', 18 October 1943, p. 1.
52. Werran, *An American Uprising in Second World War England*, p. 180.
53. Mary Louise Roberts, 'The Leroy Henry Case: Sexual Violence and Allied Relations in Great Britain, 1944', *Journal of the History of Sexuality* 26, no. 3 (2017), pp. 402–23.
54. Reynolds, *Rich Relations*, p. 234.
55. *Daily Mirror*, 'U.S. Soldier Is Sentenced to Death', 30 May 1944, p. 2.

Notes to pp. 150–158

56. Reynolds, *Rich Relations*, p. 234.
57. Ibid., p. 235.
58. Ibid.
59. *Daily Mirror*, 'Eisenhower Acts to Save Life of Condemned Negro', 16 June 1944, p. 4.
60. *The Times*, 'Death Sentence on U.S. Soldier', 19 June 1944, p. 2.
61. *Daily Express*, 'Eisenhower Rejects Negro Sentence', 19 June 1944, p. 8.
62. *Manchester Guardian*, 'Coloured Soldier's Reprieve', 19 June 1944, p. 3.
63. *The Times*, 'News in Brief', 23 June 1944, p. 2.
64. *Daily Mirror*, 'Back to Duty After Quashed Death Verdict', 22 June 1944, p. 4.
65. George Orwell, 'As I Please', *Tribune*, 3 December 1943.
66. Reynolds, *Rich Relations*, p. 228.
67. Ibid., p. 307.
68. Roberts, 'The Leroy Henry Case', p. 423.
69. Reynolds, *Rich Relations*, p. 236.

Chapter 12

1. Brett Holman, '"Bomb Back, and Bomb Hard": Debating Reprisals during the Blitz', *Australian Journal of Politics and History* 58, no. 3 (2012), pp.394–407.
2. Mark Connelly, *Reaching for the Stars: A History of Bomber Command* (London: I.B. Tauris, 2014), p. 48.
3. *Daily Telegraph*, 'Command of the Air', 12 March 1941, p. 4.
4. Algernon Charles Swinburne, 'An Autumn Vision', *The English Illustrated Magazine* 8 (1891), p. 3.
5. *Daily Mirror*, 'Berlin Gets Big Bashing Is Squealing', 9 September 1941, p. 3.
6. *Daily Mail*, 'Our Knees Shook with Fright', 9 September 1941, p. 1.
7. Henry Buckley, 'Cologne Gets It Back', *Daily Express*, 8 July 1941, p. 2.
8. Taylor, *Beaverbrook*, p. 431.
9. Ibid., p. 510.
10. Gilbert Murray and George Bernard Shaw, letter to the editor, *The Times*, 'Bombing of Cities: Military and Non-Military Objectives', 28 April 1941, p. 5.
11. Connelly, *Reaching for the Stars*, p. 55.
12. Ibid., p. 56.
13. *The Times*, '*Target for Tonight*: Review', 24 July 1941, p. 6.
14. Seton Margrave, 'Here's the Best Air War Film I Have Ever Seen', *Daily Mail*, 25 July 1941, p. 2.
15. *Daily Telegraph*, 'Exciting Film of RAF Raid', 24 July 1941, p. 3.
16. Reginald Whitley, 'RAF Raid Makes Big Film Thrill', *Daily Mirror*, 24 July 1941, p. 3.
17. Air Ministry, *Bomber Command: The Air Ministry Account of Bomber Command's Offensive Against the Axis, September 1939 – July 1941* (London: HMSO, 1941).
18. Mark Connelly, 'The British People, the Press and the Strategic Air Campaign against Germany, 1939–1945', *Contemporary British History* 16, no. 2 (2002), pp 39–58.

19. *Daily Telegraph*, 'Heavily Hit', 29 July 1943, p. 4.
20. *The Times*, leader, 31 July 1943.
21. Connelly, *Reaching for the Stars*, p. 158.
22. Richard Overy, 'Constructing Space for Dissent in War: The Bombing Restriction Committee, 1941–1945'.
23. Vera Brittain, *Seed of Chaos: What Mass Bombing Really Means* (London: Bombing Restriction Committee, 1944).
24. Vera Brittain, 'Massacre by Bombing: The Facts behind the British-American Attack on Germany', *Fellowship* X, no. 3 (1944).
25. Ibid., p. 58.
26. Ibid., p. 53.
27. Ibid., p. 60.
28. Ibid., p. 55.
29. Ibid., p. 62.
30. *Manchester Guardian*, 'Bombing Restriction', 7 December 1943, p. 6; *Manchester Guardian*, 'The Bombing of Hamburg', 12 January 1944, p. 4.
31. *New Statesman and Nation*, 'A London Diary', 5 April 1941, Vol. 21, no. 258, p. 359.
32. *New Statesman and Nation*, 'The Principle of Legitimacy', Vol. 27, no. 679 (1944), pp. 133–34.
33. Tim Luckhurst and Lesley Phippen, 'George Orwell Versus Vera Brittain: Obliteration Bombing and the Tolerance of Dissent in Weekly Political Publications', *George Orwell Studies* 2, no. 1 (2017).
34. The National Archives, AIR 2/7852, 'PUBLICITY (Code B, 84): Bomber Command offensive: publicity policy', Sir Arthur Harris, letter, 25 October 1943.
35. Anthony Clifford Grayling, *Among the Dead Cities: Was the Allied Bombing of Civilians in WWII a Necessity or a Crime?* (London: Bloomsbury, 2006), p. 183.
36. Connelly, 'The British People, the Press and the Strategic Air Campaign against Germany, 1939–1945'.
37. Tami Davis Biddle, *Rhetoric and Reality in Air Warfare: The Evolution of British and American Ideas about Strategic Bombing, 1914–1945* (Princeton, NJ, and Oxford: Princeton University Press, 2004), p. 243.
38. Howard Cowan, 'Terror Bombing Gets Allied Approval as Step to Speed Victory', *Sunday Star*, 18 February 1945, pp. 1, 4.
39. Biddle, *Rhetoric and Reality in Air Warfare*, p. 254.
40. Connelly, *Reaching for the Stars*, p. 133.
41. Calder, *The People's War*, p. 565.
42. *Daily Mirror*, 'Dresden Is a Mass of Flame', 15 February 1945, p. 1.
43. *Daily Herald*, '9,000 Plane Attack on Cities, Troops, Supplies', 15 February 1945, p. 1.
44. John Evans, 'Non-Stop Blitz to Aid Russians', *Daily Herald*, 16 February 1945, p. 1.
45. *Daily Express*, 'Dresden Bombed to Atoms', 16 February 1945, p. 1.
46. *Daily Express*, 'Berlin Coins a Word', 17 February 1945, p. 1.
47. *The Times*, 'The Air Assault', 16 February 1945, p. 5.
48. *Sunday Times*, 'Bombing Policy Stated', 18 February 1945, p. 1.

Notes to pp. 163–171

49. Tom Allbeson, 'Where Are the Pictures? Photography and British Public Perception of the Bombing of Germany, 1941–45', *PhotoResearcher*, no. 25 (2016), pp. 60–87.
50. Edgerton, *Britain's War Machine*, pp. 237–39.
51. Connelly, *Reaching for the Stars*, p. 98.
52. *Daily Mirror*, 'Torrent Rages Along Ruhr – Huns Get a Flood Blitz', 18 May 1943, p. 1.
53. Taylor, *Beaverbrook*, p. 432.
54. *Daily Express*, 'Floods Roar Down Ruhr Valley', 18 May 1943, p. 1.
55. Ibid., 'The Breach', 18 May 1943, p. 1.
56. Ibid., 'Dam Buster in Chief', 18 May 1943, p. 1.
57. *Daily Mail*, 'The Smash-Up RAF Picture Testifies to Perfect Bombing', 18 May 1943, p. 1.
58. Ibid., 'The Dams and the Men Who Smashed Them', 18 May 1943, p. 4.
59. *Daily Herald*, 'The Raid', 18 May 1943, p. 2.
60. *The Times*, 'Ruhr Dams Breached', 18 May 1943, p. 4.
61. *The Times*, 'Leader of Raid on Ruhr Dams', 28 May 1943, p. 4.
62. *The Times*, 'Devastation in the Ruhr', 19 May 1943, p. 6.
63. *Manchester Guardian*, 'Breaking of the Dams: Audacity of Leader and Crews', 18 May 1943, p. 5.
64. Ibid., 'RAF Breach Giant German Dams', 18 May 1943, p. 5.
65. *Daily Telegraph*, 'He Drew the Enemy's Fire', 18 May 1943, p. 1.
66. Ibid., 'Text of Air Ministry Statement', 18 May 1943, p. 1.
67. *Daily Express*, 'Raid a Major Victory', 18 May 1943, p. 1.
68. Cited in Connelly, *Reaching for the Stars*, p. 98.
69. McLaine, *Ministry of Morale*, p. 11.
70. Ibid., p. 37.
71. *Tribune,* Contributions by. . ., no. 350, 10 September 1943, appended to p.1
72. Vera Brittain, *Seed of Chaos: What Mass Bombing Really Means*.
73. George Orwell, 'As I Please', *Tribune*, no.386, 19 May 1944, p.11
74. George Orwell, 'As I Please', *Tribune*, no.394, 14 July 1944, p.12
75. Edgerton, *Britain's War Machine*, p. 285.
76. *Manchester Guardian*, 'Dresden Wiped Out', 5 March 1945, p. 6.
77. *Hansard*, HC Debates, Vol. 408, cols 1899–1901, 6 March 1945.
78. Ibid
79. The National Archives, CAB 120/303, 'Allied bombing policy', Prime Minister's Personal Telegram Serial No. D. 83/5.
80. Ibid., Prime Minister's Personal Minute Serial No. D. 89/5.

Chapter 13

1. Andrew Sharf, *The British Press & Jews under Nazi Rule* (London: Oxford University Press, 1962), p. 72.

2. Ibid., pp. 74–75.
3. *Manchester Guardian*, 'Nazi Concentration Camps: Official Regulations as Enforced at Lichtenburg: The Offences Punishable by Death', 10 January 1935, p. 4.
4. Sharf, *The British Press & Jews under Nazi Rule*, p. 81.
5. Ibid., p. 77.
6. Stephanie Seul, '"Herr Hitler's Nazis Hear an Echo of World Opinion": British and American Press Responses to Nazi Anti-Semitism, September 1930–April 1933', *Politics Religion & Ideology* 14, no. 3 (2013), pp. 412–30.
7. Walter Laqueur, *The Terrible Secret: An Investigation into the Suppression of Information about Hitler's "Final Solution"* (London: Weidenfeld & Nicholson, 1980), p. 204.
8. Cited in Paul David Mosley, '"Frightful Crimes": British Press Responses to the Holocaust 1944–45' (MA thesis, University of Melbourne, 2002).
9. The National Archives, FO 371/30917, 'Treatment of war criminals. Code 18 file 61 (papers 7284–8055)'.
10. Sharf, *The British Press & Jews under Nazi Rule*, p. 93.
11. *Manchester Guardian*, 'The Prison Fortress of Terezin: Reich's Clearing House for Jews', 17 September 1942, p. 4.
12. Ibid.
13. *Manchester Guardian*, 'Hitler's Anti-Jewish Fury', 5 October 1942, p. 4.
14. *Daily Telegraph*, 'Germans Murder 700,000 Jews in Poland – Travelling Gas Chambers', 25 June 1942, p. 5.
15. *Manchester Guardian*, 'Extermination', 27 October 1942, p. 4.
16. *Hansard*, HC Debates, Vol. 385, col. 2082, 17 December 1942.
17. Ibid., col. 2083.
18. *Daily Express*, 'The Little Man MPs Stood For', 18 December 1942, p. 1.
19. Ibid., '"It Might Have Been Us", Says Rothschild', 18 December 1942, p. 3.
20. *Daily Mail*, 'Jew Murders: MP Hushes Commons', 18 December 1942, p. 3.
21. *Daily Mirror*, 'Allies Brand Hun Slayers', 18 December 1942, p. 5.
22. *The Times*, 'Barbarity to Jews', 18 December 1942, p. 4.
23. *Sunday Pictorial*, 'The Foulest Crime on Earth', 20 December 1942, p. 2.
24. Ibid., 'Russia Wins New Victories', 20 December 1942, p. 1.
25. *Hansard*, HC Debates, Vol. 401, col. 1160, 5 July 1944.
26. Ibid., cols 1160–61.
27. *Daily Herald*, 'Hungary and Argentina', 6 July 1944, p. 2.
28. *The Times*, 'The Jews of Hungary', 6 July 1944, p. 5.
29. *Manchester Guardian*, 'Massacre of Jews: Mr Eden and "Barbarous Deportations"', 6 July 1944, p. 3.
30. *Daily Telegraph*, 'Frightful Crimes', 6 July 1944, p. 4.
31. *The Times*, 'Massacred Jews in Hungary: Mr Brendan Bracken's Condemnation', 7 July 1944, p. 2.
32. *The Times*, 'Hungarian Jews' Fate', 8 July 1944, p. 3.
33. *Daily Telegraph*, 'Hungarian Jews Slaughtered – Gassed in Poland', 8 July 1944, p. 3.

Notes to pp. 175–182

34. *Manchester Guardian*, 'Hungarian Jews: Estimate of Numbers Killed', 8 July 1944, p. 6.
35. *Daily Mail*, 'Make German Chiefs Pay', 7 July 1944, p. 3.
36. *Daily Express*, '1,000,000 Facing Annihilation', 15 July 1944, p. 1.
37. *Daily Express*, 8 July 1944, p. 1.
38. *The Times*, 'Stubborn Fight in East Prussia', 29 January 1945, p. 4.
39. *Sunday Times*, 'Four Miles from Konigsberg', 28 January 1945, p. 1.
40. *Manchester Guardian*, 'Russian Front: Week-End Advance', 29 January 1945, p. 6.
41. *Daily Telegraph*, 'Death Camp was Mechanised', 3 February 1945, p. 4.
42. *Manchester Guardian*, 'Nazis' Massacre of Greek Jews: Survivor's Account', 9 February 1945, p. 5.
43. Alexander Clifford, 'Blindfolded Nazis Came with Terms', *Daily Mail*, 14 April 1945, p. 1.
44. David Woodward, 'Prison Camp's Fate', *Manchester Guardian*, 14 April 1945, p. 5.
45. Alexander Buckley, 'Germans Ask British for Local Truce', *Daily Telegraph*, 14 April 1945, p. 4.
46. Our Special Correspondent, 'Typhus Causes a Truce', *The Times*, 14 April 1945, p. 4.
47. Adam Matthew Publications, *Popular Newspapers during World War II*, available online at: http://www.ampltd.co.uk/digital_guides/popular_newspapers_world_war_2_parts_1_to_5/abc-net-sales.aspx
48. Seib, *Broadcasts from the Blitz*, p. 171.
49. *Daily Mirror*, 'Didn't Everybody Know', 17 April 1945, p. 2.
50. *Daily Express*, 'The Death-Cart of Buchenwald Is Shown to Germans', 19 April 1945, p. 3.
51. Ibid., 'Ovens for the Murdered – with Stoking Rods Beside Them', 19 April 1945, p. 4.
52. Ibid., 'Vileness', 19 April 1945, p. 2.
53. *Daily Mirror*, 'Pit of Belsen', 21 April 1945, p. 5.
54. Ibid., 'Now Perhaps They'll Believe', 21 April 1945, p. 5.
55. *The Times*, 'The Victims', 20 April 1945, p. 5.
56. *Sunday Pictorial*, 'Hitler's Best Women', 22 April 1945, p. 1.
57. *Daily Express*, 'The Shackled Monster of Belsen', 21 April 1945, p. 1.
58. *Daily Express*, 'This Is the Horror We Fight', 19 April 1945, p. 1.
59. *Daily Telegraph*, 'Burgomasters at Belsen Say: "We Didn't Know"', 26 April 1945, p. 5.
60. Selkirk Parton, 'The Mayor Holds Suicide Party', *Daily Express*, 20 April 1945, p. 1.
61. *Manchester Guardian*, Letters to the Editor, 25 April 1945, p. 4.
62. *Daily Mirror*, Live Letters, 'End the Menace', 27 April 1945, p. 6.
63. *Daily Mirror*, Live Letters, 'Reminder', 30 April 1945, p. 6.
64. *Daily Mirror*, Live Letters, 'Repentance', 26 April 1945, p. 6.
65. *Daily Express*, 'Saturday Post', 28 April 1945, p. 2.
66. Ibid., 'The German Child Plays at Hanging', 28 April 1945, p. 2.
67. *The Times*, Letters to the Editor, 'History and the Facts', 21 April 1945, p. 5.
68. *Manchester Guardian*, Letters to the Editor, 25 April 1945, p. 4.
69. *Manchester Guardian*, 'The Terror in Hungary', 31 March 1944, p. 4.

232

70. *Daily Mail*, 'Doubting Thomases', 28 April 1944, p. 2.
71. David Ayerst, *Guardian: Biography of a Newspaper* (London: Collins, 1971), p. 518.

Chapter 14

1. *Daily Mirror*, 'Public Holiday Today and Tomorrow – Official', 8 May 1945, p. 1.
2. Ibid., 'On Top of the World', 8 May 1945, p. 1.
3. Ibid., 'Massacre Goes On in Prague as War Ends', 8 May 1945, p. 1.
4. Ibid., 'Celebrations Delay Due to a "Technicality"', 8 May 1945, p. 1.
5. Ibid., 'Jane', 8 May 1945, p. 7.
6. *Daily Mirror*, 'Jane', 9 May 1945, p. 7.
7. Daily Mail (1945) V E Day – It's all over, Tuesday 8 May 1945, p.1
8. Ibid., 'The Face of Victory', 8 May 1945, p. 1.
9. Ibid., 'Beacon Chain Begun by Piccadilly's Bonfires', 8 May 1945, p. 1.
10. *The Times*, 'Victory in Europe to Be Declared Today', 8 May 1945, p. 6.
11. *The Times*, 'Celebrating the Victory', 8 May 1945, p. 5.
12. *The Times*, 'Memorable Days in the War for Freedom', 8 May 1945, p. 3.
13. Ibid.
14. *Manchester Guardian*, 'Nations Rejoice at Victory', 8 May 1945, p. 5.
15. Ibid.
16. *Manchester Guardian*, 'Mr De Valera and Hitler', 9 May 1945, p. 8.
17. *Manchester Guardian*, 'First Light', 8 May 1945, p. 4.
18. *Manchester Guardian*, 'The King's Broadcast', 9 May 1945, p. 5.
19. Robert Kee, *1945: The World We Fought For* (London: Penguin, 1985), p. 170.
20. J.M. Lee and M.R.D. Foot, 'UK: Government', in Dear and Foot (eds), *The Oxford Companion to World War II*, p. 888.
21. Kee, *1945: The World We Fought For*, p. 171.
22. Gardiner, *Wartime: Britain 1939–1945*, p. 677.
23. *Daily Mirror*, 'No Vote for These Soldiers', 21 July 1945, p. 3.
24. *Sunday Pictorial*, 'Portugal Is a Tragic Sham', 22 July 1945, p. 6.
25. Ibid., 'Behind the Scenes', 22 July 1945, p. 2.
26. *Sunday Times*, 'Mr Churchill Takes the Salute', 22 July 1945, p. 1.
27. Ibid., 'Premier Returning for Election Results', 22 July 1945, p. 1.
28. *Daily Mail*, 'PM Flies Home Today for Election Results', 25 July 1945, p. 1.
29. *The Times*, Letters to the Editor, 25 July 1945, p. 5.
30. *Daily Mail*, 'Election Eve; Big Labour Claims', 26 July 1945, p. 1.
31. *Daily Mirror*, 'It's a Big Job Ahead', 26 July 1945, p. 2.
32. *Daily Mail*, 'You Will Know It All by 7.30pm', 26 July 1945, p. 1.
33. *Daily Telegraph*, 'Record Pace for Election Count', 25 July 1945, p. 1.

34. *Daily Telegraph*, 'Propaganda Tale', 23 July 1945, p. 2.
35. *Daily Telegraph*, 'U.S. Expecting a Close Finish', 26 July 1945, p. 6.
36. *The Times*, 'A Sweeping Labour Victory', 27 July 1945, p. 4.
37. *Daily Telegraph*, 'Churchill Resigns, Attlee Premier – Socialists Get Clear Majority of 153', 27 July 1945, p. 1.
38. Ibid., 'Slump in Stock Markets', 27 July 1945, p. 1.
39. Ibid., 'Troops' Vote', 27 July 1945, p. 1.
40. *Daily Herald*, 'Labour in Power', 27 July 1945, p. 1.
41. Ibid.
42. Ibid., 'Labour Bonfire Dances', 27 July 1945, p. 1.
43. Available online at: http://www.bbc.co.uk/news/special/politics97/background/pastelec/ge45.shtml
44. *The Times*, 'Great Tasks Ahead', 27 July 1945, p. 4.
45. Ibid.
46. Louis Allen, 'Burma Campaign', in Dear and Foot (eds), *The Oxford Companion to World War II*, pp. 135–39.
47. *Sunday Times*, 'Main Japan Islands May Be By-Passed', 8 July 1945, p. 7.
48. *The Times*, 'Decision to Use Atomic Bomb', 8 August 1945, p. 4.
49. Martin J. Sherwin, 'Atomic Bomb', in Dear and Foot (eds), *The Oxford Companion to World War II*, pp. 54–59.
50. *Manchester Guardian*, 'Immense Co-Operative Effort by Ourselves and US', 7 August 1945, p. 5.
51. *Daily Mail*, 'Atomic Bomb: Japs Given 48 Hours to Surrender', 7 August 1945, p. 1.
52. Ibid., 'They Toil in Secret Cities', 7 August 1945, p. 1.
53. *The Times*, 'First Atomic Bomb Hits Japan', 7 August 1945, p. 4.
54. *Daily Telegraph*, 'The Men Who Made It Possible', 7 August 1945, p. 1.
55. Los Alamos National Laboratory, Our History, available online at: https://www.lanl.gov/about/history-innovation/index.php
56. *Daily Mail*, 'Blind Girl "Saw" the First Big Flash', 7 August 1945, p. 1.
57. *The Times*, 'A Trial Bomb', 7 August 1945, p. 4.
58. Ibid., 'First Atomic Bomb Hits Japan', 7 August 1945, p. 4.
59. *Daily Mail*, 'Most Terrifying Weapon in History: Churchill's Warning', 7 August 1945, p. 1.
60. *Manchester Guardian*, 'How the Atomic Bomb Was Born: Manchester Men's Part in Fundamental Discoveries', 7 August 1945, p. 6.
61. *Manchester Guardian*, 'Our London Correspondence: The Atomic Nightmare', 8 August 1945, p. 4.
62. *The Times*, 'Decision to Use Atomic Bomb', 8 August 1945, p. 4.
63. *Daily Mirror*, 'Just Suppose It Had Happened Here', 9 August 1945, p. 1.
64. *The Listener*, 'The Atomic Bomb', 9 August 1945, p. 148.
65. *The Times*, 'Hiroshima Inferno – 4 Square Miles Obliterated – Huge Death Toll', 9 August 1945, p. 4.
66. *Daily Mail*, 'Meaning of Atomic Power', 7 August 1945, p. 2.
67. *Observer*, 'The New World: True Terror-Ridden Peace', 12 August 1945, p. 5.
68. *Daily Mirror*, 'Bomb Logic', 10 August 1945.

69. *Manchester Guardian*, 'Our London Correspondence: Thoughtful Celebration', 11 August 1945, p. 4.
70. *Manchester Guardian*, 'The Sibyl's Offer', 14 August 1945, p. 3.
71. Kee, *1945: The World We Fought For*, p. 292.
72. *Daily Mail*, '100 a Day Dying in Hiroshima', 5 September 1945, p. 1.
73. *Daily Express*, 'Atomic Plague', 5 September 1945, p. 1.
74. *The Times*, 'Controlling Use of Atomic Bombs', 7 September 1945, p. 2.
75. *New York Times*, 'Atomic Bombing of Nagasaki Told by Flight Member', 9 September 1945, pp. 1, 35.
76. *The Times*, 'Advent of the Atomic Bomb', 2 January 1946, p. 12.
77. *Sunday Times*, 'Lessons of Atom Bomb Devastation', 30 June 1946, p. 5.
78. *The Listener*, 'Mankind at the Crossroads', 4 July 1946, p. 7.
79. See, *inter alia*, Biddle, *Rhetoric and Reality in Air Warfare*; and Luckhurst and Phippen, 'George Orwell Versus Vera Brittain'.
80. Cited in Kee, *1945: The World We Fought For*, p. 289.

Conclusion

1. Herbert George Wells, *The War that Will End War* (London: Frank & Cecil Palmer, 1914).
2. Luckhurst, 'War Correspondents'.
3. MOA, 'Report on the Press', FR 126, section 4.
4. Calder, *The Myth of the Blitz* (London: Pimlico, 1991), p. 504.
5. Ibid., p. 505.
6. BBC News, 'Reporting the War: The "Fourth Arm" of Warfare', https://www.bbc.com/historyofthebbc/research/bbc-at-war/reporting-the-war/
7. BBC News, 'D-Day and War Report', https://www.bbc.com/historyofthebbc/research/bbc-at-war/d-day-and-war-report/
8. Luckhurst and Phippen, 'George Orwell Versus Vera Brittain'.
9. Peter Hennessy, *Never Again: Britain 1945–51* (London: Penguin, 1992), p. 327.
10. R.B. McCallum and Alison Readman, *The British General Election of 1945* (London: Oxford University Press, 1947), p. 181.
11. *Royal Commission on the Press, 1947–49: Report* (Cmd 7700) (London: HMSO, 1949).
12. Taylor, *Beaverbrook*, p. 584.
13. Sir Denis Hamilton, *Editor-in-Chief: The Fleet Street Memoirs of Sir Denis Hamilton* (London: Hamish Hamilton, 1989), pp. 55–59.
14. Marquand, *Britain Since 1918*, p. 403.
15. Robert W. Desmond, 'Book Review: Royal Commission on the Press, 1947–49: Report', *Journalism and Mass Communication Quarterly* 26, no. 4 (1949), pp. 470–72.
16. *Royal Commission on the Press, 1947–49: Report*, p. 3.
17. Ibid., para. 650.
18. See https://www.nctj.com/

BIBLIOGRAPHY

Action on Smoking and Health, *ASH Fact Sheet: Smoking Statistics: Who Smokes and How Much* (2016), p. 1, available online at http://ash.org.uk/wp-content/uploads/2016/06/Smoking-Statistics-Who-Smokes-and-How-Much.pdf

Adam Matthew Publications, *Popular Newspapers during World War II* (Marlborough: Adam Matthew Publications, 1993), available online at: http://www.ampltd.co.uk/digital_guides/popular_newspapers_world_war_2_parts_1_to_5/abc-net-sales.aspx

Adam Matthew Publications, *The (Sex) Bomb that Won the War* (2018), available online at: https://www.amdigital.co.uk/about/blog/item/the-sex-bomb-that-won-the-war

Addison, Adrian, *Mail Men: The Unauthorised Story of the Daily Mail* (London: Atlantic, 2017)

Addison, Paul, 'By-elections of the Second World War', in Chris Cook and John Ramsden (eds), *By-elections in British Politics* (London: Macmillan, 1973), pp. 165–97

Addison, Paul, *The Road to 1945: British Politics and the Second World War* (London: Cape, 1975)

Addison, Paul, and Jeremy Crang (eds), *Listening to Britain: Home Intelligence Reports on Britain's Finest Hour, May to September 1940* (London: Vintage Books, 2011)

Air Ministry, *Bomber Command: The Air Ministry Account of Bomber Command's Offensive Against the Axis, September 1939 – July 1941* (London: HMSO, 1941)

Alexander, Eileen, *Love in the Blitz: The Greatest Lost Love Letters of the Second World War*, ed. David McGowan and David Crane (London: Harper Collins, 2020)

Allbeson, Tom, 'Where Are the Pictures? Photography and British Public Perception of the Bombing of Germany, 1941–45', *PhotoResearcher*, no. 25 (2016), pp. 60–87

Andrew, Christopher, *The Defence of the Realm: The Authorized History of MI5* (London: Allen Lane, 2009)

Ayerst, David, *Guardian: Biography of a Newspaper* (London: Collins, 1971)

BBC, 'The Transcript of Neville Chamberlain's Declaration of War', BBC Archive Written Document (1939), available online at http://romanohistory.pbworks.com/w/file/fetch/73728956/British%20Declare%20War%20on%20Germany.pdf

BBC News, 'D-Day and War Report', https://www.bbc.com/historyofthebbc/research/bbc-at-war/d-day-and-war-report/BBC News, 'Reporting the War: The "Fourth Arm" of Warfare', https://www.bbc.com/historyofthebbc/research/bbc-at-war/reporting-the-war/

Bejerot, Nils, 'The Six-Day War in Stockholm', *New Scientist* 61, no. 886 (1974), pp. 486–87

Biddle, Tami Davis, *Rhetoric and Reality in Air Warfare: The Evolution of British and American Ideas about Strategic Bombing, 1914–1945* (Princeton, NJ, and Oxford: Princeton University Press, 2004)

Bingham, Adrian, *Family Newspapers?: Sex, Private Life and the British Popular Press 1918–1978* (Oxford: Oxford University Press, 2009)

Bingham, Adrian, 'Ignoring the First Draft of History', *Media History* 18, nos 3–4 (2012), pp. 311–26

Bingham, Adrian, 'The Woman's Realm: The *Daily Mail* and Female Readers', Daily Mail Historical Archive 1896–2004 (©Gale, a Cengage Co., 2013)

Blackett, Patrick, *Studies of War: Nuclear and Conventional*, (Edinburgh: Oliver & Boyd, 1962)

Bond, Brian (ed.), *Chief of Staff: The Diaries of Lieutenant-General Sir Henry Pownall: Volume One 1933–1940* (London: Leo Cooper, 1972)

Boyce, George, 'The Fourth Estate: The Reappraisal of a Concept', in G. Boyce, J. Curran and P. Wingate (eds), *Newspaper History: From the 17th Century to the Present Day* (London: Constable, 1978), pp. 19–40

Bibliography

Brittain, Vera, 'Massacre by Bombing: The Facts behind the British-American Attack on Germany', *Fellowship* X, no. 3 (1944)

Brittain, Vera, *Seed of Chaos: What Mass Bombing Really Means* (London: Bombing Restriction Committee, 1944)

Brookshire, Jerry, *Clement Attlee* (Manchester: Manchester University Press, 1995)

Brown, Malcolm, (ed.), *The Wipers Times: The Complete Series of the Famous Wartime Trench Newspaper* (St Albans: Little Books, 2006)

Calder, Angus, *The Myth of the Blitz* (London: Pimlico, 1991)

Calder, Angus, *The People's War: Britain 1939–1945*, 12th edn (London, Pimlico, 2008)

Calder, Peter Ritchie, *The Lesson of London* (London: Searchlight Books, Secker & Warburg, 1941)

Campbell, Kate, 'W.E. Gladstone, W.T. Stead, Matthew Arnold and a New Journalism: Cultural Politics in the 1880s', *Victorian Politics Review* 36, no. 1 (2003), pp. 20–40

Channon, Henry, *Chips: The Dairies of Sir Henry Channon* (London: Weidenfeld & Nicolson, 1967)

Childs, David, 'The British Communist Party and the War, 1939–41: Old Slogans Revived', *Journal of Contemporary History* 12, no. 2 (1977), pp. 237–53

Churchill College Cambridge, 'Sir Winston Churchill: A Biography', available online at: chu.cam.ac.uk/archives/collections/churchill-papers/churchill-biography

Cockett, Olivia, *Love and War in London: The Mass Observation Wartime Diary of Olivia Cockett*, ed. Robert Malcolmson (Stroud: The History Press, 2008)

Cockett, Richard, *Twilight of Truth: Chamberlain, Appeasement and the Manipulation of the Press* (London: Weidenfeld & Nicolson, 1989)

Collier, Richard, *The Warcos: The War Correspondents of World War Two* (London: Weidenfeld & Nicolson, 1989)

Connelly, Mark, 'The British People, the Press and the Strategic Air Campaign against Germany, 1939–1945', *Contemporary British History* 16, no. 2 (2002), pp 39–58

Connelly, Mark, *Reaching for the Stars: A History of Bomber Command* (London: I.B. Tauris, 2014)

Cooper, Duff, *Old Men Forget: The Autobiography of Duff Cooper (Viscount Norwich)* (London: Rupert Hart-Davis, 1953)

Cowles, Virginia, *Looking for Trouble* (London: Faber & Faber, 2010 [1941])

Cudlipp, Hugh, *Publish and be Damned! The Astonishing Story of the Daily Mirror* (London: Andrew Dakers Ltd, 1953)

Curran, James, 'Narratives of Media History Revisited', in M. Bailey (ed.), *Narrating Media History* (Oxford: Routledge, 2009), pp. 1–21

Curran, James, and Jean Seaton, *Power without Responsibility: Press, Broadcasting and New Media in Britain*, 6th edn (London: Routledge, 2003)

Curran, James, and Jean Seaton, *Power without Responsibility: Press, Broadcasting and the Internet in Britain*, 7th edn (London: Routledge, 2010)

Dear, I.C.B., and M.R.D. Foot (eds), *The Oxford Companion to World War II* (Oxford: Oxford University Press, 2001)

deFabrique, N., S.J. Romano, G.M. Vecchi and V.B. Van Hasselt, 'Understanding Stockholm Syndrome', *FBI Law Enforcement Bulletin* 76, no.7 (2007), pp. 10–15

Desmond, Robert W., 'Book Review: Royal Commission on the Press, 1947–49: Report', *Journalism and Mass Communication Quarterly* 26, no. 4 (1949)

Desmond, Robert W., *Tides of War: World News Reporting 1940-1945* (Iowa City: University of Iowa Press, 1984)

Dyhouse, Carol, 'The British Federation of University Women and the Status of Women in Universities, 1907–1939', *Women's History Review* 4, no. 4 (1995), pp. 465–85

Edgerton, David, *Britain's War Machine: Weapons, Resources and Experts in the Second World War* (London: Penguin, 2012)

Bibliography

Farish, Matthew, 'Modern Witnesses: Foreign Correspondents, Geopolitical Vision, and the First World War', *Transactions of the Institute of British Geographers* 26, no. 3 (2001), pp. 273–87

Feiling, Keith, *The Life of Neville Chamberlain* (London: Macmillan & Co., 1946)

Ferguson, Niall, *The Pity of War* (London: Allen Lane, 1998)

Gardiner, Juliet, *Wartime: Britain 1939–1945* (London: Headline, 2004)

Gibbs, Philip, *Adventures in Journalism* (London: W. Heinemann, 1923)

Gilbert, Martin, *Road to Victory: Winston S. Churchill 1941-1945*, (London: Heineman, 1989)

Gilbert, Martin, and Richard Gott, *The Appeasers* (London: Orion, 2000)

Goldman, Aaron, L., 'Press Freedom in Britain during World War II', *Journalism History* 22, no. 4 (1997), pp. 146–55

Grayling, Anthony Clifford, *Among the Dead Cities: Was the Allied Bombing of Civilians in WWII a Necessity or a Crime?* (London: Bloomsbury, 2006)

Griffiths, Dennis, *Fleet Street: Five Hundred Years of the Press* (London: The British Library, 2006)

Griffiths, Dennis, *A Century of Journalism 1900–2000* (Oxford: Coranto Press, 2012)

Hamilton, Denis, Sir, *Editor-in-Chief: The Fleet Street Memoirs of Sir Denis Hamilton* (London: Hamish Hamilton, 1989)

Hampton, Mark, 'Renewing the Liberal Tradition', in M. Bailey (ed.), *Narrating Media History* (Oxford: Routledge, 2009), pp. 26–35

Hanson, Neil, *Priestley's Wars* (Ilkley: Great Northern Books, 2008)

Harrison, Tom, *Living Through the Blitz* (London: Faber & Faber, 2010)

Henderson, Nevile, Sir, *Failure of a Mission: Berlin 1937–39* (London: Hodder & Stoughton, 1940)

Hennessy, Peter, *Never Again: Britain 1945–51* (London, Penguin, 1992)

Hobbs, Sandy, *Clyde Apprentices' Strikes* (1988), available online at: http://www.workerscity.org/workers_city/sandy_hobbs.html

Hodgson, Guy, 'Sir Nevile Henderson, Appeasement and the Press', *Journalism Studies* 8, no. 2 (2007), pp. 320–34

Hodgson, Guy, 'Propaganda Sheets: Trust in the Press Declined during the Second World War, as Did Its Influence', *History Today* (December 2015), available online at https://www.historytoday.com/propaganda-sheets

Hollingsworth, Clare, *The Three Week's War in Poland*, (London: Duckworth, 1940)

Holman, Brett, '"Bomb Back, and Bomb Hard": Debating Reprisals during the Blitz', *Australian Journal of Politics and History* 58, no. 3 (2012), pp.394–407

Hucker, Daniel, *Public Opinion and the End of Appeasement in Britain and France* (Farnham: Ashgate, 2011)

Hyde, Douglas, *I Believed* (London: The Reprint Society, 1952)

Hylton, Stuart, *Reporting the Blitz: News from the Home Front Communities* (Stroud: The History Press, 2012)

Jack, Ian, 'Leveson Isn't Unprecedented. The Same Issues Came up 60 Years Ago', *Guardian*, 22 June 2012, available online at: https://www.theguardian.com/commentisfree/2012/jun/22/do-failings-of-newspapers-matter

Jackson, Julian, *The Fall of France: The Nazi Invasion of 1940* (Oxford: Oxford University Press, 2003)

Kee, Robert, *1945: The World We Fought For* (London: Penguin, 1985)

Kershaw, Ian, *Fateful Choices: Ten Decisions that Changed the World, 1940–41* (London: Penguin, 2008)

King, Cecil, *Strictly Personal, Some Memoirs of Cecil H. King* (London: Weidenfeld & Nicolson, 1969)

Kitchen, Martin, *British Policy Towards the Soviet Union during the Second World War* (New York: St. Martin's Press, 1986)

Knappen, M.M., 'The Abdication of Edward VIII', *Journal of Modern History* 10, no. 2 (1938), pp. 242–50

Bibliography

Knightley, Phillip, *The First Casualty: The War Correspondent as Hero and Myth-Maker from the Crimea to Iraq*, 3rd edn (Baltimore and London: Johns Hopkins University Press, 2004)

Lammers, Donald, 'Fascism, Communism, and the Foreign Office, 1937-39', *Journal of Contemporary History* 6, no. 3 (1971), pp. 66-86

Laqueur, Walter, *The Terrible Secret: An Investigation into the Suppression of Information about Hitler's "Final Solution"* (London: Weidenfeld & Nicholson, 1980)

Lasswell, Harold, *Propaganda Technique in the World War* (Eastford, CT: Martino Fine Books, 2013)

Leveson, Brian, 'The Freedom of the Press and Democracy', in B. Leveson, *The Leveson Inquiry: The Report into the Culture, Practices and Ethics of the Press* (London: HMSO, 2012), Vol. 1, Part B, Chapter 2, para. 2.19, p. 61

Literary Digest, 'Queenly Enigma: What Will Mrs Simpson and King Edward Do? Asks Wondering World', 7 November 1936, p. 11

Lonsdale, Sarah, 'A Golden Interlude: Journalists in Early Twentieth Century British Literature', *Parliamentary Affairs* 64, no. 2 (2011), pp. 326-40

Luckhurst, Tim, '"It Is Thrown Against Me that I Have a Castle": A Portrait of Newspaper Coverage of the Central Southwark By-election, February 1940', *Journalism Studies* 13, no. 1 (2012), pp. 107-23

Luckhurst, Tim, 'Excellent but Gullible People: The Press and the People's Convention', *Journalism Studies* 14, no. 1 (2013), pp. 62-77

Luckhurst, Tim, 'War Correspondents', in *1914-1918 Online: International Encyclopedia of the First World War*, ed. by Ute Daniel, Peter Gatrell, Oliver Janz, Heather Jones, Jennifer Keene, Alan Kramer and Bill Nasson, issued by Freie Universität Berlin (2016)

Luckhurst, Tim and Lesley Phippen, 'George Orwell Versus Vera Brittain: Obliteration Bombing and the Tolerance of Dissent in Weekly Political Publications', *George Orwell Studies* 2, no. 1 (2017)

Macleod, Iain, *Neville Chamberlain* (London: Frederick Muller, 1961)

Mann, Jessica, *Out of Harm's Way: The Wartime Evacuation of Children from Britain* (London: Headline Books, 2005)

Marchant, Hilde, *Women and Children Last* (London: Gollancz, 1941)

Margach, James, *The Abuse of Power: The War between Downing Street and the Media from Lloyd George to Callaghan* (London: W.H. Allen, 1978)

Marquand, David, *Britain Since 1918: The Strange Career of British Democracy* (London: Orion Books, 2009)

Mass Observation Archive (MOA), 'Report on the Press', File Report (FR) 126 (May 1940)

Mass Observation Archive (MOA), By-elections 1937-47, Topic Collection (TC) 46

McCallum, R.B., and Alison Readman, *The British General Election of 1945* (London: Oxford University Press, 1947)

McIlroy, John, and Alan Campbell, 'Histories of the British Communist Party: A User's Guide', *Labour History Review* 68, no. 1 (2003), pp. 33-59

McInerney, Jay, *Bright Lights, Big City* (London: Jonathan Cape, 1985)

McLaine, Ian, *Ministry of Morale: Home Front Morale and the Ministry of Information in World War II* (London: George Allen & Unwin, 1979)

Milkman, Paul, *PM: A New Deal in Journalism* (New Brunswick, NJ: Rutgers University Press, 1997)

Moorhead, Alan, *The Desert War* (London: Aurum Press, 2009)

Moorhouse, Roger, *The Devils' Alliance: Hitler's Pact with Stalin, 1939-41* (London, Vintage, 2016)

Mosley, Paul David, '"Frightful Crimes": British Press Responses to the Holocaust 1944-45' (MA thesis, University of Melbourne, 2002)

National Committee of the People's Convention, *The People Speak: Official Report of the People's Convention* (London: National Committee of the People's Convention, 1941)

Nel, Philip, 'Said a Bird in the Midst of a Blitz: How World War II Created Dr Seuss', *Mosaic* 34, no. 2 (2001), pp. 65–85

Nicholas, Sian, '"There Will Be No War": The *Daily Express* and the Approach of War, 1938–39', in D. Welch and J. Fox (eds), *Justifying War: Propaganda, Politics and the Modern Age* (London: Palgrave Macmillan, 2012), pp. 200–17

Overy, Richard, 'Constructing Space for Dissent in War: The Bombing Restriction Committee, 1941–1945', *The English Historical Review* 131, no. 550 (2016), pp. 596–622

Paine, Thomas, *Rights of Man* (Mineola, NY: Dover Publications, 1999)

Painter-Downes, Mollie, *London War Notes 1939–1945* (New York: Farrar, Strauss and Giroux, 1971)

Perry, George, and Alan Aldridge, *The Penguin Book of Comics* (London: Penguin, 1967)

Pratt Boorman, H.R., *Hell's Corner 1940: Kent Becomes the Battlefield of Britain* (Maidstone: Kent Messenger, 1940)

Pugh, Martin, *State and Society: A Social and Political History of Britain 1870–1997* (London: Arnold, 1999)

Reynolds, David, *Rich Relations: The American Occupation of Britain, 1942–1945* (New York: Random House, 1994)

Roberts, Mary Louise, 'The Leroy Henry Case: Sexual Violence and Allied Relations in Great Britain, 1944', *Journal of the History of Sexuality* 26, no. 3 (2017), pp. 402–23

Robertson, Ben, *I Saw England* (New York: A.A. Knopf, 1941)

Royal Airforces Association, *History of the Battle of Britain*, available online at: https://www.rafmuseum.org.uk/research/online-exhibitions/history-of-the-battle-of-britain/

Royal Commission on the Press, 1947–49: Report (Cmd 7700) (London: HMSO, 1949)

Rudd, Fiona, 'An Unpublished Biography of Peter Ritchie Calder', available online at: https://digital.nls.uk/propaganda/calder/calder_biography.pdf

Schudson, Michael, *Why Democracies Need an Unlovable Press* (Cambridge: Polity Press, 2009)

Seib, Philip, *Broadcasts from the Blitz: How Edward R. Murrow Helped Lead America into War* (Dulles, VA: Potomac Books, 2006)

Seul, Stephanie, '"Herr Hitler's Nazis Hear an Echo of World Opinion": British and American Press Responses to Nazi Anti-Semitism, September 1930–April 1933', *Politics Religion & Ideology* 14, no. 3 (2013), pp. 412–30

Seymour-Ure, Colin, *Prime Ministers and the Media: Issues of Power and Control* (Oxford: Blackwell, 2003)

Shakespeare, Nicholas, *Six Minutes in May: How Churchill Unexpectedly Became Prime Minister* (London: Vintage, 2017)

Sharf, Andrew, *The British Press & Jews under Nazi Rule* (London: Oxford University Press, 1962)

Shawcross, William, *Queen Elizabeth The Queen Mother: The Official Biography* (London: Penguin Random House, 2010)

Siebert, Fred, 'The Press and the British Constitutional Crisis', *Public Opinion Quarterly* 1, no. 4 (1937), pp. 120–25

Swinburne, Algernon Charles, 'An Autumn Vision', *The English Illustrated Magazine* 8 (1891), p. 3

Taylor, A.J.P., *Beaverbrook* (London: Hamish Hamilton, 1972)

Taylor, A.J.P., *English History 1914–1945* (Oxford: Oxford University Press, 1990)

Taylor, D.J., *Orwell: The Life* (London: Vintage, 2004)

Temple, Mick, *The British Press* (Maidenhead: McGraw-Hill, 2008)

Thompson, George P., *Blue Pencil Admiral: The Inside Story of the Press Censorship* (London: Sampson Low, Marston & Co., 1947)

Thorburn, David, 'James W. Carey, 1934–2006' (2011), http://web.mit.edu/comm-forum/legacy/forums/carey_memoriam2.htm

Time, 'Education: Nomination', Vol. 28, no. 20 (16 November 1936), p. 85

Time, 'Foreign News: The World's Greatest Romance', Vol. 28, no. 20 (16 November 1936), p. 31

Bibliography

Time, 'Great Britain: The Crown', Vol. 28, no. 14 (5 October 1936), pp. 18–19

Toye, Richard, *Winston Churchill: A Life in the News*, (Oxford: Oxford University Press, 2020)

Trythall, A.J., 'The Downfall of Leslie Hore-Belisha', *Journal of Contemporary History* 16, no. 3 (1981), pp. 391–411

Wells, Herbert George, *The War that Will End War*, (London: Frank & Cecil Palmer, 1914)

Werran, Kate, *An American Uprising in Second World War England: Mutiny in the Duchy* (Barnsley: Pen & Sword History, 2020)

White, J. Lincoln, *The Abdication of Edward VIII* (London: George Routledge & Sons, 1937)

Wrench, John Evelyn, *Geoffrey Dawson and Our Times* (London, Hutchinson, 1955)

Young, G.M., *Stanley Baldwin* (London: Rupert Hart-Davis, 1952)

Youngs, Ian, 'Picasso's Guernica in a Car Showroom', 15 February 2012, available online at https://www.bbc.co.uk/news/entertainment-arts-16927120

List of Newspapers

Birmingham Post
Daily Express
Daily Herald
Daily Mail
Daily Mirror
Daily News (a London paper which published between 1846 and 1930)
Daily Sketch
Daily Telegraph
Daily Worker
Evening News
Evening Star
Kent Messenger
London Evening Standard
Manchester Guardian
Morning Post
News Chronicle
News of the World
News Review
New Statesman and Nation
Sunday Pictorial
The Economist
The Listener
The Observer
The People
The Scotsman
The Star
The Sunday Times
The Times
Tribune
Yorkshire Observer
Yorkshire Post

Bibliography

Parliamentary Debates

Hansard, HC Debates, Vol. 318, cols 1611–12, 4 December 1936
Hansard, HL Debates, Vol. 107, col. 424, 13 December 1937
Hansard, HC Debates, Vol. 360, cols 1150–51, 7 May 1940
Hansard, HC Debates, Vol. 362, cols 699, 713 and 747, 2 July 1940
Hansard, HC Debates, Vol. 363, cols 338–66, 17 July 1940
Hansard, HC Debates, Vol. 363, cols 394–95, 18 July 1940
Hansard, HC Debates, Vol. 364, col. 1167, 20 August 1940
Hansard, HC Debates, Vol. 365, cols 476–77, 10 October 1940
Hansard, HC Debates, Vol. 368, cols 465, 486, 506, 507, 508, 520–21 and 522, 28 January 1941
Hansard, HC Debates, Vol. 377, col. 1473, 10 February 1942
Hansard, HC Debates, Vol. 378, cols 1665–69, 19 March 1942
Hansard, HC Debates, Vol. 385, cols 187–88, 17 November 1942
Hansard, HC Debates, Vol. 385, cols 2082 and 2083, 17 December 1942
Hansard, HC Debates, Vol. 386, cols 1596, 1615 and 1616, 16 February 1943
Hansard, HC Debates, Vol. 386, cols 2021, 2032, 2040, 2049 and 2050, 18 February 1943
Hansard, HC Debates, Vol. 401, cols 1160–61, 5 July 1944
Hansard, HC Debates, Vol. 408, cols 1899–1901, 6 March 1945

The National Archives

AIR 2/7852, 'PUBLICITY (Code B, 84): Bomber Command offensive: publicity policy', Sir Arthur Harris, letter, 25 October 1943
CAB 65 Second World War conclusions
From 1939 to 1945 the internal reference for Cabinet conclusions changed to WM. Despite the introduction of a smaller War Cabinet, the notation used to identify the meetings and conclusions remained the same. WM 10 (43)1 refers to the 10th meeting in 1943 and the first agenda item or conclusion.
CAB 66/12 WP 402 (40), 'Memorandum. Type: Subversive Newspaper Propaganda. Author: Herbert Morrison'
CAB 66/14 WP (40) 482, 'Memorandum. Title: The "Daily Worker". Author: Herbert Morrison'
CAB 120/303, 'Allied bombing policy', Prime Minister's Personal Telegram Serial No. D. 83/5; and Prime Minister's Personal Minute Serial No. D. 89/5
FO 371/30917, 'Treatment of war criminals. Code 18 file 61 (papers 7284–8055)'
WP (G) (40) 145, 'War Cabinet Memorandum, Title: Compulsory Censorship. Author: Duff Cooper.'

INDEX

abdication, of King Edward VIII, 10–16
   divisions in British Press, 12–13
   foreign newspaper coverage, 13–15
Acland, Richard, 102
Adams, Harry, 99
Addison, Paul, 38, 39
   Listening to Britain, 60
Admiralty, 26, 28, 29, 45
aerial bombardment, of Britain, 22, 30–1, 198, *see also* bombing, allied of Germany
   provincial attacks, 85–9, 155
Aftonbladet (Stockholm newspaper), 159
Air Defence Cadet Corps (ADCC), 65–6
Air Ministry, 28, 43, 157, 161, 166, 168, 169
   history of campaign, 157
   objectives, 166–7
   pictures, 163, 165, 167
   supplying facts to papers, 67, 68, 72, 88, 158, 162, 198
Air-Raid Precautions Bill, 22
air raid shelters, 73–83, 85, 102–3
   Anderson, 73, 81
   basement, 75, 77, 83
   black market in private, 73
   brick surface, 85, 87, 88
   deep underground, 74, 75, 80, 81, 86, 88
   luxury hotels, 77–8
   public, 73, 74, 75, 78, 80, 81, 86, 87, 88
   shelter policy, 79–81, 83, 85, 97–8
   'strutted closes', 88
   trench, 75–7, 76*fig*
   tube stations, 74, 75, 81
Alexander, Eileen, 73, 91
Allied Forces Act 1940, 142
Allinson, Geraldine, 13
America, isolationism, 68–9
American journalists, in Britain, 68–71, *see also* American war correspondents
   censorship, 29–30
American press, coverage of abdication, 10–11, 13, 15
American service personnel, in Britain, 139–53
   arrival, 139
   censorship, 139–41, 146, 148, 149, 152, 153
   criminal offences, US and British jurisdiction, 142–3
   discrepancies, US and British soldiers, 141–2
   Launceston, street gun battle, 146–9
   racial segregation and discrimination, 146–53, 199
   sexual offences committed by, 143–6
American war correspondents, 69–71, 114, 161, 190
American War Department, 192–3
Amery, Julian, 47, 48
Anderson, Sir John, 73, 74, 80, 81–3, 89, 91, 93, 198
   suppression of *Daily Worker,* 97
Andrew, Christopher, 38, 106
Anglo-Soviet treaty (May 1942), 120
anti-Semitism, in Germany, 171
appeasement, 16–23, 46
   national newspaper support for, 17–18, 32
area bombing, 156, 158, 159, 160, 162, 163, 167, 169
   criticism of, 156, 159–60
Army Bureau of Current Affairs, 134
Arseneaux, US Private Arthur, 144
Associated Press news agency, 70, 82, 161, 168
Astor, Nancy, 17, 46
Astor, William Waldorf, Lord, 17, 46, 50
Athenia, sinking of, 26, 27
Atkin, James, Baron, 143
Atlantic Charter (August 1941), 127
atomic bombs, 191–6
   test explosion, Alamogordo, 192–3
atrocity stories, 171
Attlee, Clement, 16, 20, 30, 40, 48, 50, 93, 202
   Beveridge Report, 135
   general election (1945), 188, 189, 190, 191
   overseas evacuation, 59, 63
   press suppression, 95–6, 102
Audit Bureau of Circulations (ABC) list (1939), 10
Auschwitz (Oświęcim), 175, 176–7
Austin, Sergeant Henry, 149

Bader, Douglas Robert Stuart, 66–7
Baldwin, Stanley, 9, 11, 12, 15, 16, 17, 30
Ball, Sir Joseph, 17–18
Barham, HMS, 92
Barkley, William, 39
barons, newspaper, 9–12, 23, 156, 202
Barrett, Private Clifford, 149
Bartholomew, Guy, 95–6, 102, 105–6
Baseler Nachrichten (*Basel News*), 159
Battle of Britain, 65–72, 198
Battle of the Atlantic, 105

Index

Batty, J. Redvers, 181–2
BBC, 1, 2, 49, 70, 133, 197, 200, 201, 203
    Battle of Britain broadcasts to US, 2, 49
    Dimbleby's Belsen report, 178, 183
    evening news bulletins, 131
    invasion of Poland, 113
    papers' partnership with, 189–90, 201
    Priestley's broadcasts, 51, 57, 60
    public trust, 25
    wartime comedies, 185, 203
Beaverbrook, Max, Lord, 9, 11, 82, 93, 122, 125, 202
    British bombing of Germany, 156, 164
    intervention against suppression, 94, 95
Bech, Barbara, 63–4
BEF (British Expeditionary Force), 27–8, 36, 45, 51, 52, 53, 115, 198
Belsen, 177–8, 179, 180, 181, 182, 183
Berkeley Hotel, 77–8
Berlin Radio, 117
Berlin, RAF bombings (September 1941), 155, 159, 161
Berry, James Gomer, 1st Viscount Kemsley, 17, 166, 190, 202
Berry, William, 1st Viscount Camrose, 95, 190
Bertolet, Captain Frederick J., 151
Bevan, Aneurin, 102, 136, 167, 201
Beveridge Report (*Social Insurance and Allied Services*), 127–38, 198
    'freedom from want', 130, 131, 132
    government debate, 128–9, 135–6
    health care, 130, 131, 132
    press freedom in reporting, 137–8
    social insurance and benefits, 129, 130, 131–2, 133, 134
Beveridge, Sir William, 127, 131, 132
    marriage, 130, 131
    Moscow claim, 128, 129
    press conference, 134
    speaking tour, 135
    willingness to brief journalists, 128
Bevin, Ernest, 50, 81, 93, 94, 105, 135, 188, 202
Biddle, Tami Davis, 161
Bingham, Adrian, 4, 62
Birkenau, 175, 176
black American service personnel, 141, 144, 146, 147, 148, 149–53, 199
Blitz spirit, *see* 'Myth of the Blitz'
Blunt, the Right Reverend A.W.F., 12
Bomber Command, 157, 158, 162, 164, 165, 166, 169
    area bombing policy, 159–60, 163, 167, 168, 200
    official history, 157
    official press briefings, 167
bombing, allied of Germany, 22, 30–1, 155–69, *see also* aerial bombardment, of Britain
    Bombing Restriction Committee, 159–60, 168
    criticism, of area, 156, 159–60, 167–9, 200
    Dambusters, 164–8
    Dresden, 161–3
    Hamburg, 158
    newspaper reporting of, 166–9
    Target for Tonight (film), 156–7
    terror bombing, 160–1
Bombing Restriction Committee, 159–60, 168
bouncing bombs, 164–5
Boyce, George, 'The Fourth Estate: The Reappraisal of a Concept,' 3
Bracken, Brendan, 175, 176
British Expeditionary Force (BEF), 27–8, 36, 45, 51, 52, 53, 115, 198
British Federation of University Women, 62
Brittain, Vera, 159, 160
    Seed of Chaos (*Massacre by Bombing*, in US), 159, 167
Bronowski, Dr Jacob, 196
Brough, James, 192
Brown, William, 128
Buchenwald, 178–9, 180, 181, 182
Buckham, Bernard, 195
Buckley, Christopher, 178, 180
Buckley, Harry, 156
Burchett, Wilfred, 195
Burden, Dr Fletcher, 181

Cadogan, Sir Alexander, 109, 119
Calder, Angus, 34, 65, 69, 88, 99, 162
    Daily Worker, 124
    'Myth of the Blitz,' 57, 64, 68
Calder, Peter Ritchie, 78–9, 92
    The Lesson of London, 83
Campbell, Stuart, 93, 136
Camrose, Lord, *see* Berry, William, 1st Viscount Camrose
Canning Town, bombing, 78–9
cartoonists, 52, 104–7, 111–12, 125, 132
cartoons, 47, 132
    Low, 111–12, 111*fig*
    Strube, 48, 125
    Zec, 52, 103–7, 112*fig*, 118*fig*, 119
cartoon strips, 25, 41, 104, 185
    Pett's 'Jane,' 25, 185, 186*fig*
Case, Colonel Homer, 139–40
Cassandra (William Neil Connor), 43, 44–5, 103, 104, 105, 107
CBS Radio, 69, 71, 73, 179
censorship
    abdication crisis, 11, 14
    absence of formal power (1930's), 17
    aerial bombings, 78, 168
    Anglo-Soviet treaty, 121
    British, of American news, 34
    British press, subject to US military, 140–1

246

Index

Clydebank Blitz, 88
code of practice for American editors, 139–40
Duff Cooper's regulations (June 1940), 53–5
emergency defence regulations, 3, 54, 94, 97
government (WWI), 6
management of photography, 163
MoI, 2, 53, 65, 163, 166, 167, 199, 200
Morrison on suppression, 94–5, 96
policy, 34, 96, 148, 152
press freedom from, 34, 137–8
relaxation for Coventry raid, 87
security, 53, 65, 96, 141, 146, 148, 152, 167
US pressure for, 153
voluntary, 6, 11, 23, 27–30, 47, 53, 54, 157
censors, in MoI, 27–30, 53
Chamberlain, Neville, 16–23, 26, 34–5, 36, 37, 43, 82, 93
invasion of Denmark and Norway, 43, 44
invasion of Poland, 113
Norway debate, 45–9
reluctance to befriend USSR, 109
Zec cartoon, 104
Channon, Henry (Chips), 57, 58
Chapman, Victor John, 144
Children's Overseas Reception Board (CORB), evacuation scheme, 58–64
Christiansen, Arthur, 173
Churchill, Clementine, 123
Churchill, Winston
  aerial bombardment, 30, 161, 169
  American-British alliance, 139
  Anglo-Soviet treaty, 120
  appointment as PM, 49–51
  Atlantic Charter, 127
  atomic bombs, 193
  Battle of Britain, 65
  Beveridge Report, 135, 137
  changes in government (October 1940), 82
  Dunkirk, 51, 52
  general election (1945), 188, 189, 190, 191
  invasion of Denmark and Norway, 44
  invasion of Poland, 113
  'Jane' cartoon, 25
  newspaper suppression, 3, 92–4, 103–4, 105
  Norway debate, 45–9
  Operation Barbarossa, 116
  overseas evacuation, 63
  Soviet Union invaded by Germany, 109
  Stalingrad, 122–3
  'subversive articles', 92–4
  victory declaration, 185
City of Benares, SS, 63–4
civilian casualties, 158, 160, 162, 167, 168, 200
civilians, bombing of
  British, 30, 83, 87, 88, 91, 155, 159
  German, 155, 159–60, 162, 163, 167–8, 200

Claridge's, 77
class distinctions and discrimination
  American dislike of, 69
  in evacuation policy, 32, 41, 42
  in shelter provision, 73, 77, 79–81, 91
class equality, 68, 69, 78
  promoted by MoI, 68
class unity, 57–64, 73–4
Clifford, Alexander, 177–8
'Cliveden Set', 46
Cluse, Sampson, 173
Clydebank air raids, 88–9
Clydeside Apprentices' strike, 89
Cockburn, Claude (alias Frank Pitcairn), 46, 99
  The Week, 46, 99, 101, 102
Cockett, Olivia, 73
Cockett, Richard, 10–11, 18, 23, 37
  Twilight of Truth: Chamberlain, Appeasement and the Manipulation of the Press, 17
Cocks, Seymour, 106
Collier, Richard, 70
Common Wealth Party, 137
Communist Party of Great Britain (CPGB), 80, 88, 98, 103
  Central Southwark by-election, 37, 39, 40–1
  Clydeside Apprentices' strike, 89
  and *Daily Worker*, 96, 124
  Operation Barbarossa, 117
  People's Convention, 96–7, 98, 99–100
  during phoney war, 38
concentration camps, 171–83, 174–5
  atrocity pictures, 179–82
  Auschwitz liberation, 176–7
  Belsen, 177–8, 179, 180, 182
  Buchenwald, 178–9, 182
  final solution, 172–4, 182
  Hungarian Jews, fate of, 174–6
  inconsistent coverage, 182–3
Connelly, Mark, 155, 156–7, 162
Connor, William Neil (*Daily Mirror*'s Cassandra), 43, 44–5, 103, 104, 105, 107
Conservative Party, 134–5, 189, 202
  newspapers hostile to, 92
  St George's by-election, 9
Cooper, Duff, 9, 48, 53–5
CORB (Children's Overseas Reception Board), evacuation scheme, 58–64
courts martial, US, 142, 143–50, 151
Coventry Blitz, 85–9, 155, 161
Cowan, Howard, 161, 168–9
Cowles, Virginia, 70, 114
CPGB, *see* Communist Party of Great Britain
Crang, Jeremy, *Listening to Britain*, 60
Cripps, Sir Stafford, 114, 128, 130, 167
Crozier, W. P., 182

247

Index

Cudlipp, Hugh, 35, 92, 93, 95, 113
Cummings, A. J., 187
Cunningham-Reid, Captain Alec, 141–2
Curran, James, 105

Dachau, 171
Daily Express, 1, 5, 9, 43
    abdication crisis, 10, 12
    American troops in Britain, 139, 146, 152
    appeasement, 17–18, 19, 21
    atomic bombs, 195
    Battle of Britain, 65, 70
    bombing of Germany, 156, 162–3, 164–5
    Central Southwark by-election, 39, 41
    Churchill's appointment as PM, 49
    circulation and readership, 10, 21, 25, 26, 176
    'Cliveden Set', 46
    Clydebank air raids, 88
    concentration camps, 173, 176, 179, 180–1, 199
    Coventry Blitz, 85–6
    departure of Hore-Belisha, 36
    evacuation, 31, 32, 33
    invasion of Poland, 111
    Lord Haw-Haw, 59
    Molotov-Ribbentrop Pact, 198
    Morrison succeeds Anderson, 81, 82
    Norway debate, 47–8, 48–9
    Operation Barbarossa, 116
    overseas evacuation, 61
    RAF bombing raids (1940), 84
    second front in Europe, 122
    Soviet invasion of Finland, 115
    Stalingrad and Russian war effort, 125
Daily Herald, 1, 40, 92
    abdication crisis, 10
    American troops and racial discrimination, 147–8, 149, 153
    Beveridge Report, 131
    bombing of Germany, 162, 165
    Canning town bombing, 78–9
    Central Southwark by-election, 40, 41
    concentration camps and treatment of Jews, 171, 174, 199
    departure of Hore-Belisha, 36
    general election (1945), 191
    Operation Barbarossa, 117, 119
    People's Convention, 100
    revival of *Daily Worker,* 124
    second front in Europe, 121
    Stalingrad and Russian war effort, 125
Daily Mail, 1, 5, 9, 13, 21, 26, 178
    abdication crisis, 12
    air raid shelters, 74
    American troops in Britain, 139, 143, 144–5, 146
    appeasement, 17–18, 20, 21
    atomic bombs, 192, 193, 194, 195
    Battle of Britain, 65, 66, 68, 71
    Beveridge Report, 131–2, 137, 198
    bombing of Germany, 155, 157, 165
    changes in government (October 1940), 82
    Clydebank air raids, 89
    concentration camps, 172, 174, 176, 177–8, 182
    Coventry Blitz, 86
    Daily Worker ban, 101
    departure of Hore-Belisha, 36
    Dunkirk, 52
    general election (1945), 189
    invasion of Denmark and Norway, 44
    invasion of Poland, 110
    Molotov-Ribbentrop Pact, 110
    Norway debate, 47
    Operation Barbarossa, 119
    overseas evacuation, 62–3
    reprisals for bombing, 83–4
    Russian defence strength, 119–20
    second front in Europe, 121
    Soviet invasion of Finland, 114, 115
    Stalingrad and Russian war effort, 122, 123, 124
    VE Day, 185–6
Daily Mirror, 1, 5, 13
    abdication crisis, 10, 16
    air raid shelters, 74, 75, 79, 82–3
    American troops in Britain, 139, 143, 144, 145–6, 147, 148, 153
        and racial discrimination, 149, 150–1, 152, 153
    appeasement, 17–18, 20, 26
    atomic bombs, 193–4, 195
    Battle of Britain, 65, 67, 68, 71
    Beveridge Report, 127, 128–9, 130–1, 136–7
    bombing of Germany, 155, 157, 162, 164
    cartoons, 25, 52, 103–7, 112*fig*, 118*fig*, 119, 185, 186*fig*
    Cassandra, 43, 44–5, 103, 104, 105, 107
    Churchill's criticism of and demands for action against, 92–5, 103–7
    circulation and readership, 10, 25, 26
    Clydebank air raids, 88
    concentration camps, 174, 179, 181, 183
    Coventry Blitz, 87
    Daily Worker ban, 101
    departure of Hore-Belisha, 35
    Dunkirk, 52
    evacuation, 31–2
    general election (1945), 188, 189
    horoscope 'Message of the Stars,' 25
    invasion of Denmark and Norway, 44
    invasion of Poland, 110–11
    Norway debate, 45–6, 47
    Operation Barbarossa, 117–18, 119
    overseas evacuation, 61

Index

People's Convention, 100–1
second front in Europe, 121
Soviet invasion of Finland, 114, 115
Stalingrad and Russian war effort, 122, 123–4, 124–5
'subversive articles', 92–4
threats under Emergency Regulations, 3
VE Day, 185
Daily Sketch, 1
appeasement, 17
Dambusters Raid, 166
Daily Telegraph, 5, 203
abdication crisis, 10, 12–13, 14
air raid shelters, 75–7
American troops in Britain, 142, 146
appeasement, 17–18
atomic bombs, 192
Battle of Britain, 65, 67, 68
Beveridge Report, 127–8, 129, 198
bombing of Germany, 155, 157, 158, 167
Clydebank air raids, 88
concentration camps and treatment of Jews, 171, 173, 175, 177, 178, 180, 182, 199
Daily Worker ban, 101
general election (1945), 189–91
Morrison succeeds Anderson, 82
Operation Barbarossa, 116–17
second front in Europe, 121
Soviet invasion of Finland, 115
Stalingrad and Russian war effort, 123, 125
Daily Worker
air raid shelters, 80–1, 86, 87–8, 95, 97–8, 102–3
ban, 3, 95, 96, 97–103, 124
Central Southwark by-election, 39, 40–1
Churchill's appointment as PM, 50–1
defence regulations, censorship, 54
engagement in CPGB's campaign, 96
evacuation, 33
overseas evacuation (CORB scheme), 63, 95, 98
Scottish edition, 89, 99
Dakar, 92, 93
Dambusters raid, 164–6
Daniell, Raymond, 71, 72
Das Schwarze Korps (SS newspaper), 182
Davies, Clement, 143
Davis, US Private Lee A., 144–6
Dawson, Geoffrey, 12, 17, 18–19, 46, 52
deadlines, reporting against, 177, 178
death camps, 174–6
de Chair, Somerset, 133
defence regulations, 53–4, 65, 95, 96, 103, 104, 106–7
Defence Regulation 2D, 94, 97, 102, 106
Defence Regulation 3, 53
de Gaulle, General Charles, 92
Denmark, German invasion of, 43–5

Der Angriff (Berlin), 45
de Valera, Éamon, 187
Devers, General Jacob, 149–50
Dickins & Jones, 77
Dimbleby, Richard, 178
dissenting opinions, publishing, 2, 21, 40, 160, 167, 168, 201
Dominions, Britain's overseas, 58–64
Douhet, Giulio, 30
Dresden, 161–3
Driberg, Tom, 129
Dunkirk, 51–5

East End bombings, 78–9
The Economist, 54–5, 114
Beveridge Report, 134, 137, 153, 201
shelter policy, 81
Ecumenical Refugee Commission, 175
Eden, Anthony, 116, 117, 120, 173–4, 176, 182
Eden, Guy, 81, 122
Edgerton, David, 105, 168
editors
American, 139
Beaverbrook's, 82
censorship and suppression, 6, 28, 140
challenging ministers, 198
compliance and support, 6, 17, 37, 200
duties and objectives, 4, 42, 199
right to challenge, 34
Edwards, Mrs (Bader's mother-in-law), 67
Edwards, Murray, 147–8, 149
Edward VIII, King, 10–16, 197
Eisenhower, General Dwight David, 151–2
Elizabeth, Queen, 58
emergency reception centres, 79
ETO (European Theatre of Operations), 149, 151, 152, 153
evacuation, 30–4, *see also* overseas evacuation
Evans, Emrys, 187
Evans, John, 162
Evening News, 9, 13
Evening Star, 13
Ewer, William, 117
extraterritorial jurisdiction, 142–3, 149, 150, 152
eyewitness testimonies, 31, 201
atomic bombs, 193, 196
bombing, 78, 79, 86, 89, 155, 159, 169
concentration camps, 171, 172, 177, 182

Fabian Society, 129, 130
fairness, newspapers motivated by, 64, 89, *see also* class distinctions and discrimination
Fawden, Muriel Joyce Rosaline, 144–6
female readers, 62, 66
Field III, Marshall, 70
films, 25, 156–7, 164

249

Index

final solution, 172–4, 182
Finland, Soviet invasion, 113–15
First World War, legacy for newspapers, 6, 23, 169, 171
food rationing, 96, 98, 141
Foreign Office, 2, 28, 38, 71, 109, 113, 120, 139
France, coverage of abdication, 10, 13
free press, 2, 3, 4, 5–6, 7, 10, 53, 97, 106
Fremlin, Celia, 100

Galbraith, Professor Vivian Hunter, 181
Gallacher, Willie, 11, 102
galley proofs, 13–14, 15
Gallup poll (November 1944), 188
Gardiner, Juliet, 22, 32, 74, 80, 99, 134, 188
Garvin, James Louis, 50
gas chambers, 173, 175, 176, 177
General Council of the Press (later Press Council), 203
general election (1945), 188–91
George VI, King, 20, 58, 187–8
German press, Hitler's control of, 17
German radio, 155–6
Germany, allied bombing of, 22, 30–1, 155–69
    campaign against civilian bombing, 158–60
    criticisms of, 156–7
    Dambusters and perfect bombing, 164–6
    deliberate terror bombing, 160–1, 162, 163
    Dresden, 161–3
    Hamburg, 158–9
Gibson, Wing Commander Guy Penrose, 164, 165, 166
Gilbert, Sir Martin, 58–9
Goebbels, Joseph, 45, 117, 125, 155
Goldman, Aaron, 103
Goodhart, Arthur, 143
Gort, John Vereker, Lord, 36, 37
Gosset, Tom, 147
Gray, Bernard, 77–8
Green, Canon Peter ('Artifex'), 195
Greenwood, Arthur, 40, 43, 48, 50, 135–6, 188
Greig, Bill, 124–5, 128–9, 136–7, 185
Grenfell, Captain Russell, 191
Grierson, Colin McKay, 162
Griffiths, James, 63
Guernica, 22

Haldane, Charlotte, 33
Halifax, Edward Wood, Lord, 38, 48, 113
Hall, William, 86
Hamburg, 158–9
Hammond, US Private Travis P., 143–4
Hampton, Mark, 4
Harmsworth, Esmond Cecil (2nd Viscount Rothermere), 66, 95, 185–6
Harmsworth, Harold Sidney (1st Viscount Rothermere), 9, 66

Harris, Air Chief Marshal Sir Arthur 'Bomber,' 158, 160, 161, 163, 165, 169
Harrison, Tom, *Living Through the Blitz*, 30
Harris, Sir Percy, 102, 106
Hart, Sir Basil Liddell, 119–20
head lice infestations, 32–4
Henderson, Sir Nevile, 17
Henry, Corporal Leroy, 149–52, 153
Heydrich, Reinhard, 172
Hill, Kathleen, 103
Himmler, Heinrich, 177–8
Hiroshima, 192, 193–4, 195, 196
Hitler, Adolf, 16, 17, 20, 66, 187
    final solution, 172–4
    Mein Kampf, 182
    Operation Barbarossa, 116, 117, 118, 119
    Stalingrad, 122, 124
    Zec cartoons, 104, 118*fig*
Hoare, Sir Samuel, 20, 43
Hobbs, Mrs (Bader's mother), 66
Hobbs, Sandy, 89
Holman, Brett, 155
Home Intelligence regional reports, 60–1, 63, 91, 100, 152
Hore-Belisha, Isaac Leslie, 34–7
horoscopes, 25
Horsburgh, Florence, 33–4
Hucker, Daniel, 20–1
Hughes, Sergeant Rupert, 149
Hugh Myddelton Junior School, 31
Hull, Cordell, 176
human-interest stories, 68, 147
L'Humanité (French Communist paper), 22
Hungarian Jews, 174–6, 182
Hyde, Douglas, 97

Illingworth, Leslie Gilbert, 132
Ingersoll, Ralph, 70
International Volunteer Force, 115
Ireland, divisions in, 187
isolationism, American, 68–9, 70
Izvestia (Soviet Union national paper), 100

Jackson, Julian, *The Fall of France,* 51
Jacks, S.B.L., 33–4
'Jane' cartoon (*Daily Mirror*), 25, 185, 186
Japan, war with, 191–6
Jay, Ernest, 191
Jennings, Richard, 150
Johnson, Hewlett, Archbishop of Canterbury, 103
Jones, W. A. E., 191
Joyce, William (Lord Haw-Haw), 57, 58

Kee, Robert, 188, 195
Keitel, Field-Marshall, 186

250

Index

Kemsley, Lord, *see* Berry, James Gomer, 1st Viscount Kemsley
Kent Messenger, 12, 13–14, 15, 69–70
Kerrigan, Peter, 88
Kershaw, Ian, 64
Keyes, Sir Roger, 45–6, 47
Kimche, John, 167
King, Cecil Harmsworth, 12, 93, 95–6, 102, 103–4
King's Party (group of British Press), 13
Kipling, Rudyard, 9
Kitchen, Martin, 124
Knappen, Marshall, 10
Knightley, Philip, 39
Knox, Collie, 68
Knupffer, George, 119
Kramer, Josef, 180
Krivitsky, Walter, 38

Labour Party, 101
    Central Southwark by-election, 37, 40, 41
    in Churchill's coalition, 49–50
    and *Daily Mirror,* 16, 129
    divisions in, 99
    general election (1945), 188, 189, 190, 191, 202
    People's Convention, 100–1
    and *Sunday Pictorial,* 136
Lacey, Montague, 139
Laming, T. W., 190
Laqueur, Walter, 171
Laski, Harold, 69, 191
Lasswell, Harold, 6
Laurence, William L., 196
Lawrence, Colonel Jock, 153
Lawrence, Staff Sergeant E.R., 181
Lay, Cynthia June, 144–6
League of Coloured Peoples, 151
Leeson, Spencer, 58
Leighton-Porter, Chrystabel, 25
Lend-Lease agreement, 1, 96
letters' pages, 2, 62, 83, 150, 156, 159, 160, 181–2
Leveson, Sir Brian, 3
Liberty (American magazine), 11
Liebknecht, Karl, 96
Lilley, Irene Maude, 149–50, 151
The Listener, atomic bombs, 194, 196, 201
Literary Digest (New York), 13, 15
Lloyd George, David, 84–5, 136
Lloyd George, Megan, 136
lobby correspondents, 18
Local Defence Volunteers, 75
London Evening Standard, 9, 10, 38, 41
    abdication crisis, 10
    cartoons, 111–12, 111*fig*
    'Cliveden Set', 46
    concentration camps and treatment of Jews, 172

Lonsdale, Sarah, 7
Low, David, 111–12, 111*fig*
Luftwaffe, 65, 71, 73–4, 83, 98, 116, 131
    Coventry, 85–7 155, 161
    East End bombings, 78–9
    Stalingrad, 123
Lyons, Major, 143

MacDermot, T.W.L., 62
MacDonald, Ramsay, 18
Manchester Guardian, 12–13
    abdication crisis, 12
    American troops in Britain, 142–3, 146–7, 149, 152
    Anglo-Soviet treaty, 121
    appeasement, 21, 22
    atomic bombs, 192, 193, 195
    Battle of Britain, 67
    Beveridge Report, 133
    bombing of Germany, 159, 165–6, 168
    censorship, 54
    Central Southwark by-election, 41
    Churchill's appointment as PM, 49–50
    concentration camps and treatment of Jews, 171, 172–3, 175, 176–7, 178, 181–2, 199
    Coventry Blitz, 87
    Dunkirk, 51
    evacuation, 33–4
    Hore-Belisha's departure, 35–6
    Operation Barbarossa, 118
    overseas evacuation, 61–2
    People's Convention, 97, 100
    Stalingrad and glorification of Stalin, 123, 124
    VE Day, 187
Manhattan Project, 192, 193, 200
Mann, Arthur, 19–20, 22, 198
Mannerheim, Anastasie, 114
Mannerheim, Baron Carl Gustav Emil, 114
Mann, Jessica, *Out of Harm's Way: The Wartime Evacuation of Children from Britain,* 57–8
Marchant, Hilde, 70, 85–6
Margach, James, 18
Margesson, David, 48
Margrave, Seton, 157
Marquand, David, 127, 202
Marshall, Thurgood, 151
Marsland Gander, Leonard, 75–7
Martin, John, 38, 39
Martin, W.F., 115
Mass Observation (MO), 1, 30, 43, 49, 73
    Central Southwark by-election, 41
    general election (1945), 188
    MOA 'Report on the Press' (May 1940), 1, 23, 197
    People's Convention, 99–100

Index

McCallum, R.B., 202
McGaffin, William, 82–3
McGovern, John, 135–6
McInerney, Jay, 25–6
McLaine, Ian, 91
Mellor, Sir John, 128
MI5, 38, 106
Mickles, US Private Sammie, 144
Middleton, Drew (Associated Press), 70
Ministry of Information (MoI), 2, 27–30, 51, 54, 64, 87
    air raid shelters, 75, 81
    American Division, 71
    Battle of Britain bulletins, 65–6, 68
    censorship and control of the media, 2, 53, 65, 163, 166, 167, 199, 200
    depiction of USSR, 109, 122
    Home Intelligence regional teams, 60–1, 63, 91, 100, 152
    morale, 60, 91
    publicising German brutality, 171
Ministry of Reconstruction, 137
MO, *see* Mass Observation
Molotov-Ribbentrop Pact, 110
Molotov, Vyacheslav, 38, 109, 117–18, 120, 121, 122
Montague, Evelyn, 51
Moorhouse, Richard, 181
Moorhouse, Roger, 111
morale, 30, 38, 91, 100, 110, 197
    censorship and suppression, 6, 89
    Daily Worker and CPGB's campaign to undermine, 96, 97, 98, 100
    German, 155, 161, 200
    Home Intelligence department reports on, 60, 91
    morale-boosting news coverage, 28, 31–2, 41, 66, 85, 87, 88, 110, 198
    undermined by overseas evacuation, 59
Morning Post, 5, 14
Morrison, Herbert, 3, 32, 50, 81–3, 86, 89, 202
    Beveridge Report, 129, 130, 135, 136
    Daily Worker ban, 97–103, 124
    support for press freedom, 94–5, 96, 104
    Zec cartoon, 104–6
Moscow, Treaty of, 115
Moseley, Alderman J.A., 85
Mountain, Sir Edward, 133
Munich agreement, 18–22, 43, 109
Murray, Gilbert, 156
Murrow, Ed, 69, 71, 73, 178–9
Murrow, Janet, 69
Mussolini, Benito, 30, 110
Myers, Denis, 189
'Myth of the Blitz' (Angus Calder), 57, 64, 68

Nagasaki, 193, 194–5, 196
National Association for the Advancement of Coloured People (NAACP), 151
National Council for Civil Liberties (NCCL), 103
National Council for the Training of Journalists (NCTJ), 203
National Union of Journalists (NUJ), 103, 202, 203
naval press officers, 51, 52
Nazi propaganda, 59, 119
Nazi race laws, 171
Nazi-Soviet non-aggression pact, 38, 80, 109, 116–117, 119, 199
Neilson, Sergeant, 146
neutral countries and correspondents, reports from, 83–4, 155, 156, 159, 163, 167, 200
News Chronicle, 1
    abdication crisis, 10, 13, 16
    appeasement, 17–18
    circulation, 10, 26
    departure of Hore-Belisha, 36
    VE Day, 187
News of the World, circulation, 25, 26
newspaper barons, 9–12, 23, 156, 202
Newspaper Proprietors Association (NPA), 14, 94, 95–6, 98, 101, 199
newspapers
    circulation and readership, 1, 2, 10, 25, 26
    compliance with government, 6, 18, 37, 54, 68, 72, 125, 140–1, 200
    content, 25–6
    history, 5–7
    speaking truth to power, 2, 3, 7, 10, 42, 47, 91, 104, 136, 203
    wartime objectives, 201
New Statesman and Nation, 40, 159
New Yorker magazine, 69
New York Herald Tribune, 133
New York Times, 69, 71
    atomic bombs, 196
    Beveridge Report, 133
    Dambusters raid, 164
Nicolson, Harold, 54
North American Newspaper Alliance, 70, 190
Norway debate, 45–9
Norway, German invasion of, 43–9
NPA (Newspaper Proprietors Association), 14, 94, 95–6, 98, 101, 199
NUJ, 103, 202, 203, *see* National Union of Journalists

The Observer
    appeasement, 17
    atomic bombs, 194–5
    Churchill's appointment as PM, 50
    general election (1945), 190
Odham's Press, 40, 95

Index

official news briefings, 167
official news communiqués, 27, 30, 31, 68
Okinawa, US campaign, 192
Oliphant, Sir Lancelot, 113
Operation Barbarossa, 116–22
Operation Chastise, 164
Operation Gomorrah, 158
Operation Thunderclap, 161–2
Orwell, George, 14, 110, 141, 152, 159–60, 167–8
Oświęcim (Auschwitz), 175, 176–7
Ottum, Assistant Defence Counsel Alvin E., 148
overseas evacuation, 57–64
    CORB public scheme, 58–64, 98
    private evacuations, 57–8, 59
Owen, Frank, 107

Packe, Joyce, 148
Paine, Thomas, *Rights of Man,* 5
Painter-Downes, Mollie, 69
Panton, Selkirk, 180–1
paper shortages, impact on newspapers, 65, 199
Paris Radio, 168
Paris Soir, 13
patriotism, 6, 72, 81, 86, 192, 197, 198
    Daily Express, 65, 85
    Daily Mail, 65, 66, 86
    Daily Mirror, 105
The People, 25
People's Convention, 96–7, 98, 99–100
Pétain, Marshal, 52, 58
petrol rationing, 141
Petter, Sir Ernest, 9
Pett, Norman, 25, 185, 186*fig*
Philbin, Defence Counsel John A., 148
phoney war, 25–42
    Central Southwark by-election, 37–41
    Communist Party during, 38
    dismissal of Leslie Hore-Belisha, 34–7, 41
    evacuation, 30–4
    voluntary censorship, 27–30
Picasso, Pablo, 'Guernica,' 22
pictures, newspaper, 163, 165, 167, 186, 187, 189, 194, 201
    concentration camps and Nazi treatment of Jews, 171, 179–82
Pilcher, Hugh, 131
'Pill Box Affair,' 36
Pitt, William, 5
PM (New York newspaper), 70, 71
Poland, Soviet invasion, 110–13
Polish Jews, 173, 175
Political and Economic Planning, survey (1934), 1
Pollitt, Harry, 117, 117*fig*
Portal, Charles, 169
Post, Robert B., 69
poverty, 32

Pownall, Henry, 36
Pratt Boorman, Edwin, 13–14, 15
Pratt Boorman, H.R., 69–70
Pravda (Soviet Union national paper), 100
precision bombing, 156, 157–8, 160–1, 164, 166, 200
Press Association, 29, 36
press freedom, 22, 53, 98, 101–2, 106, 162
    American troops in Britain, 149
    Beveridge Report, 137–8
press repression (1783–1806), 5
press suppression, *see also* censorship
    Daily Mirror, demands for action against, 92–5, 107
    Daily Worker ban, 3, 95, 96, 97–103, 124
    Sunday Pictorial, demands for action against, 92–5
Prew, Bob, 66, 185–6
Priestley, J. B., 51, 57, 60, 93
Pritchard, Captain Lester, 143
Pritt, D.N., 102
propaganda, 68, 160
    Air Ministry's, 165
    Allied atrocity (WWI), 171
    Bomber Command's, 162
    CPGB and *Daily Worker*'s, 96, 97, 98, 102
    German, 88
    Lord Beaverbrook and, 82
    Nazi, 59
    state (WWI), 6–7
    Target for Tonight (film), 157
Pugh, Martin, 15–16

racial discrimination, 146–50, 152, 153
racial justice, 151
racial segregation, 141, 146–7, 152
radical media historians, 3–4
radical press (1700–1800s), 3
radio, Britain, *see* BBC
Ramsey, Guy, 186
Ransom, Lena, 181
rape trials, 143–6, 149–50
rationing, 96, 98, 141
Reach for the Sky (film), 66
Readman, Alison, 202
Red Army, 119–20, 123, 124, 125, 162, 174
    liberation of Auschwitz, 176
refugee centres, 78–9
Refugee Relief Committee, 175
repression of press freedom (1700–1800s), 5
reprisals, demands for, after German air attacks, 83–5, 86, 155
Resolution, HMS, 92
Reuters, 44, 110, 121, 123, 163
    Auschwitz, 177
Reynolds, David, 139, 142, 149, 152
Ribbentrop, Joachim von, 38, 109

Index

Riegner, Gerhart, 172
Ritchie Calder, Peter, *see* Calder, Peter Ritchie
Ritz, 78
Roberts, Mary Louise, 152–3
Robertson, Ben, 70, 71
Romilly, Giles, 44
Roosevelt, Eleanor, 61
Roosevelt, Franklin D., 14, 124, 127, 139, 161
    four freedoms, 132
Ross, Sir William David, 202
Rothermere, Lord, *see* Harmsworth, Harold Sidney, 1st Viscount
Rothschild, James de, 174
Rouse, Sir Alexander, 81
Royal Air Force (RAF), 65–8, 69–72
    bombing of Germany, 155–6, 157, 158, 160, 161–2, 163, 165, 166
    training schools, 68
Royal Commission on the Press, 23, 82, 202–3
Royal Navy, 29, 51, 52
Russia, 109–26
    invasion of Finland, 113–15
    invasion of Poland, 110–13
    Molotov-Ribbentrop Pact, 110
    Operation Barbarossa, 116–22
    second front, 119–22, 124, 125
    Stalingrad, 122–5
Russo-Finnish War, 39, 40
Russo-Japanese War (1904–5), 7
Rust, William, 124

Sassoon, Siegfried, 'Fight to a Finish,' 7
Schudson, Michael, 4
Schuster, George, 189
Scott, Captain F., 147
Scott, Captain Richard P., 147
Scott, C.P., 12, 51, 182
Scrutator (Herbert Sidebotham), 114
Searson, Charles, 37, 38, 39, 40–1
Seaton, Jean, 2, 105
second front, 119–22, 124, 125
self-censorship, *see* voluntary self-censorship
Senate House newsroom, 27–8
Seul, Stephanie, 171
sexual offences, committed by American soldiers, 143–6
Seymour-Ure, Colin, 18
Shakespeare, Geoffrey, 58–9
Shakespeare, Nicholas, *Six Minutes in May: How Churchill Unexpectedly Became Prime Minister,* 48
Sharf, Andrew, 171
Shaw, George Bernard, 103, 156
Sheean, Vincent (North American News Agency), 70–1

shelters, *see* air raid shelters
Shinwell, Manny, 106, 136
Shirer, William, 133
Sidebotham, Herbert (pen name Scrutator), 114
Silverman, Samuel, 172, 173, 174
Simmonds, Sergeant R., 146–7
Simon, John, Lord (later 1st Viscount), 105, 142
Simpson, Wallis, 11–12
Sinclair, Sir Archibald, 50, 83, 160, 161, 165
slogans, 11, 39, 96, 137
Social Insurance Committee, 127
South Hallsville School, 78–9
Southwood, Julius Elias, Lord, 95
Soviet agents, 38
Spanish Civil War, 88
The Spectator, 166, 201
Spens, William Patrick, 106
Stalingrad, 122–5
Stalin, Joseph, 109–10, 113, 115, 125–6, 161
    Operation Barbarossa, 116, 118–19, 120
    Stalingrad, 122–3
stamp duty, 5
Steer, George, 22
Stenner, Mrs K., 74
Steward, George, 18, 19, 20
St Gallen Tagblatt (Swiss newspaper), 159
Stokes, Richard, 159, 168–9
Strauss, George, 167
strip cartoons, 25, 41, 104, 185
Strube, Sidney 'George,' 48, 125
Sunday Express, 25
Sunday Pictorial, 35
    air raid shelters, 77–8, 79
    American troops in Britain, 147
    atomic bombs, 195
    Beveridge Report, 127, 129, 135–6
    concentration camps, 174, 175–6, 180
    Coventry Blitz, 87
    general election (1945), 189
    RAF bombing raids (1940), 85–6
    Soviet invasion of Finland, 113–14
    'subversive articles' and Churchill's criticism of, 92–4, 95, 103, 104
    threats under Emergency Regulations, 3
Sunday Star (Washington DC), 161
Sunday Times, 17, 124
    atomic bombs, 192, 196
    bombing of Germany, 163
    Churchill's appointment as PM, 50
    concentration camps, 176
    general election (1945), 189
    Soviet invasion of Finland, 114
Supreme Headquarters of the Allied Expeditionary Force (SHAEF), 161, 162, 163
Sweden, neutral reporters, 159, 199

Index

Swinburne, Algernon Charles, 'An Autumn Vision,' 155
Switzerland, neutral reporters, 159, 199

Target for Tonight (film), 156-7
TASS, Soviet news agency, 100, 118
Taylor, D.J., 110
Temple, Ann, 'Human Case-Book' column, 62-3
Terezin, 172
Thomas, Bert, 111
Thomas, Cecil, 93, 104, 105-6, 150
Thompson, Dorothy, 194-5
Thompson, Rear-Admiral George Pirie, 27-30, 140-1, 152
    Blue Pencil Admiral, 27
Time magazine, 13, 14, 151
The Times, 5, 203
    abdication crisis, 10, 11, 12-13, 15
    air raid shelters, 73, 74-5
    American troops in Britain, 142, 143, 144, 145, 151-2
    appeasement, 17, 18-19, 21, 32
    atomic bombs, 193, 194, 196
    Battle of Britain, 65-6, 67, 71
    Beveridge Report, 128, 129-30, 132-3, 198
    bombing of Germany, 157, 158, 163, 165
    Central Southwark by-election, 41
    Churchill's appointment as PM, 49
    circulation and readership, 21, 178
    Clydebank air raids, 88-9
    concentration camps and treatment of Jews, 171, 172, 174-5, 176, 178, 179, 181, 182, 199
    Coventry Blitz, 87
    Daily Worker ban, 101
    defence regulations, 54, 106-7
    Dunkirk, 52
    evacuation, 32-3
    general election (1945), 189
    Guernica, 22
    Hore-Belisha, departure of, 36
    invasion of Denmark and Norway, 44
    invasion of Poland, 112-13
    loyalty to Chamberlain, 44, 45, 46
    Morrison succeeds Anderson, 81-2
    Norway debate, 45, 46, 47
    Operation Barbarossa, 116, 117, 119, 120
    overseas evacuation, 60
    second front in Europe, 121-2, 125, 126
    Soviet invasion of Finland, 114, 115
    Stalingrad and Russian War effort, 123, 124, 125
    VE Day, 186
Toye, Richard, 48-9, 50, 105
Trades' Union Congress, 40
Treblinka, 175
Tribune, 114, 151, 152, 153, 159-60, 167-8, 201

Triumph, HMS, 29
trust, in newspapers, 10, 21, 23, 25, 197
Trythall, Major General A.J., 35, 37
Turner, Major C. C., 67

Ultra intelligence, 116
unemployment, 132
United Empire Party (UEP), 9
United States Army Air Force (USAAF), 158, 160-1, 163, 192
Usborne, Admiral, 27, 28
US Lend-Lease programme, 1, 96

Van der Elst, Violet, 38-9
Vatis, Leon, 177
VE Day, 185-8
Versailles, Treaty of, 17
Visiting Forces Act, 152
VJ Day, 195
Volkischer Beobachter (Nazi Party national paper), 45
voluntary self-censorship, 6, 27-30, 47, 53, 54, 157
    abdication crisis, 10-16
    American troops in Britain, 152
    Anglo-Soviet treaty, 120
    appeasement, 16-23

Wallis, Sir Barnes, 164
War Cabinet, 26, 35, 37, 49, 55, 92, 93, 125
    Beveridge Report, 129, 130, 135, 136, 137
    censorship and suppression, 53, 94-97, 102, 109
    Churchill's appointment as PM, 50
    expanded (October 1940), 81, 82
    final solution, 173
    overseas evacuation, 58
war correspondents, 4, 6, 7, 51, 114, 163, 177-8
    American, 69-71, 114, 161, 190
Warner, Phyllis, 91
War Office, 4, 28-9, 36, 134
Wartime Social Survey, 2
Washington, SS, 61
Watt, Harry, 156-7
Waugh, Evelyn, *Scoop,* 10
Webb, Maurice, 100
Weddell, Justin, 61
Wedgwood, Josiah, 62
The Week, 46, 99, 101, 102
weekly political magazines, freedom to debate, 158-9, 167-8
Wells, H. G., 69, 93, 103, 197
Werran, Kate, 147
White, J. Lincoln, 11
Whitley, Reginald, 157
Williams, Herbert, 136
Wintringham, Tom, 75
The Wipers Times, 6

255

Index

wireless, *see* BBC
Wood, Sir Kingsley, 81, 82, 136–7, 141
Woodward, David, 178
Woolton, Lord, 123–4
World Jewish Conference (WJC), 172, 182
Wrench, John Evelyn, 46

Yalta Conference, 161
Yorkshire Post

abdication crisis, 12
appeasement/Munich agreement, 19–20, 21, 22, 198
Battle of Britain, 65

Zec, Philip, 52, 104–7, 112, 112*fig*, 118*fig*, 119
Zhukov, General, 118–19
Zickel, Colonel Raymond E., 147, 148